LITIGATION
Logic

A PRACTICAL GUIDE TO EFFECTIVE ARGUMENT

PAUL BOSANAC

Cover design by ABA Publishing.

The materials contained herein represent the opinions and views of the authors and/or the editors, and should not be construed to be the views or opinions of the law firms or companies with whom such persons are in partnership with, associated with, or employed by, nor of the American Bar Association, unless adopted pursuant to the bylaws of the Association.

Nothing contained in this book is to be considered as the rendering of legal advice, either generally or in connection with any specific issue or case; nor do these materials purport to explain or interpret any specific bond or policy, or any provisions thereof, issued by any particular franchise company, or to render franchise or other professional advice. Readers are responsible for obtaining advice from their own lawyers or other professionals. This book and any forms and agreements herein are intended for educational and informational purposes only.

© 2009 American Bar Association. All rights reserved.

No part of this publication may be reproduced, stored in a retrieval system, or transmitted in any form or by any means, electronic, mechanical, photocopying, recording, or otherwise, without the prior written permission of the publisher. For permission, contact the ABA Copyrights & Contracts Department at copyright@abanet.org or via fax at 312-988-6030.

Printed in the United States of America.

13 12 11 10   5 4 3 2

Library of Congress Cataloging-in-Publication Data

Bosanac, Paul.
  Litigation logic : a practical guide to effective argument / by Paul Bosanac.
    p. cm.
  Includes index.
  ISBN 978-1-60442-571-0
  1. Trial practice—United States. 2. Forensic oratory. 3. Logic. I. Title.
  KF8915.B577 2009
  347.73'75—dc22

                                                            2009026900

Discounts are available for books ordered in bulk. Special consideration is given to state bars, CLE programs, and other bar-related organizations. Inquire at Book Publishing, ABA Publishing, American Bar Association, 321 North Clark Street, Chicago, Illinois 60654-7598.

www.ababooks.org

Contents

About the Author	xi
Acknowledgments	xiii
Introduction	xv

❦ CHAPTER ONE
The Legal Logic Flow Chart — 1

Seven Categories	5
Winona Ryder's Shoplifting	9
Majority Leader Tom Delay's Indictment	13
The Chart as an Argument Generator	18

❦ CHAPTER TWO
The Rules of Legal Logic — 19

Rule 1	19
Rule 2	19
Rule 3	21
Rule 4	21

❦ CHAPTER THREE
Prohibited Arguments — 23

Personal Belief or Opinion	26
Included Misconduct	28
Opinion as to Guilt	30

Appeals to Prejudice	33
Injecting Red Herrings	35

❦ CHAPTER FOUR
Ad Hominem (Abusive): Personal Attacks — 39

Attacks on Character	40
Exercise Discretion	41
Not from Around Here	43
Disparaging Remarks	44
Don't Call Me a Crook	46
Not Sympathetic Enough	48
Odious Comparisons	49
Pointing Fingers	51
"Unprincipled Colleagues"	53

❦ CHAPTER FIVE
Ad Hominem (Circumstantial): Bias and Prejudice — 55

Division and Epithets	56
Judicial Bias	60
Just Good Friends	62
Expert Bias	64

❦ CHAPTER SIX
Tu Quoque: Saying One Thing, Doing Another — 67

Defending Against Hypocrisy	68
Tit for Tat	70
Foul Language	71
"Clean Hands Doctrine"	72
Establishment Clause Test	75
Taking a Page from Orwell	76

❦ CHAPTER SEVEN
Poisoning the Well — 81

Pre-Trial Publicity	82
Impugning Credibility	83

Shades of Disbelief	88
What to Avoid	91

❦ CHAPTER EIGHT
Appeal to Authority — 93

Multiple Lines of Attack	94
Lower Court Decisions	95
Defining "To Carry"	96
Citing Oneself as the Expert	99
Heightened Scrutiny	101
Vouching for the Witness	102
Invoking the Judge	103

❦ CHAPTER NINE
Accent: Emphasizing Certain Words — 105

Taken Out of Context	105
Not the Whole Picture	108
Verbatim Quotes	108
Tone of Voice	110
Out of Context	115
Disagreeing with the Conclusion	117

❦ CHAPTER TEN
Equivocation: Shifts in Meaning — 119

Using the Same Word in Two Ways	121
Differing Interpretations	127

❦ CHAPTER ELEVEN
Amphiboly: Which Meaning Is Intended? — 133

Libelous Headlines	134
Higher Stakes	139
No Contradiction	144

❦ CHAPTER TWELVE
Hypostatization: Expressing Abstractions — 147

It Speaks for Itself	148

Right to Privacy	150
The Vessel as Offender	155
The Car as Wrongdoer	156

❦ CHAPTER THIRTEEN
Appealing to Ignorance — 159

Burdens of Proof	160
Nonappearing Witnesses	162
The Iceberg Metaphor	164
Responding in Kind	170
Three Responses	171

❦ CHAPTER FOURTEEN
Pity: Appealing to Sympathy — 173

Golden Rule Argument	174
Victim's Perspective	178
Victim Impact Statements	182

❦ CHAPTER FIFTEEN
Hurling Epithets — 187

Types of Lies	188
Improper Epithets	191
Catalog of Offenses	194
Courts Under Criticism	196
Unwarranted Hyperbole	199

❦ CHAPTER SIXTEEN
Humor and Ridicule — 201

Exceeding Boundaries	204
"Happy Speech"	207
Eleventh Amendment Cases	210

❦ CHAPTER SEVENTEEN
Appealing to the Mob — 215

Collective Interests	215
Appeals to Regionalism	216
Send a Message	218

CONTENTS　　　　　　　　　　　　　　　　　　　　　　　vii

Rally Round the Flag	220
Overcrowded Courtrooms	223
Pecuniary Interests	223
Biblical Authority	225
War on Drugs	227
Conscience of the Community	230
Lend Me Your Ears	234

❦ CHAPTER EIGHTEEN
Slippery Slope　　　　　　　　　　　　237

Stick to the Issues	238
Darrow on Evolution	239
The Nose of the Camel	241
Legal Floodgates	243
Point/Counterpoint	246

❦ CHAPTER NINETEEN
Reductio Ad Absurdum　　　　　　　251

Exaggerated Terms	252
Extreme Examples	254
Considerable Overstatement	256
Humor and Ridicule	258
Harsh Penalties	261
Signaling the End	262

❦ CHAPTER TWENTY
Two Wrongs Rarely Make a Right　　　265

Does the End Justify the Means?	266
The "Invited Response" Rule	270
"Plain Error" Rule	275

❦ CHAPTER TWENTY-ONE
Threats, Force, and Fear　　　　　　279

"Death for Dangerousness" Argument	282
Improper Conduct	289
Self-Incrimination Privilege	290

CHAPTER TWENTY-TWO
Begging the Question	293
Reasonable vs. Unreasonable	297
"Fair Reading"	297
Naming Names	301

CHAPTER TWENTY-THREE
The Complex Question	307
Fact Not in Evidence	318

CHAPTER TWENTY-FOUR
False Cause	323
Cause of Negligence	328
Vesting Questions	332

CHAPTER TWENTY-FIVE
False Analogy	337
Infamous Individuals	341
Apples and Oranges	344
Reliance on Foreign Law	347

CHAPTER TWENTY-SIX
Either/Or: Hobson's Choice	351
Third Alternative	357
Citing Black's Law Dictionary	360
Bright-Line Approach	362

CHAPTER TWENTY-SEVEN
Genetic: Attacking the Origin	365
A "Novel" Theory	373
Long-Standing Practices	377

CHAPTER TWENTY-EIGHT
Red Herrings	379
Divert Jury's Attention	391

CONTENTS

❦ CHAPTER TWENTY-NINE
Straw Man — 393

Impose Martial Law — 394
Cell Phone Laws — 399

❦ CHAPTER THIRTY
Division: Painting with the Same Brush — 407

Guilt by Association — 409
Gender Stereotyping — 414
Peremptory Challenges — 416

❦ CHAPTER THIRTY-ONE
Composition: One Bad Apple — 421

Taxpayer Standing — 428
Special Risk of Wrongful Execution — 430

❦ CHAPTER THIRTY-TWO
Sweeping Generalizations — 435

Overbreadth vs. Underbreadth — 441
Sweep of Criminal Statutes — 446

❦ CHAPTER THIRTY-THREE
Hasty Generalizations — 449

Sovereign Immunity — 451
Year and a Day Rule — 453
"Silly Cases" — 454
Unprovoked Flight — 462

❦ CHAPTER THIRTY-FOUR
Lies, Damn Lies, and Statistics — 463

Are Both Sides Presented? — 466
Definition of "Average" — 468
Arguing by Analogy — 472

Index — 475

About the Author

Paul Bosanac has worked for the National Labor Relations Board for more than 30 years. He has three published articles, one of which appears in the American Bar Association's *The Labor Lawyer*. As part of Marquette University's Certificate in Labor Relations Program, he taught basic and advanced Labor Law courses. He served as Chairperson of the Wisconsin State Bar Association's Labor and Employment Law Section. When the American Bar Association's Labor and Employment Law Section instituted a fellowship program, he was selected as a recipient of one of the inaugural fellowships.

Acknowledgments

This book took slightly less time than it did for Brahms to compose his Symphony No. 1 (his masterpiece was completed in 21 years). There are two reasons for this. First, I did not want to give up my day job. Second, this book is based on legal examples to illustrate more than 30 different techniques of argument. There was no shortcut to extensive reading to winnow many relevant and interesting examples of each technique. I extend my appreciation and thanks to Richard Paszkiet, Deputy Director of American Bar Association Publishing, for his consideration of my manuscript, and his role in having the ABA publish my book. Many, many thanks to Annie Beck of Lachina Publishing Services, project manager of my book, who was responsible for the day-to-day coordination of the typesetting, proofreading, and shipment of my book to the printer. Annie's gentle handling of proposed changes to the manuscript and willingness to listen to rationales for not making changes are truly appreciated. Rick and Annie's staffs also deserve inestimable credit for the careful attention they paid to every last detail of the manuscript. Any errors are my responsibility. So many of my friends encouraged me to work on this book, that I cannot name them all—but I am grateful to everyone. I would be remiss, however, not to acknowledge Cathy Roth's reading drafts of early chapters and her helpful suggestions. Patricia Ellingson willingly assisted me in proofreading the manuscript under tight deadlines. My colleague and friend, Ben Mandelman, for years too numerous to recall, patiently listened to me talk about examples I found, and offered his critiques. Finally, I would like to thank my parents, who impressed on their son the importance of education.

Introduction

Legal arguments, just as arguments in ordinary discourse, occur in patterns. Recognizing these patterns, and understanding their strengths and weaknesses, are the keys to effective argument.

Students of logic recognize these patterns as informal fallacies, arguments that are flawed, but not in a technical, formal sense. By way of illustration, an attorney may attack someone's character, rather than the substantive of his or her argument. This is known as the ad hominem (abusive) informal fallacy. Technically, there is nothing "wrong" with attacking someone's character, but what does that have to do with the soundness of the proponent's argument? A character attack is usually effective, because people believe that exhibiting a bad character is associated with untruthfulness or untrustworthiness.

Traditional books on logic treat informal fallacies as orphans, favoring concepts like inductive and deductive reasoning, and featuring Venn diagrams. The few logic books dedicated to informal fallacies are ill-suited to attorneys. First, the examples rarely involve legal subjects. Second, and more significantly, these books focus on classifying fallacies, using some variation on Aristotle's classification system, rather than recognizing the arguments.

This book is dedicated to presenting informal fallacies through legal arguments, save for a handful that are too noteworthy to pass up. Significantly, a three-page Legal Logic Flow Chart helps identify the appropriate informal fallacy by asking questions that direct the attorney to the name and relevant chapter.

This book begins with an explanation of the Legal Logic Flow Chart and offers two legal examples (a Top 10 list from actress Winona Ryder's shoplifting trial and former U.S. House of Representatives Majority Leader Tom DeLay's press conference, responding to his indictment) on which to practice using the chart. The rules of legal logic are next, followed by an examination of arguments attorneys are ethically prohibited from making. More than 30 informal fallacies are then discussed. Each chapter begins with a relevant quotation, followed by a brief explanation of the informal fallacy that includes how it is used and if it is known by other names. Many chapters have point-counterpoint examples of informal fallacies. The last chapter presents statistical uses of informal fallacies, which are, actually, no different from their non-statistical counterparts. Only U.S. Supreme Court cases are referred to by name in the text, as attorneys are likely to have a passing familiarity with them.

Among the topics discussed in this book are the following (parentheses designate the appropriate chapters):

- When is it permissible to use the analogy of an iceberg and when is it not? (ignorance)
- What parts of anatomy can trial attorneys appeal to, and what parts are forbidden? (mob/public)
- Learn about legal rules: invited response rule (two wrongs); rule of lenity (amphiboly); Golden Rule. (sympathy)
- Do quotes have to enclose verbatim statements? (accent)
- Can a judge go too far in reminding a witness of the penalties of perjury? (threats/force/fear)
- Can a witness be incredible as a matter of law? (poison the well)
- What is Occam's Razor? (rules of legal logic)
- What do Clarence Darrow's opening statement in the *Scopes* trial and the dissent from *Plessy v. Ferguson* have in common? (slippery slope)
- Why do some States prohibit attorneys from arguing that a corporation has no heart, soul, or conscience? (hypostatization)
- Committing this fallacy can have significant consequences (Rule 11 Sanctions) beyond making a bad argument. (accent)

No matter what area of law a lawyer practices, informal fallacies are readily applicable. In computer terms, informal fallacies have cross-platform application. Learning to use, and defend against, informal fallacies are the keys to effective argument.

INTRODUCTION xvii

Note

A professor of mine would exhibit a serious smile, nod his head, and exclaim, "I am being clinical, not cynical," whenever he was about to approach a contentious topic. That characterization aptly fits this book. The examples used throughout—all from the "real" world, none made up—were chosen for their suitability to illustrate the informal fallacy under discussion, not for their speaker or writer. Although all current U.S. Supreme Court Justices are cited for at least one example of an informal fallacy, none of the examples was chosen because of a Justice's particular judicial philosophy. No criticism or social commentary should be inferred from any of the examples that appear in this book. The reader must remember that all of these examples commit the fallacy of accent; that is, they are taken out of context in order to present a readable book. Citations to the sources of the arguments allow the reader to evaluate the arguments in context.

If the study of informal fallacies and the law were a course, it would be a procedural one, rather than a substantive one. The technique is important to advance (or reply to) an effective argument, regardless of which substantive area of the law is under consideration.

Finally, I have worked for more than 30 years for a Federal Government Agency. Out an abundance of caution, I note that any views that may be inferred do not represent those of the National Labor Relations Board or its General Counsel.

❧ CHAPTER ONE

The Legal Logic Flow Chart

IN THE COURTROOM, lawyers identify hearsay with a shorthand expression: an out-of-court statement offered for its truth. This expression does not cover all hearsay possibilities, of course, but it provides a starting point for detecting unreliable hearsay from a witness. The legal logic flow chart, similarly, provides a means to identify fallacious arguments. By posing a series of questions, a lawyer can zero in on the informal fallacy underpinning the opposing argument. Once the argument is identified, the page number directs the reader to the beginning of the appropriate chapter. This chart appears on the next page.

CHAPTER ONE

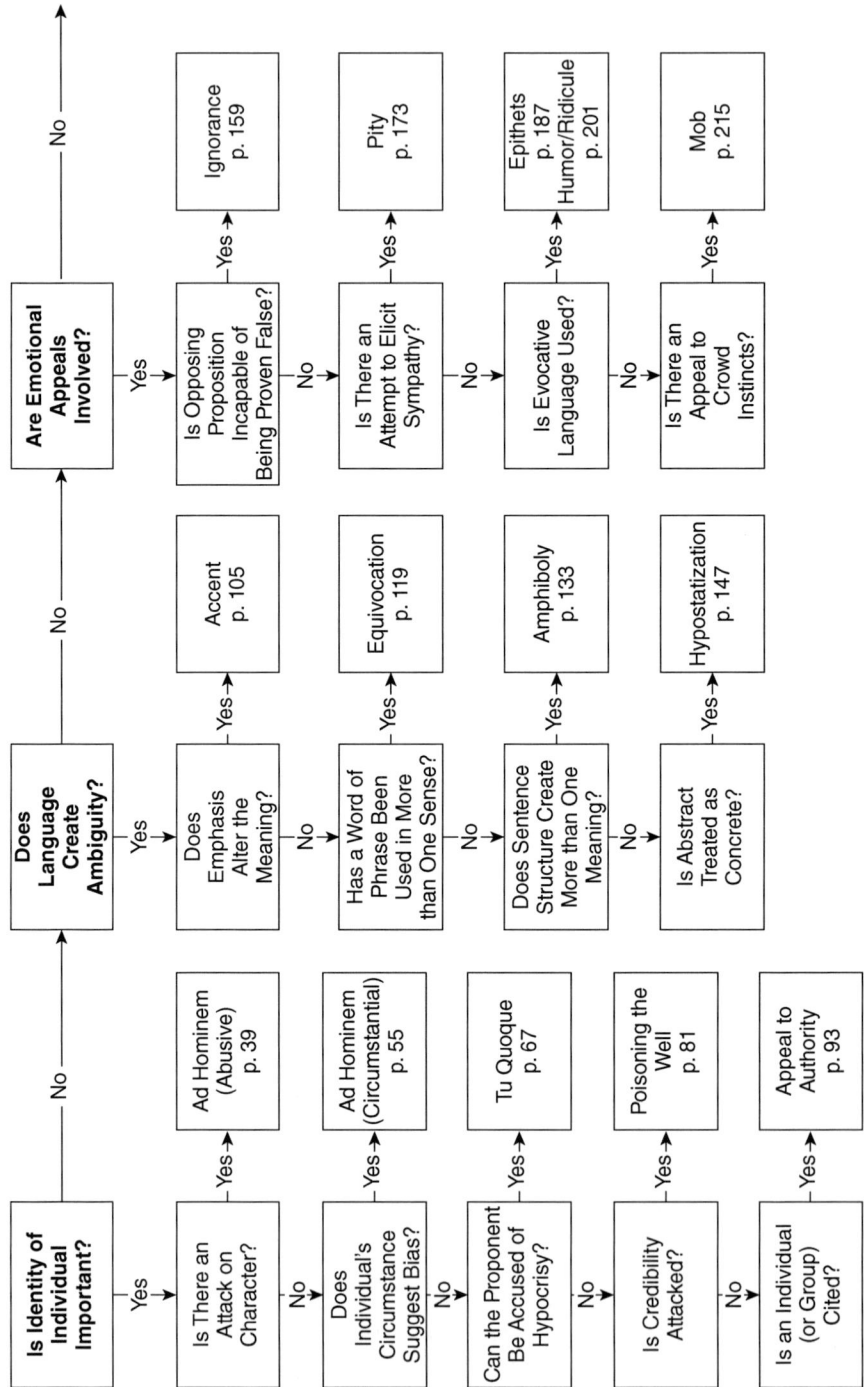

THE LEGAL LOGIC FLOW CHART

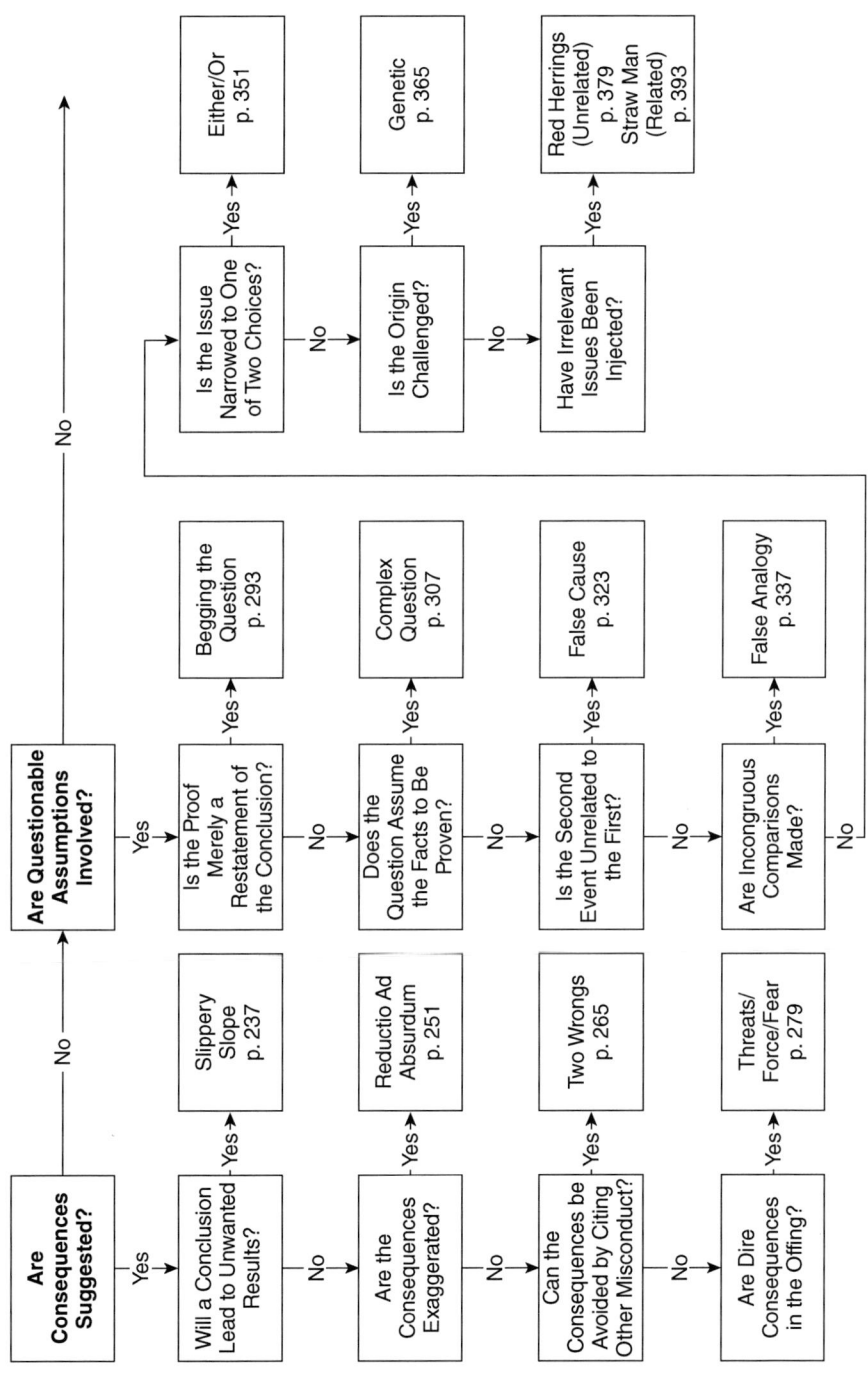

CHAPTER ONE

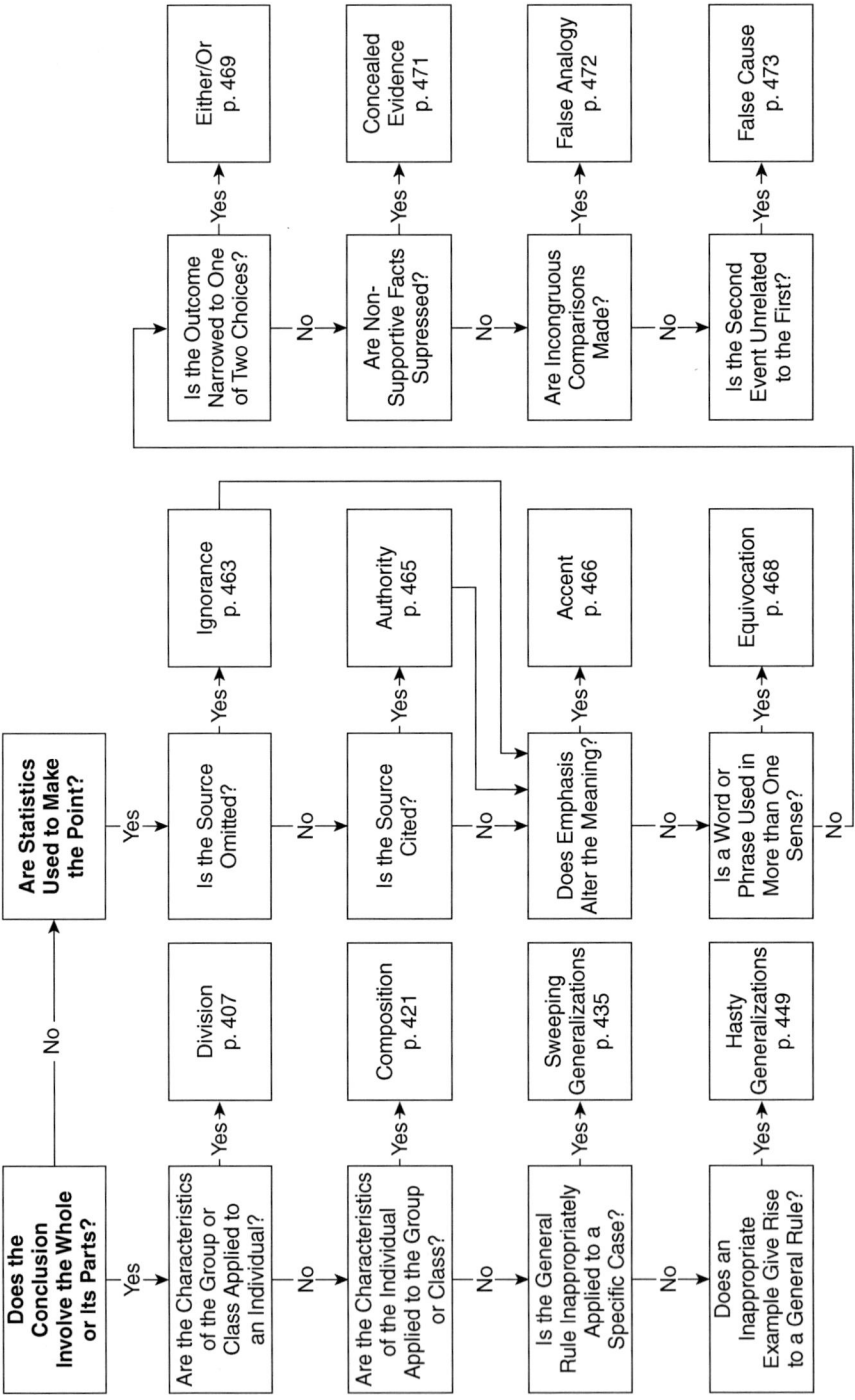

The analysis for identifying informal fallacies begins with questions intended to narrow the argument to seven main categories. These questions are:

1. Does the argument's significance depend on the identity of an individual (or group)?
2. Does language create confusion?
3. Is there an emotional appeal?
4. Are there consequences associated with an argument?
5. Does the conclusion, or result, depend on questionable assumptions?
6. Does the conclusion relate to a whole or its parts?
7. Are statistics used to make the point?

Each of these questions can be answered "yes" or "no." A "no" answer directs the reader to the right, to the next main category; a "yes" answer directs the reader to the questions below, intended to narrow the choices to the correct fallacy. A "yes" answer to any of the subsidiary questions identifies the fallacy and points the reader to the page where that fallacy is discussed and explained.

Seven Categories

The first main category of fallacy is person-specific. That is, the argument has no meaning unless the identity of the individual is known. Usually, the argument contains the person's name or some other identifying characteristic, such as his title, but the individual's identity may be obvious only from the context of the argument. An example of an argument in this category occurs when a person's character is attacked with the expectation that what this person says is not credited.

The second category involves confusion resulting from some aspect of language, either written or spoken. An attorney may declare, "Justice requires that the court . . ." Exactly what does "justice requires" mean? Attributing human characteristics (to require) to abstract concepts (justice) leaves a great deal of room for interpretation—and confusion. An attorney (or other legal professional) may either create, or take advantage of, such linguistic confusion.

The third category consists of an emotional appeal, a tug at our heart instead of our mind. Whenever an appeal is to our emotions, rather than to the facts, this fallacy is committed. Name-calling is often successful in defeating someone's argument, not because the individual's argument lacks merit, but because the emotional feelings stirred up overcome a dispassionate evaluation of the argument.

The fourth category contains arguments suggesting that advocating a certain position will have consequences, usually undesirable. A common example occurs when an attorney suggests that ruling for the other side will lead to an opening of the "floodgates" of unwanted litigation. Whether other litigation is spawned should be of no consequence to the merits of the case under consideration.

The fifth category involves conclusions, or results, that suggest questionable assumptions preceded their determination. If you find yourself scratching your head about a conclusion, chances are a questionable assumption underlies that conclusion. How often has it happened that an attorney offers an analogy, only to leave you wondering how what he described is an analogous situation?

The sixth category draws a conclusion about the whole or its parts. Either the characteristics of the whole are applied to a part, or vice versa. In referring to the "whole or its parts," it should be kept in mind that this may be a figurative as well as a literal description. The "whole" may consist of a general rule, from which a conclusion is drawn about a specific case, literally within the rule, but not within the spirit of the rule. Similarly, a conclusion may be drawn about an individual's characteristics by attributing those characteristics to the group to which the individual belongs.

The seventh category involves statistics or quantitative assertions—average, many, most, all. A certain precision is associated with statistics that gives them a self-authenticating advantage compared to nonstatistical assertions. If an argument can be reduced to mathematical quantification, the average listener will assume the argument's validity, if for no other reason than it has been "proven" statistically. Arguments based on statistics primarily employ the same fallacies as their nonstatistical counterparts, so an understanding of the first six major categories of fallacies readily transfers to statistical arguments.

After deciding which of these seven categories applies, by answering "yes" to the category's question, the next step is to work down the chart by asking the secondary questions that lead to the specific informal fallacy involved.

Connotations

Under the first heading—where the identity of the individual is important—there are five informal fallacies. Four of the five involve negative connotations; the fifth is generally positive. Attacks based on character (ad hominem (abusive)), bias (ad hominem (circumstantial)), hypocrisy (tu quoque), and credibility (poison the well) seek to undermine an argument by attacking the proponent directly. Citation to an individual or group (appeal to authority) in the hope that its prestige will lend conclusive support to the argument is the last fallacy in the person-specific column.

Ambiguity

Ambiguity created by some aspect of written or spoken English is the second heading, and there are four informal fallacies in this column. One statement can have two meanings, depending on which words are emphasized or stressed—the fallacy of accent. The tone of voice used to support an objection conveys either genuine respect or an annoying displeasure, when prefaced by the words "With all due respect, Your Honor."

Because words carry multiple meanings, a shift to another meaning of the identical word within the same argument can alter the argument substantially (equivocation). President Clinton's statement under oath questioning the meaning of "is" evoked public humor at his expense, and presents an example of equivocation. The logician's word "amphiboly" substitutes for the lay word "ambiguity": A dangling participle or an unclear reference to a pronoun creates confusion that can only be remedied by restructuring the sentence. Ascribing human characteristics to inanimate objects leads to confusion, and is a form of hypostatization.

Emotional Appeal

Emotional appeals comprise the third heading. Though there are many types of emotional appeals, some of which are found under other headings, four suitably fall under this heading. An inappropriate attempt to shift the burden of proof, to require proof of a proposition that is incapable of being proven false, is considered an appeal to ignorance. Arguments that appeal to our sympathies, rather than to our reasoning, commit the appeal-to-pity fallacy. Clarence Darrow was an effective practitioner of the art of appealing to juries' sympathies, having won many cases with this technique.

Certain words, unaccompanied by any argument, evoke strong emotions: these are known as epithets. The term "fighting words," a close cousin of epithets, describes words arousing anger and provoking a physical response. Properly timed humor can effectively persuade by disarming an adversary; ridicule makes an adversary the object of that humor. A catchall is found in the appeal to the mob, an appeal based on our desires to be acceptable to others.

Adverse Consequences

The fourth heading includes four arguments where adverse consequences are suggested. When an attorney argues that a certain decision will inevitably lead to adverse consequences, with no allowance for an intermediate result, she commits the fallacy of the slippery slope. Reducing an opponent's argument to an absurd proposition, reductio ad absurdum, exaggerates the consequences in the hope the argument will be rejected. To justify improper conduct, an attorney may argue that no consequences should befall her client, because the same or similar conduct previously was condoned. In other words, two wrongs make a right. Appeals to force or fear threaten to overcome a rational argument by focusing the opponent's attention on the dire consequences, rather than on the merits of the argument.

Questionable Assumptions

When you find yourself scratching your head, wondering how a proponent reached a particular conclusion, chances are that questionable assumptions are involved. Eight fallacies fall under the heading of questionable assumptions. In some arguments, the proof is merely a restatement of the conclusion—begging the question. When a lawyer asks a witness a question that assumes a fact not yet proven, the proper objection is: "The question assumes a fact not in evidence." In logic, this fallacy is known as a complex question.

The temporal sequence of events may lead to the conclusion that the second event was caused by the preceding event. When this is not the case, the fallacy of false cause is committed. A false analogy arises when significant, incongruous comparisons are drawn between two entities. An argument that limits the other side to one of two options, although more choices exist, commits the either/or fallacy. The validity of an argument does not depend on its origin, but many arguments are challenged because of their genesis. Irrelevant issues may arise by injecting wholly extraneous arguments (red herrings), or by raising a closely related issue and knocking it down (straw man), while claiming that the opponent's primary argument is meritless.

Erroneous Conclusions

The sixth heading includes fallacies where conclusions are applied to the whole or its parts, in a literal or figurative sense. Attributing the characteristics of the group or class to an individual (stereotyping, for example) often results in mistaken conclusions (division). Similarly, when a member's attributes are applied to the group or class, the group's diversity frequently produces erroneous conclusions (composition). A general rule may or may not apply to a specific case (sweeping generalization)—a figurative application of the whole to its parts. The hasty generalization fallacy is committed when a universal conclusion derives from an inappropriate example.

Statistical Arguments

Statistics is a category unto itself, even though the same fallacies from nonstatistical arguments carry over to statistical arguments. When the source of the statistic is omitted, the proponent relies on the appeal-to-ignorance fallacy, throwing the burden of disproving the statistic to the other party. If the source of the statistic is cited, the advocate may hope that the authority of the source overcomes any objection to the statistic itself (authority).

A statistical argument may include several statistics, only one or a few of which are presented. Accenting nonrepresentative statistics leaves, deliberately or inadvertently, a mistaken impression. The word "average" can assume several meanings, depending on the context. It may represent the sum divided by the total (average), or it may represent half of the numbers below and half above (mean). With statistics, just as with nonstatistical arguments, the fallacy of equivocation can be seductively misleading. Narrowing the outcome to one of two choices may eliminate valid arguments based on alternatives (either/or). Concealed evidence results from suppressing adverse statistical facts. Finally, statistical comparisons may not be appropriate, giving rise to a false analogy.

Two examples illustrate how the chart helps detect and identify informal fallacies. The first example involves the actress Winona Ryder; the second, former U.S. House of Representatives Majority Leader Tom DeLay.

Winona Ryder's Shoplifting

In late 2002, actress Winona Ryder was on trial for shoplifting, having been charged with grand theft, burglary, and vandalism. Deputy District Attorney Ann Rundle's closing argument presented the jury with a Top Ten list of things the law doesn't say about shoplifting.[1]

Each of the ten numbered items on Rundle's list finds a niche on the legal logic flow chart. Identifying the correct fallacy is a simple matter of following the method outlined above and applied below.

---

[1] PEOPLE, Nov. 18, 2002, at 23.

Top Ten Things the Law Doesn't Say

1. Only poor people steal.
2. No video, no crime.
3. Crime is okay if your "director" tells you to do it.
4. It's not stealing as long as you paid for some items.
5. D.A. must call every person working at Saks that day.
6. Only defense attorneys or celebrities can drive nice cars.
7. If it is not in the first report, it didn't happen.
8. If you sell $200 hair bows, you deserve to get ripped off.
9. Two wrongs make a right.
10. There's a higher standard of proof for celebrities.

1. Only poor people steal.

The first task is to decide which of the major categories can be eliminated, and which category contains the informal fallacy argued. This is not an argument that is person-specific; there is no ambiguity; there is no emotional appeal; there are no questionable assumptions; there is no suggestion of consequences. (Any doubts about whether a particular category contains the informal fallacy under analysis can be resolved by answering the questions under that heading. If the answer to all of the questions is "no," move to the next heading.) Here, answering the questions diligently should land the reader at the heading asking whether the conclusion involves the whole or its parts. The first two fallacies—division and composition—are, at first, a bit tricky to differentiate.

These fallacies require the reader to determine the members of the group or class and the identity of the individual belonging to that group or class. In this example, Rundle attempted to head off the argument that only poor people steal. Because Ryder (presumably a wealthy movie star) was not poor, she had no motive to steal. The class, as Rundle hoped to point out, is everyone who steals, and includes those who steal for reasons unrelated to ability to pay. The question then becomes: Are the characteristics of the group or class applied to an individual or vice versa? Assuming the obvious, that the characteristic is "stealing," then the group is "all who steal." By arguing that only "poor people" steal, the fallacy is one of division, which is determined by asking the question, "Are the characteristics of the group or class applied to the individual?"

2. No video, no crime.

Burden of proof is the primary issue here. Apparently, Rundle anticipated the defense would contend that with all the surveillance cameras throughout the store, at least one of them should have captured Ryder's activities. Without incriminating video evidence, the argument goes, there is no proof of a crime. This is an emotional plea to the jury, involving an appeal to ignorance: Is the opposing proposition incapable of being proven false? The defense attempted to shift the burden to the prosecution to show why the cameras did not capture Ryder in the act.

By arguing that evidence of guilt could only be proven by video, and since there was no such evidence, the defense raised a secondary argument: a straw man. Capturing a miscreant on tape engaging in illegal behavior can be evidence of wrongdoing, but it certainly is not the only method of proving guilt. Lack of video evidence would become an irrelevant argument if, for example, a credible store clerk stopped a shoplifter departing the store with an armload of unpaid merchandise.

3. Crime is okay if your "director" tells you to do it.

This argument is person-specific, not by name, but by job title: director. Rumors circulated that Ryder was researching a part in an upcoming movie, and that she wanted to experience what it was like to shoplift firsthand. To justify her shoplifting, therefore, Ryder would claim that her "director" told her to do it. Rundle sought to head off this appeal to authority by telling the jury that shoplifting is a crime, no matter who is cited as the motivation for the theft.

4. It is not stealing as long as you paid for some items.

Use of the word "some" is a clue that implicates the fallacy of accent. By accentuating the fact that Ryder paid for some items, the defense sought to redirect the jury's attention to Ryder's lawful actions. According to the defense, if Ryder were intent on shoplifting, she would not have paid for some items and not others. There must have been a mistake or, at least, reasonable doubt that she didn't intend to shoplift. Rundle correctly noted that whether some items were paid for does not excuse the fact that others were not.

5. D.A. must call every person working at Saks that day.

The unstated assumption of this argument is that the failure to call to the stand everyone who worked at Saks that day means the prosecution cannot prove Ryder was guilty of shoplifting. In other words, the defense attempted to shift to the prosecution the burden of demonstrating that every employee saw Ryder shoplift. Anything short of unanimity must result in acquittal. Just as the case with No. 2 above, the primary argument is an appeal to ignorance (prosecution incapable of eliciting incriminating testimony from all employees); the secondary argument, a straw man (testimony from all employees that is easily knocked down when they all don't appear—an irrelevant, but related issue). It is sufficient if at least one employee credibly testifies.

6. Only defense attorneys or celebrities can drive nice cars.

This argument involves individuals and groups or classes. The characteristic is "driving nice cars"; the group or class is all who drive such cars. Asking the question, "Are the characteristics of the individual (defense attorneys or celebrities) applied to the group or class (those who drive nice cars)?" yields the answer: fallacy of composition.

7. If it is not in the first report, it didn't happen.

The first report of any incident should at least mention what took place, so the reasoning goes, because it was the closest in time to the event and was based on the clearest, most accurate witness memories. Any omission of the critical event—shoplifting—suggests it didn't happen. This is another example of an appeal to ignorance and a straw man argument. The defense would have the prosecution assume the impossible burden of demonstrating Ryder shoplifted, with the proof limited to the first report's omission. There may be valid reasons why Ryder's shoplifting was not mentioned in the first report, but that does not mean a later report cannot be relied on to establish a crime took place.

8. If you sell $200 hair bows, you deserve to get ripped off.

As a consequence of selling hair bows at the outrageous price of $200, a store deserves to have them stolen, according to this argument. The word "deserves" suggests a moral justification for shoplifting. In this "two wrongs make a right" argument, the store's action (overcharging for hair bows) is an excuse for Ryder's action (not paying for them). The lawful response to overcharging is not self-help, but a refusal to purchase.

9. Two wrongs make a right.

A rose by any other name . . .

10. There's a higher standard of proof for celebrities.

This is yet another example of characteristics applied to individuals, and groups or classes. The characteristic is "higher standard of proof," and the group or class is "all celebrities." Celebrities, it is argued, because of their status, require a higher burden of proof for conviction than for the hoi polloi. Since Ryder is a celebrity (group or class), the higher burden of proof applies (characteristic applied to an individual). This argument is an example of the fallacy of division.

Majority Leader Tom DeLay's Indictment

Ronnie Earle, the district attorney for Travis County, Texas, brought an indictment against House of Representatives Majority Leader Thomas DeLay (R-TX), on September 28, 2005. DeLay, wasting no time (pun intended), called a press conference later that day to denounce the indictment. A text of his remarks appears in its entirety,[2] followed by an analysis of the informal fallacies drawn upon to condemn the indictment.

DeLay: How are you doing? You got any news today?

QUESTION: A little.

(LAUGHTER)

DeLay: Just another day at the office.

Good afternoon. Thank you all for attending.

This morning, in an act of blatant political partisanship, a rogue district attorney in Travis County, Texas, named Ronnie Earle charged me with one count of criminal conspiracy: a reckless charge wholly unsupported by the facts.

This is one of the weakest, most baseless indictments in American history. It's a sham and Mr. Earle knows it.

It's a charge that cannot hold up even under the most glancing scrutiny.

This act is the product of a coordinated, premeditated campaign of political retribution; the all-too-predictable result of a vengeful investigation led by a partisan fanatic.

Mr. Earle is abusing the power of his office to exact personal revenge for the role I played in the Texas Republican legislative campaign in 2002 and my advocacy for a new, fair and constitutional congressional map for our state in 2003.

As it turned out, those efforts were successful. Texas Republicans did, indeed, win a legislative majority. A fair and representative congressional map was drawn and it was approved by the legislature. And the Texas congressional delegation now, after the 2004 elections, fairly represents the values and attitudes of the people of the state of Texas.

---

[2]http://www.nytimes.com/2005/09/28/politics/28text-delay.html.

Over the course of this long and bitter political battle, it became clear that the retribution for our success would be ferocious. Today, that retribution is being exacted.

Mr. Earle, an unabashed partisan zealot with a well-documented history of launching baseless investigations and indictments against his political enemies, has been targeting a political action committee on whose advisory board I once served.

During his investigation, he has gone out of his way to give several media interviews in his office—the only days he actually comes to the office, I'm told—in which he has singled me out for personal attacks, in direct violation of his public responsibility to conduct an impartial inquiry.

Despite his long-standing animosity toward me and the abusive investigation that animosity has, unfortunately, rendered, as recently as two weeks ago, Mr. Earle himself publicly admitted I had never been a focus or target of his inquiry.

Soon thereafter, Mr. Earle's hometown newspaper ran a biting editorial about his investigation, rhetorically asking what the point had been, after all, if I wasn't to be indicted.

It was this renewed political pressure in the waning days of his hollow investigation that led to this morning's action, political pressure that also came from Democrat leaders.

In accordance with the rules of the House Republican Conference, I will temporarily step aside as floor leader in order to win exoneration from these baseless charges.

Now let me be very, very clear: I have done nothing wrong. I have violated no law, no regulation, no rule of the House. I have done nothing unlawful, unethical or, I might add, unprecedented, even in the political campaigns of Mr. Earle himself.

My defense in this case will not be technical or legalistic; it will be categorical and absolute. I am innocent. Mr. Earle and his staff know it. And I will prove it.

Here in Washington, there's work, very hard work ahead of our conference. We have a war to win, a region to rebuild, a budget to balance, taxes to cut, a government to reform, and a nation to lead.

In the coming weeks, the House is committed to major legislation reforming our border security and immigration laws, alleviating the rising costs of gasoline and heating fuel before the winter, and saving tens of billions of dollars through reforming federal entitlement programs.

My job right now is to serve my constituents and our nation in support of this ambitious and needed agenda.

As for the charges, I have the facts, the law, and truth on my side, just as I have against every false allegation my opponents have flung at me over the last 10 years. Once exposed to the light of objective scrutiny, every one of their frivolous accusations against me has been dismissed, and so will Mr. Earle's.

Thank you very much for this opportunity to speak to you guys today. Thank you.

The analysis follows the bolded excerpts from the transcript.

DeLay: How are you doing? You got any news today?
QUESTION: A little.
(LAUGHTER)
DeLay: Just another day at the office.

In advance of his prepared remarks, DeLay asked the reporters if there was any news, knowing full well he was there to address the top story of the day. His use of understatement brought laughter to the press conference, and emotionally disarmed the issue he was about to confront. Humor, especially self-deprecating humor, is an effective technique to deflect attention from a difficult situation.

This morning, in an act of blatant political partisanship, a rogue district attorney in Travis County, Texas, named Ronnie Earle charged me with one count of criminal conspiracy: a reckless charge wholly unsupported by the facts.

Two fallacies appear in this single sentence. First, DeLay personally attacked Earle for "blatant political partisanship." In other words, Earle, who happened to be a Democrat, brought the indictment, not because it was meritorious, but because his political circumstance as a Democrat created a bias against DeLay, a Republican (ad hominem (circumstantial)). Second, DeLay pinned Earle with the label "rogue" district attorney, and referred to the charge in the indictment as "reckless." Both words evoke strong emotions, the hallmark of epithets. Among other epithets sprinkled throughout the remarks are "baseless" indictments, "sham," "zealots," and "hollow" investigation.

As it turned out, those efforts were successful. Texas Republicans did, indeed, win a legislative majority. A fair and representative congressional map was drawn and it was approved by the legislature. And the Texas congressional delegation

now, after the 2004 elections, fairly represents the values and attitudes of the people of the state of Texas.

To buttress his argument that he was being persecuted, not prosecuted, DeLay contended his earlier actions brought about "a fair and representative congressional map" and a congressional delegation that "fairly represent the values and attitudes" of Texans. The word "fair" suggests a conclusion, but what is fair for one political party is, probably, unfair for the other. Like "beauty," "fairness" is in the eye of the beholder. As such, use of words like "fair" begs the question, because the proof of fairness depends on the conclusion that something is fair.

During his investigation, he has gone out of his way to give several media interviews in his office—the only days he actually comes to the office, I'm told—in which he has singled me out for personal attacks, in direct violation of his public responsibility to conduct an impartial inquiry.

DeLay ridiculed Earle's office attendance by linking it exclusively to the granting of media interviews. Earle may have had many valid reasons for not spending extended time in his office, but DeLay's ridicule appeal obscures those reasons. Although the exact nature of Earle's alleged "personal attacks" is unspecified, the implication (and earmark of an ad hominem attack) is clear: DeLay was indicted not for what he did, but for who he is.

Despite his longstanding animosity toward me and the abusive investigation that animosity has, unfortunately, rendered, as recently as two weeks ago, Mr. Earle himself publicly admitted I had never been a focus or target of his inquiry.

Soon thereafter, Mr. Earle's hometown newspaper ran a biting editorial about his investigation, rhetorically asking what the point had been, after all, if I wasn't to be indicted.

It was this renewed political pressure in the waning days of his hollow investigation that led to this morning's action, political pressure that also came from Democrat leaders.

According to DeLay, politics drove the indictment. As proof, he cited Earle's statement of two weeks before that DeLay was not the target of the indictment, and Earle's hometown newspaper questioned the purpose of the investigation. Reference to the newspaper was an appeal to authority. Whether the editorial writers' expressed doubts about the validity of the investigation, if DeLay was not a target, contributed to the indictment is irrelevant. It was sufficient to cite the editorial writers as a possible motivation for Earle's actions.

> **Now let [me] be very, very clear: I have done nothing wrong. I have violated no law, no regulation, no rule of the House. I have done nothing unlawful, unethical or, I might add, unprecedented, even in the political campaigns of Mr. Earle himself.**

By comparing his conduct with Earle's, DeLay sought to legitimize his actions. After all, if the prosecutor engaged in the same political conduct, it must have been legal. No one knows if Earle engaged in the identical conduct, but that will not be the issue in a trial; only DeLay's conduct will be judged. The fallacy of tu quoque accuses the proponent of hypocrisy by having engaged in the same or similar conduct.

> **My defense in this case will not be technical or legalistic; it will be categorical and absolute. I am innocent. Mr. Earle and his staff know it. And I will prove it.**

These sentences constitute an emotional appeal. DeLay will face the indictment head on—because he is innocent. He will not rely on some "technicality" to escape liability, but will fight the charges based on the facts and the law. This appeal to the public hopes to invoke our sense of fair play, and our desire to support those who have been wronged by "the system."

> **Here in Washington, there's work, very hard work ahead of our conference. We have a war to win, a region to rebuild, a budget to balance, taxes to cut, a government to reform, and a nation to lead.**

> **In the coming weeks, the House is committed to major legislation reforming our border security and immigration laws, alleviating the rising costs of gasoline and heating fuel before the winter, and saving tens of billions of dollars through reforming federal entitlement programs.**

> **My job right now is to serve my constituents and our nation in support of this ambitious and needed agenda.**

Hard work may lie ahead, but what that had to do with the indictment is anyone's guess. Balancing the budget, cutting taxes, and winning the war in Iraq are appeals to the public—our desire for fiscal responsibility and our sense of patriotism (public/mob). Because these issues have absolutely no relationship to the indictment, it is an irrelevant appeal—a red herring.

> As for the charges, I have the facts, the law, and truth on my side, just as I have against every false allegation my opponents have flung at me over the last 10 years. Once exposed to the light of objective scrutiny, every one of their frivolous accusations against me has been dismissed, and so will Mr. Earle's.

This argument involves the whole and its parts. The group or class consists of all the previously dismissed accusations leveled against DeLay. Because they were dismissed, DeLay argues, this one will be too. The characteristics of the group (dismissals) are, therefore, applied to the individual case—the current indictment—to produce the fallacy of division.

The Chart as an Argument Generator

A final word about the legal logic flow chart itself. As originally conceived, the chart was intended to decipher an argument and lead the advocate to the particular informal fallacy involved. Once identified, the informal fallacy could be examined for strengths and weaknesses, and an appropriate response could be fashioned. After working with the chart, it became apparent that the chart could be used in reverse, as an argument generator. More than 30 informal fallacies appear on the three-page chart. When confronted with the need for an argument, just look at the questions under each of the major headings, and determine if an argument could be constructed in line with the questions.

By way of example (and no matter what area of law is involved), if the other side proposes a novel argument, it can be argued that such an argument would lead to unwanted results (slippery slope), such as a flood of lawsuits. With a bit of imagination, the unwanted results could be exaggerated, leading to a reductio ad absurdum argument. Or, a genetic argument could be propounded by attacking the newness of the argument and its unsupportability in the existing body of law. Additionally, pithy humor or ridiculing some aspect of the novel argument could undercut its efficacy.

An argument need not be limited to one informal fallacy: a combination (or cluster) of informal fallacies is most effective. The greater the familiarity with informal fallacies, the easier it is to come up with an argument. Lack of imagination is the only limitation on forging an effective argument.

CHAPTER TWO

The Rules of Legal Logic

Rule 1

The number of informal fallacies in an argument is directly proportional to the fervor of the advocacy.

THE FIRST RULE OF LEGAL LOGIC is one of awareness. An attorney cannot defend against an informal fallacy if he is not aware of its use. Informal fallacies typically arise during heated arguments (often involving major social, political, or religious issues), or when the stakes are big, such as in criminal matters or high-dollar cases. The First Rule of Legal Logic does not guarantee that informal fallacies will be used under these circumstances, but it alerts the attorney that informal fallacies are likely to occur. As the temperature of the argument increases, the number of informal fallacies will likely increase, not in any direct relationship, but, rather, in a proportional one. Arguments of little consequence are not as likely to have informal fallacies cast about, but that does not mean that a lawyer can nap under these circumstances. Awareness is required at all times.

Rule 2

Informal fallacies usually travel in the company of other informal fallacies.

The Second Rule of Legal Logic can have two meanings. As a corollary to the First Rule, the Second Rule suggests that as an argument heats up, one informal fallacy will be accompanied by others, a rather insignificant conclusion. The second meaning, however, is consequential: one argument can contain multiple informal fallacies.

In the following excerpt, the author argued against the breakup of Microsoft, in antitrust litigation brought by the government, using fear, epithets, and mob appeals.

> Anyone who uses a personal computer, cares about preserving America's leadership in technology or is concerned about overreaching government regulation should take a close look at the government's proposal to break apart Microsoft and saddle it with myriad regulations and restrictions. At a time when technological advances are creating thousands of new jobs, improving productivity and helping children learn, the government's proposal would result in less innovation, fewer choices and higher prices for consumers . . . . Although the legal issues in the case won't be resolved for some time, one thing is clear: the government's plan to dismantle Microsoft and subject the remains to harsh regulatory constraints would cripple Microsoft's ability to innovate on behalf of consumers and could undermine the future success of America's high-tech industry.[1]

Appealing to fear, the author argued that nothing less than "the future success of America's high-tech industry" was at stake in the litigation. Many epithets supported the author's arguments: "overreaching government regulation," "myriad regulations and restrictions," "dismantle Microsoft," "harsh regulatory constraints," and "cripple Microsoft's ability to innovate." Public, or mob, appeals were made to "[a]nyone who uses a personal computer, [and] cares about preserving America's leadership in technology"; those who wanted to help "children learn"; and beneficiaries of "Microsoft's ability to innovate on behalf of consumers."

Multiple informal fallacies can appear in a single sentence, as demonstrated by Justice Scalia, dissenting in *Rogers v. Tennessee*,[2] a case involving the validity of imposing a requirement that a person's death occur within a year and a day from the commission of the murderous act: "I do not believe this is the system that the Framers envisioned or, for that matter, that any reasonable person would imagine."[3]

Justice Scalia's single sentence contains three informal fallacies:

---

[1] NEWSWEEK, May 22, 2000, at 42.
[2] 532 U.S. 451 (2001).
[3] *Id.* at 468.

1. An appeal to authority (citing the framers of the U.S. Constitution);
2. Begging the question (use of "reasonable" to suggest that anyone who disagrees with his argument would be "unreasonable");
3. Appeal to the public (who wants to be known as unreasonable?).

As one sentence contains three informal fallacies, there are multiple ways to respond to the argument. Being alert to the possibility of multiple informal fallacies, therefore, allows for a more effective response.

Rule 3

The best defense to an informal fallacy is an informal fallacy.

Because informal fallacies are so effective, the best defense is to respond to an argument with an informal fallacy, a "best defense is a good offense" strategy. Responding to an informal fallacy in the courtroom, or in other face-to-face situations, requires swift thinking and a ready command of many informal fallacies. In the event an appropriate responsive informal fallacy does not readily come to mind, an attorney's second option would be to understand what informal fallacy is being used by the other side, and point out the reasons why that fallacy lacks merit.

Rule 4

Use subtlety sparingly; keep the argument simple.

In the social sciences, subtlety is often valued as a sign of intellectual prowess; in the legal arena, however, subtlety can have disastrous consequences if, for example, the judge or jury fails to grasp the point of the argument. Although subtlety is an important part of argument, it is best used sparingly when making legal arguments. Complex legal arguments may suffer the same fate as subtle ones. If an argument involves many assumptions and facts, the proponent risks losing the legal audience part way through the presentation. A good principle to keep in mind is "Ockham's (Ockam's or Occam's) Razor, also called the *principle of parsimony, principle of simplicity,* or *principle of economy.*"[4]

---

[4]PETER A. ANGELES, THE HARPERCOLLINS DICTIONARY OF PHILOSOPHY 211 (HarperCollins, 2d ed. 1992).

The principle implies: . . . of two or more possible explanations for phenomena choose the one that (a) explains what is to be explained with the fewest assumptions and explanatory principles; and (b) explains all, or most, of the facts that need explaining as satisfactorily as any of the other theories.[5]

In its most basic form, Occam's Razor suggests that a lawyer's best argument is the one that is simple and direct.

---

[5]*Id.*

CHAPTER THREE

Prohibited Arguments

AN ALTERNATIVE NAME for this chapter could easily be "Ethics of Argument." That title at the top of the page, however, would broadcast a message certain to ensure this would be the least read chapter in the book. Anything to do with "ethics" must automatically be dry and boring, right? Ask any lawyer from a state requiring an ethics course as part of its continuing legal education requirements what it is like to sit through an ethics class. A three-hour course feels like time is standing still. (What were those continuing legal education people thinking when they mandated ethics as part of the perennial requirements?)

Occasionally, however, a lecturer assembles an informative and entertaining alternative to the typical presentation. This chapter modestly aspires to present interesting examples of prohibited arguments.

Prohibited arguments may roughly be divided into two classes: those that run afoul of state bar ethical canons and those that deny due process, or otherwise violate a party's rights. The lines of demarcation are not always clear, but in this chapter discussion is narrowed to prohibited arguments that are ethically improper. Later chapters discuss other prohibited arguments.

It is as important to avoid advancing improper arguments as it is to recognize when others make them—so that an objection can be made or other corrective action taken. The failure to object to an improper argument in the courtroom limits the review only for "plain error," while a contemporaneous objection permits review under the harmless error standard. In *Johnson v. United States*,[1] the United States Supreme Court laid out a four-factor test for analyzing a "plain error" challenge:

---

[1] 520 U.S. 465 (1997).

(B)efore an appellate court can correct an error not raised at trial, there must be (1) error, (2) that is plain, and (3) that affect[s] substantial rights. If all three conditions are met, an appellate court may then exercise its discretion to notice a forfeited error, but only if (4) the error seriously affect[s] the fairness, integrity, or public reputation of judicial proceedings.[2] (quotations and citations omitted; brackets in original; parentheses added).

By way of contrast, the harmless error standard only requires a consideration of the asserted error in light of the record as a whole.[3] It is far better to quickly recognize an improper argument and reduce its impact (with an appropriate objection) than to have to rely on extensive judicial review.

This chapter serves as a bridge from the Legal Logic Flow Chart to the following chapters that discuss individual informal fallacies. The emphasis is on recognizing the fallacy (improper argument) involved, but examples are also discussed to provide a logical context for the improper **argument**.

A comparison of prohibited arguments in a criminal case with those in a civil case demonstrates there are no substantial differences, although the standards are couched in slightly different terms:

Criminal Case	Civil Case	Informal Fallacies (Primary Ones)
A prosecutor . . .	An attorney . . .	
. . . should not express his or her personal belief or opinion as to the truth or falsity of any testimony or evidence . . .[4]	[shall not] . . . state a personal opinion as to the . . . credibility of a witness . . .[5]	Authority
. . . may [not] express a personal opinion as to the justice of his or her cause . . .[6]	[shall not] . . . state a personal opinion as to the justness of a cause . . .[7]	Authority

---

[2]*Id.* at 466–67.
[3]United States v. Young, 470 U.S. 1, 11–12 (1985).
[4]ABA STANDARDS FOR CRIMINAL JUSTICE PROSECUTION FUNCTION AND DEFENSE FUNCTION [hereinafter STANDARDS] 3-5.8(b) (3rd ed. 1993).
[5]MODEL RULES OF PROF'L CONDUCT [hereinafter MODEL RULES] 3.4 (e) (2008 Edition).
[6]STANDARDS 3-5.8(b), Commentary, at 108.
[7]MODEL RULES 3.4 (e).

Criminal Case	Civil Case	Informal Fallacies (Primary Ones)
. . . should not express his or her personal belief or opinion as to . . . the guilt of the defendant.[8]	[shall not] . . . state a personal opinion as to . . . the culpability of a civil litigant or the guilt or innocence of an accused . . .[9]	Authority
. . . should not make arguments calculated to appeal to the prejudices of the jury.[10]	[Exclusion of relevant evidence on grounds of prejudice . . .] (Although appeals to prejudice are not specifically restricted under the Model Rules, Federal Rule of Evidence 403 prohibits the introduction of prejudicial material.)	Ad Hominem (Abusive) Ad Hominem (Circumstantial) Red Herring Straw Man Two Wrongs Epithets Humor/Ridicule Public/Mob
. . . should refrain from argument which would divert the jury from its duty to decide the case on the evidence.[11]	[shall not] . . . allude to any matter that the lawyer does not reasonably believe is relevant or that will not be supported by admissible evidence . . .[12]	Red Herring Straw Man

ABA Standards for Criminal Justice impose similar restrictions on prosecutors and defense counsel when arguing to the jury. For example, certain standards are tailored to the interests of the parties represented by the prosecutor and defense counsel:

. . . .

(b) The prosecutor should not express his or her personal belief or opinion as to the truth or falsity of any testimony or evidence or the guilt of the defendant.[13]

. . . .

---

[8] STANDARDS 3-5.8(b).
[9] MODEL RULES 3.4 (e).
[10] STANDARDS 3-5.8(c).
[11] STANDARDS 3-5.8(d).
[12] MODEL RULES 3.4 (e).
[13] STANDARDS 3-5.8(b).

> (b) Defense counsel should not express a personal belief in his or her client's innocence . . .[14] (ellipses added).

In two other respects, the obligations are identical and substitution of "prosecutor" for "defense counsel" produces the same standard for defense counsel:

> . . . .
>
> (c) The prosecutor should not make arguments calculated to appeal to the prejudices of the jury.[15]
>
> (d) The prosecutor should refrain from argument which would divert the jury from its duty to decide the case on the evidence . . .[16] (ellipses added).

Personal Belief or Opinion

The Commentary to the Standards explains why a prosecutor should not express his or her personal belief or opinion:

> The prosecutor's argument is likely to have significant persuasive force with the jury . . . Prosecutorial conduct in argument is a matter of special concern because of the possibility that the jury will give special weight to the prosecutor's arguments, not only because of the prestige associated with the prosecutor's office, but also because of the fact-finding facilities presumably available to the office.[17] (ellipses added).

Another expression of the rationale for the prohibition is found in a Fifth Circuit decision:

> To permit counsel to express his personal belief in the testimony (even if not phrased so as to suggest knowledge of additional evidence not known to the jury), would afford him a privilege not even accorded to witnesses under oath and subject to cross-examination. Worse, it creates the false issue of the reliability and credibility of counsel. This is peculiarly unfortunate if one of them has the advantage of official backing.*
>
> *Where would this leave a criminal defendant who is entitled to representation, but whose counsel does not believe in his inno-

---

[14]STANDARDS 4-7.7(b).
[15]STANDARDS 3-5.8(c); 4-7.7(c).
[16]STANDARDS 3-5.8(d); 4-7.7(d).
[17]STANDARDS 3-5.8, Commentary, at 107.

cence? Must his counsel nevertheless assert such a belief in order to counter the expressed opinion of government counsel, or does such a defendant have an unrefuted witness against him, in the form of the prosecuting attorney? Or should a prosecutor be permitted to argue, for example, "Members of the jury, I tell you that in my opinion trained to examine evidence this defendant is guilty as hell. I know it. Even his own counsel knows it. Oh yes, his counsel asked you to find him not guilty. But I notice that not once did he suggest to you that he had even a shadow of belief in his client's innocence. Why didn't he? Because his conscience wouldn't permit him to. Even his own lawyer doesn't think he is innocent, but he wants you . . . etc., etc. That is not the argument in this case, but we see no stopping point except the one stated in the canon.[18] (parentheses and ellipses in original).

Accordingly, Standards 3-5.8(b) prohibits the prosecutor from making an appeal to authority (by expressing a personal belief or an opinion). Common to all appeals to authority is the notion that the weight of the authority will persuade, without reliance on effective arguments, or consideration of the evidence.

Most of the improper appeals to authority by prosecutors are easily recognizable because their arguments are prefaced by the first person: "I" or "me" or "my." Some statements of personal opinion, however, are not so obvious, as when a prosecutor argued to the jury: "[t]he only way I can even imagine ever acquitting this man of any of the charges is if you totally disbelieve (the government's witness) as to everything he said about (the defendant)."[19] (brackets and underlining in original; parentheses added). Having previously found that the "use of 'I think' during closing argument was improper,"[20] the First Circuit concluded, "Although the prosecutor did not use the prohibited 'I think,' language, the statement nonetheless conveyed a personal opinion to the jury and, therefore, was improper."[21]

The Commentary to Standards 3-5.8(b) suggests an alternative, for those who hope to avoid this common pitfall:

> This kind of argument is easily avoided by insisting that lawyers restrict themselves to statements such as "The evidence shows . . ." or something similar.[22] (ellipses in original).

---

[18]Hall v. United States, 419 F.2d 582, 586 (5th Cir. 1969).
[19]United States v. Auch, 187 F.3d 125, 131 (1st Cir. 1999).
[20]United States v. Smith, 982 F.2d 681, 684 & n.2 (1st Cir. 1993).
[21]*Auch*, 187 F.3d at 131.
[22]STANDARDS 3-5.8, Commentary, at 108.

Other examples of permissible language, at least according to the Third Circuit, are the following:

> It is a perfectly acceptable practice for a prosecutor to use language in addressing the jury such as "you are free to conclude," "you may perceive that," "it is submitted that," or "a conclusion on your part may be drawn," to mention only a few examples of unobjectionable phraseology. It is obligatory for prosecutors to find careful ways of inviting jurors to consider drawing argued inferences and conclusions and yet to avoid giving the impression that they are conveying their personal views to the jurors.[23] (citation omitted).

Included Misconduct

The sweep of Standards 3-5.8(b) extends beyond its literal words, and includes many forms of related conduct, all coming under the heading of appeal to authority. Again, the Commentary provides the details:

> Neither advocate may express a personal opinion as to the justice (often referred to as "justness" in court opinions) of his or her cause or the veracity of witnesses . . . The prohibition in this Standard pertains to the prosecutor's personally endorsing, vouching for, or giving an opinion. The cause should turn on the evidence, not on the standing of the prosecutor, and the testimony of witnesses must stand on its own.[24] (parentheses and ellipses added).

In a Wisconsin case involving felony theft, the defendant's counsel commented on the justness of the prosecution's case. The prosecutor objected on the basis that defense counsel engaged in a personal (ad hominem (abusive)) attack, but the court correctly recognized it as an expression of the justness of the cause:

> **[Defense Counsel]:** One of the amazing things to me in this case has been the fact that they have the guts to come in here—
>
> **[Prosecutor]:** Objection, Your Honor. Personal attacks are improper.
>
> **THE COURT:** Members of the jury, under the rules of professional conduct that govern attorneys, a lawyer is prohibited in a trial to state a personal opinion as to the justness of a cause. It's a violation of the code of judicial ethics to do so and, as such, such an argument is improper. It is wrong. You are instructed to disregard it.

Counsel is admonished not to make that argument again.

---

[23]United States v. Nersesian, 824 F.2d 1294, 1328 (2d Cir. 1987).
[24]STANDARDS 3-5.8(b), Commentary, at 108.

[**Defense Counsel**]: They came in here with the slipshod, sloppy argument—

[**Prosecutor**]: Objection. Same objection. Nothing to do with the facts of the case at all.

[**Defense Counsel**]: This is my argument.

THE COURT: Counsel, you may comment on the witness. You may comment on the evidence. You may comment on the lack of evidence. Your personal opinion is not relevant as I've indicated to this jury.[25] (brackets in original; ellipses added; citation omitted).

Preceding the argument above, the defendant's counsel sponsored several additional emotional statements, including the following comment on the evidence: "His (the prosecutor's) explanation of the 4,400 cash is pathetic, pathetic . . . . They're really grabbing at straws . . . . This in my estimation on this evidence is criminal."[26] (parentheses added; ellipses in original).

During rebuttal argument, the plaintiff's attorney, in a case involving personal injuries from a car accident, expressed his view of the justness of the defense's case:

"[t]hat's the kind of defense and evidence and forthrightness that you get from this side of the room [indicating appellants]", "[t]he last thing that the defense wants in this case is for you to be fair and reasonable. That is why they come in here with this bogus counterclaim to try and make it look like they have something to argue about . . . ." and "but [appellee] is not going to lie to you. That's my client. She is not . . . she's not going to tell you something—."[27] (brackets and ellipses in original).

The Florida Appellate Court reversed the award of damages, finding that the defendant was denied a fair trial "as the result of the cumulative nature of counsel's improper comments."[28]

A defendant convicted of conspiracy to distribute crack cocaine argued that the prosecutor improperly commented on the evidence in his closing argument. Before the parties offered their closing arguments, the District Court cautioned:

[A]ttorneys are not supposed to state their own personal feelings about credibility of witnesses or the justness of a cause, so I don't want to hear the attorneys saying: I really believe that so and so is credible, or

---

[25]http://www.wisbar.org/wisctapp2/4q98/97-2835.html; (unpublished) Wisconsin v. Kenyon, October 8, 1998, District IV Court of Appeals.

[26]*Id.*

[27]Airport Rent-A-Car, Inc. v. Lewis, 701 So. 2d 893, 896 (Fla. App. 4 Dist. 1997).

[28]*Id.* at 897.

I really think that he isn't—that he's innocent or anything like that. You can't do it.²⁹ (brackets in original).

After the court's admonition, the prosecutor stated:

> I'm not going to talk to you about things that I don't think need any more explanation. And the reason is because I think there is a lot of evidence in this case that is just absolutely beyond any doubt at all.³⁰

The Tenth Circuit held, "[T]his comment constituted, at most, de minimis error and certainly does not rise to the level of plain error needed for reversal."³¹

When a prosecutor, or defense counsel, asserts that a witness is telling the truth, the lawyer's pledge is considered improper vouching (appeal to authority):

> **[Prosecutor]:** If [the prosecution witness] is going to come in and lie to you he could have done that very, very easily. There's [sic] a million little ways they could have given it to the Defendant. But they cannot. The prosecution witnesses cannot engage in that kind of conduct. They're bound by the truth.
>
> **[Defense Counsel]:** I object to that, your Honor.
>
> **THE COURT:** Overruled.
>
> **[Prosecutor]:** They're bound by their oath and limits of honesty. The last thing you might ask yourselves—
>
> **[Defense Counsel]:** I object to that, again I have a motion.
>
> **THE COURT:** Overruled, motion denied.³² (brackets added).

The government conceded, on appeal, "that this passage contains improper witness-vouching by the prosecution."³³ Based on this passage, and another also involving witness-vouching, the First Circuit concluded that a new trial for drug and firearm offenses was warranted.³⁴

Opinion as to Guilt

A prosecutor's personal opinion regarding the guilt of the defendant creates two risks:

---

²⁹United States v. Locke, 162 F.3d 1175, 1175 (10th Cir. 1998) (unpublished).
³⁰*Id.*
³¹*Id.*
³²United States v. Manning, 23 F.3d 570, 572 (1st Cir. 1993).
³³*Id.*
³⁴*Id.* at 575.

[S]uch comments can convey the impression that evidence not presented to the jury, but known to the prosecutor, supports the charges against the defendant and can thus jeopardize the defendant's right to be tried solely on the basis of the evidence presented to the jury; and the prosecutor's opinion carries with it the imprimatur of the Government and may induce the jury to trust the Government's judgment rather than its own view of the evidence.[35] (brackets added).

It is permissible, however, "to argue the conclusion that witnesses other than the accused are guilty of a crime when evidence of such has been produced."[36] (citation omitted).

The prosecutor in the case above overstepped the boundary, into improper comment on the veracity of witnesses and their guilt, by the following two sentences in his closing argument:

I suggest you shouldn't believe Drizos and Smith because they're guilty of exactly the same bankruptcy fraud that these two defendants are guilty of. And don't you assume that they are not going to get what's coming to them either.[37]

Notwithstanding the prosecutor's use of the expression, "I suggest" (sometimes held to be the equivalent of "The evidence shows"), the Third Circuit concluded the prosecutor offered an improper opinion:

The first sentence in the prosecutor's objectionable remarks suggested that the jury should not believe Drizos and Smith because they were also guilty of the crimes of which the defendants were guilty (ad hominem (circumstantial)). This statement was clearly improper to the extent that it reflected the prosecutor's opinion concerning the guilt of Mervis and Zehrbach.[38] (parentheses added).

Even though the prosecutor exceeded the bounds of proper argument, the court found the improper commentary was cured, and declined to reverse the conviction:

Although it is true that irreparable harm may be inflicted in a moment, the comments at issue were but two sentences in a closing argument that filled forty pages of transcript. Immediately after the objection, the court gave a specific instruction to disregard the prosecutor's comment, an instruction that the court repeated just a short time later at the close of the prosecutor's argument. As a general

---

[35] United States v. Zehrbach, 47 F.3d 1252, 1265 (3d Cir. 1995), *citing* United States v. Young, 470 U.S. at 18–19.
[36] 47 F.3d at 1266.
[37] *Id.* at 1264.
[38] *Id.* at 1265.

matter, the court told the jurors to disregard any personal opinion of counsel and to base their decision solely on the evidence. And, in its final instructions, the court cautioned the jury members that the arguments of counsel are not evidence . . . and that they must not consider any evidence that they were earlier instructed to disregard. We believe that this extensive cautioning by the court was sufficient to cure the prosecutor's error.[39] (ellipses added).

A prosecutor's expression of his belief in the guilt of the defendant was not reversed on appeal, although the prosecutor stated:

> Now, Eddie Vega, in his testimony, and I think maybe Albert said that there was always a Mr. Big in the heroin business, and that he takes the profits and the little guys go to jail or words to that effect. Albert said that he had done enough time for other people, and *in this case I think that you have sitting before you a genuine certified Mr. Big in the heroin business, and he is the Defendant* . . .[40] (italics in original; ellipses added).

This case was decided before *United States v. Young*,[41] in which the U.S. Supreme Court approved the "invited response" doctrine (two wrongs). Before *Young*, the Tenth Circuit did not countenance the idea that a party could respond to improper argument with another improper argument: "We must agree that the effect of this rebuttal argument was to impress the jury with the prosecuting attorney's personal conclusion that the appellant was guilty. Such remarks expressing the personal opinion of the prosecuting attorney have been emphatically disapproved."[42]

The outcome of this case, had it arisen after *Young*, is anyone's guess.

In a case where the defendant was charged with theft of government property, the prosecutor concluded her argument to the jury with the following:

> I think, ladies and gentlemen, that when you finish examining all these materials, you will be able to find, I suggest to you, that there is ample evidence there for you to find beyond any reasonable doubt that (defendant) did in fact commit the acts that the government charges her with. And I would ask you, therefore, to do your duty and return a verdict of guilty. Thank you.[43] (parentheses added).

---

[39] *Id.* at 1267.
[40] United States v. Rios, 611 F.2d 1335, 1343 (10th Cir. 1979).
[41] 470 U.S. 1 (1985).
[42] 611 F.2d at 1343.
[43] United States v. Mandelbaum, 803 F.2d 42, 43 (1st Cir. 1986).

The defense counsel did not contemporaneously object to the remarks, but after rebuttal, in a side bar, argued that the remarks were improper and asked for a "corrective instruction." The court denied this request. Finding that the remarks improperly commented on the guilt of the defendant, the First Circuit, nonetheless, concluded they were not severe, and were isolated. In the face of strong evidence of guilt, the court declined to reverse the conviction.[44]

Appeals to Prejudice

The Commentary to Standards 3-5.8(c) discusses the importance of avoiding appeals to prejudice:

> Remarks calculated to evoke bias or prejudice should never be made in a court by anyone, especially the prosecutor. Where the jury's predisposition against some particular segment of society is exploited to stigmatize the accused or the accused's witnesses, such argument clearly trespasses the bounds of reasonable inference or fair comment on the evidence. There are many cases in which courts have reversed convictions as the result of inflammatory remarks made by a prosecutor containing references to the defendant's race, religion, or ethnic background.[45]

Because remarks appealing to prejudice are based on a particular individual's circumstances, the ad hominem (circumstantial) fallacy may be implicated. Also, appeals to prejudice play to the mob mentality of rejecting individuals belonging to different races or nationalities (mob/public). Another possible fallacy is the fallacy of division, in which the characteristics of the group are applied to the individual—in other words, stereotyping:

> **[Deputy Prosecutor:]** There was one thing [that defense counsel mentioned] about, you know, it was the parents who wanted the conviction and somehow she was coached. Yeah, you can bet the parents wanted a conviction. *This is every mother's nightmare. Leave your daughter for an hour and a half, and you walk back in, and here's some black, military guy on top of your daughter.* That's what she's saying . . .
>
> **[Defense Counsel]:** Objection, your Honor. This is an appeal to racism.
>
> **THE COURT:** Overruled.[46] (italics, brackets, and ellipses in original).

---

[44]*Id.* at 44–46.
[45]*Id.* at 108.
[46]State v. Rogan, 984 P.2d 1231, 1238 (Haw. 1999).

In reversing the conviction, the Hawaii Supreme Court noted the evil in appealing to racial prejudice:

> In this case the deputy prosecutor's reference to Rogan as a "black, military guy" was clearly inflammatory inasmuch as it raised the issue of and cast attention to Rogan's race. Because there was no dispute as to the identity of the perpetrator in this case, Rogan's race was not a legitimate area of inquiry inasmuch as race was irrelevant to the determination of whether Rogan committed the acts charged . . . . Indeed, the deputy prosecutor's comment had the potential of distracting the jury from considering only the evidence presented at trial. It is therefore inescapable that the deputy prosecutor's reference to Rogan as a "black, military guy" was an improper emotional appeal that could foreseeably have inflamed the jury.[47] (ellipses added).

The deputy prosecutor's comments also violated the "golden rule" prohibition (pity) by asking the jury to assume the role of the complainant's mother:

> The deputy prosecutor's inflammatory reference to Rogan's race was further compounded by the statement that the incident was "every mother's nightmare," which was a blatantly improper plea to evoke sympathy for the Complainant's mother and represented an implied invitation to the jury to put themselves in her position. Like the deputy prosecutor's reference to Rogan's race, the "every mother's nightmare" comment was not relevant for purposes of considering whether Rogan committed the acts charged.[48]

Prejudicial remarks are not confined to arguments by the parties, but may result from a witness's testimony. In questioning a witness, the prosecutor elicited testimony that the defendant owned a gay nightclub:

> **Q:** Now, in the beginning of the restaurant when it first opened, how often did you speak with the defendant about the Galleria II Restaurant?
>
> **A:** On a daily basis.
>
> **Q:** When you say "daily basis," was that on the phone or in person?
>
> **A:** Usually in person.
>
> **Q:** Where was that?
>
> **A:** At the club that he owns in Providence, Gerardo's.

---

[47]*Id.* at 1240.
[48]*Id.*

Q: What type of club is that?
A: A gay night club.[49]

The defendant objected to the answer and moved for a mistrial, contending the comment was "gratuitous" and intended to "inflame the passions and prejudices of [the] jury."[50] (brackets added). The judge was concerned whether the jury could set aside any prejudice against gays, and spoke to each juror individually to ask whether the juror could render a fair decision, notwithstanding that the defendant owned a gay nightclub. Satisfied with the questioning of the jurors, the district court judge (and, later, the Court of Appeals) found nothing improper with the remarks.[51]

The admonition in Standards 3-5.8(d)—the prosecutor should not divert the jury from deciding the case on the evidence—prevents the prosecutor from using at least three informal fallacies: red herring, two wrongs, and ad hominem (abusive). The Commentary notes the prohibited arguments:

> References, for example, to the likelihood that other authorities, such as a governor or the appellate courts, will correct an erroneous conviction are impermissible efforts to lead the jury to shirk responsibility for its decision. Predictions about the effect of an acquittal on lawlessness in the community also go beyond the scope of the issues in the trial and are to be avoided.
>
> Of course, the restriction must be reciprocal; a prosecutor may be justified in making such a reply to an improper argument of defense counsel if made without provocation by the prosecutor . . .
>
> The prosecutor should not, moreover, use arguments which are, in essence, personal attacks on defense counsel. The prosecutor should abstain from any allusion to the personal peculiarities and idiosyncrasies of opposing counsel. The duty to avoid such a personal attack is also, obviously, reciprocal.[52] (footnote omitted; ellipses added).

Injecting Red Herrings

Interjecting an irrelevant, unrelated argument into the case gives rise to a red herring fallacy. The first of the two examples mentioned in

---

[49]United States v. DiSanto, 86 F.3d 1238, 1248–1249 (1st Cir. 1996).
[50]*Id.* at 1249.
[51]*Id.*
[52]STANDARDS 3-5.8(d), Commentary, at 109.

the Commentary concerns arguments to the jury that it is not the decision maker in a death penalty case. In 1985, the U.S. Supreme Court was confronted with this issue—a case in which a defendant shot and killed the owner of a small grocery store in the course of a robbery. During the capital sentencing proceeding, the prosecution, responding to the defense argument that the jury held the awesome responsibility of deciding whether the defendant should receive the death penalty, advanced the following argument:

> **Assistant District Attorney:** Ladies and gentlemen, I intend to be brief. I'm in complete disagreement with the approach the defense had taken. I don't think it's fair. I think it's unfair. I think the lawyers know better. Now, they would have you believe that you're going to kill this man and they know—they know that your decision is not the final decision. My God, how unfair can you be? Your job is reviewable. They know it. Yet they . . .
>
> **Counsel for Defendant:** Your Honor, I'm going to object to this statement. It's out of order.
>
> **Assistant District Attorney:** Your Honor, throughout their argument, they said this panel was going to kill this man. I think that's terribly unfair.
>
> **THE COURT:** Alright, go on and make the full expression so the Jury will not be confused. I think it proper that the Jury realizes that it is reviewable automatically as the death penalty commands. I think that information is now needed by the Jury so they will not be confused.
>
> **Assistant District Attorney:** Throughout their remarks, they attempted to give you the opposite, sparing the truth. They said "Thou shalt not kill." If that applies to him, it applies to you, insinuating that your decision is the final decision and that they're gonna take [the defendant] out in the front of this Courthouse in moments and string him up and that is terribly, terribly unfair. For they know, as I know, and as Judge Baker has told you, that decision you render is automatically reviewable by the Supreme Court. Automatically, and I think it's unfair and I don't mind telling them so.[53] (ellipses in original; brackets added; citation omitted).

Justice Thurgood Marshall, writing for the Supreme Court majority, held "that it is constitutionally impermissible to rest a death sentence on a determination made by a sentencer who has been led to believe that the responsibility for determining the appropriateness of the defendant's death rests elsewhere."[54]

---

[53] *Caldwell v. Mississippi*, 472 U.S. 320, 325–26 (1985).
[54] *Id.* at 328–29.

His rationale follows: "[F]or a sentencer to impose a death sentence out of a desire to avoid responsibility for its decision presents the specter of the imposition of death based on a factor wholly irrelevant to legitimate sentencing concerns."[55]

The second diversion example mentioned in the Commentary involves predictions of lawlessness in the community if the defendant is acquitted. Where a youth assaulted two police officers with a table knife, the prosecutor argued that acquitting the defendant would result in a new form of government: "[A]cquittal 'would leave police powerless to protect against' such behavior short of resort to martial law."[56] (brackets added).

The D.C. Circuit reversed the conviction, finding that an argument "raising the specter of martial law" was irrelevant to any issue in the case (red herring) and was an improper appeal to the jury's passion and prejudice.[57]

In the following, the prosecution replied to a defense argument (two wrongs) by unleashing a personal attack on the defense counsel (ad hominem (abusive)):

> Responding to defense counsel's closing argument in which he intimated that other individuals, including (a) prosecution witness ... might have murdered the (victims), the prosecutor stated that "[c]asting suspicion in [a] trial like that is completely irresponsible. It's irresponsible of the defense to make that accusation against somebody who has to live in this area, without anything whatsoever to back it up." (parentheses and ellipses added; brackets in original).

The prosecutor also faulted the defense counsel for arguing that a prosecution witness was lying about witnessing these murders, characterizing the defense view as "ludicrous" and "a smoke screen."[58]

The court carefully considered the challenges raised to the prosecutor's arguments:

> Here, although the prosecutor called defense counsel "irresponsible" for raising suspicions about (a prosecution witness), the point of her criticism was counsel's lack of evidentiary support for such a claim. Because the focus of her comment was on the evidence adduced at trial, rather than on the integrity of defense counsel, it was proper. Nor was it objectionable for the prosecutor to characterize defense counsel's challenge to (a witness's) credibility as "ludicrous" and "a smoke screen." The record shows that the prosecutor made this charge

---

[55] *Id.* at 332.
[56] Brown v. United States, 370 F.2d 242, 246 (D.C. Cir. 1966).
[57] *Id.*
[58] People v. Frye, 959 P.2d 183, 228 (Cal. 1998).

in the context of reviewing the evidence pertaining to the time of day the murders took place. She argued that there was no evidence tying the murders to the earlier time frame on which defense counsel had based its challenge to (a witness's) veracity. Read in the context of her broader argument, the prosecutor's remarks were a fair response to defense argument challenging (a witness's) testimony, and reflected the prosecutor's belief in the inadequacy of the evidence relied on by the defense. Her statement did not constitute misconduct.[59] (parentheses added; citation omitted).

Comments about the consequences of a jury's verdict also divert the jury from limiting its consideration to the evidence in the case. A prosecutor argued to the jury that it should consider the impact of its decision on other kids: "[Darryl Whiting] also brought the kids of Roxbury the guns, the drugs, the violence[;] don't 'let other kids be succored [sic] in by that flash, that cash, that deception.'"[60] (first brackets in original).

The First Circuit, conducting a "plain error" review, found the remarks improperly commented about the consequences of the jury's verdict, but did not reverse the conviction, as the remarks were isolated and direct responses to defense counsel's portrayal of the defendant as a philanthropist:

> This statement was prejudicial, defendants argue, because "it sought to deflect [the jurors'] attention from the issues that they were sworn to decide, . . . and attempted to foist onto the jury responsibility for the extra-judicial consequences of a not guilty verdict." We agree that the "other kids" reference was improper for "[t]he prosecutor should refrain from arguments [predicting] the consequences of the jury's verdict."[61] (brackets and ellipses in original).

---

[59] *Id.*
[60] United States v. Whiting, 28 F.3d 1296, 1302 (1st Cir. 1994).
[61] *Id.*

CHAPTER FOUR

Ad Hominem (Abusive): Personal Attacks

When you have no basis for argument, abuse the plaintiff.

Cicero, 106-43 B.C.
Louis Levinson, *Bartlett's Unfamiliar Quotations*, 1971[1]

THE AD HOMINEM INFORMAL FALLACY takes its name from the Latin, "to the man." Lawyers generally recognize an "ad hominem" argument as attacking the person, rather than the argument, but rarely distinguish between the different types of personal attack. The difference lies in the means of attack. The "abusive" ad hominem variety involves an assault on someone's character; the "circumstantial" variety (discussed in the next chapter) criticizes an individual's circumstance, by suggesting that circumstance creates a bias or prejudice.

It is far easier to attack someone's character than the substance of his argument. Refuting an argument often requires a thorough investigation, a complete knowledge of the facts, and an understanding of nuanced law; denigrating someone's character swiftly dispenses with these requirements. Character traits are highly visible and, when singled out, represent a shorthand for personal faults. Because society at large, and juries, tends to disbelieve people of "bad character," the temptation to launch an ad hominem (abusive) attack is often irresistible, particularly in the heat of a courtroom battle.

---

[1] *Cited in* DAVID SHRAGER AND ELIZABETH FROST, THE QUOTABLE LAWYER 74 (Facts on File Publications 1986).

Attacks on Character

Attacks on character frequently involve other informal fallacies. Epithets and ridicule, for example, can brutally strike at the heart of an individual's character. Another technique is to attribute an individual's character to a nationality or other group trait (division). Since 9/11, individuals of certain ethnic groups are more likely to be branded as terrorists. Not all attacks need be explicit; implicit character assaults may be equally effective.

Outside the courtroom, the only restriction on ad hominem (abusive) attacks is the self-restraint of the speaker. In the following example, elevated to prominence by the parties involved, columnist William Safire reports on an exchange between former Speaker of the House Newt Gingrich and then Deputy Secretary of State Richard Armitage:[2]

> In a Washington speech, Gingrich had blazed away at "ineffective and incoherent" State for "six months of diplomatic failure" and its "propensity for appeasing dictators and propping up corrupt regimes." In contrast, he noted, the Defense Department "delivered diplomatically and then the military delivered militarily."
>
> The former Republican Speaker berated State bureaucrats for undue deference to the U.N. and for tolerance of terrorism in Syrian-occupied Lebanon. Because much of his unofficial view is shared by what many liberals call "the neocon cabal" around Bush, Gingrich's broadside was taken by le tout Washington as damning evidence of internal war between Rumsfeldian hawks and Powellite doves.[3]

Safire duly noted, "The State response was ad hominem, attacking the speaker rather than his speech."[4] After dismissing rejoinders by an assistant secretary of state as "not of an adept vituperator," Safire wrote:

> It fell to Colin Powell's longtime best friend, Deputy Secretary of State Richard Armitage, to slam back in the classic tradition.
>
> "It's clear that Mr. Gingrich is off his meds and out of therapy," said America's second-ranking diplomat. All of us observing "the Shootout at the Neocon Cabal" agree that was a good one. The rhythm of Armitage's memorable phrase—reminiscent of Adlai Stevenson's "out of sorts and out of office"—suggests that an unbalanced Gingrich is in need of, and running from, psychiatric care. The deputy secre-

---

[2] *Invective's Comeback*, N.Y. TIMES, April 28, 2003, at A.23.
[3] *Id.*
[4] *Id.*

AD HOMINEM (ABUSIVE): PERSONAL ATTACKS

tary's riposte offends only psychiatrists, and there are no Republican psychiatrists.[5]

Exercise Discretion

Outside the courtroom, there may be no consequences for implying that someone needs psychiatric care, but inside the courtroom, appropriate discretion must be exercised. An attorney who filed a pending substitution motion against a judge found himself in criminal contempt for suggesting that the judge needed to be examined by a psychiatrist:

> **THE COURT:** Also I am going to sua sponte enter an order ordering Mr. Kaeding to be examined by a psychiatrist of the choice of the Court, because I do not know whether he is competent to stand trial.
>
> **MR. SPEARS:** You cannot rule since there has been a Motion for leave—
>
> **THE COURT:** (Interrupting) I can; anybody can request a psychiatric examination. I am going to do that.
>
> **MR. SPEARS:** I will be asking for one for you, Judge; have that on the record.
>
> **MR. SCHARF:** Judge, I would ask he be found in contempt for that.
>
> **THE COURT:** I am going to hold you in contempt, $500 dollar fine.
>
> **MR. SPEARS:** Praise God, praise the Lord Almighty God. May you—
>
> **MR. SCHARF:** (Interrupting) I ask for jail.
>
> **MR. SPEARS:** May you reap what you sow, Judge, by the good book.
>
> **THE COURT:** You have 24 hours to pay the fine, or you are going to jail.
>
> **MR. SPEARS:** Thank you, Judge.
>
> **MR. SCHARF:** Thank you.
>
> **MR. SPEARS:** See you there, Judge.[6]

The Illinois Appellate Court upheld the trial court's imposition of criminal contempt:

---

[5]*Id.*
[6]People v. Kaeding, 607 N.E.2d 580, 582 (Ill. App. 2d 1993).

> In the instant case, we find that Spears' comments were calculated to embarrass the court and to derogate from the court's authority and dignity. Accordingly, we hold that based on this conduct, the trial court's finding of direct criminal contempt was proper.[7]

In the courtroom, especially in the case of a criminal trial, the dangers of allowing a character attack may extend beyond discrediting a witness's testimony:

> These dangers include the risk that the jury will convict the defendant because his criminal disposition makes it more likely he committed the crime on trial, or because the defendant is a bad person deserving of punishment, whether or not he committed the charged crime.[8] (citations omitted).

To prevent abuse, Federal Rule of Evidence 404(a) greatly restricts the use of character evidence: "Evidence of a person's character or a trait of character is not admissible for the purpose of proving action in conformity therewith on a particular occasion."

Rule 404(b) similarly circumscribes the use of other types of character evidence: "Evidence of other crimes, wrongs, or acts is not admissible to prove the character of a person in order to show action in conformity therewith."

In a bank robbery trial, the defense counsel argued in summation "that the police charged the defendants because they were 'undesirables to law enforcement agencies,' and not because they were guilty of the offenses charged."[9] Lifting the term "undesirable" from defense counsel's statement, the prosecutor replied:

> Mr. Barker's attorney admits that these defendants are not desirable people, that they're undesirable people. Now I submit to you that desirable people don't rob banks; undesirable people do rob banks, and they admit that they're undesirable. Because they're undesirable doesn't mean they robbed this bank, but you should consider that along with all this other evidence.[10]

The Sixth Circuit reversed the conviction, finding the term "undesirables" was used to prove guilt, when the defense had not sought to prove the defendant's good character:

> As a general rule, the prosecution may not rely upon the defendants' bad character to prove guilt unless the defense has sought to excul-

---

[7]*Id.* at 583.
[8]United States v. Powers, 59 F.3d 1460, 1467 n.1 (4th Cir. 1995).
[9]United States v. Barker, 553 F.2d 1013, 1025 (6th Cir. 1977).
[10]*Id.*

pate them by proof of good character. The record does not indicate that defendants had sought to prove their good character. Even if they had, "that character or disposition offered, whether for or against the [defendant], must involve the *specific trait* related to the act charged." We do not believe that such a broad generality as "undesirables" is sufficiently probative of whether defendants committed the particular offense charged to permit reliance upon it.[11] (italics and brackets in original; citations omitted).

In closing argument, a prosecutor fleetingly referred to the defendants as "bad people":

> There are bad people in the world, ladies and gentlemen. We are lucky where we live (North Dakota) not to come in contact with as many as there may be in other parts of the country. But there are still some around here.[12] (parentheses added).

The Eighth Circuit found that the reference to "bad people" constituted prosecutorial misconduct, and reversed the conviction:

> Referring to defendants as "bad people" simply does not further the aims of justice or aid in the search for truth, and is likely to inflame bias in the jury and result in a verdict based on something other than evidence. Therefore the remarks were highly improper.[13]

Not from Around Here

The court also concluded that the prosecution improperly appealed to the mob instincts of the jury (public/mob), by pointing out that the defendants were not from the area:

> We believe that by twice calling the African-American Defendants "bad people" and by calling attention to the fact that the Defendants were not locals, the prosecutor gave the jury an improper and convenient hook on which to hang their verdict, and we are not prepared to say that the evidence was so overwhelming that the court's error in permitting the improper remarks to stand was harmless beyond a reasonable doubt. We conclude that the Defendants are entitled to a new trial on all counts.[14]

To explain the character of the witnesses who testified against the defendant, and where they could be found, a prosecutor commented,

---

[11] *Id.*
[12] United States v. Cannon, 88 F.3d 1495, 1502 (8th Cir. 1996).
[13] *Id.*
[14] *Id.* at 1503.

"If you're going to try the devil, you've got to go to hell to get your witnesses."[15] Labeling the defendant "the devil" was not grounds to overturn the conviction.[16]

During closing arguments in the May 2006 trial against former Enron Corporation chiefs Jeffrey Skilling and Kenneth Lay, prosecutor Kathryn Ruemmler argued that the two former CEOs were arrogant (and, therefore, not credible witnesses):

> Ruemmler asked jurors to compare the demeanor of witnesses who had accepted responsibility for their actions with that of Skilling and Lay, who she said offered "a series of excuses, convenient memory lapses" and blame games.
>
> "On cross-examination, they fought, argued, made long speeches, evaded questions," she said. "Nobody else is smart enough . . . . That is extraordinary arrogance. It is the exact same tactic they used when they were running Enron."[17] (ellipses added).

Disparaging Remarks

In a case involving a triple murder, a prosecutor, who read from a prepared text during opening summation, disparaged both the defendant and his codefendant with the terms "murderous fiends," "rats," "utterly merciless killers," and "inhumane, unfeeling and reprehensible creatures":

> I implore you not to forget that . . . the lives of three good men . . . were literally sacrificed to satisfy the greed of two murderous fiends.
>
> Now, it did not take you long, did it, ladies and gentlemen, to discover that this was not a case about cats and mice. No, ladies and gentlemen. It was a case about rats. And what else would you call some people who would lay in wait and shoot three men in the back except maybe cowards.
>
> After asking the dutiful wife [Donna Couture] a number of questions, the officers walked through the kitchen and entered the bedroom and found Couture beneath the bed garbed in only a pair of shorts, the macho, despicable coward number one.
>
> We have learned . . . they are cold blooded and merciless killers that took the lives of three good, decent and hardworking men . . . .

---

[15]State v. Hudson, 245 S.E.2d 686, 692 (N.C. 1978).
[16]*Id.* at 692–93.
[17]*Enron's Defense Team Gives Jury Instructions,* http://www.washingtonpost.com/wp-dyn/content/article/2006/05/16AR2006051600795.html (May 16, 2006).

AD HOMINEM (ABUSIVE): PERSONAL ATTACKS 45

>What kind of person would lay in wait and attack three unsuspecting and almost defenseless men but shoot them in the back? They must be the most inhumane, unfeeling and reprehensible creatures that God has damned to set loose upon us.[18] (ellipses and brackets in original).

The Supreme Court of Connecticut described the improper character attack:

> It is no part of a district attorney's duty, and it is not his right, to stigmatize a defendant. He has a right *to argue* that *the evidence* proves the defendant guilty as charged in the indictment, but for the *district attorney himself to characterize* the defendant as 'a cold-blooded killer' is something quite different. No man on trial for murder can be officially characterized as a murderer or as 'a cold-blooded killer,' until he has been adjudged guilty of murder or pleads guilty to that charge.[19] (italics in original; citation omitted).

Where the evidence against a defendant is considered strong, courts are loathe to overturn the conviction, even when the prosecution steps out of the ring, but not here:

> [A]ppeals to passion and prejudice may so poison the minds of jurors even in a strong case that an accused may be deprived of a fair trial. The prosecutor cannot pollute the waters and then claim that we should ignore his actions because the fish are not worth saving. Given the egregious nature of the prosecutor's remarks, a failure on our part to reverse the defendant's conviction would suggest that in a strong case the defendant is not entitled to a fair trial and therefore anything goes. We conclude that in his opening summation the prosecutor's character assassination of the defendant so tainted the trial as to deny the defendant due process of law.[20] (brackets in original; citations omitted).

In a case where the defendant was accused of interstate transportation of a stolen vehicle, a prosecutor began his final argument by vouching for the credibility of the police and the F.B.I. (authority), and followed by attacking the defendant's character—branding him "a hoodlum":

> Now, gentlemen, I get a little tired of the police and the F.B.I. being the whipping boys of criminals and liars. I just don't believe that Harry Degnan who took Beck's statement and whom you have seen in this courtroom all this time would force anybody to make a statement.

---

[18]State v. Couture, 482 A.2d 300, 317 n.17 (Conn. 1984).
[19]*Id.* at 317–18.
[20]*Id.* at 318–19.

I know him to be a fine F.B.I. officer—absolutely the finest I know. A man of absolute integrity. And I get a little tired of the F.B.I. being whipping boys for hoodlums. And that is the only way I know how to describe the defendant Donald Hall, he is a hoodlum.[21]

The Fifth Circuit reversed the conviction, based in part on this misconduct:

This type of shorthand characterization of an accused, not based on evidence, is especially likely to stick in the minds of the jury and influence its deliberations. Out of the usual welter of grey facts it starkly rises—succinct, pithy, colorful, and expressed in a sharp break with the decorum which the citizen expects from the representative of his government.[22]

A teenager convicted of rape challenged the prosecutor's characterization of him in summation as a "teenage hoodlum walking the streets of Washington. . . ."[23] (ellipsis in original). The Court of Appeals for the District of Columbia upheld the conviction, despite reservations over the characterization:

Surely this sort of argument should be avoided. The trial of appellant was for rape, not for being a hoodlum. It is odd that the United States through its representative should be put in the position of trying in this way to prejudice the jury by going beyond the scope of the evidence and the trial. Such tactics are inconsistent with the civilization of the law and endanger the integrity of its administration. They should be condemned by the trial court sua sponte in the presence of the jury. But we feel certain the jury convicted in this case on the basis of its view of the evidence. We add that had objection been made we are confident the court would have instructed the jury to disregard this extraneous characterization of the accused.[24]

Don't Call Me a Crook

Along with "hoodlums," people often think of the term "crooks." The latter term, too, has been found to be an improper character attack, but not sufficient to warrant overturning a conviction for conspiracy to sell stolen goods and theft of an interstate shipment.[25] Similarly, a prosecu-

---

[21]Hall v. United States, 419 F.2d 582, 585 (5th Cir. 1969).
[22]*Id.* at 587.
[23]United States v. Jenkins, 436 F.2d 140, 145 (D.C. Cir. 1970).
[24]*Id.*
[25]United States v. Singer, 660 F.2d 1295, 1304 (8th Cir. 1981).

AD HOMINEM (ABUSIVE): PERSONAL ATTACKS

tor's closing argument, which included the epithets "liar, crook, and wheeler and dealer," was deemed improper but harmless error.[26]

A defendant charged with assault with intent to commit rape and labeled by the prosecution as a "parasite" successfully won a reversal, based in part on the following character attack:

> Additionally, his (the prosecutor's) further comments, i.e., that appellant is "like a parasite . . . never works . . . stays at people's homes . . . [d]rives people's cars . . . steals from his own parents to get anything . . . won't work for it," had nothing to do with the crimes alleged and inferred that people who do not work, live with others, and drive other people's cars are bad people and more likely to do criminal acts. This argument directed at appellant's character invited the jury to decide the case based upon its own value judgment and not on the law.[27] (ellipses and brackets in original; parentheses added).

Even corporate symbols are not immune from a character attack, as when the plaintiff's attorney attacked Borden's Elsie the Cow, as a cold, calculating, big corporation:

> What you decide today is going to determine on [sic] not only whether Eddie and Debbie are monetarily taken care of because, sure, that's part of the deal. There's no question about it.
>
> . . . .
>
> *They say, but don't hold it against us. Don't hold it against Elsie.*
>
> Well, I got to tell you something. Elsie isn't the sweet little cow you see on the milk can. Obviously, Elsie is a great big corporation and they are there to do one thing, lay it off on somebody else to take care of this man and this lady for the rest of their lives, lay it off on anybody you can lay it off to. Well, fair—lay it off anyplace but don't lay it off on us because we just don't want to hear about it and that is not right and that is not proper . . .[28] (italics in original; first ellipsis added).

The appellate court, though citing this portion of the argument, believed the vice was not the character attack on Elsie, but the plaintiff's attorney's assertion of "personal knowledge (authority) of nefarious activities supposedly engaged in by the large corporate defendant which

---

[26]United States v. Hoffman, 415 F.2d 14, 21 (7th Cir. 1969).
[27]People v. Herring, 25 Cal. Rptr. 2d 213, 218 (Cal. App. 2 Dist. 1993).
[28]Borden, Inc. v. Young, 479 So. 2d 850, 851 n.4 (Fla. App. 3 Dist. 1985).

were not only not in evidence but did not in fact exist . . ."[29] (ellipsis added).

Not Sympathetic Enough

Kmart similarly came under an ad hominem (abusive) attack by the plaintiffs' counsel for having too little sympathy for the injury it caused:

> [Plaintiffs'] . . . counsel argued at one point that Kmart and its doctors "don't care at all" about Smith personally, which is quite different than arguing that Kmart did not care about or take steps to prevent the possibility of injury. There were other instances in which plaintiffs' counsel argued that Kmart "does not care," in the present tense, which has little bearing on the question of Kmart's negligence at the time of the accident. Counsel also argued that Kmart did not even care enough to make Guffy available to give a deposition in the case. Finally counsel argued that Kmart did not care because it was not paying the true amount of damages that it caused. The import of these remarks was to stain the corporate character of Kmart in front of the jury. This is improper argument.[30] (brackets and ellipsis added).

The First Circuit, nevertheless, concluded that the improper argument was harmless.[31]

> [Parties to legal proceedings are not the only targets of ad hominem (abusive) attacks. Attorneys often denigrate opposing counsel by employing this time-tested technique, even though the rules of professional conduct prohibit such personal attacks:] The prosecutor should not, moreover, use arguments which are, in essence, personal attacks on defense counsel. The prosecutor should abstain from any allusion to the personal peculiarities and idiosyncrasies of opposing counsel. The duty to avoid such a personal attack is also, obviously, reciprocal.[32]

In a criminal case for extortion and RICO violations, the prosecutor ". . . addressed defense counsel at one point as 'you sleaze,' at another as 'you hypocritical son -- ---,' as being 'so unlearned in the law,' and on several occasions the prosecutor objected to questions by the defense

---

[29] *Id.* at 851.
[30] Smith v. Kmart, 177 F.3d 19, 26 (1st Cir. 1999).
[31] *Id.* at 28.
[32] STANDARDS 3-5.8(d), Commentary, at 109.

AD HOMINEM (ABUSIVE): PERSONAL ATTACKS

as 'nonsense.' "[33] (ellipsis added). Although the remarks were improper, the Second Circuit did not overturn the convictions.[34]

A defendant was convicted of four counts of capital sexual battery and one count of lewd and lascivious act on a child under 16 years of age. During jury voir dire, the prosecutor stated:

> And I'm going to be presenting to you the State of Florida versus Theodore Kellogg . . . Obviously you know my name, and the fact that I'm an attorney and what type of law I practice. You know Mr. Howell is a public defender and the fact that he defends criminals.[35] (ellipses in original).

According to the court (which reversed the conviction), "The prosecutor's statement was a clearly improper character attack on both defense counsel and (the defendant)."[36]

The plaintiff's counsel engaged in so many unprovoked personal attacks on the defendant's counsel, in the presence of the jury, that an appellate court felt it was unnecessary to list more than the following to reverse the decision in favor of the plaintiff:

> "You think you got a monopoly on intelligence.
>
> "He not only makes an objection, but he makes a misstatement of fact every time he makes an objection.
>
> "What is all this 'four-flushing?'
>
> "That is very unfair, you see, how he makes it difficult, he puts a knife in your back.
>
> "Then why do you open your mouth and raise a lot of fuss about it?
>
> "He makes an objection and it sounds like an elevator is going to climb.
>
> "Judge, I never heard such an asinine objection."[37]

Odious Comparisons

Likening opposing counsel to someone or something opprobrious provides another means to carry out a character attack. The Ninth Circuit

---

[33]United States v. Biasucci, 786 F.2d 504, 514 n.9 (2d Cir. 1986).
[34]*Id.* at 514–15.
[35]Kellogg v. State, 761 So. 2d 409, 409 (Fla. App.2 Dist. 2000).
[36]*Id.*
[37]Vujovich v. Chicago Transit Authority, 126 N.E.2d 731, 735 (1955).

concluded that the prosecutor's comparison of the defense counsel to "a magician and a squid" were not sufficient to overturn the conviction, especially when the attacks were not one-sided:

> [T]he prosecutor's comments comparing defense counsel to both a magician and a squid were not likely to have prejudiced the jury against [the defendant], particularly in light of defense counsel's comparison of the prosecutor to the Wizard of Oz. Viewed in context, the prosecutor's remarks were acceptable—though not highly desirable—advocacy.[38] (brackets added).

During closing argument, a prosecutor referred to defense counsel as "a professional criminal defense lawyer."[39] The Illinois Supreme Court had previously held that "it is error to refer to defense counsel as a 'hired gun,' as the term and its connotations are in fact . . . pejorative."[40] (ellipses added). But here, the appellation was not improper:

> The remarks in this case do not suggest deception or trickery on the part of defense counsel, a factor which is dominant in the cases we have found on this point. Frankly, defense counsel *was* "a professional criminal defense attorney," just as the attorney for the State was a professional prosecutor. The jurors are not so naive that they fail to recognize these distinctions, and we do not believe that these comments, without more, warrant the label of "error."[41]

Expert witnesses, like parties and opposing counsel, are not spared character attacks. A doctor, qualified at the trial as a medical expert, experienced this attack during closing argument:

> Now, that brings us to to [sic] Dr. Jindrich. The hired gun from Hot Tub Country. Have stethoscope, will travel.
>
> . . . .
>
> I think Dr. Jindrich is a living example of Lincoln's law. You can fool all of the people enough of the time.
>
> He is a politician. He runs for office.[42] (ellipsis in original).

The defense counsel did not object to this characterization; nevertheless, the Nevada Supreme Court found that "[i]n this case, the prosecutorial misconduct was so prejudicial as to require court intervention

---

[38]United States v. Lopez-Alvarez, 970 F.2d 583, 598 (9th Cir. 1992).
[39]People v. Johnson, 803 N.E.2d 405, 437 (Ill. 2003).
[40]*Id.* at 438.
[41]*Id.*
[42]Sipsas v. State, 716 P.2d 231, 234 (Nev. 1986).

sua sponte to protect the defendant's right to a fair trial. Failure to do so was error."[43] (italics in original; citations omitted).

Pointing Fingers

The highest Court in the land is not impervious to character attacks, either. Certainly, the U.S. Supreme Court comes under attack from outside critics, but a significant number of character attacks originate with the Justices themselves. In the excerpts that follow, various members of the Court note the shortcomings of their colleagues: casual, clever, ignorant, deceptive, and unprincipled.

In the aftermath of the 2000 U.S. general election, *Bush v. Gore*[44] was decided by the Supreme Court. Chief Justice Rehnquist cited three cases that Justice Ginsburg felt not only were inapposite but were misleading ("casual citation"), because their citation suggested they were representative of a larger body of case law:

> The Chief Justice's casual citation of these cases might lead one to believe they are part of a larger collection of cases in which we said that the Constitution impelled us to train a skeptical eye on a state court's portrayal of state law. But one would be hard pressed, I think, to find additional cases that fit the mold.[45]

Nothing fires up a debate like a disagreement over religion, and the Supreme Court jumped into the fire, in 1989, in *Allegheny County v. Greater Pittsburgh ACLU*,[46] when it decided the appropriateness of two holiday displays (a creche and a menorah) on public property in downtown Pittsburgh. Justice Blackmun, writing for the majority, announced that Justice Kennedy was "clever" (not in the sense of "adroit," but more in the sense of "crafty"):

> Justice Kennedy is clever but mistaken in asserting that the description of the menorah purports to turn the Court into a "national theology board." Any inquiry concerning the government's use of a religious object to determine whether that use results in an unconstitutional religious preference requires a review of the factual record concerning the religious object—even if the inquiry is conducted pursuant to Justice Kennedy's "proselytization" test. Surely, Justice Kennedy cannot mean that this Court must keep itself in ignorance of the symbol's

---

[43]*Id.* at 235.
[44]531 U.S. 98 (2000).
[45]*Id.* at 140.
[46]492 U.S. 573 (1989).

conventional use and decide the constitutional question knowing only what it knew before the case was filed.[47] (citations omitted).

Justice Scalia, never one to mince words, especially when he is in the minority, criticized his colleagues in the majority as being "ignorant," and "willfully" so, in *Hill v. Colorado*,[48] involving the legality of an 8-foot, no-approach zone around clinics providing abortion services:

> The Court displays a willful ignorance of the type and nature of communication affected by the statute's restrictions. It seriously asserts, for example, that the 8-foot zone allows a speaker to communicate at a "normal conversational distance[.]" I have certainly held conversations at a distance of eight feet seated in the quiet of my chambers, but I have never walked along the public sidewalk—and have not seen others do so—"conversing" at an 8-foot remove. The suggestion is absurd.[49] (citation omitted, brackets added).

Dissenting in *Webster v. Reproductive Health Services*,[50] Justice Blackmun accused the members of the plurality of deception in the way they treated *Roe v. Wade*:[51]

> Nor in my memory has a plurality gone about its business in such a deceptive fashion. At every level of its review, from its effort to read the real meaning out of the Missouri statute, to its intended evisceration of precedents and its deafening silence about the constitutional protections that it would jettison, the plurality obscures the portent of its analysis. With feigned restraint, the plurality announces that its analysis leaves *Roe* "undisturbed," albeit "modif[ied] and narrow[ed]." But this disclaimer is totally meaningless. The plurality opinion is filled with winks, and nods, and knowing glances to those who would do away with *Roe* explicitly, but turns a stone face to anyone in search of what the plurality conceives as the scope of a woman's right under the Due Process Clause to terminate a pregnancy free from the coercive and brooding influence of the State. The simple truth is that *Roe* would not survive the plurality's analysis, and that the plurality provides no substitute for *Roe*'s protective umbrella.[52] (brackets in original; citation omitted).

---

[47]*Id.* at n.60.
[48]530 U.S. 703 (2000).
[49]*Id.* at 756.
[50]492 U.S. 490 (1989).
[51]410 U.S. 113 (1973).
[52]*Webster*, 492 U.S. at 538.

"Unprincipled Colleagues"

Justice Scalia, dissenting in *Atkins v. Virginia*,[53] accused his colleagues of being unprincipled, for having concluded that the execution of mentally retarded prisoners is "cruel and unusual punishment," based merely on their personal views, without regard to the law:

> Today's decision is the pinnacle of our Eighth Amendment death-is-different jurisprudence. Not only does it, like all of that jurisprudence, find no support in the text or history of the Eighth Amendment; it does not even have support in current social attitudes regarding the conditions that render an otherwise just death penalty inappropriate. Seldom has an opinion of this Court rested so obviously upon nothing but the personal views of its members.
>
> . . . .
>
> [I]n the end, it is the *feelings* and *intuition* of a majority of the Justices that count the perceptions of decency, or of penology, or of mercy . . . entertained by a majority of the small and unrepresentative segment of our society that sits on this Court.[54] (brackets, ellipses, and italics in original, citations omitted).

A final note. It would be wise to remember the words of Justice Felix Frankfurter: "It is a fair summary of history to say that the safeguards of liberty have frequently been forged in controversies involving not very nice people."[55]

---

[53] 536 U.S. 304 (2002).
[54] *Id.* at 337–38.
[55] United States v. Rabinowitz, 339 U.S. 56, 69 (1950) (Frankfurter, J., dissenting).

CHAPTER FIVE

Ad Hominem (Circumstantial): Bias and Prejudice

> *Bias is a term used in the "common law of evidence" to describe the relationship between a party and a witness which might lead the witness to slant, unconsciously or otherwise, his testimony in favor of or against a party. Bias may be induced by a witness' like, dislike, or fear of a party, or by the witness' self-interest.*[1]

THE SECOND TYPE OF ATTACK directed "to the man" suggests that an individual's "circumstance" creates a self-interest (bias or prejudice), which negates the legitimacy of his testimony or argument. Any "circumstance" suggesting a relationship (friendship, membership in an organization, pecuniary interest in the outcome of a case, fear of retaliation, for example) may be used to raise the specter of bias. In the legal arena, no one is spared from claims of bias: not witnesses, not jurors, not attorneys, not judges. Proof of actual bias is not required; potential (or the appearance of) bias is often sufficient.

The key to an effective ad hominem (circumstantial) argument is finding, and highlighting, the right circumstance giving rise to a claim of bias. Responding to a claim of bias is not easy, as the proof often requires proving a negative: the individual is not biased despite the circumstance. Of course, it is possible for individuals to set aside their biases or prejudices, but the suspicion will linger that their views were dictated by their circumstances.

In a trial, the trier of fact (jury or judge) is responsible for assessing the impact of potential or actual bias on credibility. Once a witness has been challenged as biased, counsel can seek to "rehabilitate" that

---

[1] United States v. Abel, 469 U.S. 45, 52 (1984).

witness, and the only restriction on the evidence is that it must meet the relevance standard of Federal Rule of Evidence 402.[2] ("All relevant evidence is admissible, except as otherwise provided . . . .") Because bias is not a collateral issue, extrinsic evidence may be employed as a lever to dislodge the bias claim.[3]

Division and Epithets

An effective ad hominem (circumstantial) argument often involves two other informal fallacies, either individually or in combination: division and epithets. Attributing the characteristics of a group to an individual member (division) may be manifestly unfair, but it permissibly raises a claim of bias in the legal system. If the group can be labeled with an epithet, evoking a strong emotional reaction, so much the better. The facts in *United States v. Abel*,[4] the precedent-setting case on bias, involved both of these fallacies.

Defendant Abel and two others were indicted for bank robbery. Unlike the other two, who pleaded guilty, Abel stood trial. Ehle, one of the two indictees who reached a plea agreement, agreed to testify against Abel. Abel's counsel announced to the district court that he would seek to impeach Ehle's testimony by producing a witness, Mills, who would testify that after the robbery, Ehle told Mills that he (Ehle) was going to falsely accuse Abel, to receive a favorable deal from the government. Responding, the prosecutor stated he intended to recall Ehle, who would testify that he, Abel, and Mills were all members of the "Aryan Brotherhood," a secret prison gang sworn to perjury, theft, murder, and self-protection.

The prosecutor's cross-examination of Mills included the following:

Q: Mr. Mills, do you belong to any secret type of prison organization which is restrictive somewhat in its membership?

A: No, I don't.

Q: Do you belong to any secret-type organization which has as part of its creed or tenants [sic] or oath of that organization that

---

[2]United States v. Lindemann, 85 F.3d 1232, 1243 (7th Cir. 1996).
[3]*Id.*
[4]469 U.S. 45 (1984).

members thereof will first of all deny they belong to that secret organization?

A: No, I don't.

Q: And do you belong to any secret organization which has as part of its creed that those members who belong to it will lie to protect the members that are in the secret organization?

A: I know of no organization like that.[5]

Ehle was then recalled to the stand, and testified about the gang and his, Abel's, and Mills's membership in the gang. The jury convicted Abel of bank robbery. The Ninth Circuit reversed Abel's conviction, finding that Ehle's rebuttal testimony was improperly admitted because it not only showed that Mills's membership might cause him to slant his testimony but also was used to show that Mills's membership must have caused him to lie on the stand. Because Abel did not take the stand and, therefore, the testimony about gang membership could not have been offered to impeach him, the Ninth Circuit concluded the testimony prejudiced Abel "by mere association."[6]

Contrary to the Ninth Circuit, the U.S. Supreme Court found that Mills's and Abel's membership in the "Aryan Brotherhood" was sufficiently probative to show that Mills was biased in favor of Abel. The Court noted the Federal Rules of Evidence do not explicitly sanction impeachment by bias: "[T]he Rules do not by their terms deal with impeachment for 'bias,' although they do expressly treat impeachment by character evidence and conduct, Rule 608, by evidence of conviction of a crime, Rule 609, and by showing of religious beliefs or opinion, Rule 610."[7]

Even without explicit authorization under the Federal Rules of Evidence to raise bias, the Court concluded that impeachment by bias is "almost always relevant because the jury, as finder of fact and weigher of credibility, has historically been entitled to assess all evidence which might bear on the accuracy and truth of a witness' testimony."[8]

In this case, the Court willingly attributed the group's characteristics to individual members: "A witness' and a party's common membership

---

[5]United States v. Abel, 707 F.2d 1013, 1016 (9th Cir. 1983).
[6]*Id.* at 1017.
[7]469 U.S. at 49.
[8]*Id.* at 52.

in an organization, even without proof that the witness or party has personally adopted its tenants [sic], is certainly probative of bias."⁹

The name of the group, "Aryan Brotherhood," was deemed "unduly prejudicial" by the district court, and so the prosecutor, in the transcript citation above, euphemistically referred to the organization as "a secret type of prison organization."¹⁰

Plea agreements played a role in the Enron trial, when the defense counsel argued many of the prosecution's witnesses could not be believed because they struck deals with the government:

> Petrocelli urged the jury of eight women and four men to reject testimony from government witnesses, who he said pleaded guilty under duress.
>
> "The only time anybody in this case acted guilty is when they were forced to sign contracts with the government to buy back their lives."¹¹

Defendants, of course, have a great deal at risk in a criminal trial, but does that fact, alone, compromise their credibility if they take the stand? Prosecutors frequently argue "to the effect that, if the defendant is innocent, government agents must be lying," an argument that has repeatedly drawn fire from reviewing courts.¹² Here, a prosecutor argues the defendants are biased, and should not be credited, because they have the most to lose:

> Ladies and gentlemen, in order to find these defendants not guilty in this case, you have to discredit all of the testimony that the government witnesses gave to you, and you will have to believe what the two people who have the most to lose here have said happened, and you'll also have to believe that the records that were produced, pursuant to what the witnesses have told the government, have absolutely no bearing whatsoever on the proof in this case.¹³

The Ninth Circuit reversed the conviction (for assisting federal offenders to avoid apprehension), finding, among other things, that the prosecutor improperly vouched for the government's witnesses.¹⁴

---

⁹*Id.*

¹⁰*Id.* at 48.

¹¹www.washingtonpost.com/wp-dyn/content/article/2006/05/16/AR2006051600795.html.

¹²United States v. Richter, 826 F.2d 206, 209 (2nd Cir. 1987).

¹³United States v. Sanchez, 176 F.3d 1214, 1224 (9th Cir. 1999).

¹⁴*Id.* at 1225.

Participants in the legal process are frequently the targets of bias claims. The defense counsel was not so subtly accused of bias by a prosecutor during this rebuttal argument:

> Now, Ms. Carothers went on at length about the evidence the government presented where there were no tapes of this, no videotapes of that, no da da da da, da da da. Well, can you imagine if we left the investigation of this case to a criminal defense attorney what kind of evidence we would have?[15]

At the trial, defense counsel failed to object to this remark. On appeal, the Seventh Circuit dismissed the comment as an isolated incident that did not improperly influence the outcome of the trial.[16]

Another prosecutor commented to the jury that defense counsel's role is to obfuscate the facts and the issues:

> It's a very common thing to expect the defense to focus on areas which tend to confuse. That is—and that's all right, because that's [defense counsel's] job. If you're confused and you're sidetracked, then you won't be able to bring in a verdict.... It's his job to throw sand in your eyes, and he does a good job of it, but bear in mind at all times, and consider what [defense counsel has] said, that it's his job to get this man off. He wants to confuse you.[17] (brackets in original; ellipses added).

The California Supreme Court concluded that the remarks accurately served as "a reminder to the jury that it should not be distracted from the relevant evidence and inferences that might properly and logically be drawn therefrom,"[18] and did not require reversal.

Should a jury composed exclusively of federal government employees, in a case involving a federal law, be considered too biased to render a fair verdict? That was the issue before the U.S. Supreme Court, where the defense counsel argued:

> Now, I have exhausted my ten challenges, and here I have twelve Government jurors who are to decide this defendant's case, which is a violation of the Federal statute, being brought in a Federal Court, prosecuted by a Federal prosecutor, and the case is being presented by Federal agents.[19]

---

[15]United States v. Emenogha, 1 F.3d 473, 481 (7th Cir. 1993).
[16]*Id.*
[17]People v. Bell, 778 P.2d 129, 149 (Cal. 1989).
[18]*Id.*
[19]Frazier v. United States, 335 U.S. 497, 504–505 (1948).

Justice Rutledge, writing for a 5–4 majority of the U.S. Supreme Court, held that government employees are subject to challenge only for "actual bias," not because of their status as federal employees.[20] Justice Jackson, author of the dissenting opinion, concluded that a jury of all government employees would be biased: "On one proposition I should expect trial lawyers to be nearly unanimous: that a jury, every member of which is in the hire of one of the litigants, lacks something of being an impartial jury."[21]

The U.S. Supreme Court has ruled that every conceivable circumstance suggesting jury bias effectively cannot be eliminated, but a fair trial can be held, nevertheless:

> [D]ue process does not require a new trial every time a juror has been placed in a potentially compromising situation. Were that the rule, few trials would be constitutionally acceptable. The safeguards of juror impartiality, such as *voir dire* and protective instructions from the trial judge, are not infallible; it is virtually impossible to shield jurors from every contact or influence that might theoretically affect their vote. Due process means a jury capable and willing to decide the case solely on the evidence before it, and a trial judge ever watchful to prevent prejudicial occurrences and to determine the effect of such occurrences when they happen. Such determinations may properly be made at a hearing . . .[22] (ellipses added).

Rarely does the U.S. Supreme Court entertain a claim that a judge's alleged bias violates the Due Process Clause of the Fourteenth Amendment. Issues involving "kinship, personal bias, state policy, remoteness of interest" are generally left to state legislatures.[23]

Judicial Bias

In *Aetna Life Insurance Co. v. Lavoie*,[24] however, the Supreme Court considered the constitutional issue of judicial bias. This "case within a case" involved an insurer's refusal to completely pay a hospital bill, and a resultant lawsuit for payment and punitive damages. The jury awarded $3.5 million in punitive damages, and the Alabama Supreme Court affirmed, 5–4, in an unsigned per curiam opinion, authored by Justice Embry. During the pendency of an application for rehearing, the insurer

---

[20] *Id.* at 510.
[21] *Id.* at 514.
[22] Smith v. Phillips, 455 U.S. 209, 217 (1982).
[23] Tumey v. Ohio, 273 U.S. 510, 523 (1927).
[24] 475 U.S. 813 (1986).

learned that while the case was pending before the Alabama Supreme Court, Justice Embry filed two lawsuits, against different insurance companies, seeking punitive damages for their alleged bad-faith failure to pay claims. One lawsuit was a class action on behalf of all state employees, and swept within its ambit the remaining justices on the Alabama Supreme Court.

The insurer raised three claims of bias before the U.S. Supreme Court: (1) Justice Embry's general bias against insurance companies that were dilatory in paying claims; (2) Justice Embry's participation in a case involving the identical issue pending in Alabama's lower courts, in suits filed by him; and (3) all the justices on the Alabama Supreme Court were biased because of their interests as potential class members as state employees.

One of Justice Embry's lawsuits required him to provide a deposition, which fell into the insurer's hands. To support its claim that Justice Embry was generally biased against insurance companies, the insurer noted his response to the question whether he ever had any difficulty processing claims: "[T]hat is a silly question. For years and years."[25]

The U.S. Supreme Court held that this allegation of general bias did not disqualify Justice Embry based on constitutional grounds, stating that "it is likely that many claimants have developed hostile feelings of frustration in awaiting settlement of insurance claims."[26]

Participation in a case before the Alabama Supreme Court involving an issue Justice Embry was pressing in the lower state courts, however, was a different matter. According to the U.S. Supreme Court, "Justice Embry's opinion for the Alabama Supreme Court had the clear and immediate effect of enhancing both the legal status and the settlement value of his own case."[27]

Two other conclusions buttressed the Supreme Court's opinion that Justice Embry's failure to recuse himself amounted to a violation of Due Process under the Fourteenth Amendment:

> We hold simply that when Justice Embry made that judgment, he acted as "a judge in his own case."[28]

> We also hold that his interest was "'direct, personal, substantial, [and] pecuniary.'"[29] (brackets in original; citations omitted).

---

[25] *Id.* at 818.
[26] *Id.* at 821.
[27] *Id.* at 824.
[28] *Id.*
[29] *Id.*

All the other justices of the Alabama Supreme Court (two withdrew from participation in the class action lawsuit during the motion for rehearing) were also charged with having an interest in this case. The U.S. Supreme Court rejected these allegations of bias, employing three techniques: (1) reductio ad absurdum; (2) de minimis; and (3) slippery slope.

First, the Court exaggerated the consequences (the possibility that all state judges would be disqualified):

> [A]ccepting [the insurer's] expansive contentions might require the disqualification of every judge in the State. If so, it is possible that under a "rule of necessity" none of the judges or justices would be disqualified.[30] (citation omitted; brackets added).

Second, the Court minimized the financial consequences to the other justices:

> [W]hile these justices might conceivably have had a slight pecuniary interest, we find it impossible to characterize that interest as "'direct, personal, substantial, [and] pecuniary.'"[31] (footnote and citations omitted; brackets in original).

Third, the Court said accepting the claim of bias against the other justices would invariably lead to unwanted results:

> With the proliferation of class actions involving broadly defined classes, the application of the constitutional requirement of disqualification must be carefully limited. Otherwise constitutional disqualification arguments could quickly become a standard feature of class action litigation.[32] (citation omitted).

If a judge rejects all of a party's testimony and evidence, is that confirmation of bias? "[T]otal rejection of an opposed view cannot of itself impugn the integrity or competence of a trier of fact."[33]

Just Good Friends

In early 2004, the Sierra Club filed a motion asking Justice Scalia to recuse himself from certain pending cases involving Vice President Cheney,[34] because the two of them recently participated in a Louisiana

---

[30] *Id.* at 825.
[31] *Id.* at 825–26.
[32] *Id.* at 826.
[33] NLRB v. Pittsburgh S.S. Co., 337 U.S. 656, 659 (1949).
[34] Cheney v. U.S. Dist. Court for the Dist. of Columbia, 541 U.S. 913 (2004).

duck hunting trip (not to be confused with the February 2006 quail hunting trip, where the Vice President accidentally shot a member of his hunting party). The recusal motion prompted a Memorandum, authored by Justice Scalia, in which he declined to sideline himself during the consideration of the cases.[35] Justice Scalia's defenses to claims of bias based on friendship and benefit to his relatives are noteworthy.

Agreeing that his recusal would be required if his "impartiality might reasonably be questioned," Justice Scalia began his defense with a question suggestive of circular reasoning:

> Why would that result follow from my being in a sizeable group of persons, in a hunting camp with the Vice President, where I never hunted with him in the same blind or had other opportunity for private conversation? The only possibility is that it would suggest I am a friend of his. But while friendship is a ground for recusal of a Justice where the personal fortune or the personal freedom of the friend is at issue, it has traditionally *not* been a ground for recusal where *official action* is at issue, no matter how important the official action was to the ambitions or the reputation of the Government officer.[36] (italics in original).

As to the claim that his relatives benefited from the flight from Washington, D.C. to Louisiana, on the Vice President's jet, concededly "more comfortable and more convenient than flying commercially," Justice Scalia defended by arguing that any hunter would have been extended that same courtesy:

> My married son and son-in-law were given a ride—not because they were relatives and as a favor to me; but because there were other hunters leaving from Washington, and as a favor to them (and to those who would have had to go to New Orleans to meet them). Had they been unrelated invitees to the hunt, the same would undoubtedly have occurred. Financially, the flight was worth as little to them as it was to me.[37] (parentheses in original).

(Justice Scalia was part of a 7–2 majority that remanded the case to the court of appeals to consider whether that court should issue a mandamus to the district court in connection with discovery preceding litigation of the suit.)[38]

---

[35] *Id.*
[36] *Id.* at 916.
[37] *Id.* at 921 n.2.
[38] 542 U.S. at 392.

Expert Bias

Experts play an important role in the judicial process, which is to bring their specialized knowledge to bear on a case, so that the jury and judge have a better understanding of the facts and issues. Though experts are unlikely to have a direct stake in the outcome of a case, they are not exempt from claims of bias. Early on, as the next example reveals, lawyers subjected experts to derision for their alleged bias.

In an accident case, the plaintiff's counsel offered his contemptuous view of expert witnesses, and argued that an automobile brake expert was biased because he was in the brake business and expected all brakes to be in perfect working order:

> Now, as to whether Joe Waren was driving his automobile without having it equipped with adequate brakes; you have the testimony of this expert, testifying that he examined the brakes a few days after the wreck and found them in serious condition. When I hear experts testify it reminds me of an old saying that there are just three kinds of liars, first we have the plain liars, then we have damn liars, and then we have the expert testimony. Now, this fellow is in the brake business, he fixes brakes all the time, and he thinks the brakes on a car should be in apple pie order, and unless they were he wouldn't think they would stop a car; but you have the actual facts about the brakes on that car from Mrs. Waren, who told you that it always stopped when they wanted to stop . . .[39] (ellipses added).

The Texas Court of Civil Appeals held that the comparison of experts to liars was improper, but because counsel did not interpose a timely objection, the error was waived.[40]

Questioning an expert about his fee and expense arrangement is a legitimate trial tactic to determine bias:

> We reject defendant's claim that the prosecutor committed misconduct by questioning Dr. Blinder about the fee he was receiving for his testimony. "The compensation and expenses paid or to be paid to an expert witness by the party calling him [or her] is a proper subject of inquiry by any adverse party as relevant to the credibility of the witness and the weight of his [or her] testimony."[41] (citations omitted; brackets in original).

During the Enron trial, the prosecution argued that the sizeable fee paid to an expert witness created a bias:

---

[39]McGregor Milling & Grain Co. v. Waren, 175 S.W.2d 476, 480 (Tex. App. 1943).
[40]*Id.*
[41]People v. Price, 821 P.2d 610, 688 (Cal. 1991).

Ruenmmler reminded the jury of testimony that Enron's highly touted retail unit was instead "a basket case," according to the executive hired to rescue it. She showed jurors a conference-call script in which Skilling chose to omit mention of losses. And she sketched out a last-minute scheme to meet Wall Street earnings expectations for the fourth quarter of 1999.

"Abracadabra. Just like that. A penny to meet the consensus estimate. That's fraud. It's wrong," she said. "The only people who said something different were Mr. Skilling and his $600,000 expert."[42]

An expert's bias can also arise from participation in the investigation of a criminal defendant.

[W]e are of the opinion that if a witness has been extensively involved in a criminal investigation against a defendant, and is presented at trial as a neutral, detached expert against that defendant, then the witness's previous involvement qualifies as "bias," and the defendant is entitled to expose such bias pursuant to Fed. R. Evid. 607.[43]

(Rule 607 states: "The credibility of a witness may be attacked by any party, including the party calling the witness.")

An attorney need not directly argue that the opposition is biased, but may accomplish this objective indirectly—by begging the question with facts suggesting what an unbiased presentation would look like. President Clinton's attorneys employed this technique against the Special Prosecutor (OIC; Office of Independent Counsel):

Accordingly a fair report from the OIC would, inter alia, provide all exculpatory evidence, assess the credibility of witnesses in terms of bias, reason to falsify, prior inconsistent statements, etc., and draw reasonable inferences. A fair report would identify shortcomings in the investigation itself, including any excesses, mistakes, errors in judgment, or impermissible tactics. A fair report would demonstrate that every possible effort had been made to identify all possibly exculpatory evidence, and that all such evidence had been given appropriate weight. And a fair report would address honestly and answer truthfully the following questions . . .[44]

Effective use of questions can cast doubt on a witness's objectivity. Attorneys for President Clinton suggested Linda Tripp was biased against the President by asking questions that assumed she was biased:

---

[42] www.washingtonpost.com/wp-dyn/content/article/2006/05/16/AR2006051600795.html.
[43] Schledwitz v. United States, 169 F.3d 1003, 1015 (6th Cir. 1999).
[44] CHICAGO TRIBUNE, Sept. 13, 1998, at 33.

What were Linda Tripp's motives in seeking out the OIC in January, 1998? Did she articulate a fear of being prosecuted in Maryland under that State's anti-taping laws? Why did she request immunity from prosecution? Why was she given immunity?

. . . .

What assessment has the OIC made of Ms. Tripp's ideological motivations? Was the OIC aware she had submitted an anti-Clinton book proposal to avowed Clinton hater Lucianne Goldberg? Was the OIC aware of Goldberg's role in Ms. Tripp's taping and arrangement for Ms. Lewinsky's use of a messenger service?[45]

---

[45] *Id.*

CHAPTER SIX

Tu Quoque: Saying One Thing, Doing Another

"*Ken Starr has engaged in precisely the same conduct—that is, making statements that are technically accurate but intentionally misleading—that he contends are grounds for impeachment for the president of the United States[.]*"

James Jordan, a spokesman for the Democrats on the Judiciary Committee.[1]

NO ONE WANTS TO BE ACCUSED of hypocrisy—saying one thing, but doing another. The moral force behind an argument derives from the belief that the proponent accepts the argument, as demonstrated by her actions consistent with that argument. Acting contrary to an argument, however, should not diminish the value of that argument. Indeed, the argument may actually be meritorious, but in the eyes of nearly everyone, that argument is worthless because the proponent does not attach enough value to it to act consistently with her beliefs.

Tu quoque, in Latin, means "you also."[2] There are two closely related variations of this fallacy. The first, as described above, involves an advocate whose actions are inconsistent with her declarations. The second involves the assertion that a proponent cannot criticize others' conduct, because she engages in the criticized conduct. This latter argument is similar to the "two wrongs make a right" fallacy, except that the disputed conduct need not be improper, illegal, or otherwise "wrong."

---

[1] http://www.nytimes.com/library/politics/100598clinton-starr.html (10-5-98).
[2] S. MORRIS ENGEL, WITH GOOD REASON: AN INTRODUCTION TO INFORMAL FALLACIES 222 (Bedford/St. Martins 6th ed. 2000).

Several common adages give expression to this fallacy. How often has the expression, "People in glass houses should not throw stones,"[3] been spoken or written? Or, the politically incorrect expression: "Our skirts are clean!"? When caught acting contrary to a stated position ("He doesn't practice what he preaches."), people rely on the common refrain: "Do as I say, not as I do."

Defending Against Hypocrisy

If there is a single, most effective fallacy for all occasions, the tu quoque argument would certainly be a strong candidate. How do you defend against hypocrisy? Immediately upon being challenged for engaging in tu quoque conduct, the proponent must convincingly demonstrate that his behavior is distinguishable from the challenged conduct. A weak or ineffective response (or no response) leaves the impression the proponent has conceded the argument.

In the quotation at the beginning of this chapter, James Jordan was not suggesting that Special Prosecutor (OIC; Office of Independent Counsel) Ken Starr should be impeached, because his conduct was identical to President Clinton's. Jordan implied that the President's conduct was proper, because the Special Prosecutor engaged in the identical conduct. How can the Special Prosecutor complain about the President's conduct when he (Starr) engaged in the same behavior? In other words, the Special Prosecutor could not be heard to complain about the President's conduct, because he (Starr) lacked the moral authority to do so.

The tu quoque conduct need not be identical to the conduct being compared; the use of similar words can substitute for the lack of identical conduct. President Clinton's lawyers accused the OIC of "abuse of authority," when comparing it to the allegation that the President was "abusing his power":

> In truth, the OIC's decision to invade the confidential relationship between the President and his most senior advisors and lawyers was unprecedented. It reflects a patent abuse of authority by the OIC and a wholesale abandonment of any prosecutorial judgment in a campaign to prevent the President from consulting meaningfully with his advisors. At bottom, the Independent Counsel seems to believe that, merely because he chooses to seek confidential information from the Office of the President, the President may not contest that demand without risking a charge that he is abusing his power.[4]

---

[3]*Id.* at 224.
[4]CHICAGO TRIBUNE, Sept. 13, 1998, at 40.

If the opposing party engaged in allegedly improper (and even though unrelated) conduct, his moral authority to act with regard to any matter may be seriously undermined. That was the picture President Clinton's attorneys attempted to portray, as they alleged the OIC engaged in questionable "tactics, illegal leaking, and manifest intent to cause [the President] damage":

> The OIC suggests that the President's delay in acknowledging a relationship with Ms. Lewinsky somehow contributed to an obstruction of justice because it affected how the prosecutors would conduct the investigation. This claim is unfounded, as a matter of law. The President had no legal obligation to appear before the grand jury absent compulsion and every reason not to do so, given the OIC's tactics, illegal leaking, and manifest intent to cause him damage.[5]

When the opposing party's conduct is alleged to be illegal, it is more difficult for that party to claim the moral high ground:

> In a letter from the Independent Counsel to the President's personal counsel, dated February 6, 1998, the Independent Counsel wrote: "From the beginning, I have made the prohibition of leaks a principal priority of the Office. It is a firing offense, as well as one that leads to criminal prosecution." However, Chief Judge Johnson has entered a series of orders finding prima facie reason to believe that persons in the OIC violated Rule 6(e), Fed. R. Crim. P., by illegal leaking (for example, "[t]he Court finds that the serious and repetitive nature of disclosures to the media of Rule 6(e) material strongly militates in favor of conducting a show cause hearing"). Has anyone been fired or disciplined by the OIC for illegal leaking? What steps have been taken to investigate and discipline OIC personnel who have engaged in illegal leaking?[6] (brackets and parentheses in original; citation omitted).

Taking a position contrary to acknowledged facts does not enhance a party's ability to pursue a course of action, or to avoid charges of hypocrisy. The OIC, according to President Clinton's attorneys, knew the President had nothing to do with the assertion of a claim of Secret Service privilege, yet the OIC, nevertheless, proceeded to allege an abuse of power:

> Further, the OIC charges the President with abusing his power despite the fact that the OIC knew that he had nothing to do with the decision to assert the privilege or to pursue the appeal from Judge Johnson's decision. Indeed, the OIC itself had argued (in contesting the

---

[5]*Id.*
[6]*Id.* at 33.

claim of the Secret Service in the district court) that the failure of the President to involve himself in the matter was itself a reason for the court to reject the Service's claim. The OIC cannot have it both ways.[7] (parentheses in original).

Tit for Tat

The most forceful tu quoque argument arises when the opposition can (credibly) be accused of the identical conduct he complains of. Here, the Special Prosecutor is accused of dilatory conduct:

> The OIC's apparent argument that the assertions of privilege were for purposes of delay lacks any evidentiary support and, more significantly, overlooks the OIC's own dilatory conduct. After Mr. Lindsey was subpoenaed and before he was scheduled to testify, the Office of the President attempted to avoid litigating these issues by reaching an accommodation that would provide the OIC with access to the information to which it was entitled while maintaining the legitimate confidentiality interests of the President. The OIC rejected those efforts and instead filed its motion to compel. The OIC has continued to reject any attempt by the White House to compromise, choosing instead to litigate these issues. The Office of the President has sought to avoid any delay by agreeing to expedited briefing schedules involving privilege litigation, and the courts, appreciating the time-sensitivity of the issues, have ruled swiftly on these matters.[8] (citations omitted).

Examples of alleged dilatory conduct effectively enhance the comparison between the parties' actions:

> Finally, substantial delay in the investigation has been self-inflicted. The OIC has wandered aimlessly down more alleys and byways than any federal prosecutor would appropriately do. The OIC has called current and former White House staffers before the grand jury, and interviewed many others. The OIC has called presidential advisers before the grand jury four, five and six times; sometimes for only one- or two-hour sessions. Some witnesses appeared to testify only to find themselves waiting for hours and then being told to return on another day. The OIC has also insisted on exploring such irrelevant subjects as White House contacts with the press, and has required tes-

---

[7] *Id.* at 40.
[8] *Id.* at 35.

timony from attorneys whose primary function was to deal with the OIC. Such actions are highly unusual, if not unprecedented.⁹

In response to his indictment, on September 28, 2005, then U.S. House of Representatives Majority Leader Tom DeLay asserted that Texas prosecutor Ronnie Earle could not prosecute him (DeLay), because DeLay's political campaign conduct was no different from his (Earle's):

> Now let [me] be very, very clear: I have done nothing wrong. I have violated no law, no regulation, no rule of the House. I have done nothing unlawful, unethical or, I might add, unprecedented, even in the political campaigns of Mr. Earle himself.¹⁰ (brackets in original).

The Second Circuit, in a 2–1 ruling, refused to enforce a Federal Communications Commission fine involving the broadcast of "fleeting expletives."¹¹ One commentator noted that tu quoque vulgarity by President Bush and Vice President Cheney was central to the court's decision:

> If President Bush and Vice President Cheney can blurt out vulgar language, then the government cannot punish broadcast television stations for broadcasting the same words in similarly fleeting contexts.
>
> That, in essence, was the decision on Monday, when a federal appeals panel struck down the government policy that allows stations and networks to be fined if they broadcast shows containing obscene language.¹²

Foul Language

Notably, the Second Circuit cited instances where the President and Vice President used language that would have run afoul of the FCC's ruling:

> But the judges said vulgar words are just as often used out of frustration or excitement, and not to convey any broader obscene meaning. "In recent times even the top leaders of our government have used variants of these expletives in a manner that no reasonable person would believe referenced sexual or excretory organs or activities."

---

⁹*Id.*
¹⁰http://www.nytimes.com/2005/09/28/politics/28text-delay.html.
¹¹Fox Television Stations v. Fed. Commc'ns Comm'n, 489 F.3d 444 (2nd Cir. 2007).
¹²http://www.nytimes.com/2007/06/05/business/media/05decency.html.

Adopting an argument made by lawyers for NBC, the judges then cited examples in which Mr. Bush and Mr. Cheney had used the same language that would be penalized under the policy. Mr. Bush was caught on videotape last July using a common vulgarity that the commission finds objectionable in a conversation with Prime Minister Tony Blair of Britain. Three years ago, Mr. Cheney was widely reported to have muttered an angry obscene version of "get lost" to Senator Patrick Leahy on the floor of the United States Senate.[13]

During the spring of 2005, when the Democrats had 44 U.S. Senators (plus one independent) and the Republicans had 55 Senators, Republicans threatened to change the Senate's rules to ban judicial filibusters, a tactic the Democrats were successfully using to prevent a vote on some of President Bush's judicial nominees. Republicans claimed history was on their side: "Never in the history of the Senate before now has filibustering been used to stop a federal court nomination."[14]

However, one Republican, Senator Chuck Hagel (R-NE), in a rare admission of tu quoque conduct, conceded Republicans, while enjoying majority status in the Senate, had tactically prevented some of President Clinton's judicial nominees from reaching the bench: "The Republicans' hands aren't clean on this either. What we did with Bill Clinton's nominees—about 62 of them—we just didn't give them votes in committee or we didn't bring them up[.]"[15]

"Clean Hands Doctrine"

Judicial recognition of tu quoque conduct can be found in the "clean hands doctrine": The principle that a party cannot seek equitable relief or assert an equitable defense if that party has violated an equitable principle, such as good faith.[16]

Although the "clean hands doctrine" requires a party in equity to be free of improper conduct, the principle is not susceptible to mechanical application:

> We may assume that because of the clean hands doctrine a federal court should not, in an ordinary case, lend its judicial power to a plaintiff who seeks to invoke that power for the purpose of consummating a transaction in clear violation of law. But this does not mean that courts

---

[13] *Id.* See 489 F.3d at 459–60.
[14] *Filibustering Federal Court Nominees,* http://www.mrcranky.com/movies/houseofwax/42.htm (05/09/05).
[15] *Id.*
[16] BLACK'S LAW DICTIONARY, 208 (spec. abr. 8th ed. 2006).

must always permit a defendant wrongdoer to retain the profits of his wrongdoing merely because the plaintiff himself is possibly guilty of transgressing the law in the transactions involved. The maxim that he who comes into equity must come with clean hands is not applied by way of punishment for an unclean litigant but "upon considerations that make for the advancement of right and justice." It is not a rigid formula which "trammels the free and just exercise of discretion." Therefore, before deciding the applicability of the maxim to the case at hand, we must examine the particular transactions and circumstances involved together with the federal laws which are alleged to taint these transactions with illegality.[17] (citations and footnotes omitted).

Tu quoque conduct need not be limited to specific individuals. Government, at all levels, was accused by a representative of R. J. Reynolds Tobacco Company of complicity in enacting legislation that promoted cigarette smoking. Having done so, what moral authority did the government command to turn around and sue the tobacco companies?

Even a cursory review of the legislative history of laws dealing with tobacco products reveals that legislation has been enacted by federal, state and locally elected representatives with full awareness that there are health risks associated with the use of cigarettes.

Having fully participated in deliberate, societal decisions that cigarettes are a lawful product which adults may choose to use, a number of states—through their attorneys general—now seek to change the rules and effectively eliminate tobacco by suing to recover hundreds of millions of dollars in Medicaid lawsuits.[18]

Justices on the U.S. Supreme Court often note the tu quoque writings of their colleagues on the opposing side of a case. In *Hill v. Colorado*,[19] Justice Stevens, writing for the Court, pointed out that dissenting Justices Scalia and Kennedy rejected legislation proposed by partisans they disapproved of, but upheld legislation enacted by partisans they approved of:

Similarly, the contention that a statute is "viewpoint based" simply because its enactment was motivated by the conduct of the partisans on one side of a debate is without support. The antipicketing ordinance upheld in *Frisby v. Schultz*, a decision in which both of today's dissenters joined, was obviously enacted in response to the activities of anti-abortion protesters who wanted to protest at the home of a particular

---

[17]Johnson v. Yellow Cab Transit Co., 321 U.S. 383, 387–88 (1944).
[18]Daniel W. Donahue, *The States Are Asking Courts to Abolish Principles of Factual and Legal Proximate Cause*, A.B.A. J., Jan. 1997, at 56.
[19]530 U.S. 703 (2000).

doctor to persuade him and others that they viewed his practice of performing abortions to be murder. We nonetheless summarily concluded that the statute was content neutral.[20] (citation omitted).

Bush v. Gore,[21] the case that determined the winner of the 2000 presidential election, elicited many references to tu quoque conduct. Justice Stevens argued that the majority did not follow "their own reasoning":

> Even assuming that aspects of the remedial scheme might ultimately be found to violate the Equal Protection Clause, I could not subscribe to the majority's disposition of the case. As the majority explicitly holds, once a state legislature determines to select electors through a popular vote, the right to have one's vote counted is of constitutional stature. As the majority further acknowledges, Florida law holds that all ballots that reveal the intent of the voter constitute valid votes. Recognizing these principles, the majority nonetheless orders the termination of the contest proceeding before all such votes have been tabulated. Under their own reasoning, the appropriate course of action would be to remand to allow more specific procedures for implementing the legislature's uniform general standard to be established.[22]

In another passage, Justice Stevens quotes the majority's declaration that equal protection guarantees should not be sacrificed to speed, but contends that is precisely what the majority did:

> In the interest of finality, however, the majority effectively orders the disenfranchisement of an unknown number of voters whose ballots reveal their intent—and are therefore legal votes under state law—but were for some reason rejected by ballot-counting machines. It does so on the basis of the deadlines set forth in Title 3 of the United States Code. But, as I have already noted, those provisions merely provide rules of decision for Congress to follow when selecting among conflicting slates of electors. They do not prohibit a State from counting what the majority concedes to be legal votes until a bona fide winner is determined. Indeed, in 1960, Hawaii appointed two slates of electors and Congress chose to count the one appointed on January 4, 1961, well after the Title 3 deadlines. Thus, nothing prevents the majority, even if it properly found an equal protection violation, from ordering relief appropriate to remedy that violation without depriving Florida voters of their right to have their votes counted. As the majority notes, "[a] desire for speed is not a general excuse for ignoring equal protection guarantees."[23] (citations omitted).

---

[20]*Id.* at 724–25.
[21]531 U.S. 98 (2000).
[22]*Id.* at 126–27.
[23]*Id.* at 127.

Justice Ginsburg, also a dissenter, cited a law review article authored by Justice O'Connor, in which she (Justice O'Connor) argued (contrary to her position in this case) that the Court may reasonably defer to constitutional interpretations by a state supreme court:

> This Court more than occasionally affirms statutory, and even constitutional, interpretations with which it disagrees.
>
> . . . .
>
> O'Connor, Trends in the Relationship Between the Federal and State Courts from the Perspective of a State Court Judge, 22 Wm. & Mary L. Rev. 801, 813 (1981) ("There is no reason to assume that state court judges cannot and will not provide a 'hospitable forum' in litigating federal constitutional questions.").[24] (parentheses in original; ellipses added).

The majority, according to Justice Ginsburg, also ignored its customary practice regarding dual sovereignty:

> The extraordinary setting of this case has obscured the ordinary principle that dictates its proper resolution: Federal courts defer to state high courts' interpretations of their state's own law. This principle reflects the core of federalism, on which all agree. "The Framers split the atom of sovereignty. It was the genius of their idea that our citizens would have two political capacities, one state and one federal, each protected from incursion by the other." The Chief Justice's solicitude for the Florida Legislature comes at the expense of the more fundamental solicitude we owe to the legislature's sovereign. U. S. Const., Art. II, §1, cl. 2 ("*Each State* shall appoint, in such Manner as the Legislature *thereof* may direct," the electors for President and Vice President). Were the other members of this Court as mindful as they generally are of our system of dual sovereignty, they would affirm the judgment of the Florida Supreme Court.[25] (citations omitted; parentheses and italics in original).

Establishment Clause Test

Similarly, Justice Brennan faulted Justices Blackmun and O'Connor, in *Allegheny County v. Greater Pittsburgh ACLU*,[26] for not following their customary practice of examining a "message conveyed by objects" in context, citing previous cases by the two Justices:

---

[24] *Id.* at 136–37.
[25] *Id.* at 142–43.
[26] 492 U.S. 573 (1989).

In asserting that the Christmas tree, regardless of its surroundings, is a purely secular symbol, Justices Blackmun and O'Connor ignore the precept they otherwise so enthusiastically embrace: that context is all important in determining the message conveyed by particular objects. (Blackmun, J.) (relevant question is "whether the display of the creche and the menorah, in their respective 'particular physical settings,' has the effect of endorsing or disapproving religious beliefs") (O'Connor, J.) ("'[E]very government practice must be judged in its *unique circumstances* to determine whether it constitutes an endorsement or disapproval of religion'") (O'Connor, J., concurring)); (O'Connor, J.) ("Establishment Clause analysis depends on sensitivity to the context and circumstances presented by each case"); (O'Connor, J.) (emphasizing "the need to focus on the specific practice in question in its particular physical setting and context"). In analyzing the symbolic character of the Christmas tree, both Justices Blackmun and O'Connor abandon this contextual inquiry. In doing so, they go badly astray.[27] (citations omitted; italics and parentheses in original).

In the same case, Justice Blackmun offered a tu quoque critique of Justice Kennedy's Establishment Clause test:

But because Justice Kennedy's formulation of this essential Establishment Clause inquiry is no less fact intensive than the "endorsement" formulation adopted by the Court, Justice Kennedy should be wary of accusing the Court's formulation as "using little more than intuition and a tape measure," lest he find his own formulation convicted on an identical charge.[28]

Taking a Page from Orwell

Justice Blackmun also wrote that Justice Kennedy's opinion could have taken a page from George Orwell's famous novel:

A secular state, it must be remembered, is not the same as an atheistic or antireligious state. A secular state establishes neither atheism nor religion as its official creed. Justice Kennedy thus has it exactly backwards when he says that enforcing the Constitution's requirement that government remain secular is a prescription of orthodoxy. It follows directly from the Constitution's proscription against government affiliation with religious beliefs or institutions that there is no orthodoxy on religious matters in the secular state. Although Justice Kennedy

---

[27]*Id.* at 640–41.
[28]*Id.* at 608.

accuses the Court of "an Orwellian rewriting of history," perhaps it is Justice Kennedy himself who has slipped into a form of Orwellian newspeak when he equates the constitutional command of secular government with a prescribed orthodoxy.[29] (citations omitted).

Whether Miranda rights are rooted in the Constitution created a disagreement between Chief Justice Rehnquist and Justice Scalia, in *Dickerson v. United States*.[30] The Chief Justice quoted a previous decision by Justice Scalia, seemingly contradicting his position in this case:

> We do not think there is such justification for overruling *Miranda*. *Miranda* has become embedded in routine police practice to the point where the warnings have become part of our national culture. See *Mitchell v. United States*, 526 U. S. 314, 331-332 (1999) (Scalia, J., dissenting) (stating that the fact that a rule has found "'wide acceptance in the legal culture'" is "adequate reason not to overrule" it). While we have overruled our precedents when subsequent cases have undermined their doctrinal underpinnings, see, e.g., *Patterson v. McLean Credit Union*, 491 U. S. 164, 173 (1989), we do not believe that this has happened to the *Miranda* decision. If anything, our subsequent cases have reduced the impact of the *Miranda* rule on legitimate law enforcement while reaffirming the decision's core ruling that unwarned statements may not be used as evidence in the prosecution's case in chief.[31] (parentheses in original).

Justice Scalia answered this tu quoque argument with his own tu quoque argument, noting previous opinions from the Justices in the majority, to the effect that *Miranda* was not based on the Constitution:

> [B]ut also that Justices whose votes are needed to compose today's majority are on record as believing that a violation of *Miranda* is not a violation of the Constitution. See *Davis v. United States*, 512 U. S. 452, 457-458 (1994) (opinion of the Court, in which Kennedy, J., joined); *Duckworth v. Eagan*, 492 U. S. 195, 203 (1989) (opinion of the Court, in which Kennedy, J., joined); *Oregon v. Elstad*, 470 U. S. 298 (1985) (opinion of the Court by O'Connor, J.); *New York v. Quarles*, 467 U. S. 649 (1984) (opinion of the Court by Rehnquist, J.).[32] (ellipses added; parentheses in original).

Supreme Court decisions and law review articles are not the only sources of tu quoque writings for the Justices on the Court. Justice

---

[29] *Id.* at 610–11.
[30] 530 U.S. 428 (2000).
[31] *Id.* at 443–44.
[32] *Id.* at 445.

Ginsburg, dissenting in *Muscarello v. United States*,[33] quoted from an opinion by Justice Breyer when he sat on the First Circuit Court of Appeals:

> To be more specific, as cogently explained on another day by today's opinion writer:
>
> "The special 'mandatory minimum' sentencing statute says that anyone who '*uses or carries*' a gun 'during and in relation to any . . . drug trafficking crime' must receive a mandatory five-year prison term added on to his drug crime sentence. At the same time, the Sentencing Guidelines, promulgated under the authority of a different statute, provide for a two-level (i.e., a 30% to 40%) sentence enhancement where a 'firearm . . . was possessed' by a drug offender, U. S. S. G. §2D1.1(b)(1), unless the possession clearly was not 'connected with the [drug] offense.'" *McFadden*, 13 F. 3d, at 467 (Breyer, C. J., dissenting).[34] (citations omitted; italics, ellipses, and parentheses in original).

Similarly, Justice Stevens, in *Morse v. Frederick*,[35] a case involving a First Amendment challenge to a high school student's public banner, noted a previous circuit court decision by Justice Alito, seemingly contradicting his Supreme Court position:

> Certainly where there is no finding and no showing that engaging in that conduct would materially and substantially interfere with the requirements of appropriate discipline in the operation of the school, the prohibition cannot be sustained. As other federal courts have long recognized, under *Tinker*,
>
> "regulation of student speech is generally permissible only when the speech would substantially disrupt or interfere with the work of the school or the rights of other students. . . . *Tinker* requires a specific and significant fear of disruption, *not just some remote apprehension of disturbance.*" *Saxe v. State College Area School Dist.*, 240 F.3d 200, 211 (CA3 2001)(Alito, J.)[36] (italics and ellipses in original).

Ridicule may accompany a tu quoque argument, as practiced by members of the Supreme Court. Justice Scalia ridiculed Justice Breyer's theory of stare decisis, in *College Savings Bank v. Florida Prepaid Postsecondary Education Expense Board*:[37]

---

[33]524 U.S. 125 (1998).
[34]*Id.* at 140–41.
[35]127 S. Ct. 2618 (2007).
[36]*Id.* at 2645.
[37]527 U.S. 666 (1999).

> First, Justice Breyer and the other dissenters have adopted a decidedly perverse theory of *stare decisis*. While finding themselves entirely unconstrained by a venerable precedent such as *Hans*, imbedded within our legal system for over a century, at the same time they cling desperately to an anomalous and severely undermined decision (*Parden*) from the 1960's. Surely this approach to *stare decisis* is exactly backwards—unless, of course, one wishes to use it as a weapon rather than a guide, in which case any old approach will do.[38] (citations omitted; parentheses in original).

A tu quoque argument need not derive from statements solely by the proponent. Quoting the writings of a source cited by the proponent may, effectively, cast the source as a surrogate proponent. Justice White employed this technique in *Harmelin v. Michigan*,[39] a case involving the Eighth Amendment's "cruel and unusual" language, where the defendant was convicted of possessing more than 650 grams of cocaine and was sentenced to life in prison without possibility of parole:

> Thus, Benjamin Oliver, cited by Justice Scalia, observed with respect to the Eighth Amendment:

> No express restriction is laid in the constitution, upon the power of imprisoning for crimes. But, as it is forbidden to demand unreasonable bail, which merely exposes the individual concerned, to imprisonment in case he cannot procure it; as it is forbidden to impose unreasonable fines, on account of the difficulty the person fined would have of paying them, the default of which would be punished by imprisonment only, it would seem, that imprisonment for an unreasonable length of time, is also contrary to the spirit of the constitution.[40] (citation omitted).

Justice White then remarked: "Justice Scalia concedes that the language of the Amendment bears such a construction. His reasons for claiming that it should not be so construed are weak."[41] (citation omitted).

---

[38] *Id.* at 689.
[39] 501 U.S. 957 (1991).
[40] *Id.* at 1009–10.
[41] *Id.*

CHAPTER SEVEN

Poisoning the Well

"Falsus in uno, falsus in omnibus"

(False in one thing, false in everything)

Legal maxim

"POISON THE WELL" did not originate as a term of logic: The expression goes back to the Middle Ages, when waves of anti-Jewish prejudice and persecution were common. If a plague struck a community, the people blamed it on the Jews, whom they accused of "poisoning the wells."[1]

Nowadays, the phrase "poison the well" signifies, in logic terms, an overwhelming personal attack, yielding little or no opportunity to mount a comeback. Raising serious doubts about an individual's credibility is the usual form of attack. This may be accomplished by proclaiming that someone who failed to tell the truth once cannot be trusted to tell the truth about anything, ever again, as typified by the legal maxim above. Even if it cannot be proven that an individual has prevaricated previously, a declaration to that effect, followed by a challenge to veracity on other issues, is often equally effective.

Defending against a successful poison-the-well attack is exceedingly difficult. How do you un-poison a well? One solution may be to sell bottled water—a bit more expensive, but far safer. In other words, an effective defense strategy could be a deft switch in topics away from what poisoned the well. Perhaps it can be argued that the attack on

---

[1] S. MORRIS ENGEL, WITH GOOD REASON: AN INTRODUCTION TO INFORMAL FALLACIES 225 (Bedford/St. Martins 6th ed. 2000).

credibility is manifestly unfair, in the hopes of attracting sympathy. Or you can emphasize a weakness in the opponent's case which, hopefully, overshadows the assault on credibility. Better still, recognize a poison-the-well argument early, and neutralize it before it succeeds.

Pre-Trial Publicity

Besides attacks on credibility, a poison-the-well argument may arise in the context of a jury's ability to render an impartial decision. Pre-trial publicity, in news reports, is often cited as a reason for a change in venue. An attorney's media comments may also prejudice the jury, and could subject him to possible discipline. The ABA's Model Rules of Professional Conduct strictly limit extrajudicial statements that "the lawyer knows or reasonably should know . . . will have a substantial likelihood of materially prejudicing an adjudicative proceeding in the matter."[2] In other words, poisoning the well.

A poison-the-well argument is usually limited to two outcomes: it is successful or it is not. (Not to be confused with the either/or fallacy, which limits the choice to one of two alternatives, while ignoring other options.) Either the poison in the well is so overwhelming none of the water is potable, or it is so diluted it does not pollute the well. Courts, called upon to decide whether statements or conduct denies a defendant or party due process, cannot simply split the difference, but must decide that the well was poisoned or it was not.

Outside the courtroom, poison-the-well arguments take many forms. Columnist Cal Thomas, inveighing against cloning, advances a poison-the-well argument against the *New York Times* editorial writers in this example:

> The New York Times editorializes against cloning, but that newspaper, which regularly endorses abortion for any reason and at any stage, long ago gave up any right to be heard on this subject. . . . We are now viewed as complex machines to be dissected and used for whatever purpose the majority may wish.[3] (ellipses added).

Thomas argued that the editorial writers' support for abortion rights disqualified them from even commenting about cloning—despite their

---

[2]ABA MODEL RULES OF PROFESSIONAL CONDUCT, Rule 3.6, *Trial Publicity* 70 (2008 ed.).

[3]*Bush Action: Fruit of the Poisoned Tree*, MILWAUKEE JOURNAL SENTINEL, Aug. 12, 2001, at 3J.

agreement with him on that subject. Here, the well is poisoned by an earlier stance the editorial writers espoused.

A more traditional example of the poison-the-well argument occurs when someone is accused of not telling the truth. In the May 2005 British elections, where Prime Minister Tony Blair sought—and won—a third term, he was attacked for his support of the Iraq war. (His name was even twisted into B-liar.)[4] During the election campaign, the leader of the Conservatives, Michael Howard, did not outright accuse the Prime Minister of lying, but it was implicit in this poison-the-well attack: "If you can't trust Mr. Blair on the decision to take the country to war—the most important decision a prime minister can take—how can you trust Mr. Blair on anything else ever again?"[5]

Impugning Credibility

Howard's argument sought not only to impugn Blair's credibility over the Iraq war but also to extend that lack of credibility to any other issue. This is also an example of begging the question, where the conclusion is a restatement of the proof: It is assumed, without proving, that Blair could not be trusted to take the country to war; therefore, he could not be trusted with any decision.

In court, the Federal Rules of Evidence strictly define the limits of attacking a witness's credibility and, by implication, limit the ability to poison the well. Sometimes (unexpectedly) a "friendly" witness offers testimony favorable to the other side. In that circumstance, an attorney may wish to challenge her witness's credibility. Such a challenge is allowed: "The credibility of a witness may be attacked by any party, including the party calling the witness."[6]

An attack on a witness's credibility may be "in the form of opinion or reputation," but that attack is not open ended:

> (1) the evidence may refer only to character for truthfulness or untruthfulness, and (2) evidence of truthful character is admissible only after the character of the witness for truthfulness has been attacked by opinion or reputation evidence or otherwise.[7]

---

[4]An early example of this usage appeared in *The Times* (United Kingdom), June 10, 2003, at 9.
[5]N.Y. TIMES, *Blair, on Defensive, Releases a Secret Memo on the Iraq War*, http://www.nytimes.com/2005/04/29/international/europe/29britain.html.
[6]Fed. R. Evid. 607. Who May Impeach.
[7]Fed. R. Evid. 608. Evidence of Character and Conduct of a Witness.

Conviction of a crime may be used to undermine a witness's credibility, but, here too, restrictions are placed on the use of such evidence. Assuming it is not prejudicial, confusing, or a waste of a time,[8] evidence of a crime "punishable by death or imprisonment in excess of one year"[9] may be used to attack the credibility of witness, other than an accused. A defendant's credibility may be attacked by the same evidence, provided "the probative value of admitting this evidence outweighs its prejudicial effect to the accused . . ."[10]

Evidence that a witness has been convicted of *crimen falsi* also may be admitted:

> (2) evidence that any witness has been convicted of a crime shall be admitted if it involved dishonesty or false statement, regardless of the punishment.[11]

Generally, evidence involving a conviction of a crime or *crimen falsi*

> is not admissible if a period of more than ten years has elapsed since the date of the conviction or of the release of the witness from the confinement imposed for that conviction, whichever is the later date, unless the court determines, in the interests of justice, that the probative value of the conviction . . . substantially outweighs its prejudicial effect.[12] (ellipses added).

Though not couched in terms of "poisoning the well," the admissibility of criminal conviction evidence is always dependent on its lack of "prejudicial effect." Therefore, whenever this type of evidence is offered to attack a witness's credibility, an attorney should argue that its introduction would poison the well, i.e., it will have a "prejudicial effect."

The legal maxim "falsus in uno, falsus in omnibus" suggests that a witness who has lied about a material fact cannot be trusted to tell the truth about anything. Courts have generally rejected this form of the poison-the-well argument:

> The maxim "*Falsus in uno, falsus in omnibus*" has been well said to be itself "absolutely false as a maxim of life." The correct principle was stated by Judge Campbell more than a century ago:
>
>> There never has been any positive rule of law which excluded evidence from consideration entirely, on account of the wilful falsehood

---

[8]Fed. R. Evid. 403. Exclusion of Relevant Evidence on Grounds of Prejudice, Confusion, or Waste of Time.
[9]Fed. R. Evid. 609. Impeachment by Evidence of Conviction of Crime.
[10]*Id.*
[11]*Id.*
[12]*Id.*

of a witness as to some portions of his testimony. Such disregard of his oath is enough to justify the belief that the witness is capable of any amount of falsification, and to make it no more than prudent to regard all that he says with strong suspicion, and to place no reliance on his mere statements. But when testimony is once before the jury, the weight and credibility of every portion of it is for them, and not for the Court to determine.[13] (italics in original; citations omitted).

A Federal District Court Judge's refusal to give a jury instruction that included the "falsus in uno, falsus in omnibus" charge resulted in an appeal to the Second Circuit. The case involved a defendant found guilty of (among other things) "conspiracy to commit murder in connection with the shooting deaths of two rival drug dealers."[14] Evidence of the defendant's guilt was provided almost exclusively from cooperating codefendants. The defendant exercised his constitutional right not to testify, and offered no witnesses to rebut the government's case. "Instead, defense counsel's strategy was to attack the credibility of the government witnesses."[15]

At the charge conference, the judge agreed to give the following instruction concerning the witnesses' credibility:

> If you believe that a witness has given false testimony with respect to a material fact, you may disregard the testimony of the witness in whole or in part. A witness may have been mistaken or may have lied as to part of the testimony, and yet be accurate and truthful as to other parts.[16]

Based on his belief that the instruction would be given to the jury, the defense counsel argued:

> That was just another lie he made here on the stand, and when a witness lies in front of you on the stand, you can take that, you can consider it and if you feel it's appropriate you can say, You know what, I'm going to disregard everything this person says, because they are insulting me, they are lying to me right here on the stand.[17]

When the judge charged the jury, he omitted the agreed-upon instruction. The defense counsel complained about the omission, and the judge conceded he knowingly did not include the instruction:

---

[13]United States v. Weinstein, 452 F.2d 704, 713–14 (2nd Cir. 1971).
[14]United States v. James, 239 F.3d 120, 121–22 (2nd Cir. 2000).
[15]*Id.* at 122.
[16]*Id.*
[17]*Id.*

> **THE COURT:** You asked for it, and I went back and read all the cases and learned something, frankly, that charge is generally disfavored. I never was comfortable with that charge but I used to give it routinely.
>
> I am not blaming you but it caused me to do more research, and having done the research I was at liberty to remove it, and it is a disfavored charge, and for good reason.[18] (footnote omitted).

During jury deliberations, a juror submitted a note to the judge: "Please clarify. If a juror believed that a witness lied on the witness stand, should the juror ignore the entire testimony from that witness?"[19]

After speaking with counsel, the judge recalled the jury, read the juror's question aloud, and responded:

> Well, ladies and gentlemen, that is really for the juror. And ultimately for the jury, to decide. That's not a question we decide. That's a question you individually as jurors and collectively as a jury decide. After considering all the evidence you decide on the basis of what you heard whether to believe in whole or in part the testimony of a particular witness. I really can't, that's your duty, that's your authority, and I think that's the best way to handle that.[20] (footnote omitted).

The Second Circuit, in reviewing the conviction, was troubled by the omission of the promised instruction. However, the court found that the defendant did not show that "he was substantially misled in formulating his arguments or otherwise prejudiced."[21] Additionally, the court concluded that the judge's response to the juror's question "conveyed the practical substance of a *falsus in uno* instruction, even though the judge did not use the traditional prefatory phrase."[22] The conviction was upheld.[23]

Can a witness's testimony be incredible as a matter of law—the ultimate poison-the-well argument? During grand jury testimony, an assistant United States attorney attempted to get Michael Huber to identify Richard Gervasio as his bookie:

> **AUSA:** When you went back to [Tommy Briscoe] you asked him if he was betting with someone?
>
> **Huber:** Yes.

---

[18] *Id.*
[19] *Id.* at 123.
[20] *Id.*
[21] *Id.* at 125.
[22] *Id.*
[23] *Id.* at 127.

AUSA: What did he tell you?

Huber: He said that he was.

AUSA: Did he give a name at that time?

Huber: Yes, he did.

AUSA: Who was it?

Huber: I think the guy's name was Tom. I just knew him by sort of a synonym.

(Oops!)

AUSA: Tom?

Huber: Yes.

AUSA: How about Richie?

Huber: Richie. That sounds right. Richie it is.

AUSA: Is it Richie?

Huber: Richie. That's correct.[24] (brackets in original; parentheses added).

Gervasio argued on appeal that this grand jury testimony, and other inconsistencies, demonstrated that Huber was "a chronic liar whose testimony was incredible as a matter of law."[25] The Seventh Circuit noted that Huber's "identification of Gervasio may have been something less than a prosecutor's dream," but held that credibility was within the jury's realm, and "Huber's testimony was [not] so unreliable that the jury was not allowed to credit it."[26] As far as determining whether a witness's testimony is incredible as a matter of law, the court held:

> A witness' testimony is only incredible as a matter of law when it is unbelievable on its face—that is, when it would have been "physically impossible for the witness to observe what he described, or impossible under the laws of nature for those events to have occurred at all."[27] (citation omitted).

Judge Learned Hand expressed his view that it is perfectly rational to believe only portions of a witness's testimony:

> It is no reason for refusing to accept everything that a witness says, because you do not believe all of it; nothing is more common in all kinds of judicial decisions than to believe some and not all.[28]

---

[24] United States v. Zizzo, 120 F.3d 1338, 1359 (7th Cir. 1997).
[25] Id.
[26] Id.
[27] Id.
[28] N.L.R.B. v. Universal Camera Corp., 179 F.2d 749, 754 (2nd Cir. 1950).

Even if a witness tenders misleading testimony, that does not provide a basis for dismissing all of that witness's testimony:

> Piraino's strategy on appeal is to claim that the court should disregard in its entirety (the testimony of three opposing witnesses). Piraino argues that these three lied about the existence of an unwritten policy governing leaves of absences for employees with less than a year of service. In light of this so-called "perjury," Piraino argues that the court should not have credited any of their testimony. The Supreme Court has warned that such attacks on credibility rarely succeed: "[W]hen a trial judge's finding is based on his decision to credit the testimony of one or two or more witnesses, each of whom has told a coherent and facially plausible story that is not contradicted by extrinsic evidence, that finding, if not internally inconsistent, can virtually never be clear error." Additionally, it is within the district court judge's discretion to believe or disbelieve testimony based on the overall credibility of the witness; a misleading statement does not require the judge to disbelieve everything the witness says.[29] (parentheses added; brackets in original; citation omitted).

Shades of Disbelief

In *Calderone v. Thompson*,[30] Justice Kennedy's use of detail and expressions of disbelief left no room to credit the defendant, Thompson. First, Justice Kennedy discussed instances where Thompson was caught lying:

> Contrary to the emphatic advice of trial counsel, Thompson chose to testify. The result was by all accounts a disaster for his claim that he did not rape or murder Fleischli. The prosecution got Thompson to admit he lied to police after his arrest, when he denied having sex with Fleischli. He also admitted having lied to police about Fleischli's whereabouts the night of the murder, telling them she had left his apartment with Kashani. When asked about this lie, Thompson replied, "Mr. Kashani seemed as likely a candidate [as] anybody at that time."[31] (brackets in original).

Second, Justice Kennedy laid out facts that, by themselves, suggested Thompson's version of the events was not believable:

> He then presented his most recent, and perhaps most fantastic, account of the events of the night of the murder. Thompson testi-

---

[29]Piraino v. Int'l. Orientation Resources, Inc., 137 F.3d 987, 991 n.2 (7th Cir. 1998).
[30]523 U.S. 538 (1998).
[31]*Id.* at 561–62.

fied that, after having consensual sex with Fleischli, he fell asleep and remained asleep while, not more than six feet away, someone else stabbed Fleischli five times in the head, wrapped her head and body with duct tape, two towels, a sheet, her jacket, a sleeping bag, and a rope, moved her body from the apartment, and scrubbed the carpet to remove her blood. The District Court found Thompson's testimony "was riddled with inconsistencies and outright falsehoods." The District Court further stated: "Thompson's testimony no doubt affected the jury's verdict."[32] (citations omitted).

Based on the recitation above, Justice Kennedy removed any doubt that the well had been poisoned, and that only one conclusion was possible: "The point is beyond dispute; since Thompson lied about almost every other material aspect of the case, the jury had good reason to believe he lied about whether the sex was consensual."[33]

Poison-the-well arguments are not limited to attacking an individual's credibility, but may include an attorney's extrajudicial statements about an upcoming, or ongoing, trial. In this situation, the poisoned well is the jury's ability to render a fair and impartial verdict, based exclusively on the facts presented at the trial. This is still a person-specific argument, but instead of assaulting an individual's credibility, the attack is carried out against the members of the jury, in an attempt to have them disregard the facts elicited at the trial.

In *Gentile v. State Bar of Nevada*,[34] the U.S. Supreme Court considered whether an attorney's remarks at a press conference merited punishment by the Nevada State Bar because they materially prejudiced (poisoned) the jury. Grady Sanders owned Western Vault, where large amounts of cocaine and travelers' checks, used in an undercover operation, went missing from a deposit box. The day after his client (Sanders) was indicted, Gentile, an attorney, called a press conference, where he read a prepared statement and fielded questions from the press. Sanders was acquitted some six months later, following a jury trial. Thereafter, Gentile was disciplined by the State Bar of Nevada for violating a Nevada Supreme Court rule, based on ABA Model Rule of Professional Conduct 3.6, and the discipline was upheld by the Nevada Supreme Court.[35]

Gentile's punishment stemmed mainly from the following prepared remarks at the press conference:

---

[32] *Id.* at 562.
[33] *Id.*
[34] 501 U.S. 1030 (1991).
[35] *Id.* at 1033.

> When this case goes to trial, and as it develops, you're going to see that the evidence will prove not only that Grady Sanders is an innocent person and had nothing to do with any of the charges that are being leveled against him, but that the person that was in the most direct position to have stolen the drugs and money, the American Express Travelers' checks, is Detective Steve Scholl.
>
> There is far more evidence that will establish that Detective Scholl took these drugs and took these American Express Travelers' checks than any other living human being.
>
> . . . .
>
> Now, with respect to these other charges that are contained in this indictment, the so-called other victims, as I sit here today I can tell you that one, two—four of them are known drug dealers and convicted money launderers and drug dealers; three of whom didn't say a word about anything until after they were approached by Metro and after they were already in trouble and are trying to work themselves out of something.[36]

There was no dispute that Gentile's

> admitted purpose for calling the press conference was to counter public opinion which he perceived as adverse to his client, to fight back against the perceived efforts of the prosecution to poison the prospective juror pool, and to publicly present his client's side of the case.[37]

Before the Supreme Court, Gentile argued that the test for an attorney's extrajudicial statements was the same as that for restricting media coverage: "clear and present danger" of "actual prejudice or an imminent threat."[38] A 5–4 majority of the Court rejected that test in favor of the one which appears in ABA Model Rules 3.6(a): "the substantial likelihood of materially prejudicing that proceeding."[39] A different 5–4 majority found that Nevada's State Court Rule was vague and, therefore, Gentile did not violate the state's proscription on extrajudicial conduct.[40]

---

[36] *Id.* at 1059.
[37] *Id.* at 1064.
[38] *Id.* at 1069.
[39] *Id.* at 1076.
[40] *Id.* at 1048.

What to Avoid

In the Comment to ABA Model Rule 3.6, a listing of subjects that may very well poison the jury pool provides a guide to what an attorney should avoid to steer clear of disciplinary proceedings, and what to recognize if an opponent exceeds the proper bounds:

> (1) The character, credibility, reputation or criminal record of a party, suspect in a criminal investigation or witness, or the identity of a witness, or the expected testimony of a party or witness;
>
> (2) In a criminal case or proceedings that could result in incarceration, the possibility of a plea of guilty to the offense or the existence or contents of any confession, admission, or statement given by a defendant or suspect or that person's refusal or failure to make a statement;
>
> (3) The performance or results of any examination or test or the refusal or failure of a person to submit to an examination or test, or the identity or nature of physical evidence expected to be presented;
>
> (4) Any opinion as to the guilt or innocence of a defendant or suspect in a criminal case or proceeding that could result in incarceration;
>
> (5) Information that the lawyer knows or reasonably should know is likely to be inadmissible as evidence in a trial and that would, if disclosed, create a substantial risk of prejudicing an impartial trial; or
>
> (6) The fact that a defendant has been charged with a crime, unless there is included therein a statement explaining that the charge is merely an accusation and that the defendant is presumed innocent until and unless proven guilty.[41]

Gentile is also significant for possible defenses that can be raised to charges that an attorney's extrajudicial statements poisoned the jury pool. Timing of the statement, in proximity to the trial, is crucial. In *Gentile*, the trial occurred some six months after the press conference, and "not a single juror indicated any recollection of [Gentile] or his press conference."[42] (citations omitted; brackets added). Therefore, the further from the trial date the statements are made, the stronger the argument they did not poison the well.

An attorney fearing that an opponent has poisoned the well can request that jurors be sequestered, the trial be continued, or the venue be changed.[43] The Supreme Court also noted that "[v]oir dire can play

---

[41] ABA MODEL RULES OF PROFESSIONAL CONDUCT (hereinafter MODEL RULES) 85 (2008 ed.).
[42] *Gentile, supra* note 34 at 1047.
[43] *Id.* at 1057.

an important role in reminding jurors to set aside out-of-court information and to decide the case upon the evidence presented at trial."[44]

In 2006, a well-established organization of lawyers changed its name from the Association of Trial Lawyers of America—a name that sufficed for 34 years—to the American Association for Justice. A prominent plaintiff's attorney explained the organization's name was changed in response to the poisoned well:

> We tip our hat to the insurance companies and others in corporate America who spent millions of dollars over a lot of years to poison the well for the name *trial attorney*—and with some other choice terms they've bestowed on us . . . But now we're going to be telling people what we do, instead of just labeling ourselves with a title. The other side won't find it so easy coming after us if they have to talk about what we do.[45] (italics and ellipses in original).

---

[44] *Id.* at 1055.
[45] *New Name, New Strategies*, A.B.A. J. 39 (Feb. 2007).

CHAPTER EIGHT

Appeal to Authority

Ipse Dixit

... a bare assertion resting on the authority of an individual.[1]

THE LATIN NAME FOR AN APPEAL to authority is argumentum ad verecundiam (argument to veneration). When citing an authority, the expectation (and hope) is that the reader or listener will pay more attention to who is making the statement than to the statement itself. An authority may be a group (a court); an individual (Blackstone); or a nonlegal source (a physician). Often, the authority will be an expert, but that is not always the case. Sometimes an authority is an entity that does not disclose its source, as when a news organization quotes an unidentified individual, with the expectation that the news organization's reputation (unstated appeal to authority) will vouch for the accuracy and reliability of the facts presented.

In the legal arena, attorneys are viewed by laypersons as authority figures, which creates potential ethical issues. Prosecutors, for example, must be careful not to suggest to juries that a defendant is guilty based on evidence gathered during a police investigation, but not presented at the trial. Attorneys are prohibited from volunteering their own views of the evidence or the veracity of witnesses. Likewise, attorneys cannot offer personal assurances of a witness's credibility (vouching), or offer personal assurances that extra-record evidence supports the witness's testimony (bolstering).

---

[1] BLACK'S LAW DICTIONARY 961 (rev. 4th ed. 1968).

Multiple Lines of Attack

An attorney has multiple lines of attack when defending against an appeal to authority. Obviously, the authority—like the expert witness—is subject to cross-examination over his or her qualifications: education, experience, training, scholarly writings, etc. Presenting another authority, equally qualified, who offers a contrasting view of the evidence, may diminish the impact of the opposing side's authority. The facts which form the basis of the authority's opinion can also be challenged.

Other informal fallacies (ad hominem (abusive)), ad hominem (circumstantial)), for example) may be used to challenge the character or the bias of an authority. In the courtroom, improper appeals to authority are subject to objections. In appellate cases, the parties often defend against improper appeals to authority by claiming the other side tipped the scales first, and they were merely "righting the scales"—the "invited response" doctrine (two wrongs).

Constitutional arguments invariably rely on the writings or statements of the "Founding Fathers," the "Founders," or the "Framers." Hamilton, Jay, Jefferson, Adams, and others can certainly be considered authorities on the Constitution, given their involvement in creating that document, but citing one of the founders does not end the argument. As Justice Souter notes, dissenting in *Alden v. Maine*,[2] there are legitimate limits to appealing to the framers as authorities:

> The Framers' intentions and expectations count so far as they point to the meaning of the Constitution's text or the fair implications of its structure, but they do not hover over the instrument to veto any application of its principles to a world that the Framers could not have anticipated.[3]

Justice Souter was responding to Justice Kennedy, writing for the majority, who invoked the framers' perceived understandings concerning sovereign immunity, as authority for his arguments that the Constitution bans an individual suit against a state to enforce a federal statutory right under the Fair Labor Standards Act:

> These holdings reflect a settled doctrinal understanding, consistent with the views of the leading advocates of the Constitution's ratification, that sovereign immunity derives not from the Eleventh Amendment but from the structure of the original Constitution itself.
>
> . . . .

---

[2] 527 U.S. 706 (1999).
[3] *Id.* at 807.

> The Framers of the Constitution did not share our dissenting colleagues' belief that the Congress may circumvent the federal design by regulating the States directly when it pleases to do so, including by a proxy in which individual citizens are authorized to levy upon the state treasuries absent the States' consent to jurisdiction.[4] (ellipses added; citations omitted).

Justice Kennedy invoked an even higher authority than the framers to support his arguments: Blackstone.

> In reciting the prerogatives of the Crown, Blackstone—whose works constituted the preeminent authority on English law for the founding generation—understood the close and necessary relationship understood to exist between sovereignty and immunity from suit . . .[5] (ellipses added).

An appeal to authority need not always be to a higher (or the highest) authority. Justice Ginsburg, in *Buckhannon v. West Virginia*,[6] appealed to the "authority of the many"[7] when she cited the Federal Circuit Courts of Appeal: "When this Court rejects the considered judgment prevailing in the Circuits, respect for our colleagues demands a cogent explanation. Today's decision does not provide one."[8]

Lower Court Decisions

The limits of citing the courts of appeals, when arguing to the Supreme Court, are noted by Justice Scalia, dissenting in *CBOCS West, Inc. v. Humphries*:[9]

> Of course, lower court decisions may be persuasive, and when the Court rejects the unanimous position of the courts of appeals, it is fair to point out that fact. But the point has traction only to the extent it tends to show that the Court's reasoning is flawed on the merits, as demonstrated by the number of judges who have reached the opposite conclusion. (citing Justice Ginsburg's quotation above). Unlike decisions of this Court, decisions of the courts of appeals, even when unanimous, do not carry *stare decisis* weight, nor do they relieve us of our obligation independently to decide the merits of the question

---

[4]*Id.* at 728, 759.
[5]*Id.* at 715.
[6]532 U.S. 598 (2001).
[7]Also called "argument by consensus." S. Morris Engel, With Good Reason: An Introduction to Informal Fallacies 241 (Bedford/St. Martins 6th ed. 2000).
[8]*Buckhannon, supra* note 6, at 643–44.
[9]128 S. Ct. 1951 (2008).

presented. That is why, when we have affirmed a view unanimously held by the courts of appeals, we have done so (at least until today) not because we gave precedential weight to the lower courts' decisions, but because we agreed with their resolution of the question on the merits.[10] (first parentheses added; citations omitted).

Justice Scalia's analysis of the import of courts of appeals' decisions is an example of begging the question: Under what circumstance does the Supreme Court affirm the rulings of the courts below? When the courts of appeals' reach the same decision as the Supreme Court, having considered the case *de novo*.

Justice O'Connor cited state court decisions as authority in a case involving the "year-and-a-day rule," prohibiting prosecution if the victim didn't die within a year of sustaining the causal injury:

> At the same time, however, the fact that a vast number of jurisdictions have abolished a rule that has so clearly outlived its purpose is surely relevant to whether the abolition of the rule in a particular case can be said to be unexpected and indefensible by reference to the law as it then existed.[11]

Responding to Justice O'Connor, Justice Scalia appealed to two higher authorities—Blackstone and the framers:

> What occurred in the present case, then, is precisely what Blackstone said—and the Framers believed—would not suffice. The Tennessee Supreme Court made no pretense that the year-and-a-day rule was bad law from the outset; rather, it asserted, the need for the rule, as a means of assuring causality of the death, had disappeared with time. Blackstone—and the Framers who were formed by Blackstone—would clearly have regarded that *change* in law as a matter for the legislature, beyond the *power* of the court.[12] (italics in original).

Defining "To Carry"

A logomachy broke out between Justices Breyer and Ginsburg, in *Muscarello v. United States*,[13] over the meaning of "to carry," and whether Congress intended it to include transportation of a firearm in a vehicle. Justice Breyer, who argued "to carry" is not limited to conveyance on

---

[10] *Id.* at 1969–70.
[11] Rogers v. Tennessee, 532 U.S. 451 (2001).
[12] *Id.* at 477.
[13] 524 U.S. 125 (1998).

one's person, first turned to the tried and true authorities for word definitions—various dictionaries:

> The origin of the word "carries" explains why the first, or basic, meaning of the word "carry" includes conveyance in a vehicle. See The Barnhart Dictionary of Etymology 146 (1988) (tracing the word from Latin "carum," which means "car" or "cart"); 2 Oxford English Dictionary, *supra*, at 919 (tracing the word from Old French "carier" and the late Latin "carricare," which meant to "convey in a car"); The Oxford Dictionary of English Etymology 148 (C. Onions ed. 1966) (same); The Barnhart Dictionary of Etymology, *supra*, at 143 (explaining that the term "car" has been used to refer to the automobile since 1896).[14] (parentheses in original).

Not content to rely solely on the dictionary definition of "to carry," Justice Breyer also appealed to literary authorities:

> The greatest of writers have used the word with this meaning. See, e.g., The King James Bible, 2 Kings 9:28 ("[H]is servants carried him in a chariot to Jerusalem"); *id.*, Isaiah 30:6 ("[T]hey will carry their riches upon the shoulders of young asses"). Robinson Crusoe says, "[w]ith my boat, I carry'd away every Thing." D. Defoe, Robinson Crusoe 174 (J. Crowley ed. 1972). And the owners of Queequeg's ship, Melville writes, "had lent him a [wheelbarrow], in which to carry his heavy chest to his boardinghouse." H. Melville, Moby Dick 43 (U. Chicago 1952). This Court, too, has spoken of the "carrying" of drugs in a car or in its "trunk." *California v. Acevedo*, 500 U.S. 565, 572-573 (1991); *Florida v. Jimeno*, 500 U.S. 248, 249 (1991).[15] (parentheses and brackets in original).

In reply, Justice Ginsburg first argued that Justice Breyer committed the fallacy of accent (Chapter 9): selectively quoting only those authorities who support his position, while ignoring those who do not: "On lessons from literature, a scan of Bartlett's and other quotation collections shows how highly selective the Court's choices are."[16]

Then, Justice Ginsburg argued that equally (or, perhaps better) qualified authorities supported the limited definition of "to carry":

> If "[t]he greatest of writers" have used "carry" to mean convey or transport in a vehicle, so have they used the hydra-headed word to mean, *inter alia*, carry in one's hand, arms, head, heart, or soul, sans vehicle. Consider, among countless examples:

---

[14] *Id.* at 128.
[15] *Id.* at 129.
[16] *Id.* at 143.

> "[H]e shall gather the lambs with his arm, and carry them in his bosom." The King James Bible, Isaiah 40:11.
>
> "And still they gaz'd, and still the wonder grew, That one small head could carry all he knew." O. Goldsmith, The Deserted Village, ll. 215-216, in The Poetical Works of Oliver Goldsmith 30 (A. Dobson ed. 1949).
>
> "There's a Legion that never was 'listed, That carries no colours or crest." R. Kipling, The Lost Legion, st. 1, in Rudyard Kipling's Verse, 1885-1918, p. 222 (1920).
>
> "There is a homely adage which runs, 'Speak softly and carry a big stick; you will go far.'" T. Roosevelt, Speech at Minnesota State Fair, Sept. 2, 1901, in J. Bartlett, Familiar Quotations 575:16 (J. Kaplan ed. 1992).[17] (brackets in original).

Among the members of the Court, Justice Breyer's arguments carried the day, relegating Justice Ginsburg to the minority.

In Chapter 1, the following example from Winona Ryder's trial was identified as an appeal to authority: "Crime is okay if your 'director' tells you to do it." The cited authority is an unnamed "director," who allegedly instructed the actress to research a part for an upcoming movie by having a real-life shoplifting experience. Even if an anonymous "director" instructed Ryder to actually experience shoplifting, it would not excuse breaking the law.

A corporate CEO cited her position as authority for believing her testimony under oath:

> Hewlett Packard Co. chief Carly Fiorina became agitated on the witness stand Wednesday under questioning about company documents that allegedly show the purchase of Compaq Computer Corp. would fall short of its financial goals. At one point during the tense exchange, [Hewlett Attorney Stephen] Neal said somewhat curtly, "Let me ask the questions."
>
> Fiorina responded, "Sir, you are accusing the CEO of a publicly traded company of lying."
>
> "I am only asking you questions right now," Neal replied.[18] (brackets in original).

After the lessons of Enron, WorldCom, and Tyco, statements by high corporate officials might not project the same authority they once may have.

---

[17]*Id.* at 143–44.
[18]MILWAUKEE JOURNAL SENTINEL, Apr. 25, 2002, at 3D.

Citing Oneself as the Expert

A variation on the self-declaration theme occurs when decision makers cite their own publications or presentations as authority for their decisions. Justice Scalia has cited several of his own law reviews in his Supreme Court opinions: "Assorted Canards of Contemporary Legal Analysis";[19] "Sovereign Immunity and Nonstatutory Review of Federal Administrative Action: Some Conclusions from the Public Lands Cases";[20] "Originalism: the Lesser Evil."[21] A former chairman of the National Labor Relations Board cited speeches he presented as authority for his opinions.[22] Quoting one's self as authority is also a form of circular reasoning or begging the question: Why is it so? Because I say so.

Courtroom appeals to authority usually involve three types of lawyer conduct: expressing personal beliefs, vouching, and bolstering. Besides having a winning case overturned on appeal, attorneys risk ethical sanctions by these improper appeals to authority.

Defense lawyers in criminal cases may not offer their opinions concerning the guilt or innocence of their clients to the jury.[23] Usually, the improper appeal takes some form of the following: "I believe this man is innocent because otherwise I would not be here defending him."[24]

The prosecutorial counterpart declares that she would not be associated with a criminal case unless the defendant was guilty:

> I still believe and knew prior to the time that I became associated in this particular prosecution in the month of October, that this particular Defendant was guilty of this particular offense. I would not have been associated with the prosecution of this particular case unless I had so believed.[25]

Defendants, in urging reversal of their convictions, claimed a prosecutor (as in the preceding quotation) improperly argued for guilt on the basis of evidence not placed before the jury. They also argued that the prosecutor believed they were guilty from the beginning, and contended that he would not have taken the case if he thought they were innocent:

---

[19]Harmelin v. Michigan, 501 U.S. 957, 986 n.11 (1991).
[20]Hess v. Port Authority Trans-Hudson Corp., 513 U.S. 30, 54 (1994).
[21]McCreary County, KY v. American Civil Liberties, 545 U.S. 844, 899 n.7 (2005).
[22]Beverly Enterprises-Hawaii, Inc., 326 NLRB 335, 365 n.31 (1998).
[23]ABA STANDARDS FOR CRIMINAL JUSTICE PROSECUTION FUNCTION AND DEFENSE FUNCTION (hereinafter STANDARDS) 4-7.7 (3rd ed. 1993).
[24]U.S. v. Swanson, 943 F.2d 1070, 1078 (9th Cir. 1991).
[25]People v. Kirkes, 249 P.2d 1, 3 (Cal. 1952).

I've lived with the case for quite some time and I've looked at it from every angle, as have you—but not as long as I have. I won't try to superimpose my views of what I see in the case on you, but rather, maybe the things I say you can use as a different reference point, as a different way of looking at things. Take it as I hope you will take the views of each of the other jurors when you are back there. Stand in the person's shoes, stand in my shoes. Look at it the way I look at it, and decide for yourself whether it's reasonable to look at it that way, if I bring up something that you hadn't thought of. And: I hope to make it a very brief, because, as I said, the case is a very, very strong one, if ever there was.[26]

Rejecting the defendants' argument, the court stated:

A prosecutor's statement that he believes the defendant to be guilty is improper if it is tantamount to a testimonial assertion that the prosecutor believed the defendant guilty from the inception of the prosecution; any such assertion implies that the district attorney possesses proof of guilt beyond that which the jury has examined. Here the prosecutor did not allude to any hidden facts nor did he state that he had always believed the defendants were guilty. He simply commented on the strength of the evidence and stated that he had lived with and looked at the case longer than the jury, which is reasonable and to be expected. We find no misconduct in these statements.[27] (citations omitted).

A district attorney concluded his argument to the jury by stating:

I appreciate your attention, your being here, and I ask you to consider carefully all of that evidence, the instructions, and reach a fair, just, honest conclusion. I'm convinced in my mind it will be the same conclusion I reached several months ago.[28]

The defendant argued that the prosecutor's remark, "the same conclusion I reached several months ago," amounted to a pronouncement of guilt, but the court rejected this argument:

A review of the prosecutor's entire argument to the jury persuades us that the defendant exaggerates the effect of this remark. In contrast to the cases relied on by defendant, the district attorney did not expressly tell the jury that he would not have prosecuted defendant unless he personally believed him guilty.[29] (citations omitted).

---

[26]People v. Brown, 261 Cal. Rptr. 262, 271 n.6 (Cal. App. 2d 1989).
[27]*Id.* at 271.
[28]People v. Green, 609 P.2d 468, 488 (Cal. 1980).
[29]*Id.* at 483.

Heightened Scrutiny

In addition to their roles as advocates, prosecutors carry authority because of their office, and, consequently, their statements are subject to heightened scrutiny:

> [Because] [i]t is well established that a prosecutor may not argue his personal belief in a witness's credibility or in a defendant's guilt as juries "will normally place great confidence in the faithful execution of the obligations of a prosecuting attorney, improper insinuations or suggestions are apt to carry more weight against a defendant than such statements by witnesses."[30] (citations omitted).

The Eighth Circuit was asked to consider whether a prosecutor improperly appealed to authority by his comments on a required element of proof:

> In arguing that the evidence supported a finding the crime was committed with "depravity of mind," an aggravating circumstance, the prosecutor stated, "it's disgusting and it's as cold as anything I've ever seen."[31]

The court found,

> The . . . remark was clearly improper. It invited the jury to rely on the prosecutor's personal opinion about the relative coldness of this crime and compared the circumstances of this crime to other crimes that were not in the record.[32] (ellipses added).

Nevertheless, the court was unwilling to overturn the conviction: "After taking all of the aggravating and mitigating circumstances into account, we see no probability that the sentence would have been any different. The error was harmless beyond a reasonable doubt."[33]

On appeal to the First Circuit, defendants claimed a prosecutor "improperly placed his own character at issue" when he argued: "[a]n attack on me and my colleagues and our ethics and our approach to this case not only [is] an affront to me personally, but a smoke screen."[34] (brackets in original).

The court rejected the defendants' argument:

> Although a prosecutor may not pledge his own character as a basis for inferring the defendant's guilt, the statement in this case referred to

---

[30] United States v. Humphrey, 287 F.3d 422, 433 (6th Cir. 1991).
[31] Young v. Bowersox, 161 F.3d 1159, 1162 (8th Cir. 1998).
[32] *Id.*
[33] *Id.*
[34] United States v. Whiting, 28 F.3d 1296, 1303 (1st Cir. 1994).

the government's conduct of its investigation, not the guilt or innocence of the defendants. The prosecutor's isolated remark responded to far harsher remarks of defense counsel that the government had suborned perjury. Finally, the trial judge properly instructed the jury to disregard the prosecutor's statement that he felt affronted.[35] (citation omitted).

Vouching for the Witness

Vouching occurs when an attorney pledges her personal assurance that a witness is telling the truth. Again, prosecutors' arguments are susceptible to extra scrutiny: "Improper vouching occurs when the prosecutor places 'the prestige of the government behind the witness' by providing 'personal assurances of [the] witness's veracity.'"[36] (brackets in original). Often vouching happens when a witness has been successfully attacked on cross-examination, and the attorney wishes to assure the jury that the witness was telling the truth. Whether the attorney is vouching or merely arguing a conclusion about the witness's credibility, based on record evidence, can often be a close question, as the next two examples demonstrate.

In closing argument, the prosecutor stated, "Why, ladies and gentlemen, if [Gibson's] lying, isn't she doing a better job of it? I submit to you, ladies and gentlemen, that she's not lying. I submit to you that she's telling the truth"[37] (brackets in original).

This statement was found not to be improper vouching:

> These 'I submit' statements do not constitute vouching. The prosecutor here, argued that Gibson told the truth because, if she were lying, she would have done a better job. This is simply an inference from evidence in the record. These statements do not imply that the government is assuring Gibson's veracity, and do not reflect the prosecutor's personal beliefs.[38] (citations omitted).

In contrast, the following statements transgressed the line of proper behavior:

I think he (Jim Ludden) was very candid.

I don't think it was a pat story, because there are variations.

---

[35] *Id.*
[36] United States v. Kerr, 981 F.2d 1050, 1053 (9th Cir. 1992).
[37] United States v. Nicoechea, 986 F.2d 1273, 1279 (9th Cir. 1993).
[38] *Id.*

APPEAL TO AUTHORITY

> I think he (Al Butler) was candid. I think he was honest.
>
> Al Butler was candid with you folks.
>
> The question is, were they hoodwinking you when they testified? I think not.[39] (parentheses in original).

According to the Ninth Circuit,

> Here, an experienced United States attorney deliberately introduced into the case his personal opinion of the witnesses' credibility. He repeatedly ignored his special obligation to avoid improper suggestions and insinuations. A prosecutor has no business telling the jury his individual impressions of the evidence. Because he is the sovereign's representative, the jury may be misled into thinking his conclusions have been validated by the government's investigatory apparatus.[40]

Vouching is not limited to explicit declarations of support for a witness, but may also include implicit endorsements, as the Sixth Circuit found when the prosecutor remarked about a witness: "I've got to say it's real satisfying to see that this community lost an angry law breaker and may soon get back a productive, law-abiding man who will rejoin his family as a hardworking taxpayer and a positive role model for both the community and for his family."[41]

Invoking the Judge

A variation on the traditional vouching theme involves the invocation of the judge as part of the prosecution team:

> [T]he government's job is to . . . ferret through all the smoke screens and lead you to the truth.
>
> . . . .
>
> [I]f I did anything wrong in this trial I wouldn't be here. The court wouldn't allow that to happen.[42] (first brackets and ellipses in original).

The Ninth Circuit, under the plain error standard, held the prosecutor's latter statement was clearly improper:

> That statement, in effect, attributed to the court some independent knowledge regarding the government's decision to prosecute Smith

---

[39]*Kerr, supra* note 36, at 1053.
[40]*Id.*
[41]United States v. Modena, 302 F.3d 626, 634 (6th Cir. 2002).
[42]United States v. Smith, 962 F.2d 923, 928 (9th Cir. 1992).

and its subsequent conduct of the trial. Moreover, it suggested to the jury that the court also was satisfied as to the truth of Brown's testimony. Just as the prosecutor may not take advantage of this special role as representative of the sovereign to imply that the government's investigatory apparatus is satisfied of the defendant's guilt, even more so he may not abuse his position and his obligation to see justice done by imputing such satisfaction to the court.[43] (citation omitted).

In a later case, the Ninth Circuit again confronted this issue when a prosecutor argued,

It is also not his [defense counsel's] job to ask you to look at all of the evidence. And he is asking you to look at little bits and pieces. The Government and the Judge will be asking you to consider all of the evidence in making your decision.[44] (brackets added).

The court found the prosecutor

was not only allying herself with the court, she was also arguing that both the government and the court had one view of the jury's responsibilities and the defendant's lawyer another. Even the prosecutor [in the case immediately above] did not go quite so far as to directly put the defense on a "different team" from the government and the judge. The potential effect on the jury of the prosecutor's implication that the government and the court are allied in opposition to the defendant and his lawyer is serious indeed.[45] (brackets added).

Bolstering is a close sibling of vouching. An attorney (usually the prosecutor, who has access to extensive investigatory resources) intimates that he or she possesses information not presented to the jury, but which bears on the credibility of the witness (appeal to ignorance). The jury is asked to trust the attorney's judgment that even though the evidence is not offered in the courtroom, it is sufficient to credit or discredit the witness. These cases are decided by an examination of the record, and whether the attorney drew inferences "as to credibility on the basis of evidence presented to the jury."[46]

---

[43]*Id.* at 934.
[44]United States v. Frederick, 78 F.3d 1370, 1379 (9th Cir. 1996).
[45]*Id.* at 1380.
[46]People v. Padilla, 906 P.2d 388, 421 (Cal. 1995).

CHAPTER NINE

Accent: Emphasizing Certain Words

> "The first thing we do, let's kill all the lawyers."
>
> William Shakespeare (1564-1616), *King Henry VI, Part II* (1591), act 4, sc. 2, line 83.

> "There are 100 jails in this state and I'm proud to say that nobody in my family has ever been in one of them," boasted the political candidate.
>
> Shouted a heckler, "And which one is that?"
>
> Lance Davidson, *The Ultimate Reference Book: The Wit's Thesaurus 1* (1994).

THE FALLACY OF ACCENT occurs when words (or even a single word) are stressed or emphasized, and confusion results because the intent of the speaker or writer is not discernible without knowing the circumstances surrounding the accented words.

Taken Out of Context

A passage taken out of context is the most common example of the fallacy of accent. The first quote above is frequently cited as evidence that Shakespeare despised lawyers so much that he wanted to kill all of them. Quoting Shakespeare is, obviously, an appeal to authority. But the remark is also an example of the fallacy of accent, because it was taken out of context and given a meaning that was not intended. The speaker was Dick the Butcher, responding to ex-convict Jack Cade, an advocate of anarchy. Butcher understood that before there could be anarchy, the legal system, and those who administer it, would have to be eliminated. In context, Shakespeare's quote did not advocate killing all the lawyers because they were bad, greedy, or caused distress among the populace, usually the modern-day context:

> **Cade:** I thank you, good people; there shall be no money; all shall eat and drink on my score; and I will apparel them all in one livery, and that they may agree like brothers, and worship me their Lord.
>
> **Dick:** The first thing we do, let's kill all the lawyers.
>
> **Cade:** Nay, that I mean to do. Is not this a lamentable thing, that of the skin of an innocent lamb should be made parchment? That parchment, being scribbled o'er, should undo man? Some say the bee stings; but I say, 'tis the bee's wax; for I did but seal once to a thing, and I was never mine own man since. How now! Who's there.[1]

"Selective quotation," often considered synonymous with quoting out of context, can also mean citing various sources, to the exclusion of other relevant, and contrary, sources.

The second quotation at the beginning of this chapter illustrates another form of the fallacy of accent, where the word "one" is given an unintended meaning by emphasis, suggesting the politician's family had been in one state jail, to the exclusion of all the others. The politician's intended meaning of "one" jail was in the collective sense: No member of the family, not even one, had been in any of the state jails.

A third type of fallacy of accent involves the speaker's tone of voice, and determining the intent of that tone. For example, an individual passing through a crowd may say, "Excuse me." Depending on the tone of voice, the individual could be truly apologetic, maybe for having stepped on someone's foot. On the other hand, the individual could be jostling through the crowd, with "excuse me" meaning, "Make way! I'm coming through."

In the courtroom, attorneys must be aware of the various circumstances producing the fallacy of accent. An expert cross-examiner will force a witness to concede critical facts, facts that must be contradicted or explained on recross or redirect, by putting them in their appropriate context. Similarly, an attorney who wants a witness to convey the particular tone of a statement should not only ask what was said, but should elicit facts (anger, sadness, indifference, for example) providing

---

[1] *King Henry, id.* at lines 79–91.

the statement's context. The selective introduction of documents can be countered immediately, by invoking the "rule of completeness":

> Rule 106. Remainder of or Related Writings or Recorded Statements
>
> When a writing or recorded statement or part thereof is introduced by a party, an adverse party may require the introduction at that time of any other part or any other writing or recorded statement which ought in fairness to be considered contemporaneously with it.[2]

President Clinton's attorneys, responding to Special Prosecutor Kenneth Starr's Report,[3] accented facts that, while arguably true, had little relevance to the point at issue.

To rebut the claim that President Clinton committed perjury, his lawyers emphasized that he provided truthful answers, even though they may not have been responsive to the questions asked:

> The law defines perjury very clearly. Perjury requires proof that an individual knowingly made a false statement while under oath. Answers to questions that are literally true are not perjury. Even if an answer doesn't directly answer the question asked, it is not perjury if it is true—no accused has an obligation to help his accuser. Answers to fundamentally ambiguous questions also can never be perjury. And nobody can be convicted of perjury based on only one other person's testimony.[4]

The President's cooperation in the investigation was also stressed, implying that his cooperation meant he had nothing to hide, and he did not commit any crimes:

> During the past four and a half years, the President has cooperated extensively with this investigation. He has given testimony by deposition at the White House to the Independent Counsel on four separate occasions, and on two other occasions, he gave videotaped deposition testimony for Whitewater defendants and was cross-examined by the Independent Counsel. He has submitted written interrogatory answers, produced more than 90,000 pages of documents and other items, and provided information informally in a variety of ways. The OIC subpoenaed from the President, and reviewed, virtually every personal financial record and gubernatorial campaign finance record that exists for the period from the mid-1980s to the present, in its endless search

---

[2]Fed. R. Evid. 106.

[3]In anticipation of the Starr Report, the President's lawyers issued a Response, on September 11, 1998, and a Rebuttal to the Report, on September 12, 1998. CHICAGO TRIBUNE, Sept. 13, 1998, at 32, 38.

[4]*Id.* at 32.

to find something to use against the President. This comprehensive and thorough financial review yielded the OIC nothing.[5]

Not the Whole Picture

Another way to defend against legal charges is to argue that the prosecutor's case doesn't present the entire picture, because the prosecutor engaged in the fallacy of accent. According to the President's lawyers, the Special Prosecutor engaged in the fallacy of accent by emphasizing certain facts, without putting them in context:

> Third, by selectively presenting the facts and failing to set out the full context of the answers that it claims may have been perjurious, the OIC has presented a wholly misleading picture. This tactic is most pronounced in the OIC's astonishing failure to set out the initial definition of "sexual relations" presented by the Jones lawyers at President Clinton's deposition, two parts of which were eliminated by Judge Wright as being "too broad." The OIC also fails to mention that the Jones lawyers were fully able, and indeed were invited by President Clinton's counsel, to ask the President specific questions about his sexual encounters, but they chose not to do so.[6] (citations omitted).

President Clinton's lawyers also argued that the depiction presented in Kenneth Starr's report was, at best, only half complete, because the grand jury evidence that was relied on (accented) included no exculpatory evidence:

> Use of a federal grand jury to compile evidence for possible impeachment proceedings in Congress raises numerous troubling questions regarding the credibility of that evidence. Indeed, given the limited role of a grand jury in our system and the total absence of procedural protections in the process, the Independent Counsel's insistence that his investigation has been a search for "truth" is deeply misleading. In fact, it has been a one-sided effort to present the worst possible version of a limited set of facts.[7]

Verbatim Quotes

When a writer encloses a statement in quotes, or when someone states, "Quote . . . end quote," he or she accents what a speaker or writer has said. Must a quoted statement be a verbatim rendition of what that indi-

---

[5] *Id.* at 33.
[6] *Id.* at 38.
[7] *Id.* at 33.

vidual said? May a quote be "cleaned up" to make grammatical sense out of a garbled statement? Does the writer or speaker have license to enclose a statement in quotation marks, even though the quoted individual never made the statement, so long as the quoted statement accurately conveys the speaker's or writer's intent?

The U.S. Supreme Court considered these issues in the context of California's libel law, in *Masson v. New Yorker Magazine, Inc.*,[8] where Masson, a psychoanalyst, sued the *New Yorker* for publication of allegedly defamatory material. The Court stated,

> In general, quotation marks around a passage indicate to the reader that the passage reproduces the speaker's words verbatim. They inform the reader that he or she is reading the statement of the speaker, not a paraphrase or other indirect interpretation by an author. By providing this information, quotations add authority to the statement and credibility to the author's work. Quotations allow the reader to form his or her own conclusions, and to assess the conclusions of the author, instead of relying entirely upon the author's characterization of her subject.[9]

Because *Masson* was before the Court on a summary judgment motion, the issue was whether "the evidence suffices to show that respondents acted with the requisite knowledge of falsity or reckless disregard as to the truth or falsity."[10] Additionally, the Court stated, "We must consider whether the requisite falsity inheres to the attribution of words to the petitioner which he did not speak."[11] The Court then analyzed the practical impact of altering a quote:

> In some sense, any alteration of a verbatim quotation is false. But writers and reporters, by necessity, alter what people say, at the very least to eliminate grammatical and syntactical infelicities. If every alteration constituted the falsity required to prove actual malice, the practice of journalism, which the First Amendment standard is designed to protect, would require a radical change, one inconsistent with our precedents and First Amendment principles.[12]

Other practical difficulties in rendering an accurate quote are also noted:

> Even if a journalist has tape-recorded the spoken statement of a public figure, the full and exact statement will be reported in only rare

---
[8] 501 U.S. 496 (1991).
[9] *Id.* at 511.
[10] *Id.* at 513.
[11] *Id.*
[12] *Id.* at 514.

circumstances. The existence of both a speaker and a reporter; the translation between two media, speech and the printed word; the addition of punctuation; and the practical necessity to edit and make intelligible a speaker's perhaps rambling comments, all make it misleading to suggest that a quotation will be reconstructed with complete accuracy.[13]

The Court then analyzed the relationship between quotations and the fallacy of accent (not using that term, of course):

The use or absence of punctuation may distort a speaker's meaning, for example, where that meaning turns upon a speaker's emphasis of a particular word. In other cases, if a speaker makes an obvious misstatement, for example by unconscious substitution of one name for another, a journalist might alter the speaker's words but preserve his intended meaning. And conversely, an exact quotation out of context can distort meaning, although the speaker did use each reported word.[14]

Accordingly, the Court concluded: "We reject the idea that any alteration beyond correction of grammar or syntax by itself proves falsity in the sense relevant to determining actual malice under the First Amendment."[15]

Proving malice must, therefore, meet the following test:

We conclude that a deliberate alteration of the words uttered by a plaintiff does not equate with knowledge of falsity for purposes of *New York Times v. Sullivan,* unless the alteration results in a material change in the meaning conveyed by the statement. The use of quotations to attribute words not in fact spoken bears in a most important way on that inquiry, but it is not dispositive in every case.[16] (citations omitted).

Tone of Voice

Tone of voice can certainly determine whether a statement constitutes a threat or an innocent statement. Should an appellate court make that determination, or is that a judgment best made by the sitting judge, who can observe the witness's demeanor firsthand? In *J.C. Penney Co.*

---

[13]*Id.* at 515.
[14]*Id.*
[15]*Id.* at 514.
[16]*Id.* at 517.

v. NLRB,[17] the Seventh Circuit overruled the National Labor Relations Board and concluded that a supervisor did not threaten an employee when he stated he was glad she had a husband, after learning of her union activity. At the hearing before the administrative law judge, the employee was questioned about the statement:

Q: Now, after you began wearing this union button, Teamsters button to work, did any member of management ever talk to you about the button or comment on the button in any way?

A: Yes, they did.

Q: Who was that supervisor that commented to you?

A: Mark Smith.

. . . .

Q: So it was about the end of the work day for you?

A: Yes.

Q: When you were working, was anyone else in the area?

A: Joanne Wells.

Q: And who started the conversation between yourself and Mr. Smith, you or Mr. Smith?

A: Mr. Smith.

Q: And what did he do to start up the conversation?

A: He said, "Hi. How are you doing?"

Q: Then what did he say?

A: Then he says something about the fact about, "When are you getting married?" I said, "Well, we set the year but not the date." And he looked—do you want me to go on?

Q: Yes.

A: Okay. And during the conversation he looked down and saw I was wearing a union button and he stepped back like, "Oh, you're for the union?" And I didn't say anything.

Q: First of all, he saw the union button.

A: Yes.

---

[17]123 F.3d 988 (7th Cir. 1997).

Q: And did he stop or pause for a minute or did he start talking right away?

A: He paused for a second. I don't know. I can't give how long, but he stopped and he looked at the button and he says, "Oh, you're for the union?" And I didn't say anything.

Q: Did his tone of voice change when he asked you, "Are you for the union," compared to the first statement that he made to you about getting married?

A: Yes, he did.

Q: And how did that tone of voice change?

A: It was disappointment. It was harder, like, "Oh, you're for the union."

MR. ROWE [outside counsel for J.C. Penney]: I'd object to the characterization of the tone of voice. This witness is trying to put herself in the place of another person. Object—

ADMINISTRATIVE LAW JUDGE METZ: Overruled. I think she can testify to what she heard, characterize it.

BY MS. STUART [*counsel for the General Counsel of the NLRB*]:

Q: Okay.

A: I didn't say anything after that, and he says, "Oh, I'm glad you got a husband." And after that, after he said that, Joanne Wells said, "Oh, you won't live long." And then Mark with a face on him like, "Oh, she shouldn't have said that," you know, and he turned around and walked away. He didn't say anything to Joanne.

Q: Now, after this conversation that you've just testified about with Mr. Smith, did you change your practice with regard to wearing union buttons to work?

A: Yes, I did. I started not wearing them on me, but I'd start putting them in my purse. And I kept my purse in my desk. And at work when I go in now, they could be seeing at the time clock, but I never carried it. The only time I carry my purse is when I got in the building and out the building.

Q: So your purse wouldn't be out during the work day?

A: No.[18] (ellipses, italics, and brackets in original).

---

[18] *Id.* at 994–95.

The supervisor "denied he ever saw (the employee) wear a union button, that he had any conversation with her about the union, and that he ever threatened her with discharge because of her support for the union."[19] (parentheses added). The administrative law judge credited the employee's testimony.

Judge Cudahy dissented from the majority's finding regarding this conversation:

> The majority recites the proper incantation of deference to the NLRB, but does not live by that time-honored maxim. The ALJ found that Mark Smith threatened Diana Jaccard when he saw Jaccard's pro-union pin and said, "I'm glad you got a husband." It is possible that Smith meant no harm. Perhaps after noting Jaccard's pro-union pin he shrugged, paused and tried to return to the topic of Jaccard's impending wedding. But it's also possible that Smith looked, sounded and was menacing.[20]

The administrative law judge, argued Judge Cudahy, was in the best position to determine the import of the challenged statement:

> It is a question of tone and temperament, and of whom you believe. The ALJ heard Jaccard and Smith; this court has not. And the ALJ believed Jaccard and not Smith, who flatly denied that the conversation ever took place. The credibility of a witness—and our deference to the ALJ—goes beyond the bare fact that words were spoken . . . A witness' credibility also can inform a factfinder's understanding of what those words meant.[21] (citations omitted).

Protecting the trial record from a tone of voice misinterpretation may require an attorney's intervention, as in this case when the defense counsel orally moved for a mistrial, and described the prosecutor's conduct:

> If Your Honor please, I think the record should note that during his closing argument Mr. Satti not only pounded on the table on a couple of occasions, I would say he fairly shouted to the jury when he said a point Your Honor has already ruled on that he's the kind of man who raped a child. At this point he pounded on the table and shouted, and the tenor of his remarks with regard to what kind of person the accused was with gestures and raising his voice as he did I think is inconsistent with the dispassionate administration of justice as is required by the prosecuting authority, and it was to such extreme, I submit to the Court, that as to inflame this jury with regard to Mr.

---

[19] *Id.* at 995.
[20] *Id.* at 999.
[21] *Id.*

Satti's passion in connection with this case; and I, therefore, move for a mistrial.[22]

Sometimes the record does not need explicit protection:

> We cannot accept the government's contention that references to defense counsel were made as compliments about his skill at cross-examination. It is clear even from a cold record that the statement was not laudatory and the "compliment" a back-handed one at best.[23]

In this case, the prosecutor remarked:

> **Prosecutor:** Sorry. I'm trying to compliment him [Mr. Jacobson, defense counsel] that he did a very good job of confusing her on the stand.
>
> **Mr. Jacobson:** Excuse me, Your Honor, I object, comments about me are not appropriate.
>
> **THE COURT:** Proceed with your argument, that's enough.[24]

(brackets added).

How do Supreme Court Justices defend against selective quotation by their colleagues? After all, opinions sometimes go on at length on insignificant points, and contain statements that later may be used against one of the Justices.

In *Allegheny County v. Greater Pittsburgh ACLU*,[25] Justice Stevens, supporting Justice O'Connor's concurring opinion, noted that Justice Kennedy selectively cited scholarly articles that, nevertheless, undercut the argument he advanced: "(Justice Kennedy) neglects to mention that 1 of the 2 articles he cites as disfavoring the endorsement test itself cites no fewer than 16 articles and 1 book lauding the test."[26] (citation omitted).

Justice Kennedy, in turn, accused the majority of selective quotation:

> But that is not the history or the purpose of the Establishment Clause. Government policies of accommodation, acknowledgment, and support for religion are an accepted part of our political and cultural heritage. As Chief Justice Burger wrote for the Court in *Walz v. Tax Comm'n of New York City*, we must be careful to avoid "[t]he hazards

---

[22]State v. Fullwood, 484 A.2d 435, 442 n.7 (Conn. 1984).
[23]United States v. Frederick, 78 F.3d 1370, 1380 n.5 (9th Cir. 1996).
[24]*Id.* at 1379.
[25]492 U.S. 573 (1989).
[26]*Id.* at 650 n.6.

of placing too much weight on a few words or phrases of the Court," and so we have "declined to construe the Religion Clauses with a literalness that would undermine the ultimate constitutional objective as illuminated by history."[27] (citations omitted; brackets in original).

Justice O'Connor, in *Rogers v. Tennessee*,[28] acknowledged there was language in a previous Supreme Court decision that supported the petitioner's position, but she deflected the language's impact by labeling it "dicta":

> To the extent petitioner argues that the Due Process Clause incorporates the specific prohibitions of the *Ex Post Facto* Clause as identified in *Calder*, petitioner misreads *Bouie*. To be sure, our opinion in *Bouie* does contain some expansive language that is suggestive of the broad interpretation for which petitioner argues. Most prominent is our statement that "[i]f a state legislature is barred by the *Ex Post Facto* Clause from passing a law, it must follow that a State Supreme Court is barred by the Due Process Clause from achieving precisely the same result by judicial construction." This language, however, was dicta.[29] (citations omitted; brackets in original).

Justice Scalia, dissenting, argued that Justice O'Connor was mistaken in labeling the language in *Bouie* as "dicta":

> The Court seeks to avoid the obvious import of this language by characterizing it as mere dicta . . . Only a concept of dictum that includes the very reasoning of the opinion could support this characterization. The *ratio decidendi* of *Bouie* was that the principle applied to the legislature though the *Ex Post Facto* Clause was contained in the Due Process Clause insofar as judicial action is concerned. I cannot understand why the Court derives such comfort from the fact that later opinions applying *Bouie* have referred to the Due Process Clause rather than the *Ex Post Facto* Clause. That is entirely in accord with the rationale of the case, which I follow and which the Court discards.[30] (citations omitted).

Out of Context

Justice Scalia then accused Justice O'Connor of committing the fallacy of accent, by taking language from *Bouie* out of context:

---

[27] *Id.* at 657.
[28] 532 U.S. 451 (2001).
[29] *Id.* at 458–59.
[30] *Id.* at 469.

The Court attempts to cabin *Bouie* by reading it to prohibit only "'unexpected and indefensible'" judicial law revision, and to permit retroactive judicial changes so long as the defendant has had fair warning that the changes might occur. This reading seems plausible because *Bouie* does indeed use those quoted terms; but they have been wrenched entirely out of context.[31] (citation omitted).

Chief Justice Rehnquist, in *Bennis v. Michigan*,[32] involving the forfeiture of a wife's car because it was used by her husband to engage in illicit sex, also labeled language from another decision as "dicta":

> Petitioner relies on a passage from *Calero-Toledo*, that "it would be difficult to reject the constitutional claim of . . . an owner who proved not only that he was uninvolved in and unaware of the wrongful activity, but also that he had done all that reasonably could be expected to prevent the proscribed use of his property." . . . But she concedes that this comment was *obiter dictum*, and "[i]t is to the holdings of our cases, rather than their dicta, that we must attend."[33] (first ellipses in original; brackets in original; citations omitted).

Citation to foreign law came under scathing criticism by Justice Scalia in *Lawrence v. Texas*,[34] involving the legality of anti-sodomy laws:

> The Court's discussion of these foreign views (ignoring, of course, the many countries that have retained criminal prohibitions on sodomy) is therefore meaningless dicta. Dangerous dicta, however, since "this Court . . . should not impose foreign moods, fads, or fashions on Americans."[35] (parentheses and ellipses in original; citations omitted).

Another technique, employed by Justice Breyer, dissenting in *Ewing v. California*,[36] involving a three strikes law, is to first concede the accented case, and then minimize its import:

> The third case, *Sims*, is on point both factually and legally, for the Nevada Supreme Court (by a vote of 3 to 2) found the sentence constitutional. I concede that example—a single instance of a similar sentence imposed outside the context of California's three strikes law, out of a prison population now approaching two million individuals.
>
> The upshot is that comparison of other sentencing practices, both in other jurisdictions and in California at other times (or in respect to

---

[31] *Id.* at 469–70.
[32] 516 U.S. 442 (1996).
[33] *Id.* at 449–50.
[34] 539 U.S. 558 (2003).
[35] *Id.* at 598.
[36] 538 U.S. 11 (2002).

other crimes), validates what an initial threshold examination suggested. Given the information available, given the state and federal parties' ability to provide additional contrary data, and given their failure to do so, we can assume for constitutional purposes that the following statement is true: Outside the California three strikes context, Ewing's recidivist sentence is virtually unique in its harshness for his offense of conviction, and by a considerable degree.[37] (citations omitted; parentheses in original).

Disagreeing with the Conclusion

A similar technique involves acknowledging the accented language, but then disagreeing with the conclusion to be drawn. Chief Justice Rehnquist, writing for the majority, employed this technique in *Dickerson v. United States*,[38] concerning the constitutionality of the *Miranda* decision.

> We disagree with the Court of Appeals' conclusion, although we concede that there is language in some of our opinions that supports the view taken by that court. But first and foremost of the factors on the other side—that *Miranda* is a constitutional decision—is that both *Miranda* and two of its companion cases applied the rule to proceedings in state courts—to wit, Arizona, California, and New York.[39] (citations omitted).

Justice Kennedy also used this technique in *Alden v. Maine*[40]:

> There are isolated statements in some of our cases suggesting that the Eleventh Amendment is inapplicable in state courts. This, of course, is a truism as to the literal terms of the Eleventh Amendment. As we have explained, however, the bare text of the Amendment is not an exhaustive description of the States' constitutional immunity from suit. The cases, furthermore, do not decide the question presented here—whether the States retain immunity from private suits in their own courts notwithstanding an attempted abrogation by the Congress.[41] (citations omitted).

The fallacy of accent can have consequences beyond a bad argument. The Seventh Circuit sanctioned an attorney under Rule 11 of the Federal Rules of Civil Procedure for deliberately misquoting (taking out of context) a case in a brief:

---

[37]*Id.* at 47.
[38]Dickerson v. United States, 530 U.S. 428 (2000).
[39]*Id.* at 438.
[40]527 U.S. 706 (1999).
[41]*Id.* at 735–36.

Perhaps most objectionable to us is the Company's practice of misstating the law. In the Company's brief to this court, for example, it states, "This Court has further stressed that a Rule 11 motion requires: 'judges to make findings and give explanations every time a party seeks sanctions under Rule 11,'" citing our decision in *Szabo Food Service*. In fact, *Szabo Food Service* states the following: "We do not now join the Fifth Circuit in requiring judges to make findings and give explanations every time a party seeks sanctions under Rule 11. Sometimes the reason is obvious." *Szabo Food Service*, 823 F.2d at 1084 (citations omitted). It is obvious to us that when counsel engages in this type of deliberate mischaracterization of precedent, sanctions are warranted.[42] (parentheses in original; citation omitted).

The tone of voice used in a courtroom can also occasion rather severe sanctions. A defense lawyer, upset with the jury's finding that his client was guilty, engaged in the following colloquy with the judge:

Mr. Jerry Milano: I want to say a little more before you start with your show for your television.

THE COURT: My show?

Mr. Jerry Milano: Your show.

THE COURT: You are now guilty of contempt.

Mr. Jerry Milano: Do what you have to do.

THE COURT: I will.[43]

The Supreme Court of Ohio sanctioned defense counsel with a sizeable fine ($2,000 in 1984 dollars) and a suspended jail term for being in contempt.[44] The court's finding was based on a videotape that revealed "that respondent's remarks were made heatedly and in a raised voice."[45]

---

[42]Teamsters Local 579 v. B&M Transit, 132 LRRM 2255, 2260 (7th Cir. 1989).
[43]Bar Association of Greater Cleveland v. Milano, 459 N.E.2d 496, 497 (Ohio 1984).
[44]*Id.* at n.6.
[45]*Id.*

CHAPTER TEN

Equivocation: Shifts in Meaning

"It depends on what the meaning of the word 'is' is."

President Clinton in his Paula Jones deposition.[1]

A SHIFT IN THE MEANING of a word or phrase in a given context gives rise to the fallacy of equivocation. Defending against an equivocation first requires recognizing what word or phrase underwent a change in meaning, not necessarily an easy task, as the example involving President Clinton below illustrates. An attorney must pay particularly close attention to a witness's answers when questioning about critical facts in the case, and not hesitate to ask follow-up questions. Second, responding to an equivocation requires placing the word or phrase in context, and explaining how the meaning was switched and why it was unfair to do so.

The quotation by President Clinton above has been the subject of many jokes and frequent public discussion, and is perhaps one of the best known equivocations. President Clinton explained his understanding of his testimony in the Paula Jones deposition as follows:

> If the—if he—if "is" means is and never has been, that is not—that is one thing. If it means there is none, that was a completely true statement. . . . Now, if someone had asked me on that day, are you having any kind of sexual relations with Ms. Lewinski, that is, asked me a question in the present tense, I would have said no. And it would have been completely true.[2] (ellipses in original).

---

[1] CHICAGO TRIBUNE, Sept. 13, 1998, at 19 n.1128.
[2] *Id.*

Accordingly, President Clinton, when asked if he was having an affair, answered that on that particular day he was not. "Is" can also mean in the present, as an ongoing relationship—such as, "Are you having an affair?"—not necessarily referring to a particular day.

With the benefit of hindsight, one way for Paula Jones's lawyers to have avoided this problem with "is" would have been to ask if the President ever had a "sexual affair" with Ms. Lewinski. Additionally, because the President did not agree with the definition of "sexual affair," further questioning was necessary to establish if there was any physical contact between the President and Ms. Lewinski, and the nature of that contact:

> The President was asked (at the Jones' deposition) whether he had "an extramarital sexual affair" with Ms. Lewinski and responded that he did not. That term was undefined and ambiguous. The President understood the term "sexual affair" to involve a relationship involving sexual intercourse. He had no such relationship with Ms. Lewinski.[3] (parentheses added; citations omitted).

Just as the word "is" can have more than one meaning, so too can the word "you." A prosecutor asked the defendant (Lighte) the following questions:

> **Q:** And Grand Jury Exhibit—Check number 405, Grand Jury Exhibit—
>
> **A:** Yes, this is remuneration for a trip I made to Washington.
>
> **Q:** So this is one that you received the proceeds of?
>
> **A:** That's my endorsement, yes.
>
> (8) **Q:** And you did not receive the proceeds of the others?
>
> **A:** No, these are not mine.[4]

As explained by the Second Circuit, the defendant did not commit perjury:

> The sequence preceding question (8) referred to the appellant as an individual but question (8) uses "you" without indication that, unlike the prior two questions, the appellant was now being questioned in his role as trustee. Lighte contends that his negative response was designed to state that he had not personally received the proceeds of other checks. Although the record shows that Lighte received some

---

[3]*Id.* at 36.
[4]United States v. Lighte, 782 F.2d 367, 376 (2nd Cir. 1986).

money in a personal capacity, during oral argument the Assistant United States Attorney stated that question (8) was falsely answered because Lighte received proceeds in his capacity as trustee. Since the question does not tell Lighte that he should answer it based on his actions as trustee, the response cannot be perjurious under the theory advanced by the government. Rather, the ambiguous use of the pronoun "you" rose to the level of a fundamental ambiguity and thus should have not been submitted to the trial jury.[5]

On the humorous side, the following war story relates a shift in meaning of the words "doing now": "During voir dire, Judge Benjamin Mackoff of Chicago made a practice of asking potential jurors what their adult children were 'doing now.' One prospective juror in a criminal case gave a candid answer about his son: 'Two to six in Stateville.'"

That's an Illinois prison. The prospective juror was excused.[6]

Using the Same Word in Two Ways

In early October 2005, Iraq's parliament made a critical ruling concerning the number of votes required for passage of the newly proposed constitution that was scheduled for a vote later that month. The parliament held that for purposes of ratification, "voters" consisted of those who showed up at the polls and actually voted, but that for purposes of rejection, "voters" consisted of all those who were registered voters:

> In other words, the parliament was interpreting the word "voters" in the interim constitution in two different ways in the same article. That critical article reads:

> The general referendum will be successful and the draft constitution ratified if a majority of the voters in Iraq approve and if two-thirds of the voters in three or more governorates do not reject it.[7]

Interpreting the second definition of "voters" as "registered voters" had the effect of enlarging the number of voters who had to reject the constitution—two-thirds of those eligible to vote versus two-thirds of those actually voting. Those who opposed the constitution would have been required to overcome those who did not vote. Each "registered" voter who did not appear at the polls, in effect, became a vote for ratification.

---

[5]*Id.*
[6]A.B.A. J. 146 (Oct. 1989).
[7]http://www.nytimes.com/reuters/news/news-iraq-referendum.htm (Oct. 4, 2005).

The significance of this switch in meaning was not lost on the world community, and after a few days of condemnation, the Iraqi parliament reversed itself, and interpreted the second reference to "voter" to be someone who showed up at the polls to vote.[8] Of course, the constitution passed, even with one definition of "voters."

A counterpart to the 2005 Iraqi constitutional election was the U.S. 2000 presidential election, ultimately resolved by the U.S. Supreme Court. A November 29, 2000, newspaper editorial lamented the continuing campaign after the ballots were cast:

> Bill Clinton may have invented the notion of the permanent campaign, but even he could never have imagined anything like the post-election hurricane in the Sunshine State. This is the campaign that will not die. At a moment when the fate of the 43rd president of the United States is about to be decided by lawyers and judges, the campaign goes on, with both principals laying claim to principle and the partied interests on each side repeating the same message over and over and over again:
> - Bush et al. The votes have been counted at least three times and, in some cases as many as five times. The count has been certified, and Bush is the winner.
> - Gore et al. A full and fair count has not been completed in Miami-Dade and Palm Beach counties and, who knows, perhaps elsewhere, too. Count them all, and Gore will win.[9]

For their part, the Bush supporters argued that "counted" meant all the ballots had been tabulated up to five times, and there were no more ballots to consider. The Gore supporters countered that not all the ballots had been "counted" because there were ballots that expressed the voters' choice, but had not been accepted by the voting machines because of difficulties with the punch cards. Thus, for the Bush supporters, "counted" referred to an accurate arithmetic tabulation of the votes; for the Gore supporters, "counted" referred to all ballots not previously considered by voting machines.

Before the U.S. Supreme Court, which reviewed the Florida Supreme Court's decision to continue counting the ballots, the issue again involved equivocation: What did the Florida legislature mean by the term "legal votes"? The Florida Secretary of State's brief argued that

---

[8]http://www.washingtonpost.com/wp-dyn/content/article/2005/10/05/AR2005100500256_pf.html (Oct. 5, 2005).

[9]MILWAUKEE JOURNAL SENTINEL, Nov. 29, 2000, at 14A.

[i]n this case, legal votes were not rejected. "Legal votes," as that term is used in section 102.168(3)(c), means votes properly executed in accordance with the instructions provided to all registered voters in advance of the election and in the polling places. By properly executing their ballots, voters can ensure that their vote will be counted by the tabulation machinery. Otherwise, these same voters risk having their vote disregarded. No other definition for "legal votes" fits the legislature's scheme.[10]

Chief Justice Rehnquist, concurring with his colleagues' per curiam opinion, argued that there could be only one meaning for "legal vote":

It is inconceivable that what constitutes a vote that must be counted under the 'error in the vote tabulation' language of the protest phase is different from what constitutes a vote that must be counted under the 'legal votes' language of the contest phase.[11]

Justice Souter disagreed, contending that the Florida Supreme Court could not have engaged in equivocation, because the definition of "legal vote" did not change:

The statute does not define a "legal vote," the rejection of which may affect the election. The State Supreme Court was therefore required to define it, and in doing that the court looked to another election statute, §101.5614(5), dealing with damaged or defective ballots, which contains a provision that no vote shall be disregarded "if there is a clear indication of the intent of the voter as determined by a canvassing board." The court read that objective of looking to the voter's intent as indicating that the legislature probably meant "legal vote" to mean a vote recorded on a ballot indicating what the voter intended. It is perfectly true that the majority might have chosen a different reading. But even so, there is no constitutional violation in following the majority view; Article II is unconcerned with mere disagreements about interpretive merits.[12] (citations omitted).

Atlantic Cleaners & Dyers v. United States[13] is often cited for the establishment of rules governing the use of identical words in different parts of the same statute. There, the Attorney General charged the defendants with "a combination and conspiracy in restraint of trade and commerce," under the Sherman Anti-Trust Act, for having entered an agreement "to maintain prices and allot customers" in the District of Columbia. Sections 1 and 3 of the Sherman Anti-Trust Act read:

---

[10]news.findlaw.com/cnn/docs/election2000/uscharrisbrf1210.pdf at 10.
[11]Bush v. Gore, 531 U.S. 98, 119 n.4 (2000).
[12]*Id.* at 131–32.
[13]286 U.S. 427 (1932).

Section 1. Every contract, combination in the form of trust or otherwise, or conspiracy, in restraint of trade or commerce among the several states, or with foreign nations, is declared to be illegal.

. . . .

Section 3. Every contract, combination in form of trust or otherwise, or conspiracy, in restraint of trade or commerce in any Territory of the United States or the District of Columbia, or in restraint of trade or commerce between any such Territory or Territories and any State or States or the District of Columbia, or with foreign nations, or between the District of Columbia and any State or States or foreign nations, is declared illegal.[14]

The defendants denied they were engaged in "trade or commerce" within the meaning of the Sherman Act, and argued that the same words describing illegal activity were used in both sections: "restraint of trade or commerce." Accordingly, since the words in Section 1 and Section 3 were identical, and because Section 1 was based on the commerce clause of the Constitution, "the words 'trade or commerce' in section 1 cannot be broader than the single word 'commerce' as used in that clause; and that commerce does not include a business such as that carried on by (the defendants)."[15] (parentheses in original).

The Supreme Court acknowledged that a "natural presumption" occurs whenever the same word is used more than once in a statute:

> Most words have different shades of meaning and consequently may be variously construed, not only when they occur in different statutes, but used more than once in the same statute or even in the same section. Undoubtedly, there is a natural presumption that identical words used in different parts of the same act are intended to have the same meaning.[16] (citation omitted).

Nevertheless, that

> presumption is not rigid and readily yields whenever there is such variation in the connection in which the words are used as reasonably to warrant the conclusion that they were employed in different parts of the act with different intent. Where the subject-matter to which the words refer is not the same in the several places where they are used, or the conditions are different, or the scope of the legislative power exercised in one case is broader than that exercised in another,

---

[14] 15 U.S.C. §§ 1, 3.
[15] *Atlantic Cleaners, supra* note 13, at 432.
[16] *Id.* at 433.

the meaning well may vary to meet the purposes of the law, to be arrived at by a consideration of the language in which those purposes are expressed, and of the circumstances under which the language was employed.[17] (citations omitted).

The Court continued:

> It is not unusual for the same word to be used with different meanings in the same act, and there is no rule of statutory construction which precludes the courts from giving to the word the meaning which the Legislature intended to have in each instance.[18] (citations omitted).

Notwithstanding the Court's finding that there is no "rule of statutory construction which precludes the courts" from giving separate meanings to identical words in the same act, *Atlantic Cleaners*, in its modern context, is cited for the contrary proposition: "Such a conclusion runs counter to the basic rule of statutory construction that identical words used in different parts of the same Act are intended to have the same meaning. *Atlantic Cleaners & Dyers, Inc. v. United States.*"[19] (citation omitted).

On the merits, the Supreme Court, in *Atlantic Cleaners*, concluded that Section 1 of the Sherman Act was passed under the power to regulate commerce, and the meaning of "trade or commerce" could not be broader than that power. Section 3, however, was not limited to the power to regulate commerce, but came under Congress's "plenary power to legislate for the District of Columbia."[20] The only restriction, therefore, on Congress would have been another provision of the Constitution, which the Court found there was none. Accordingly, the Court determined that it was

> free to interpret § 3 dissociated from § 1 as though it were a separate and independent act, and, thus viewed, there is no rule of statutory construction which prevents our giving the word "trade" its full meaning, or the more extended of two meanings, whichever will best manifest the legislative purpose.[21] (citations omitted).

Ruling on the summary judgment motion before it, the Court adopted the expanded meaning of "trade," and found against the defendants.

---

[17] *Id.*
[18] *Id.*
[19] Dep't of the Treasury v. Fabe, 508 U.S. 491, 515 (1993).
[20] *Id.* at 434.
[21] *Id.* at 435.

A corollary to the *Atlantic Cleaners* ruling—identical words in a statute can have different meanings—holds that different words addressing the same subject matter are presumed to have dissimilar meanings:

> Justice White suggests that because the Framers prohibited "excessive fines" (which he asserts, and we will assume for the sake of argument, means "disproportionate fines"), they must have meant to prohibit "excessive" punishments as well. This argument apparently did not impress state courts in the 19th century, and with good reason. The logic of the matter is quite the opposite. If "cruel and unusual punishments" included disproportionate punishments, the separate prohibition of disproportionate fines (which are certainly punishments) would have been entirely superfluous. When two parts of a provision (the Eighth Amendment) use different language to address the same or similar subject matter, a difference in meaning is assumed. See *Walton v. Arizona*. (Scalia, J., concurring in part and concurring in judgment).[22] (parentheses in original; citations omitted).

A legal commentator humorously described "equivocation" in the following manner:

> The tendency to assume that a word which appears in two or more legal rules, and so in connection with more than one purpose, has and should have precisely the same scope in all of them, runs all through legal discussions. It has all the tenacity of original sin and must be constantly guarded against.[23]

The term "Legislature" in the Constitution is subject to different meanings, depending on the context:

> The use in the Federal Constitution of the same term in different relations does not always imply the performance of the same function. The Legislature may act as an electoral body, as the choice of United States Senators under Article 1, section 3, prior to the adoption of the Seventeenth Amendment. It may act as a ratifying body, as in the case of proposed amendments to the Constitution under article 5. It may act as a consenting body, as in relation to the acquisition of lands by the United States under Article 1, section 8, paragraph 17. Whenever the term "legislature" is used in the Constitution, it is necessary to consider the nature of the particular action in view.[24] (citations omitted).

---

[22]Harmelin v. Michigan, 501 U.S. 957, 978 n.9 (1991).
[23]Cook, *"Substance" and "Procedure" in the Conflict of Laws*, 42 YALE L.J. 333, 337 (1933), *cited in* Gustafson v. Alloyd Co., 513 U.S. 561, 598 (1995).
[24]Smiley v. Holm, 285 U.S. 355, 365–66 (1932).

Differing Interpretations

Opinions of the U.S. Supreme Court often turn on differing interpretations of the same word or words. Justice Ginsburg, dissenting in *Muscarello v. United States*,[25] argued that "carries" is not limited to having a gun on someone's person, but can mean transporting a gun in a car's glove compartment, and cited an example of equivocation from an earlier case:

> Noting the paradoxical statement, "'I *use* a gun to protect my house, but I've never had to *use* it,'" the Court in *Bailey*, emphasized the importance of context—the statutory context. Just as "uses" was read to mean not simply "possession," but "active employment," so "carries," correspondingly, is properly read to signal the most dangerous cases—the gun at hand, ready for use as a weapon.[26] (italics in original; citations omitted).

Oliver Cromwell equivocated the word "conscience" to preclude Catholics from celebrating Mass in Ireland: "As to freedom of conscience, I meddle with no man's conscience; but if you mean by that, liberty to celebrate the Mass, I would have you understand that in no place where the power of the Parliament of England prevails shall that be permitted."[27]

Similar words are often passed off as having the same meaning. "People," "person," and "accused" may be interchangeable, depending on the context in which they are used. But these words may also have distinct meanings which, when commingled, produce equivocations. Chief Justice Rehnquist, writing for the Court, in *United States v. Verdugo-Urquidez*,[28] stated: "The question presented by this case is whether the Fourth Amendment applies to the search and seizure by United States agents of property that is owned by a nonresident alien and located in a foreign country."[29]

The Fourth Amendment provides:

> The right of the people to be secure in their persons, houses, papers, and effects, against unreasonable searches and seizures, shall not be violated, and no Warrants shall issue, but upon probable cause,

---

[25] 524 U.S. 125 (1998).
[26] *Id.* at 144–45.
[27] *Cited in* Abington School Dist. v. Schempp, 374 U.S. 203, 250 n.14 (1963), from HOOK, THE PARADOXES OF FREEDOM 23 (1962).
[28] 494 U.S. 259 (1990).
[29] *Id.* at 261.

supported by Oath or affirmation, and particularly describing the place to be searched, and the persons or things to be seized.[30]

Is a nonresident alien protected by the Fourth Amendment's term "people"? The Chief Justice considered the use of the word "people" in the Constitution:

> [The Fourth Amendment], by contrast with the Fifth and Sixth Amendments, extends its reach only to "the people." Contrary to the suggestion of *amici curiae* that the Framers used this phrase "simply to avoid [an] awkward rhetorical redundancy," . . . "the people" seems to have been a term of art employed in select parts of the Constitution. The Preamble declares that the Constitution is ordained and established by "the people of the United States." The Second Amendment protects "the right of the people to keep and bear Arms," and the Ninth and Tenth Amendments provide that certain rights and powers are retained by and reserved to "the people." See also U.S. Const., Amdt. 1 ("Congress shall make no law . . . abridging . . . the right of the people peaceably to assemble"); Art. I, 2, cl. 1 ("The House of Representatives shall be composed of Members chosen every second Year *by the people of the several States*").[31] (first brackets added; citations omitted; ellipses and italics in original).

In concluding that the defendant did not receive the Fourth Amendment's protections, the Chief Justice wrote:

> While this textual exegesis is by no means conclusive, it suggests that "the people" protected by the Fourth Amendment, and by the First and Second Amendments, and to whom rights and powers are reserved in the Ninth and Tenth Amendments, refers to a class of persons who are part of a national community or who have otherwise developed sufficient connection with this country to be considered part of that community.[32] (citation omitted).

Therefore, as written in the Constitution, the term "people" does not include a nonresident alien, for purposes of Fourth Amendment protection.[33]

A lawyer, on behalf of his paralegal, complained that the owner of their building refused to prevent smoke from the smokers' lounge from irritating his paralegal's allergies. The lawyer wrote a letter to the building's owner demanding that the smoking stop and insisted on $25,000

---

[30] U.S. Const.
[31] *Verdugo-Urquidez, supra* note 28, at 265.
[32] *Id.*
[33] *Id.* at 274–75.

as a settlement. When the owner refused this request, the attorney withdrew the offer and stated his paralegal would proceed with all available legal remedies. The lawyer obtained an ex parte TRO, to ban smoking on the second floor, and the local newspaper published an article on the lawsuit and the TRO. In a follow-up article, the newspaper quoted the owner: "He tried to extort money out of me because I refused to pay his demands."[34]

The attorney sued the building owner, and the newspaper, alleging defamation, invasion of privacy, and intentional infliction of emotional distress. The attorney argued that the word "extort" conveyed the idea that he was guilty of "extortion", a crime under Alabama law. The Alabama court disagreed:

> The crime of extortion is defined as "knowingly obtain[ing] by threat control over the property of another, with intent to deprive him of the property."
>
> . . . The verb "extort," however, includes the meaning "to obtain from a person by force, intimidation, or undue or illegal power" and the meaning "to gain especially by ingenuity or compelling argument." *Miriam* [sic] *Webster's Collegiate Dictionary* 412 (10th ed. 1997). In addition, the word "extort," in the context of Barnes' (the owner) remarks, is what the United States Supreme Court has characterized as "rhetorical hyperbole, a vigorous epithet used by [Barnes] who considered [Blevins's] negotiating [tactics] extremely unreasonable."[35] (parentheses added; brackets in original; citations omitted).

Deciding in favor of the building owner, and the newspaper, the Alabama court held:

> Because the word "extort" is not confined to its meaning that suggests the crime of extortion and because the use of the word in the context in which it was spoken indicates that it was rhetorical hyperbole, we concluded that Barnes' statement did not amount to slander per se because it did not charge Blevins with an indictable offense.[36]

In *Buckhannon v. West Virginia*,[37] the U.S. Supreme Court, by a 5–4 majority, declined to award attorney's fees to the plaintiffs because their lawsuit was mooted by a state legislature's actions. The question before the Court was whether a party that brings about a change in the other side's position, but does not obtain a judgment, can claim attorney's fees

---

[34] Blevins v. W.F. Barnes Corp., 768 So. 2d 386, 389 (Ala. Civ. App. 1999).
[35] *Id.* at 391.
[36] *Id.*
[37] 532 U.S. 598 (2001).

as the "prevailing party," under the appropriate statutes. Justice Ginsburg, writing for the dissent, lamented—

> The Court today holds that a plaintiff whose suit prompts the precise relief she seeks does not "prevail," and hence cannot obtain an award of attorney's fees, unless she also secures a court entry memorializing her victory. The entry need not be a judgment on the merits. Nor need there be any finding of wrongdoing. A court-approved settlement will do.[38]

Justice Scalia, concurring with the majority, dissected the term "prevailing party" and distinguished it from "prevail":

> It is undoubtedly true, as the dissent points out by quoting a nonlegal dictionary, that the word "prevailing" can have other meanings in other contexts: "prevailing winds" are the winds that predominate, and the "prevailing party" in an election is the party that wins the election. But when "prevailing party" is used by courts or legislatures in the context of a lawsuit, it is a term of art. It has traditionally—and to my knowledge, prior to enactment of the first of the statutes at issue here, *invariably*—meant the party that wins the suit or obtains a finding (or an admission) of liability.[39] (citation omitted; italics in original).

He continued:

> If a nuisance suit is mooted because the defendant asphalt plant has gone bankrupt and ceased operations, one would not normally call the plaintiff the prevailing party. And it would make no difference, as far as the propriety of that characterization is concerned, if the plant did not go bankrupt but moved to a new location to avoid the expense of litigation. In one sense the plaintiff would have "prevailed"; but he would not be the prevailing party in the lawsuit. Words that have acquired a specialized meaning in the legal context must be accorded their *legal* meaning.[40] (italics in original).

In *Simmons v. South Carolina*,[41] the U.S. Supreme Court held that a jury considering the imposition of the death penalty should be told if, under state law, a defendant is parole ineligible. The defendant in *Ramdass v. Angelone*[42] was not parole ineligible at the time of his sentencing trial for murder, even though he had been convicted of unrelated rob-

---

[38] *Id.* at 622.
[39] *Id.* at 615.
[40] *Id.*
[41] 512 U.S. 154 (1994).
[42] 530 U.S. 156 (2000).

beries (which would bring him within the three strikes law), because final judgments had not been entered. The Supreme Court majority held that, because the defendant was not parole ineligible as of his sentencing trial, there was no basis for extending *Simmons* to this situation.

Justice Stevens, in dissent, wrote that the *Simmons* plurality assumed, without deciding, the defendant's parole ineligibility, based on the meaning of "accurate":

> The *Simmons* plurality did say that "an instruction informing the jury that petitioner is ineligible for parole is legally accurate." But in the very next sentence the plurality wrote: "Certainly such an instruction is *more accurate* than no instruction at all." This made it clear that "accuracy," in the sense used there, is a relative term, not an absolute conclusive determination of legal status.[43] (citations omitted; italics in original).

Are "gender" and "sex" interchangeable in the context of "discrimination"? Not according to Justice Scalia, who dissented in *J.E.B. v. Alabama*:

> Throughout this opinion, I shall refer to the issue as sex discrimination, rather than (as the Court does) gender discrimination. The word "gender" has acquired the new and useful connotation of cultural or attitudinal characteristics (as opposed to physical characteristics) distinctive to the sexes. That is to say, gender is to sex as feminine is to female and masculine to male. The present case does not involve peremptory strikes exercised on the basis of femininity or masculinity (as far as it appears, effeminate men did not survive the prosecution's peremptories). The case involves, therefore, sex discrimination plain and simple.[44]

---

[43]*Ramdass, supra* note 42, at 188 n.9.
[44]511 U.S. 127, 157 n.1 (1994).

🌊 CHAPTER ELEVEN

Amphiboly: Which Meaning Is Intended?

> *Ejusdem generis*
>
> *Under the principle of ejusdem generis, when a general term follows a specific one, the general term should be understood as a reference to subjects akin to the one with specific enumeration.*[1]

IN THE LOGICIAN'S LEXICON, "amphiboly" is another word for "ambiguity"—but not just any ambiguity. Amphiboly is an ambiguity caused by grammatical or syntactical construction, creating doubt about which of several meanings was intended. A meaning may be unclear for many reasons: because a pronoun could refer to more than one antecedent, because there is faulty parallelism, or because a dangling modifier could refer to multiple words. The fallacy of accent can be remedied by referring to the context of the accented words; the fallacy of equivocation can be remedied by understanding what meaning has been ascribed to a word or phrase. Amphiboly, by contrast, requires a grammatical restructuring of the phrase or sentence (or multiple phrases or sentences) to eliminate the confusion.

Untangling an amphiboly may require reference to basic rules of grammar, contract interpretation rules, or constitutional interpretative canons. *Ejusdem generis*, for example, cited at the top of this chapter, is intended to resolve statutory ambiguities caused by a string of enumerated instances, followed by a general description. How to treat the

---

[1] Norfolk & Western R. Co. v. Train Dispatchers, 499 U.S. 117, 129 (1991).

general description becomes the issue. Can it include only those enumerated items preceding the general description, or can it include like items, but not enumerated? The latter is preferred under the *ejusdem generis* interpretation rule.

By way of example, the Sierra Club sued the Illinois Department of Conservation to prevent logging, or inviting bids for logging, in a state park, where the Department had the authority to sell "gravel, sand, earth or other material."[2] The Illinois Supreme Court, relying on the doctrine of *ejusdem generis*, held: "Timber, like sand, gravel and earth fill, is part of the bounty of the earth's surface. But it would both defy common sense and render the other statutes on timber sales surplusage to include timber in this section. We decline to do so."[3]

To defend against an amphiboly, an attorney should first argue that there is no ambiguity, and no interpretation is required.

Libelous Headlines

Headline writers often commit the fallacy of accent in their efforts to attract readers, but they may also attract lawsuits for libel or defamation, by committing the fallacy of amphiboly. On October 3, 1995, O. J. Simpson was acquitted, in a criminal trial, of the murders of his former wife, Nicole Brown Simpson, and her friend, Ronald Goldman.[4] A week later, the *National Examiner* newspaper ran the following headline, referring to Brian "Kato" Kaelin, Simpson's house guest, and a witness at the trial:[5]

COPS THINK KATO DID IT!

. . . he fears they want him for perjury, say pals

The inside headline appearing over the article, on page 17, read:[6]

KATO KAELIN . . .

COPS THINK HE DID IT!

. . . he fears they want him for perjury, say pals

The article's first four paragraphs stated:

---

[2]Sierra Club v. Kenney, 429 N.E.2d 1214, 1222 (1981).
[3]*Id.*
[4]Kaelin v. Globe Commc'ns Corp., 162 F.3d 1036 (9th Cir. 1998).
[5]*Id.* at 1037.
[6]*Id.* at 1038.

Kato Kaelin is still a suspect in the murder of Nicole Brown Simpson and Ron Goldman, friends fear.

They are worried that LAPD cops are desperately looking for a way to put Kato behind bars for perjury.

"We're sure the cops have been trying to prove that Kato didn't tell them everything he knows, that somehow he spoiled their case against O.J.," says one pal. "It's not true, but we think they're out to get even with Kato."

"I'm worried that Kato will get a persecution complex. He'll end up looking around every corner and thinking he sees a cop."[7]

When the newspaper publisher refused a demand to retract the article, Kaelin filed a libel action. During discovery, the newspaper's designated representative testified at a deposition:

Q: What did you think, [when reviewing the article before publication] about the words "Cops Think He Did It" meant? What is the "it" to which this statement—

A: Perjury.

Q: Perjury?

A: Mm-hmm.

Q: Did you have any concern that a reader might connect the "Cops Think He Did It" with the other information in the article that refers to allegations that Mr. Kaelin was involved in the murders themselves?

A: I was a bit concerned about it, yes, but in fact I thought the second part of the headline coped with that . . . .[8] (brackets added; ellipses in original).

The Ninth Circuit, reviewing the district court's grant of summary judgment for the publisher, held:

This case is about the headlines, especially the one appearing on the cover. The first issue is whether the headlines alone are susceptible of a false and defamatory meaning and, if so, whether they can be the basis of a libel action even though the accompanying story is not defamatory.[9]

---

[7] *Id.*
[8] *Id.* at 1038–39.
[9] *Id.* at 1039.

The Ninth Circuit's analysis included the following:

> As already seen, the front page headline consists of two sentences. The first—"COPS THINK KATO DID IT!"—states what the cops supposedly think. The second—" . . . he fears they want him for perjury, says pals"—is what Kato's pals supposedly said. These two sentences express two different thoughts and are not mutually exclusive.[10] (ellipses in original).
>
> . . . .
>
> Since the publication occurred just one week after O.J. Simpson's highly publicized acquittal for murder, we believe that a reasonable person, at that time, might well have concluded that the "it" in the first sentence of the cover and internal headlines referred to the murders. Such a reading of the first sentence is not negated by or inconsistent with the second sentence as a matter of logic, grammar, or otherwise. In our view, an ordinary reader reasonably could have read the headline to mean that the cops think that Kato committed the murders and that Kato fears that he is wanted for perjury.
>
> Globe argues that the "it" refers to perjury. Even assuming that such a reading is reasonably possible, it is not the only reading that is reasonably possible as a matter of law. So long as the publication is reasonably susceptible of a defamatory meaning, a factual question for the jury exists.[11] (citations omitted; ellipses added).

Overturning the district court's summary judgment ruling, the Ninth Circuit concluded there was sufficient evidence for a jury to find that the headlines were defamatory, and that the publisher acted with actual malice.[12]

In 1988, Congress passed the Anti-Drug Abuse Act, which, after later amendments, provided:

> [Each] public housing agency shall utilize leases which . . . provide that any criminal activity that threatens the health, safety, or right to peaceful enjoyment of the premises by other tenants or any drug-related criminal activity on or off such premises, engaged in by a public housing tenant, any member of the tenant's household, or any guest or other person under the tenant's control, shall be cause for termination of tenancy.[13] (brackets added).

---

[10] *Id.* at 1039–40.
[11] *Id.* at 1040.
[12] *Id.* at 1042–43.
[13] 42 U.S.C. § 1437(d)(l)(6) (Supp. V 1994).

AMPHIBOLY: WHICH MEANING IS INTENDED?

Implementing regulations by HUD (United States Department of Housing and Urban Development) required "public housing authorities (PHAs) to impose a lease obligation on tenants":

> To assure that the tenant, any member of the household, a guest, or another person under the tenant's control, shall not engage in:
>
> (A) Any criminal activity that threatens the health, safety, or right to peaceful enjoyment of the PHA's public housing premises or by other residents or employees of the PHA, or
>
> (B) Any drug-related criminal activity on or near such premises.
>
> Any criminal activity in violation of the preceding sentence shall be cause for termination of tenancy, and for eviction from the unit.[14]

Four public housing tenants were evicted pursuant to lease provisions that obligated them to ensure that no "member of the household, a guest, or another person under the tenant's control, shall not engage in . . . [a]ny drug-related criminal activity on or near such premise[s]."[15] (ellipses and brackets in original).

A significant issue determining the rights of the evictees was whether the words "under a tenant's control" referred solely to "another person," or whether they also referred to "member of the household" and "guest." An en banc panel of the Ninth Circuit found that "under a tenant's control" referred to all three terms.

The U.S. Supreme Court reversed, and held that the Anti-Drug Abuse Act permitted eviction of household members and guests— whether or not the tenants were aware of the drug activity (or should have known of the activity). In rejecting the argument that the tenants were required to have known of the drug activity, the Supreme Court found: "Congress' decision not to impose any qualification in the statute, combined with its use of the term 'any' to modify 'drug-related criminal activity,' precludes any knowledge requirement."[16]

The Court also rejected the argument that "under a tenant's control" applied to "member of the tenant's household" and "guest":

> [T]his interpretation runs counter to basic rules of grammar. The disjunctive "or" means that the qualification applies only to "other person." Indeed, the view that "under the tenant's control" modifies

---

[14]Dep't of Hous. and Urban Dev. v. Rucker, 535 U.S. 125, 129 n.2 (2002).
[15]Id. at 128.
[16]Id. at 130–31.

everything coming before it in the sentence would result in the nonsensical reading that the statute applies to a "public housing tenant . . . under the tenant's control."[17] (ellipses in original).

Aside from basic grammar rules, the Court considered four other defenses:

1. The legislative history of the statute.[18]
2. The plain reading of the statute creating absurd results.[19]
3. The canon of constitutional avoidance.[20]
4. Reliance on other Supreme Court decisions to cast doubt on the statute's constitutionality under the Due Process Clause.[21]

When the text of a statute is unambiguous, it is inappropriate to refer to the legislative history.[22] In this case, the Supreme Court's reading of the statute to be unambiguous obviated a search of the legislative history. Nevertheless, the Court also rejected arguments based on the legislative history of the statute.[23]

The Ninth Circuit held that a plain reading of the statute *required* local public housing authorities to evict tenants, an absurd result. The Supreme Court disagreed:

> It is not "absurd" that a local housing authority may sometimes evict a tenant who had no knowledge of the drug-related activity. Such "no-fault" eviction is a common "incident of tenant responsibility under normal landlord-tenant law and practice."[24] (citation omitted).

As in the case involving legislative history, when the statute is unambiguous, the canon of constitutional avoidance does not apply.[25] According to the Court,

> There are, moreover no "serious constitutional doubts" about Congress' affording local public housing authorities the discretion to conduct no-fault evictions for drug-related crime.[26] (citation omitted).

---

[17] *Id.* at 131.
[18] *Id.* at 132.
[19] *Id.* at 133.
[20] *Id.* at 134.
[21] *Id.* at 135.
[22] *Id.* at 132.
[23] *Id.* at 133 n.4.
[24] *Id.* at 134.
[25] *Id.*
[26] *Id.* at 135.

AMPHIBOLY: WHICH MEANING IS INTENDED?   139

Finally, the Ninth Circuit found a violation of the Due Process Clause because the lease permits "tenants to be deprived of their property interest without any relationship to individual wrongdoing."[27] Rejecting the cases relied upon by the Circuit, the Supreme Court held:

> The government is not attempting to criminally punish or civilly regulate respondents as members of the general populace. It is instead acting as a landlord of property that it owns, invoking a clause in a lease to which respondents have agreed and which Congress has expressly required.[28]

Higher Stakes

Criminal statutes are subject to the same ambiguities as civil statutes—only the stakes for the individual are usually higher. In *Jones v. United States*,[29] the U.S. Supreme Court divided 5–4 over the correct interpretation of the following statute for carjacking:

> Whoever, possessing a firearm as defined in section 921 of this title, takes a motor vehicle that has been transported, shipped, or received in interstate or foreign commerce from the person or presence of another by force and violence or by intimidation, or attempts to do so, shall—
>
> (1) be fined under this title or imprisoned not more than 15 years, or both,
>
> (2) if serious bodily injury (as defined in section 1365 of this title) results, be fined under this title or imprisoned not more than 25 years, or both, and
>
> (3) if death results, be fined under this title or imprisoned for any number of years up to life, or both.[30] (parentheses in original).

The ambiguity results from the three numbered subsections. Do they define "three distinct offenses or a single crime with a choice of three maximum penalties, two of them dependent on sentencing factors exempt from the requirements of charge and jury verdict"?[31] Justice

---

[27]*Id.*
[28]*Id.*
[29]526 U.S. 227 (1999).
[30]18 U.S.C. § 2119 (Supp. V 1988).
[31]*Jones, supra* note 29, at 229.

Souter, writing for the majority, found that the carjacking statute set out three distinct offenses.[32]

This case arose when a grand jury indicted the defendant, Jones, for, among other things, "carjacking or aiding and abetting carjacking, in violation of 18 U.S.C. § 2119 . . . ."[33] The indictment did not specify any numbered subsections, and did not contain any facts set forth in subsections (2) or (3). At the arraignment, "the Magistrate Judge told Jones that he faced a maximum sentence of 15 years on the carjacking charge."[34] (citation omitted).

The district court's jury instructions referred only to the elements in the first paragraph of the statute. Jones was found guilty.

The presentence report recommended that Jones be sentenced to 25 years, because he caused serious bodily injury to one of the victims during the carjacking. Jones argued that serious bodily injury was an element of the offense, and had been ". . . neither pleaded in the indictment nor proven before the jury."[35] Nevertheless, the district court sentenced Jones to 25 years for the carjacking.[36]

The Ninth Circuit, in accord with the Eleventh,[37] concluded that the structure of the statute, where the numbered subsections were grammatically dependent on the first paragraph, demonstrated that the subsections were not separate crimes.

> For its [the Ninth Circuit's] view that the subsections provided sentencing factors, the court found additional support in the statute's legislative history. The heading of the subtitle of the bill creating § 2119 was "Enhanced Penalties for Auto Theft," which the court took as indicating that the statute's numbered subsections merely defined sentencing enhancements.[38] (brackets added; citation omitted).

Justice Souter rejected the "look" of the statute as conclusive evidence of one crime with three sentencing provisions, by noting that the first paragraph contains elements and could possibly stand alone. The first numbered subsection, he wrote, could be a sentencing provision, because it did not add any additional elements to prove. However, the second and third subsections add enhanced penalties, conditioned on

---

[32]*Id.*
[33]*Id.* at 230.
[34]*Id.* at 230–31.
[35]*Id.* at 231.
[36]*Id.*
[37]United States v. Williams, 51 F.3d 1004, 1009–10 (11th Cir. 1995).
[38]*Jones, supra* note 29, at 232.

additional facts (injury, death), suggesting they are not merely sentencing considerations.

Justice Souter then acknowledged the Ninth Circuit's argument that the numbered subsections could not stand alone (thereby constituting three separate offenses), but are structurally integrated with the first paragraph, suggesting a single offense with sentencing provisions.

Additionally, he noted the argument that "shall" precedes the numbered subsections, "which often divides offense-defining provisions from those that specify sentences."[39]

Wielding logic counter to the Ninth Circuit, Justice Souter argued,

> if the shorter subsection (2) of § 2119 does not stand alone, neither does the section's more voluminous first paragraph. In isolation, it would merely describe some very obnoxious behavior, leaving any reader assuming that it must be a crime, but never actually told that it is. Only the numbered subsidiary provisions complete the thought.[40]

As for the "shall" argument, he noted that "although it frequently separates offense-defining clauses from sentencing provisions, it hardly does so invariably."[41] To further bolster his arguments, Justice Souter looked to other statutes,[42] state practices,[43] and legislative history,[44] and concluded they supported his reading of the statute.

Justice Kennedy, writing for the dissenters, offered a contrary view of the statute:

> Section 2119 begins by setting forth in its initial paragraph elements typical of a robbery-type offense. For all ordinary purposes, this is a complete crime. If, for instance, there were only a single punishment, as provided in clause (1), I think there could be no complaint with jury instructions drawn from the first paragraph of § 2119, without reference to the punishment set forth in clause (1). The design of the statute yields the conclusion that the following numbered provisions do not convert each of the clauses into additional elements. These are punishment provisions directed to the sentencing judge alone.[45]

The structure of the statute, argued Justice Kennedy, lent itself to a single crime, with three sentencing options:

---

[39] *Id.* at 233.
[40] *Id.* at 233.
[41] *Id.* at 234.
[42] *Id.*
[43] *Id.* at 236.
[44] *Id.* at 237–39.
[45] *Id.* at 256.

Even as written, though, the statute sets forth a complete crime in the first paragraph. It is difficult to see why Congress would double back and insert additional elements for the jury's consideration in clauses (2) and (3).[46]

Even the choice of verbs came into play:

In addition, there is some significance to the use of the active voice in the main paragraph and the passive voice in clauses (2) and (3) of § 2119. In the more common practice, criminal statutes use the active voice to define prohibited conduct.[47] (citations omitted).

Additionally, Justice Kennedy rejected the majority's argument that the statute created doubt:

[T]he constitutional doubt canon of construction is applicable only if the statute at issue is "genuinely susceptible to two constructions after, and not before, its complexities are unraveled. Only then is the statutory construction that the constitutional question a 'fair' one."[48] (citations omitted).

With minimal changes to the statute, Justice Kennedy asserted, it would unambiguously reflect the dissenters' view. He then offered a way to avoid the amphiboly:

Congress could leave the initial paragraph of § 2119 intact, and provide that one who commits the conduct described there shall "be imprisoned for any number of years up to life." It could then add that "if the sentencing judge determines that no death resulted, one convicted under this section shall be imprisoned not more than 25 years" and "if the sentencing judge determines that no serious bodily injury resulted, one convicted under this section shall be imprisoned not more than 15 years."[49]

Title VII of the Omnibus Crime Control and Safe Streets Act of 1968,[50] in relevant part, reads:

Any person who—

(1) has been convicted by a court of the United States or of a State or any political subdivision thereof of a felony . . . and who receives, possesses, or transports in commerce or affecting commerce . . . any

---

[46] *Id.*
[47] *Id.* at 258.
[48] *Id.* at 266.
[49] *Id.* at 267.
[50] 18 U.S.C. app. § 1202(a).

firearm shall be fined not more than $10,000 or imprisoned for not more than two years, or both. (ellipses added).

A defendant, who was a felon, was prosecuted for a violation of the above statute for "possessing" a pistol and a shotgun at different times, in *United States v. Bass*.[51] The prosecution did not attempt to establish that either of the defendant's firearms was possessed "in commerce or affecting commerce." According to the Supreme Court, the issue was

> whether the statutory phrase "in commerce or affecting commerce" applies to "possesses" and "receives" as well as to "transports." If it does, then the Government must prove an essential element of the offense that a possession, receipt, or transportation was "in commerce or affecting commerce"—a burden not undertaken in this prosecution for possession.[52]

Justice Thurgood Marshall, writing for the majority, found that "the natural construction of the language suggests" that "in commerce or affecting commerce" applies not only to "transports," but also to the two other antecedents: "receives" and "possesses."[53] After examining the legislative history of this provision, as well as its grammatical structure, Justice Marshall concluded that the statute was ambiguous. Because this was a criminal statute, he applied the rule of lenity:

> In various ways over the years, we have stated that "when choice has to be made between two readings of what conduct Congress has made a crime, it is appropriate, before we choose the harsher alternative, to require that Congress should have spoken in language that is clear and definite."[54] (citation omitted).

The narrower reading (i.e., the more lenient interpretation) compelled a finding that "in commerce or affecting commerce" was a "part of all three offenses."[55] As the government had not demonstrated a linkage between the defendant's possession of firearms and interstate commerce, the Court upheld the circuit court and reversed the conviction.[56]

In *District of Columbia v. Heller*,[57] the U.S. Supreme Court considered the meaning of the Second Amendment:

---

[51] 404 U.S. 336 (1971).
[52] *Id.* at 339.
[53] *Id.*
[54] *Id.* at 347.
[55] *Id.*
[56] *Id.* at 351.
[57] 128 S. Ct. 2783 (2008).

> A well regulated Militia, being necessary to the security of a free State, the right of the people to keep and bear Arms, shall not be infringed.

The immediate issue confronting the Justices involved the District of Columbia's ban on handgun ownership; the broader issue involved the right of individuals, apart from service in a militia, to own and possess "guns for nonmilitary purposes like hunting and personal self-defense."[58] Justice Scalia, writing for the 5–4 majority, concluded that there is no difference between the Second Amendment, as written, and the following:

> The right of the people to keep and bear Arms shall not be infringed.

No Contradiction

To reach his conclusion, and thus untangle the amphiboly created by the initial clause, Justice Scalia first analyzed the operative clause, and then returned to the prefatory clause. Having concluded there was nothing in the operative clause—"the right of the people to keep and bear Arms, shall not be infringed"—suggesting a collective right to maintain arms, Justice Scalia wrote that individuals could own handguns and other firearms. Returning to the prefatory clause—"A well regulated Militia, being necessary to the security of a free State"—Justice Scalia found it did not contradict the operative clause: "We reach the question, then: Does the preface fit with an operative clause that creates an individual right to keep and bar arms? It fits perfectly, once one knows the history that the founding generation knew and that we have described above."[59]

Justice Stevens, dissenting, argued that the Court should not have casually jettisoned the prefatory clause:

> The preamble thus both sets forth the object of the Amendment and informs the meaning of the remainder of its text. Such text should not be treated as mere surplusage, for "[i]t cannot be presumed that any clause in the constitution is intended to be without effect." *Marbury v. Madison*.[60] (brackets in original; citation omitted).

He then chided the majority for its inverted analysis:

---

[58] *Id.* at 2822.
[59] *Id.* at 2801.
[60] *Id.* at 2826.

The Court today tries to denigrate the importance of this clause of the Amendment by beginning its analysis with the Amendment's operative provision and returning to the preamble merely "to ensure that our reading of the operative clause is consistent with the announced purpose." That is not how this Court ordinarily reads such texts, and it is not how the preamble would have been viewed at the time the Amendment was adopted. While the Court makes the novel suggestion that it need only find some "logical connection" between the preamble and the operative provision, it does acknowledge that a prefatory clause may resolve an ambiguity in the text. Without identifying any language in the text that even mentions civilian uses of firearms, the Court proceeds to "find" its preferred reading in what is at best an ambiguous text, and then concludes that its reading is not foreclosed by the preamble. Perhaps the Court's approach to the text is acceptable advocacy, but it is surely an unusual approach for judges to follow.[61]

The order of a Supreme Court Justice's analysis has been derided previously, and suggests that careful scrutiny should attach to any real (or perceived) ambiguities, whenever an unusual analytical technique is employed. Justice Scalia, for example, in *Zuni v. Department of Education*,[62] criticized Justice Breyer's majority opinion for its lack of linearity:

> The very structure of the Court's opinion provides an obvious clue as to what is afoot. The opinion purports to place a premium on the plain text of the Impact Aid statute, but it first takes us instead on a round-about tour of "[c]onsiderations other than language"—page after page of unenacted congressional intent and judicially perceived statutory purpose. Only after we are shown "why Zuni concentrates its argument upon language alone, (impliedly a shameful practice, or at least indication of a feeble case), are we informed how the statute's plain text does not unambiguously *preclude* the interpretation the Court thinks best . . . This is a most suspicious order of proceeding, since our case law is full of statements such as "We begin, as always, with the language of the statute, and replete with the affirmation that, when "[g]iven [a] straightforward statutory command, there is no reason to resort to legislative history. Nor is his cart-before-the-horse approach justified by the Court's excuse that the statute before us is, after all, a technical one.
>
> . . . .

---

[61] *Id.*
[62] 167 L. Ed. 2d 449 (2007).

As almost a majority of today's majority worries, "[w]ere the inversion [of inquiry] to become systemic, it would create the impression that agency policy concerns, rather than the traditional tools of statutory construction, are shaping the judicial interpretation of statutes."[63] (citations omitted; ellipses added; italics, brackets, and parentheses in original).

Similarly, Justice Thomas (a member of the majority in *Heller*), in *Gustafson v. Alloyd Co., Inc.*,[64] critiqued the majority's upside-down analysis:

> From the majority's opinion, one would not realize that § 12(2) was involved in this case until one had read more than half-way through. In contrast to the majority's approach of interpreting the statute, I believe the proper method is to begin with the provision actually involved in this case, § 12(2), and then turn to the 1933 Act's definitional section, § 2(1), before consulting the structure of the Act as a whole. Because the result of this textual analysis shows that § 12(2) applies to secondary or private sales of a security as well as to initial public offerings, I dissent.[65]

---

[63]*Id.* at 470.
[64]513 U.S. 561 (1995).
[65]*Id.* at 584.

CHAPTER TWELVE

Hypostatization: Expressing Abstractions

"Objection. The document speaks for itself."

A common trial objection

CERTAIN WORDS—justice, due process, liberty, property, for example—convey abstract thoughts, ideas, or expressions that vary in meaning from individual to individual. When abstractions are treated as if they had concrete meanings, confusion may result from the lack of a common understanding of what is intended. Hypostatization is the term used to denote the treatment of abstract words as though they had concrete meanings. A closely related term, reification, is the assignment of human characteristics to inanimate things. For ease of use, these two related terms—hypostatization and reification—will be treated interchangeably.

When an attorney declares, "Justice requires . . . ," what does that mean exactly? To "require" something is a characteristic of human behavior, not a characteristic of an abstraction. Although confusion may arise over the precise meaning of "justice requires," attorneys understand the concept argued, even though room for disagreement remains.

Attorneys express abstractions as though they had concrete meanings for many reasons. As exemplified in the next paragraph, shorthand locutions have developed that are understood by all attorneys. Why change what seems to work? Hypostatizations also permit attorneys to argue based on euphonious expressions, such as "fundamental fairness requires," which tend to carry more weight than "the facts in this case . . . ."

One way to turn a hypostatization against opposing counsel is to use the same expression, but disagree as to its application. For example, an attorney might argue, "Your Honor. While counsel may believe fundamental fairness requires you to decide in his (or her) favor, it is not fundamentally fair in light of the facts in this case, because . . . ."

The objection above—"The document speaks for itself"—is not meant literally, for a document has no vocal chords and cannot speak. (Given the advanced state of technology, however, documents someday may mimic human speech.) This objection usually arises when a witness is asked to relate the contents of a document before it is introduced into evidence. Opposing counsel objects because the witness often is unable to relate the contents word-for-word, but instead characterizes the contents. Characterizing the document is not the best evidence of its contents; the document, itself, is. The objection, invoking the "best evidence rule," is grounded in a Federal Rule of Evidence:

> Rule 1002. Requirement of Original
>
> To prove the content of a writing, recording, or photograph, the original writing, recording, or photograph is required, except as otherwise provided in these rules or by Act of Congress.

Instead of a document speaking for itself, Justice Kennedy, dissenting in part, in *Allegheny County v. Greater Pittsburgh ACLU*,[1] contended that the religious test offered by the majority pointed to its own self-flaws:

> But for the most part, Justice Blackmun's and Justice O'Connor's objections are not well taken. As a practical matter, the only cases of symbolic recognition likely to arise with much frequency are those involving simple holiday displays, and in that context *Lynch* provides unambiguous guidance. I would follow it. The majority's test, on the other hand, demands the Court to draw exquisite distinctions from fine detail in a wide range of cases. The anomalous result the test has produced here speaks for itself.[2]

It Speaks for Itself

As any first-year law student can relate, there is a tort doctrine whose English translation sounds similar to "the document speaks for itself":

---

[1] 492 U.S. 573 (1989).
[2] *Id.* at 675 n.11.

> Res ipsa loquitur is applied in negligence actions as a permissible inference that literally means "the thing speaks for itself." Res ipsa loquitur is "merely a short way of saying that the circumstances attendant upon an accident are themselves of such a character as to justify a [court or] jury in inferring negligence as the cause of that accident." The doctrine allows a plaintiff the opportunity to establish a prima facie case "when he could not otherwise satisfy the traditional requirements for proof of negligence." The jury is thereby permitted, but not compelled to infer a defendant's negligence without the aid of any direct evidence. Even when the doctrine applies, however, the burden of proving the defendant's negligence remains upon the plaintiff.[3] (brackets in original; citations omitted).

The "thing" that supposedly "speaks for itself" is the accident resulting from the defendant's negligence. Even though the circumstances of the negligence suggest the defendant was negligent, there is a great deal of room for interpretation and confusion. Generally, a plaintiff must demonstrate proof of three elements to successfully rely on the *res ipsa loquitur* doctrine:

1. A casualty of a sort which usually does not occur in the absence of negligence.
2. Caused by an instrumentality within the defendant's exclusive control.
3. Under circumstances indicating that the casualty did not result from the act or omission of the plaintiff.[4]

An apt illustration of the difficulties inherent in ascribing concrete meaning to abstract terms appeared in the jousting between Justice Kennedy (for the majority) and Justice Scalia (for the dissenters) in *Lawrence v. Texas*,[5] involving the validity of Texas's law prohibiting private, homosexual conduct. Justice Kennedy wrote.

> Liberty protects the person from unwarranted government intrusions into a dwelling or other private places. In our tradition the State is not omnipresent in the home. And there are other spheres of our lives and existence, outside the home, where the State should not be a dominant presence. Freedom extends beyond spatial bounds. Liberty presumes an autonomy of self that includes freedom of thought, belief, expression, and certain intimate conduct. The instant case involves liberty of the person both in its spatial and more transcendent dimensions.[6]

---

[3]Dover Elevator Co. v. Swann, 638 A.2d 762, 765 (Md. 1993).
[4]*Id.*
[5]539 U.S. 558 (2003).
[6]*Id.* at 562.

The next passage from Justice Kennedy expansively interpreted the meaning of liberty:

> These matters, ("personal decisions relating to marriage, procreation, contraception, family relationships, child rearing, and education") involving the most intimate and personal choices a person may make in a lifetime, choices central to personal dignity and autonomy, are central to the liberty protected by the Fourteenth Amendment. At the heart of liberty is the right to define one's own concept of existence, of meaning, of the universe, and the mystery of human life. Beliefs about these matters could not define the attributes of personhood were they formed under compulsion of the State.[7] (parentheses added).

Justice Scalia took issue with Justice Kennedy's definition of liberty:

> And if the Court is referring not to the holding of *Casey*,[8] but to the dictum of its famed sweet-mystery-of-life passage. ("'At the heart of liberty is the right to define one's own concept of existence, of meaning, of the universe, and of the mystery of human life'"): That "casts some doubt" upon either the totality of our jurisprudence or else (presumably the right answer) nothing at all. I have never heard of a law that attempted to restrict one's "right to define" certain concepts; and if the passage calls into question the government's power to regulate *actions based on* one's self-defined "concept of existence, etc.," it is the passage that ate the rule of law.[9] (parentheses in original; citations omitted; italics in original).

Right to Privacy

The notion of "liberty" is enshrined in the Fourteenth Amendment; the right to "privacy" is nowhere to be found in the Constitution. Nevertheless, the ill-defined, abstract concept of "privacy" ranks as one of the most important rights of the individual. Certain aspects of the right to privacy have arisen in the case law: "The cases sometimes characterized as protecting 'privacy' have in fact involved at least two different kinds of interests. One is the individual interest in avoiding disclosure of personal matters, another is the interest in independence in making certain kinds of important decisions."[10] (footnotes omitted).

---

[7]*Id.* at 574.
[8]Planned Parenthood v. Casey, 505 U.S. 833 (1992).
[9]*Lawrence, supra* note 5, at 588.
[10]Whalen v. Roe, 429 U.S. 589 (1977).

As Justice Stewart noted, "the Constitution affords protection against certain kinds of government intrusions into personal and private matters, [but] there is no general constitutional 'right to privacy.'"[11] (brackets added).

In *Whalen v. Roe*,[12] the U.S. Supreme Court considered the extent of the right to privacy in the context of the following issue: "The constitutional question presented is whether the State of New York may record, in a centralized computer file, the names and addresses of all persons who have obtained, pursuant to a doctor's prescription, certain drugs for which there is both a lawful and an unlawful market."[13]

The district court enjoined enforcement of portions of the legislation, deciding that they violated the plaintiffs' "protected rights of privacy."

At the district court hearing, plaintiffs introduced evidence of the impact of the statute on privacy:

> Two parents testified that they were concerned that their children would be stigmatized by the State's central filing system. One child had been taken off his Schedule II medication because of this concern. Three adult patients testified that they feared disclosure of their names would result from central filing of patient identifications. One of them now obtains his drugs in another State. The other two continue to receive Schedule II prescriptions in New York, but continue to fear disclosure and stigmatization. Four physicians testified that the prescription system entrenches on patients' privacy, and that each had observed a reaction of shock, fear, and concern on the part of their patients whom they had informed of the plan. One doctor refuses to prescribe Schedule II drugs for his patients. On the other hand, over 100,000 patients per month have been receiving Schedule II drug prescriptions without their objections, if any, to central filing having come to the attention of the District Court.[14]

And they argued that "the statute threatens to impair both their interest in the nondisclosure of private information and also their interest in making important decisions independently."[15]

Justice Stevens, writing for the majority, found that the statute, on its face, does not "pose a sufficiently grievous threat to either interest to establish a constitutional violation."[16] In rejecting the plaintiffs'

---

[11] *Id.* at 607–608.
[12] *Supra.*
[13] *Id.* at 591.
[14] *Id.* at 595 n.16.
[15] *Id.* at 600.
[16] *Id.*

argument that their privacy rights were invaded by the statute, Justice Stevens wrote:

> Even without public disclosure, it is, of course, true that private information must be disclosed to the authorized employees of the New York Department of Health. Such disclosures, however, are not significantly different from those that were required under the prior law. Nor are they meaningfully distinguishable from a host of other unpleasant invasions of privacy that are associated with many facets of health care. Unquestionably, some individuals' concern for their own privacy may lead them to avoid or to postpone needed medical attention. Nevertheless, disclosures of private medical information to doctors, to hospital personnel, to insurance companies, and to public health agencies are often an essential part of modern medical practice even when the disclosure may reflect unfavorably on the character of the patient. Requiring such disclosures to representatives of the State having responsibility for the health of the community, does not automatically amount to an impermissible invasion of privacy.[17] (footnote omitted).

A prosecutor's use of hypostatization in closing argument drew an objection from defense counsel, and an instruction from the judge to disregard it:

> **[Prosecutor]:** Convict the Defendant fairly because the facts and the law compel conviction. Convict the Defendant because justice compels conviction.
>
> **[Defense Counsel]:** I object to that, too . . .
>
> **THE COURT:** I direct the jury to ignore the last statement of the United States Attorney. Your responsibility, as I told you at the beginning, is to determine whether or not, in light of the law that is given to you by the Court, the government has met its burden of proving the Defendant guilty beyond a reasonable doubt . . .[18] (ellipses in original).

The prosecutor urged the jury to convict the defendant because "justice compels" conviction. The judge correctly noted that conviction must rest on the facts, not on abstract concepts. The First Circuit held that the prosecutor's comment was an "[i]mproper (appeal) to the jury to act in ways other than as a dispassionate arbiter of the facts."[19] Although jurors can disagree on the facts, and their significance under

---

[17] *Id.* at 602.
[18] United States v. Manning, 23 F.3d 570, 573 (1st Cir. 1994).
[19] *Id.* at 573.

the law, at least the defendant's fate is not left to the jurors' notions of abstract nouns.

Both Special Prosecutor Kenneth Starr and President Clinton employed hypostatization to make their respective cases. In his referral to Congress, under the heading—"C. The President repeatedly and unlawfully invoked the Executive Privilege to conceal evidence of this personal misconduct from the grand jury."—the Special Prosecutor wrote: "In a very real and significant way, the objectives of William J. Clinton, the person, and his Administration (the Clinton White House) are one and the same."[20] (parentheses in original).

In other words, the Special Prosecutor personified the abstract noun "Administration" to allow it to have "objectives." Did the Special Prosecutor intend to convey the idea that everyone in the administration shared the President's objectives? Perhaps. But that was not necessarily the case.

Arguing that the Special Prosecutor did not make out a case for perjury, the President's lawyers asserted: "The law simply does not require the witness to aid his interrogator. The Referral seeks to punish the President for being unhelpful to those trying to destroy him politically."[21]

"The law" is an abstraction, about which reasonable individuals can disagree. The President's lawyers could have asserted, "A witness is not required to aid his interrogator," but that does not project as much majesty as "The law" does not require.

In response to the Special Prosecutor's Referral, the President's lawyers sought to give a concrete meaning to the abstract noun "fundamental fairness":

> Spectacularly absent from the Referral is any discussion of contradictory or exculpatory evidence or any evidence that would cast doubt on the credibility of the testimony the OIC cites (but does not explicitly quote). This is a failure of fundamental fairness which is highly prejudicial to the President and it is reason alone to withhold judgment on the Referral's allegations until all the prosecutor's evidence can be scrutinized—and then challenged, as necessary, by evidence from the President.[22]

Before the Special Prosecutor's Referral was submitted to Congress, President Clinton's lawyers argued that the Constitution and "simple justice" have certain minimal "demands":

---

[20] CHICAGO TRIBUNE, Sept. 13, 1998, at 27.
[21] Id. at 36.
[22] Id. at 38.

For these reasons, the impeachment process must be painstaking and deliberate. It must focus only on such harms as the Framers intended to be redressed by the incomparably severe act of impeachment. And most importantly, it must be understood for what it is—a process of inquiry. That process is itself the exercise of a public trust "of delicacy and magnitude." Accordingly, if the process is begun it is only just that the members engaged in this solemn task withhold judgment until the process is complete and all the facts are known. Our Constitution's most basic values and the requirements of simple justice together demand no less.[23]

A plaintiff sued Shell Oil Company for injuries suffered in a vehicle collision.[24] The plaintiff's counsel, in closing argument to the jury, argued that the

> defendant was a corporation, had no soul, could neither go to heaven nor hell and that "the way that the law punishes a corporation for not paying their debts in a case like this, if you find that they owe actual damage, is to require them to pay a punitive damage."[25]

The Mississippi Supreme Court held that the closing argument, previously condemned,[26] together with other trial errors, required that the judgment for the defendant be reversed, and a new trial be held.[27]

Alabama, too, prohibits attorneys from arguing that corporations do not have certain body parts or spiritual accouterments. A plaintiff's lawyer argued to the jury: "A corporation, like I said is a legal entity . . . but it's not a human being. It has no conscience. The only way you can punish a corporation is through monetary damages."[28] (ellipses in original).

The Alabama Supreme Court compared the argument to one in an earlier case, in which the court found the following jury remarks to be "improper and highly prejudicial": "A corporation has no heart, it has no soul. It has got no fear of Hell and Damnation in the hereafter."[29]

The court reached the same conclusion as in the earlier case: the argument "was improper, highly prejudicial, and irrelevant to the issues . . ."[30]

---

[23]*Id.* at 33.
[24]Shell Oil Co. v. Pou, 204 So. 2d 155 (Miss. 1967).
[25]*Id.* at 157.
[26]Brush v. Laurendine, 150 So. 818 (1933).
[27]*Shell Oil, supra* at 157.
[28]Southern Life and Health Ins. v. Smith, 518 So. 2d 77, 80 (1987).
[29]*Id.*
[30]*Id.* at 81.

Under Admiralty Law, a ship is bestowed with human attributes, complete with gender:

> A ship is born when she is launched, and lives so long as her identity is preserved. Prior to her launching she is a mere congeries of wood and iron—an ordinary piece of personal property. . . . In the baptism of launching she receives her name, and from the moment her keel touches the water she is transformed, and becomes a subject of admiralty jurisdiction. She acquires a personality of her own; becomes competent to contract, and is individually liable for her obligations, upon which she may sue in the name of her owner, and be sued in her own name.
>
> . . . .
>
> She is capable, too, of committing a tort, and is responsible in damages therefor. She may also become quasi bankrupt; may be sold for the payment of her debts, and thereby receive a complete discharge from all prior liens, with liberty to begin a new life, contract further obligations, and perhaps be subjected to a second sale.[31] (ellipses added).

The Vessel as Offender

Admiralty law also treats the vessel as the offender, regardless of the culpability of the ship's owner, if the ship's mission was unlawful:

> The vessel which commits the aggression is treated as the offender, as the guilty instrument or thing to which the forfeiture attaches, without any reference whatsoever to the character or conduct of the owner. The vessel or boat (says the act of Congress) from which such piratical aggression, etc., shall have been first attempted or made shall be condemned. Nor is there any thing new in a provision of this sort. It is not an uncommon course in the admiralty, acting under the law of nations, to treat the vessel in which or by which, or by the master or crew thereof, a wrong or offence has been done as the offender, without any regard whatsoever to the personal misconduct or responsibility of the owner thereof. And this is done from the necessity of the case, as the only adequate means of familiarly applied to cases of smuggling and other misconduct under revenue laws; and has been applied to other kindred cases, such as cases arising on embargo and non-intercourse acts. In short, the acts of the master and crew, in cases of this sort, bind the interest of the owner to the ship, whether he be innocent or guilty; and he impliedly submits to whatever the

---

[31]Tucker v. Alexandroff, 183 U.S. 424, 438 (1902).

law denounces as a forfeiture attached to the ship by reason of their unlawful or wanton wrongs."[32] (parentheses in original).

The Car as Wrongdoer

The U.S. Supreme Court held that a car was a wrongdoer in *Bennis v. Michigan*,[33] and that Michigan could abate the vehicle as a public nuisance. The husband used the vehicle, without his wife's knowledge, to have a tryst with a prostitute. His wife argued that she should have been compensated for her interest in the car, and that Michigan's unwillingness to provide an innocent-owner defense denied her rights under the Due Process Clause of the Fourteenth Amendment or the Takings Clause of the Fifth Amendment. A 5-4 Supreme Court majority denied the wife's constitutional claims.

Chief Justice Rehnquist, writing for the majority, noted a long line of Supreme Court opinions, beginning in the 1800s, in which property was forfeited even though the owner did not know of the illicit use:

> Our earliest opinion to this effect is Justice Story's opinion for the Court in *The Palmyra*. The Palmyra, which had been commissioned as a privateer by the King of Spain and had attacked a United States vessel, was captured by a United States war ship and brought into Charleston, South Carolina, for adjudication ... On the Government's appeal from the Circuit Court's acquittal of the vessel, it was contended by the owner that the vessel could not be forfeited until he was convicted for the privateering. The Court rejected this contention, explaining: "The thing is here primarily considered the offender, or rather the offence is attached primarily to the thing."[34] (citations omitted).

Writing for the dissenters, Justice Stevens advanced several arguments why Michigan should not have been allowed to abate the car in this case. In one argument, he cautioned that the majority's ruling would expose owners of property to confiscation, for minor illegal acts of others (reductio ad absurdum):

> The logic of the Court's analysis would permit the States to exercise virtually unbridled power to confiscate vast amounts of property where professional criminals have engaged in illegal acts. Some air-

---

[32]Bennis v. Michigan, 516 U.S. 442, 461 n.5 (1996).
[33]*Id.*
[34]*Id.* at 446–47.

line passengers have marijuana cigarettes in their luggage; some hotel guests are thieves; some spectators at professional sports events carry concealed weapons; and some hitchhikers are prostitutes. The State surely may impose strict obligations on the owners of airlines, hotels, stadiums, and vehicles to exercise a high degree of care to prevent others from making illegal use of their property, but neither logic nor history supports the Court's apparent assumption that their complete innocence imposes no constitutional impediment to the seizure of their property simply because it provided the locus for a criminal transaction.[35]

Justice Stevens rejected the need for remedial relief and, implicitly, attacked the majority's hypostatization—that the car was the wrongdoer:

> The remedial rationale is even less convincing according to the State's "nuisance" theory, for that theory treats the car as a nuisance only so long as the illegal event is occurring and only so long as the car is located in the relevant neighborhood. The need to "abate" the car thus disappears the moment it leaves the area. In short, therefore, a remedial justification simply does not apply to a confiscation of this type . . .[36] (citations omitted).

As additional support for this argument, Justice Stevens wrote:

> In fact, the rather tenuous theory advanced by the Michigan Supreme Court to uphold this forfeiture was that the neighborhood where the offense occurred exhibited an ongoing "nuisance condition" because it had a reputation for illicit activity, and the car contributed to that "condition." On that view, the car did not constitute the nuisance of itself; only when considered as a part of the particular neighborhood did it assume that character. One bizarre consequence of this theory, expressly endorsed by the Michigan high court, is that the very same offense, committed in the very same car, would not render the car forfeitable if it were parked in a different part of Detroit, such as the affluent Palmer Woods area.[37] (citations omitted).

Next, he employed his own hypostatization, by giving a concrete meaning to the words "fundamental fairness": "Apart from the lack of a sufficient nexus between petitioner's car and the offense her husband committed, I would reverse because petitioner is entirely without

---

[35] *Id.* at 458–59.
[36] *Id.* at 465.
[37] *Id.* at 464 n.9.

responsibility for that act. Fundamental fairness prohibits the punishment of innocent people."[38]

The Michigan statutes in this case were drafted in terms of hypostatization, i.e., several classes of inanimate objects could be declared a nuisance under the Michigan statute authorizing abatement:

> Any building, vehicle, boat, aircraft, or place used for the purpose of lewdness, assignation or prostitution or gambling, or used by, or kept for the use of prostitutes or other disorderly persons, . . . is declared a nuisance, . . . and all . . . nuisances shall be enjoined and abated as provided in this act and as provided in the court rules.[39] (ellipses in original).
>
> . . . .
>
> Any vehicle, boat, or aircraft found by the court to be a nuisance within the meaning of this chapter is subject to the same order and judgment [abatement] as any furniture, fixtures and contents as herein provided.[40] (brackets and ellipses added).

---

[38] *Id.* at 466.
[39] *Id.* at 444 n.2, citing Mich. Comp. Laws Ann. § 600.3801.
[40] *Id.* at n.3, citing § 600.3825 (1987).

CHAPTER THIRTEEN

Appealing to Ignorance

"Of Course, absence of evidence is not always evidence of absence."

Machinists Lodge 964 v. B.F. Goodrich Aerospace, 387 F.3d 1046, 1055 (9th Cir. 2004).

"There are things we know that we know. There are known unknowns; that is to say there are things that we now know we don't know. But there are also unknown unknowns. There are things we do not know we don't know."

Former Secretary of Defense Donald Rumsfeld explaining that the "absence of evidence is not evidence of absence," at a press conference in June 2002, when the "Bush Administration started pushing hard for war with Iraq by focusing on fears of the unknown—terrorists and weapons of mass destruction . . ."[1]

THE THREE HALLMARKS of an appeal to ignorance (argumentum ad ignorantiam) are:

1. A lack of evidence to prove a particular assertion, allegation, or proposition;
2. A shifting of the burden to the opposing side to disprove the assertion, allegation, or proposition; and
3. A claim that the failure to respond to, provide evidence in support of, or declare proof of, the assertion, allegation, or proposition, therefore, proves it.

---

[1]NEWSWEEK, May 8, 2006, at 38.

In the courtroom, a suspicion that opposing counsel is appealing to ignorance should arise anytime the asserted burden is to disprove some fact or argument.

Burdens of Proof

Attorneys should have an easier time recognizing and responding to these arguments than laypersons, because as part of their legal training, attorneys learn about presumptions and burdens of proof. There are even rules of evidence that assign burdens of proof:

> Rule 301. Presumptions in General in Civil Actions and Proceedings.
>
> In all civil actions and proceedings not otherwise provided for by Act of Congress or by these rules, a presumption imposes on the party against whom it is directed the burden of going forward with evidence to rebut or meet the presumption, but does not shift to such party the burden of proof in the sense of the risk of non-persuasion, which remains throughout the trial upon the party on whom it was originally cast.[2]

The Federal Rules of Evidence also specify what must be done to demonstrate a lack of evidence, for example, in the case of public records:

> Rule 803(10). Absence of public record or entry.
>
> To prove the absence of a record, report, statement, or data compilation, in any form, or the nonoccurrence of nonexistence of a matter of which a record, report, statement, or data compilation, in any form, was regularly made and presented by a public office or agency, evidence in the form of a certification in accordance with rule 902,[3] or testimony, that diligent search failed to disclose the record, report, statement, or data compilation, or entry.

Notwithstanding any advantage attorneys may have over laypersons in determining who has what burden of proof, it does not mean the task is effortless or uncomplicated:

> In summary, there is no key principle governing the apportionment of the burdens of proof. Their allocation, either initially or ultimately, will depend upon the weight that is given to any one or more of sev-

---

[2]Federal Rule of Evidence 301.
[3]Federal Rule of Evidence 902 is titled "Self-authentication."

eral factors, including: (1) the natural tendency to place the burdens on the party desiring change, (2) special policy considerations such as those disfavoring certain defenses, (3) convenience, (4) fairness, and (5) the judicial estimate of the probabilities.[4]

Certain obvious defenses to an appeal to ignorance come readily to mind. In the courtroom, an attorney may rely on statutes, rules of procedure, or decisions to properly lay the burden of proof at the doorstep of the opposing side. Also, it is always important to ask whether the issue subject to the appeal to ignorance is relevant to the case. If not, no additional evidence is required.

Three examples raised in Chapter 1, from the Winona Ryder trial, demonstrate this point: "No video, no crime"; "DA must call every person working at Saks that day"; "If it is not in the first report, it didn't happen."

Each of these appeals seeks to have the prosecutor disprove some fact, but are these facts and issues relevant? Does it matter if Ryder's actions were not captured by surveillance cameras, if there is other proof to establish her guilt? Must every employee working that day be called to establish guilt, or is it sufficient if there is credible testimony from a few eyewitness employees? Might there be a good reason why the first report did not refer to the illegal behavior? In each instance, the defense would hope to argue that the prosecution failed to present evidence of guilt, but the prosecutor could point to strong, independent evidence, without having to respond to the defense arguments.

Can an attorney win a case merely by attacking the opposing side's witnesses, without calling any "friendly" witnesses? A Fifth Circuit decision describes three instances where the plaintiff's counsel directed the jury's attention to the respondent's failure to call witnesses from the national company:

> It bothers me and I hope it bothers you, that if what I presented to you in this case about the corporate negligence in security was not true, why didn't we . . . see someone from the national company come into this courtroom and try to explain their conduct.

> Immediately after the court sustained Kmart's objection and gave a curative instruction (that a defendant has no obligation to produce any witnesses), the Whiteheads' counsel returned to this tactic, in total defiance of the district court's ruling, until counsel was interrupted by the same objection. Before being interrupted, he stated: "We heard no one from the national corporation—the national cor-

---

[4]McCormick on Evidence, 952 (3rd ed. 1984).

poration come here and explain why——." The district court reminded the Whiteheads' counsel that it had sustained the objection and gave another curative instruction.

In his rebuttal closing argument, and notwithstanding the court's having earlier sustained Kmart's objections, the Whiteheads' counsel returned to this improper tactic:

> [Kmart's] whole ploy in this case was to come in and attack the plaintiffs' case, attack their witnesses, be critical of them and have a nice man from Jackson [Kmart's local loss prevention manager/corporate representative] and a nice, good, mild-mannered lawyer trying to make you think: Well, they are just real nice folks, and they just didn't do anything wrong.
>
> . . . .
>
> Shame on Kmart. *Shame on the corporation for not sending representatives here to testify about why they don't have a policy. Shame on them for having a local man sit here and take the fall. . . .* [5] (italics, ellipses, parentheses, and brackets in original).

Once again, the district court sustained the objection by Kmart. Petitioner's counsel sought to shift the burden to the respondent to produce witnesses in support of its defense, a tactic the Fifth Circuit disapproved of:

> In short, counsel twice violated the court's ruling on Kmart's objection. Counsel's continued improper references to Kmart using a local representative/witness served to do nothing but appeal to prejudice and passion. It goes without saying that such conduct and comments have no place in a federal court. Worse still, they prevent a fair trial.[6] (footnote omitted).

Nonappearing Witnesses

A related approach involves an attorney's appeal to the jury to believe that witnesses who did not appear would have provided supportive testimony. This puts opposing counsel in the position of having to disprove testimony never offered at the trial. A prosecutor closed his case with this argument:

---

[5] Whitehead v. Food Max of Ms., 163 F.3d 265, 277 (5th Cir. 1998).
[6] *Id.*

[D]efendant had a problem. There was too much irrefutable evidence. For example, you can't call 10 or 12 agents, surveilling agents, liars. It just doesn't work. You can maybe call one or two liars, but can't call 10 or 12. So being an intelligent man, defendant created a story . . .[7] (brackets and ellipses in original; citation omitted).

The Ninth Circuit explained why this appeal to ignorance was improper:

Unlike statements concerning the veracity of witnesses, this comment cannot be considered an inference based on the evidence. While it is true that Agent Reyes testified that several of the meetings leading to the transaction were under surveillance, the government only called three witnesses—Reyes, Alvaro, and Agent Leppla, the arresting officer. The prosecutor's assertion that there were as many as nine other law enforcement officials who would support their testimony is an improper reference to inculpatory evidence not produced at trial.[5]

---

[5] While it is true that the testimony of these ten other government witnesses would have concerned only what they saw while conducting surveillance, and therefore would not have corroborated the government's case on the contested issues in the case, the jury had no way of knowing that. So far as the jury was concerned, this statement indicated that these uncalled witnesses were prepared to testify to the same facts as Alvaro and Reyes. The impact of such an assertion in a case where the credibility of the witnesses is crucial has been noted by this Court.[8] (citation omitted).

In contrast to the argument above (implying that other, nontestifying witnesses would provide supportive testimony), a different prosecutor explicitly vouched (improperly) for witnesses who did not testify:

In closing argument, defense counsel criticized the state's investigation and questioned the lack of testimony from officers who were present at the crime scene. Defense counsel specifically emphasized that the arresting and searching police officers had not been called by the state.

The state responded to this defense tactic by arguing to the jury:

"Now the state could have called the police officers in this case but was it necessary? They were just going to come in here and reiterate to you—

---

[7] United States v. Molina, 934 F.2d 1440, 1446 (9th Cir. 1991).
[8] *Id.*

> [Objection.] What the police officers would have told you is exactly the same thing the witnesses would have told you. . . . There was no need to call them."[9] (brackets and ellipses in original).

A defendant argued that a prosecutor's remark during closing argument improperly shifted the burden to the defendant to come forth with evidence:

> Scott's second claim is that the prosecutor improperly shifted the burden of proof at trial. He points to the prosecutor's statement during closing arguments that "there's no evidence of heat of the moment, heat of passion, of some sudden unexplainable impulse." Scott argues that this statement improperly placed the burden on Scott to show some evidence of a factor that would reduce the crime from first degree murder, rather than leaving the burden with the prosecutor to prove the elements of premeditation and deliberate killing beyond a reasonable doubt. The district court concluded that this claim was barred by procedural default and, alternatively, lacked merit.[10]

The Sixth Circuit agreed the claim was barred, as no contemporaneous objection was raised, and the remark was not so severe as to require a new trial.[11]

The Iceberg Metaphor

Everyone recognizes that the majority of an iceberg's mass lies beneath the surface of the water, out of sight. Consequently, an iceberg can serve as an interesting metaphor for what is unknown. The next two examples illustrate proper and improper use of this metaphor.

In a case involving a violation of the Anti-Kickback Act, the prosecutor argued:

> I don't know; you know, the beer and the candy and the other stuff that was testified about here kind of *reminds me of an iceberg; Mr. Strayhorn (defendant's counsel) would lead you to believe it was just a little block of ice floating down, but to me it's just the tip of a big iceberg.* You know why I say that? It's hard for me to believe that Mr. Sinhel or anybody else could be influenced by this alone. . . . I don't believe that Sinhel could be bought for as little as we have been able to show that he received here. . . .[12] (ellipses, parentheses, and italics in original).

---

[9]Tillman v. State, 647 So. 2d 1015, 1015 (Fla.App.4 Dist. 1994).
[10]Scott v. Elo, 302 F.3d 598, 603 (6th Cir. 2002).
[11]*Id.* at 604.
[12]United States v. Grossman, 400 F.2d 951, 955–56 (4th Cir. 1968).

The Fourth Circuit concluded that the prosecutor's argument invited conviction on extra-record facts, and reversed the conviction based on this prejudicial argument:

> It is sufficient that the former provided the setting for implanting in the minds of the jury the notion that Sinhel had engaged in other related crimes and making that notion explicit with regard to defendant by the "tip of the iceberg" argument.
>
> In short, the prosecutor insinuated that Sinhel had been given many gifts and gratuities for an illegal purpose, probably from defendant, beyond those for which defendant was charged and beyond those for which proof was offered at the trial. The prejudice to a defendant of inviting conviction on facts—if they be such—dehors the record is counter to the basic concept of fairness.[13]

In the second case of an iceberg metaphor, the defendants advanced the identical argument: "that the use of the metaphor 'iceberg' to describe the criminal enterprise intimated that the evidence adduced at trial was only the 'tip' of the 'iceberg' or other unproven criminal activity."[14]

The Second Circuit disagreed with the defendants:

> The Use of the term "iceberg" was not improper. The government is not barred from using rhetorical devices during the trial. Here, the "iceberg" metaphor was used for the limited purpose of describing the structure of the loansharking operation: the "tip" of the "iceberg" being the business front, and the submerged segment, concealed from view, representing the rest of the enterprise. The use of the metaphor was not, as appellants contend, a reference to evidence of other crimes not adduced at trial.[15] (citations omitted).

A defendant challenged this statement in the prosecutor's closing argument: "the long road of the trial is almost done, in this phase anyway."[16]

According to the defendant, the prosecutor's remark "impermissibly communicated to the jury her belief that the penalty phase of the trial would occur because a guilty verdict was inevitable."[17] That view was not shared by the California Supreme Court:

---

[13]*Id.* at 956.
[14]United States v. Biasucci, 786 F.2d 504, 513 (2nd Cir. 1986).
[15]*Id.*
[16]People v. Frye, 959 P.2d 183, 226 (Cal. 1998).
[17]*Id.*

A prosecutor may not give a personal opinion or belief as to the defendant's guilt if it will suggest to the jury the prosecutor has information bearing on guilt that has not been disclosed at trial. However, a prosecutor is permitted to offer an opinion on the state of the evidence. This is precisely what occurred here. There was no misconduct.[18] (citations omitted).

The absence of evidence can be argued as either a failure to establish a proposition, or as evidence to prove the proposition. The Ninth Circuit, reviewing a California Supreme Court decision, considered the following statements by the prosecutor in closing argument:

> Another category or factor that you can consider and then give the appropriate weight to is . . . "Whether or not the offense was committed while the defendant was under the influence of extreme mental or emotional disturbance."
>
> I submit to you that there is absolutely no evidence Mr. McDowell was under the influence of extreme mental or emotional disturbance.
>
> It is People's contention that the fact that there was no influence of a strain, mental or emotional disturbance, is a factor in aggravation, and you should give it the proper weight.
>
> . . . .
>
> [With respect to factor (h)], [w]ell if Mr. McDowell was able to do it, what he did, . . . with no evidence of intoxication . . . then you know that it didn't exist.
>
> And I submit to you that this is a factor in aggravation because it tells you the degree to which Mr. McDowell planned out and foresaw and designed a scheme to meet his sexual urgings on May 20th, 1992.[19] (ellipses and brackets in original).

According to the Ninth Circuit, the appeal was improper, but it did not affect the outcome:

> The prosecutor properly could have argued that there was no evidence of mental impairment or intoxication and the jury could consider this lack of evidence. The prosecutor could not argue, however, that under California law this lack of evidence constituted a positive aggravating factor.

---

[18] *Id.* at 226–27.
[19] McDowell v. Calderon, 107 F.3d 1351, 1364 (9th Cir. 1997), *withdrawn* 173 F.3d 1186 (9th Cir. 1999).

APPEALING TO IGNORANCE 167

Nevertheless, in the present case, the California Supreme Court determined any error was harmless. We agree with the California Supreme Court: there is not a reasonable possibility that the argument affected the verdict.[20] (citations omitted).

Minuscule evidence in support of a party's position may be exploited by asserting there is, effectively, a lack of evidence to meet the burden. Justice Breyer employed this technique in *Ewing v. California*,[21] involving California's "three strikes" law:

> We also know that California, the United States, and other States supporting California in this case, despite every incentive to find someone else like Ewing who will have to serve, or who has actually served, a real prison term anywhere approaching that imposed upon Ewing, have come up with precisely three examples. The Govt. points to *Ex parte Howington*, where an Alabama court sentenced an offender with three prior burglary convictions and two prior grand theft convictions to "life" for the theft of a tractor-trailer. The Govt. also points to *State v. Heftel*, where a South Dakota court sentenced an offender with seven prior felony convictions to 50 years' imprisonment for theft. And the Govt. cites *Sims v. State*, where a Nevada court sentenced a defendant with three prior felony convictions (including armed robbery) and nine misdemeanor convictions to life without parole for the theft of a purse and wallet containing $476.[22] (parentheses in original; citations omitted).

Justice Scalia used the identical technique in *College Savings v. Fla. Prepaid Postsecondary Education*,[23] where he minimizes the only supporting case by labeling it "dicta":

> Unsurprisingly, petitioner points to no decision of this Court (or of any other court, for that matter) recognizing a property right in freedom from a competitor's false advertising about its own products. The closest petitioner comes is dicta in *International News Service v. Associated Press*, where the Court found equity jurisdiction over an unfair-competition claim because "[t]he rule that a court of equity concerns itself only in the protection of property rights treats any civil right of a pecuniary nature as a property right."[24] (parentheses and brackets in original; citations omitted).

---

[20] *Id.* at 1364–65.
[21] 538 U.S. 11 (2003).
[22] *Id.* at 46.
[23] 527 U.S. 666 (1999).
[24] *Id.* at 673.

In *Alden v. Maine*,[25] a 5-4 decision, the U.S. Supreme Court tackled the issue whether nonconsenting states could be subject to private suits for damages in state courts. The case arose when a group of probation officers sued the State of Maine in a Federal District Court, alleging a violation of the Fair Labor Standards Act. (While this action was pending, the Court decided *Seminole Tribe of Fla. v. Florida*,[26] which held that "Congress lacks power under Article 1 to abrogate the States' sovereign immunity from suits commenced or prosecuted in the federal courts.")[27]

The probation officers "then filed the same action in state court,"[28] and when their suit was rebuffed they turned to the U.S. Supreme Court. The Court held "[t]hat the powers delegated to Congress under Article I of the United States Constitution do not include the power to subject nonconsenting States to private suits for damages in state courts."[29] (brackets added).

Both the majority and minority discussed the scope of the Eleventh Amendment, with each side appealing to ignorance, and responding to the other's arguments.

Justice Kennedy, writing for the majority, argued that the dissent offered no evidence to support its argument:

> Although the sovereign immunity of the States derives at least in part from the common-law tradition, the structure and history of the Constitution make clear that the immunity exists today by constitutional design. The dissent has provided no persuasive evidence that the founding generation regarded the States' sovereign immunity as defeasible by federal statute. While the dissent implies this view was held by Madison and Marshall, nothing in the comments made by either individual at the ratification conventions states, or even implies, such an understanding.[30] (citation omitted).

Justice Kennedy also asserted that the lack of commentary by the founders resulted from a basic understanding that the existing principle would not be altered by the Constitution:

---

[25] 527 U.S. 706 (1999).
[26] 517 U.S. 44 (1996).
[27] *Alden, supra* at 712.
[28] *Id.*
[29] *Id.*
[30] *Id.* at 733.

We believe, however, that the founders' silence is best explained by the simple fact that no one, not even the Constitution's most ardent opponents, suggested the document might strip the States of the immunity. In light of the overriding concern regarding the States' war-time debts, together with the well known creativity, foresight, and vivid imagination of the Constitution's opponents, the silence is most instructive. It suggests the sovereign's right to assert immunity from suit in its own courts was a principle so well established that no one conceived it would be altered by the new Constitution.[31]

Writing for the dissent, Justice Souter answered this appeal to ignorance defense:

The Court says, "the founders' silence is best explained by the simple fact that no one, not even the Constitution's most ardent opponents, suggested the document might strip States of the immunity." In fact, a stalwart supporter of the Constitution, James Wilson, laid the groundwork for just such a view at the Pennsylvania Convention. For the most part, it is true, the surviving records of the ratifying conventions do not suggest that much thought was given to the issue of suit against States in their own courts. But this silence does not tell us that the Framers' generation thought the prerogative so well settled as to be an inherent right of States, and not a common-law creation. It says only that at the conventions, the issue was not on the participants' minds because the nature of sovereignty was not always explicitly addressed.[32] (citations omitted).

Justice Souter also responded to the majority's ignorance argument by arguing that there is, indeed, evidence to support the dissenters' position:

The Court says "there is no evidence that [the proposed amendments] were directed toward the question of sovereign immunity or that they reflect an understanding that the States would be subject to private suits without consent under Article III as drafted." No evidence, that is, except the proposed amendments themselves, which would have omitted the Citizen-State Diversity Clause. If the proposed omission is not evidence going to sovereign immunity to private suits, one wonders what would satisfy the Court.[33] (brackets in original; citation omitted).

---

[31] *Id.* at 741.
[32] *Id.* at 772 n.12.
[33] *Id.* at 780 n.20.

Responding in Kind

Another technique, employed by Justice Souter, is to respond in kind, i.e., lodge an appeal to ignorance claim against the other side (a tu quoque argument):

> On this account, the Framers of the Eleventh Amendment said nothing about sovereign immunity in state court because it never occurred to them that such immunity could be questioned; had they thought of this possibility, they would have considered it absurd that States immune in federal court could be subjected to suit in their own courts.[34]

Justice Scalia, dissenting in *Boy Scouts of America v. Dale*,[35] a case involving the revocation of an adult assistant scoutmaster's position upon learning he was "an avowed homosexual and gay rights activist," argues that there is no evidence the organization disapproves of homosexuality:

> The evidence before this Court makes it exceptionally clear that BSA has, at most, simply adopted an exclusionary membership policy and has no shared goal of disapproving of homosexuality. BSA's mission statement and federal charter say nothing on the matter; its official membership policy is silent; its Scout Oath and Law—and accompanying definitions—are devoid of any view on the topic; its guidance for Scouts and Scoutmasters on sexuality declare that such matters are "not construed to be Scouting's proper area," but are the province of a Scout's parents and pastor; and BSA's posture respecting religion tolerates a wide variety of views on the issue of homosexuality. Moreover, there is simply no evidence that BSA otherwise teaches anything in this area, or that it instructs Scouts on matters involving homosexuality in ways not conveyed in the Boy Scout or Scoutmaster Handbooks. In short, Boy Scouts of America is simply silent on homosexuality. There is no shared goal or collective effort to foster a belief about homosexuality at all—let alone one that is significantly burdened by admitting homosexuals.[36]

Justice Breyer, dissenting in *Bush v. Gore*,[37] similarly argued there was no evidence to support the majority's rationale in this case:

---

[34] *Id.* at 793 n.29.
[35] 530 U.S. 640 (2000).
[36] *Id.* at 684.
[37] 531 U.S. 98 (2000).

As far as the first issue is concerned, petitioners presented no evidence, to this Court or to any Florida court, that a manual recount of overvotes would identify additional legal votes. The same is true of the second, and, in addition, the majority's reasoning would seem to invalidate any state provision for a manual recount of individual counties in a statewide election.[38]

Harmelin v. Michigan[39] involved the scope of the Eighth Amendment's cruel and unusual language. Justice Scalia, author of the majority opinion, responds to Justice White's appeal to ignorance argument by asserting the burden lies with Justice White:

> Justice White apparently agrees that the Clause outlaws particular "modes" of punishment. He goes on to suggest, however, that because the Founders did not specifically *exclude* a proportionality component from words that "could reasonably be construed to include it," the Eighth Amendment *must* prohibit disproportionate punishments as well. Surely this is an extraordinary method for determining what restrictions upon democratic self-government the Constitution contains. It seems to us that our task is not merely to identify various meanings that the text "could reasonably" bear, and then impose the one that from a policy standpoint pleases us best. Rather, we are to strive as best we can to select from among the various "reasonable" possibilities *the most plausible* meaning. We do not bear the burden of "proving an affirmative decision against the proportionality component,"; rather, Justice White bears the burden of proving an affirmative decision in its favor. For if the Constitution does not affirmatively contain such a restriction, the matter of proportionality is left to state constitutions or to the democratic process.[40] (citations omitted).

Three Responses

The final examples raise three distinct responses to appeals to ignorance: *sui generis*, judicial discretion, and compliance with the law.

Judge Birch, in *Schiavo v. Schiavo*,[41] (involving the removal of Terry Schiavo's feeding tube) argued that there was a dearth of case support because the statute under consideration was unique:

---

[38] *Id.* at 145.
[39] 501 U.S. 957 (1991).
[40] *Id.* at 976–77 n.6.
[41] 404 F.3d 1270 (11th Cir. 2005) (Birch, J., specially concurring).

In his dissenting opinion, Judge Tjoflat questions why we have not cited any cases for the proposition that Congress cannot, in a statute, withdraw our ability to use the doctrines of abstention, exhaustion and waiver. As I have explained, the Act is unprecedented in nature, and therefore a lack of controlling case law is unremarkable.[42]

There would have been no need for a statute, argued Justice Souter, in *Jones v. United States*,[43] because judges exercised wide discretion:

> The fact that we point to no statutes of the earlier time exemplifying the distinction between elements and facts that elevate sentencing ranges is unsurprising, given the breadth of judicial discretion over fines and corporal punishment in less important, misdemeanor, cases.[44] (citations omitted).

To explain the lack of relevant First Amendment case law, Seventh Circuit Judge Richard Posner argued it was nothing more than a reflection of legal compliance:

> This is such an elementary violation of the First Amendment that the absence of a reported case with similar facts demonstrates nothing more than widespread compliance with well-recognized constitutional principles.
>
> . . . .
>
> "The easiest cases don't even arise."[45] (citations omitted; ellipses added).

---

[42]*Id.* at 1274 n.4.
[43]526 U.S. 227 (1999).
[44]*Id.* at 244.
[45]Eberhardt v. O'Malley, 17 F.3d 1023, 1028 (7th Cir. 1994).

CHAPTER FOURTEEN

Pity: Appealing to Sympathy

> *Sympathy for suffering and indignation at wrong are worthy sentiments, but they are not safe visitors in the courtroom, for they may blind the eyes of Justice. They may not enter the jury box, nor be heard on the witness stand, nor speak too loudly through the voice of counsel.*
>
> F.W. Woolworth Co. v. Wilson, 74 F.2d 439, 443 (5th Cir. 1934).

THE *ARGUMENTUM AD MISERICORDIAM* FALLACY appeals to our sense of sympathy or pity. Implicit within any appeal to sympathy is the question: "How would you feel if . . . ?" The ending to the question could take many forms: ". . . you were confined to a wheelchair for the rest of your life?"; ". . . *your* child had been walking along the sidewalk?"; ". . . you lost a loved one because the corporation didn't use proper safety devices?"

An appeal to sympathy in the courtroom must be guarded against to prevent an unjust outcome, based on this emotion, rather than the facts of the case. The following Federal Rule of Evidence may be invoked in response to many informal fallacies, but it is particularly useful whenever the appeal is to the jury's sympathies:

> Rule 403. Exclusion of Relevant Evidence on Grounds of Prejudice, Confusion, or Waste of Time.
>
> Although relevant, evidence may be excluded if its probative value is substantially outweighed by the danger of unfair prejudice . . .

A motion in limine may also be an appropriate defense to keep prejudicial evidence from reaching the jury.

If evidence is presented to the jury that has not been objected to, there is another avenue left to consider:

> In the event that evidence is introduced that is so unduly prejudicial that it renders the trial fundamentally unfair, the Due Process Clause of the Fourteenth Amendment provides a mechanism for relief.[1] (citation omitted).

Golden Rule Argument

One of the most common forms of the appeal to sympathy used by trial lawyers is the Golden Rule argument:

> The "golden rule" argument suggests to jurors that they place themselves in the position of a party or victim. The golden rule argument is impermissible because it tends to subvert the objectivity of the jury. It is seen as an attempt to dissuade the jurors from their duty to weigh the evidence and instead to view the case from the standpoint of a litigant or party. The rule is applied to criminal cases as well as civil cases.[2] (citations omitted).

Professor James W. McElhaney, writing about the Golden Rule argument, notes:

> The law only says that it is improper to *ask* the jury to put themselves in the shoes of one of the parties. It does not say they cannot do it on their own. And it does not say you cannot try your case so they instinctively stand in his shoes. It only says you cannot ask them to do it.[3] (italics in original).

Professor McElhaney suggests that an attorney can avoid an improper Golden Rule argument, while still creating an identification with the jury, by placing the jury "right in the center of the action"[4]:

> "Ladies and gentlemen, it is July 23, 1986. You are standing on the corner of 5th and Wells, in downtown Milwaukee. It is 2:30 in the afternoon. There, on the southeast corner, is an elderly gentleman with a cane, waiting for the light to turn green. Off to his left, a block away, a black and silver Chevrolet Corvette is approaching the intersection of 5th and Wells at a high rate of speed.

---

[1] Payne v. Tennessee, 501 U.S. 808, 825 (1991).
[2] King v. State, 877 S.W.2d 583, 586 (Ark. 1994).
[3] A.B.A. J. 106 (Dec. 1, 1987).
[4] *Id.*

PITY: APPEALING TO SYMPATHY

"You are about to see what will happen when those two forces—the man and the car—come together. Let me tell you about the man who is about to step off the curb . . . ."⁵ (ellipses added).

A plaintiff's counsel, appealing to the jury to award significant damages, declared:

> The incident took approximately two hours from when they were abducted to when they were released. And I calculated it, and that's 7,200 seconds. And I want for you to just for a couple of seconds to see—when I say start, that's ten seconds. Ten seconds.
>
> *And can you imagine how it would feel to have a knife in your side or a knife on your leg or a pistol at your neck for ten seconds?*⁶ (italics in original).

The Fifth Circuit concluded the argument was improper.

Finally, counsel engaged in an improper "Golden Rule" argument.

> This court has forbidden plaintiff's counsel to explicitly request a jury to place themselves in the plaintiff's position and do unto him as they would have him do unto them.

Such arguments encourage the jury to

> decide the case on the basis of personal interest and bias rather than on the evidence.
>
> . . . .
>
> Even assuming (counsel) was not explicitly invoking the Golden Rule, counsel was clearly inviting the members of the jury to put themselves in the place of the plaintiffs when deciding damages.⁷ (citations omitted; parentheses and ellipses added).

Additionally, the size of the damage awards was a signal to the circuit that counsel had exceeded the proper bounds of argument:

> Without deciding that the awards are excessive, we note that, at the very least, they are at the high end of the spectrum for such damages. This large verdict, when accompanied by counsel's improper arguments, further indicates that the jury was influenced by the prejudicial statements.⁸ (citation omitted).

On advice of counsel, a father delivered title of his car to his ex-wife, who neglected to register the car in her name. After the transfer,

---

⁵*Id.*
⁶Whitehead v. Food Max of Mississippi, Inc., 163 F.3d 265, 278 (5th Cir. 1999).
⁷*Id.*
⁸*Id.*

the son (who was living with his mother) got in an accident, and the father was sued for "negligent entrustment of (an) automobile" to his son.[9] Counsel for the father argued to the jury:

> Frank did what was reasonable under the situation, what his attorney had told him to do. And I think that sometimes it is helpful if you put yourself in the same shoes as the party that's doing something . . . Anyway, what would you have done in the same situation?[10] (ellipses in original).

The Idaho Appeals Court drew an important distinction when making a Golden Rule argument:

> We hold that the "golden rule" argument is only appropriate when used to ask the jury to assess the reasonableness of a party's actions by relying upon their own common sense and life experiences. The "golden rule" argument is never appropriate when used to influence the damage award. Our holding is in accord with the majority of courts which have decided this issue.[11]

Significant rights can be lost by failing to recognize a Golden Rule argument, and by not requesting appropriate relief. The attorney defending against a claim that his corporate client "negligently or wantonly" left an air compressor in the middle of the road, where the plaintiff drove into it, argued to the jury:

> I want you to consider the importance of that last statement. He didn't even see what he hit. What if a child, for example, was standing on the edge of the road, was on the blacktop that night near where that air compressor was? That child is not wearing reflective ribbon. That child is not fronted by a barricade on the front and back. That child doesn't have red barrels telling you you are about to come up on a construction site or a child playing site. What if that child had been standing on the blacktop, on the edge of the blacktop, even closer to the road than the shoulder, up on the blacktop? If that was your grandchild or your child—
>
> **[Plaintiff's Counsel]:** Objection.
>
> **THE COURT:** I sustain.
>
> **[Defense Counsel]:** If that was someone's grandchild or someone's child, that child today would have been struck by this vehicle and

---

[9] Lopez v. Langer, 761 P.2d 1225, 1230 (Idaho App. 1998).
[10] *Id.*
[11] *Id.*

PITY: APPEALING TO SYMPATHY

he never would have seen the child. And he's telling you that he did everything fine and he drove his vehicle correctly in order for you to give him money. Think about that.

I don't have a chance to talk to you again. The way it is structured, they get to open. I talk and now they will go up and talk again and I can't respond any more. But, as I said to you at the outset, I don't think this case is about money damages. I want you to look at the fault involved and listen to the law on negligence and contributory negligence because that has been the law here in Alabama for a long, long time, a hundred and sixty-two years, for people like yourselves who decide the issues and follow the law. And think about that child not even on the shoulder but standing on the blacktop—

[Plaintiff's Counsel]: I object to that. That is improper.

THE COURT: I will sustain.[12] (brackets in original).

The plaintiffs' counsel "did not request a curative instruction and did not move for a mistrial."[13] The plaintiffs argued that the reference to "your grandchild or your child" was a plea to put the jurors in the defendant's shoes. The Alabama Supreme Court affirmed the judgment in favor of the defendant, concluding that any prejudice that might have resulted from this remark was not so great that it could not have been remedied by a proper curative instruction.[14]

After the defendant's counsel argued that the jury should consider mitigating circumstances, the prosecutor explicitly appealed for sympathy—but for the victim, not the defendant:

> It may be suggested to you, well, be merciful, be merciful not because of any merit the defendant may present to you but because of the sort of people you are. Be merciful. Let mercy flow. Where does mercy belong? Where does mercy belong in these cases? The ancient Greek philosopher, Aristotle, once said, "Pity may be defined as a feeling of pain caused by the sight of some evil, destructive or painful event which benefits someone who does not deserve it." Who does not deserve it? Who did not deserve to die?
>
> Did Minh Linda Luong Rogers deserve to die? Did Linda Minh Rogers deserve to die?
>
> . . . .

---

[12] Walker v. Asbestos Abatement Servs., Inc., 639 So. 2d 513, 514 (Ala. 1994).
[13] *Id.*
[14] *Id.* at 515.

The defendant did what he wanted to do with the knowledge that these things were wrong, but now calls upon you not to do what I submit, you need to do, in the name of mercy.[15] (ellipses in original).

The North Carolina Supreme Court rejected the defendant's appeal:

> Defendant contends that by this argument the State directly linked important evidentiary facts offered by defendant in mitigation with sympathy, and it advised jurors that they should decide these cases by following the law without sympathy. We disagree with this characterization of the State's argument. The State did not tell the jury to reject sympathy arising from the evidence; to the contrary, it told the jury to be merciful but to consider where mercy belongs in these cases. Such an argument is within the scope of permissible arguments.[16]

Victim's Perspective

A related approach asks the jury to view the crime from the victim's perspective. During the penalty phase of the trial, the prosecutor observed:

> He didn't have to kill these people under any scenario you can conjure up. *Imagine the pain that they went through both physically and mentally.* Mr. Nail, knowing that his life is being snuffed out and worried about his wife in the other room, he doesn't know what happened, he never did know that she was murdered. And Mrs. Nail the same. Somebody strangling her from behind and she doesn't know what happened in the garage and she's dying and she knows she's dying but she doesn't even know what happened to her husband and will never know.[17] (italics in original).

This was a proper argument, concluded the Nevada Supreme Court:

> A "Golden Rule" argument asks the jury to place themselves in the shoes of the victims, and has repeatedly been declared to be prosecutorial misconduct. Here, the prosecutor asked the jury to imagine the final moments of the victims' lives, and we do not consider this a "Golden Rule" argument. Further, the prosecutor's remarks were reasonable inferences from the evidence presented.[18] (citations omitted).

---

[15]State v. Conner, 480 S.E.2d 626, 633 (N.C. 1997).
[16]*Id.*
[17]Williams v. State, 945 P.2d 438, 445 (Nev. 1996).
[18]*Id.*

PITY: APPEALING TO SYMPATHY

A year earlier, the Nevada Supreme Court considered the death sentence appeal of a defendant convicted of murder and attempted sexual assault. During the closing argument in the penalty phase, the prosecutor remarked:

> Do I make these statements to excite you or to remind you of the violence that encompasses the defendant? For a moment, we recreate that crime because this punishment has to fit that crime.
>
> But how aggravating is it to sit there and this man get in your car, the vehicle that you own, and begin to perpetrate these crimes on you?[19]

The defendant argued on appeal

> that the language cited above, along with the prosecutor's comment that anything less than the death penalty would be disrespectful to the dead and irresponsible to the living, amounts to an improper "Golden Rule" plea as well as a plea to the jury to return a death penalty verdict on behalf of the victim in this case.[20]

Disagreeing with the defendant, the court held:

> In commenting that anything less than the death sentence would be disrespectful to the dead, we conclude that the prosecutor was merely pointing out to the jury that our society values human life, and in order to respect the value of human life, one who takes a human life in the manner that (the defendant) did should have to pay for his crime with his own life. Furthermore, the prosecutor's statements painted a vivid picture for the jury, and any reference to "you" appears to be merely rhetorical. For these reasons, we conclude that the prosecutor's statements were proper.[21] (parentheses added).

Can a prosecutor go too far, for example, by assuming the role of the victim?

The prosecutor delivered most of his closing argument in the first-person voice of the deceased, Mr. Alameda. In the first sentence of his initial closing argument, the prosecutor announced to the jury that "I on behalf of Mr. Alameda have an opportunity to speak to you." Then, after explaining the nature of the circumstantial evidence, the prosecutor returned to the theme of speaking for Mr. Alameda. The argument rambled through aspects of Mr. Alameda's life, including his good works for the community's young people, his planned trip to visit his parents,

---

[19] Witter v. State, 921 P.2d 886, 899 (Nev. 1996).
[20] *Id.*
[21] *Id.* at 899–900.

his hopes to live to be 60 years old and to die from natural causes, and suggestions that he was a homosexual.[22]

The District of Columbia Court of Appeals then described the crime:

> In focusing on the murder, the prosecutor, still speaking as Mr. Alameda, described how he answered the door and let appellants into his apartment, how he felt when he was being stabbed, how he had not screamed because he could not believe it was happening to him, and how his throat was cut "as people often do in sacrifices."[23]

The narrative continued:

> The prosecutor told the jury, still as Mr. Alameda, that he was not angry at William Hawthorne but thought "it wasn't fair. I shouldn't have died that way." The argument graphically portrayed the brutality of the killing and highlighted Mr. Alameda's kindliness. The prosecutor told the jury that Mr. Alameda's eyes were open while he was being stabbed and that he had asked appellants why they were doing this to him, since he would have given them the things they had taken if they had asked. The prosecutor continually told the jury about what Mr. Alameda knew after he had died, and repeated that Mr. Alameda could not comprehend that William Hawthorne would do this to him since Mr. Alameda had taken him into his home.[24] (footnote omitted).

According to the court, the prosecutor exceeded the bounds of the permissible:

> In our view, the rhetorical device was ill-founded because it placed the prosecutor in the shoes of the victim and expressed the prosecutor's personal opinion about Mr. Alameda's thoughts, before and after his death, which were not, and as to the latter obviously could not be, evidence in the case.
>
> . . . .
>
> The first person singular rhetorical device had the dual effect of placing the prosecutor in the victim's shoes and turning the prosecutor into Mr. Alameda's personal representative. A prosecutor may no more represent the victim in this fashion than he may urge the jurors to place themselves in the victim's shoes. The prosecutor is also for-

---

[22]Hawthorne v. United States, 476 A.2d 164, 170 (D.C. App. 1984).
[23]*Id.*
[24]*Id.* at 170–71.

PITY: APPEALING TO SYMPATHY

bidden from appealing to the jury's emotions and sympathy for the victim of a crime.[25] (citations and footnotes omitted; ellipses added).

The court then overturned the conviction:

We hold appellants were substantially prejudiced by the prosecutor's use of the first-person rhetorical device which transformed him into the victim begging for the jury's sympathy. Accordingly, we reverse appellants' convictions and remand for a new trial.[26]

Instead of asking the jury to assume the roles of the parties to the proceeding, what if an attorney asks the jury to put themselves in the place of an eyewitness? During summation, a prosecutor remarked:

The statement concerned Mohan's ability to identify the driver of the oncoming Chevrolet where the distance between Mohan's car and the other car was approximately 3 to 4 feet and both cars were travelling in opposite directions between 30 and 35 miles per hour. The prosecutor said to the jury, "I'm not going to talk in terms of feet or seconds or milliseconds. I want you to put yourselves in the place that [Mohan] was in."[27] (brackets in original).

The First Circuit held that since defense counsel did not object to the remarks, the court could only conduct a review under the plain error standard.[28] The court then rejected the defendant's arguments:

Kirvan's brief relies primarily on cases that forbid so-called "golden rule" arguments in which plaintiffs or prosecutors ask the jury to put itself in the place of the victim. But "golden rule" cases do not apply where, as here, the jury is asked to put itself in the place of an *eyewitness*. In this situation, the invitation is not an improper appeal to the jury to base its decision on sympathy for the victim but rather a means of asking the jury to reconstruct the situation in order to decide whether a witness' testimony is plausible.[29] (italics in original; citation omitted).

A direct appeal to sympathy occurred during the Enron trial, when former CEO Kenneth Lay's defense counsel, Bruce Collins, urged the jury not to find Lay guilty. Collins created the image of a caged animal, certainly not an appropriate destiny for a former CEO of a large

---

[25] *Id.* at 171–72.
[26] *Id.* at 173.
[27] United States v. Kirvan, 997 F.2d 963, 964 (1st Cir. 1993).
[28] *Id.*
[29] *Id.*

corporation: "Today you decide whether Ken Lay will be locked up in a cage for the rest of his life. Today you decide if Ken Lay is a criminal."[30]

Victim Impact Statements

In 1987, the U.S. Supreme Court, in *Booth v. Maryland*,[31] by a 5 (Powell, Brennan, Marshall, Blackmun, and Stevens) to 4 (Rehnquist, White, O'Connor, and Scalia) majority, held that Maryland's statute permitting a victim impact statement to be introduced at the sentencing phase of a capital murder trial violated the Eighth Amendment. Two years later, another 5 (Brennan, White, Marshall, Blackmun, and Stevens) to 4 (Rehnquist, O'Connor, Kennedy, and Scalia) majority "extended the rule announced in *Booth* to statements made by a prosecutor to the sentencing jury regarding the personal qualities of the victim."[32]

Four years after its 1987 decision in *Booth*, the Court's composition had changed: Justices Powell and Brennan were replaced by Justices Kennedy and Souter. When the Court again confronted the issues raised by a victim impact statement, in *Payne v. Tennessee*,[33] a 6-3 majority overruled *Booth* and *Gathers*.

The facts in *Payne* were:

> Defendant was convicted of first degree murder in the killing of a 28-year old woman and her 2-year old daughter, and one count of assault with intent to commit murder in the first degree for the stabbing of her 3-year old son. The mother, who refused defendant's sexual advances, lived across the hall from the defendant's girlfriend. When the mother resisted the defendant's advances he became violent, and stabbed her with a butcher knife 41 times. Her daughter was also stabbed to death in the attack. Despite stab wounds that penetrated completely through his body, the 3-year old son survived.

During the sentencing phase of the trial, the prosecution called the 28-year-old's mother to the stand, and asked her how the murders of his mother and sister affected her grandson:

> He cries for his mom. He doesn't seem to understand why she doesn't come home. And he cries for his sister Lacie. He comes to me many times during the week and asks me, Grandmama, do you miss my

---

[30]"Enron's Defense Team Gives Jury Instructions," http://www.washingtonpost.com/wp-dyn/content/article/2006/05/16AR2006051600795.html (May 16, 2006).
[31]482 U.S 496 (1987).
[32]South Carolina v. Gathers, 490 U.S. 805 (1989).
[33]501 U.S. 808 (1991).

PITY: APPEALING TO SYMPATHY

Lacie. And I tell him yes. He says, I'm worried about my Lacie.[34] (citation omitted).

As part of his argument in favor of the death penalty, the prosecutor explicated the continuing impact of the grandson's experience:

> But we do know that Nicholas was alive. And Nicholas was in the same room. Nicholas was still conscious. His eyes were open. He responded to the paramedics. He was able to follow their directions. He was able to hold his intestines in as he was carried to the ambulance. So he knew what happened to his mother and baby sister.
>
> There is nothing you can do to ease the pain of any of the families involved in this case. There is nothing you can do to ease the pain of Bernice or Carl Payne, and that's a tragedy. There is nothing you can do basically to ease the pain of Mr. and Mrs. Zvolanek, and that's a tragedy. They will have to live with it the rest of their lives. There is obviously nothing you can do for Charisse and Lacie Jo (mother and daughter). But there is something that you can do for Nicholas.
>
> Somewhere down the road Nicholas is going to grow up, hopefully. He's going to want to know what happened. And he is going to know what happened to his baby sister and his mother. He is going to want to know what type of justice was done. He is going to want to know what happened. With your verdict, you will provide the answer.[35] (citations omitted; parentheses added).

After Payne's attorney offered his closing argument, the prosecutor argued in rebuttal:

> No one will ever know about Lacie Jo because she never had the chance to grow up. Her life was taken from her at the age of two years old. So, no there won't be a high school principal to talk about Lacie Jo Christopher, and there won't be anybody to take her to her high school prom. And there won't be anybody there—there won't be her mother there or Nicholas' mother there to kiss him at night. His mother will never kiss him good night or pat him as he goes off to bed, or hold him and sing him a lullaby.
>
> . . . .
>
> [Petitioner's attorney] wants you to think about a good reputation, people who love the defendant and things about him. He doesn't want you to think about the people who love Charisse Christopher, her mother and daddy who loved her. The people who loved little Lacie Jo, the grandparents who are still here. The brother who mourns for

---

[34] *Id.* at 814–15.
[35] *Id.* at 815.

her every single day and wants to know where his best little playmate is. He doesn't have anybody to watch cartoons with him, a little one. These are the things that go into why it is especially cruel, heinous, and atrocious, the burden that that child will carry forever.[36] (brackets in original; citation omitted).

The Supreme Court majority upheld the right to introduce victim impact evidence at the sentencing stage of a criminal trial, finding that the Eighth Amendment does not prohibit such evidence:

> We thus hold that if the State chooses to permit the admission of victim impact evidence and prosecutorial argument on that subject, the Eighth Amendment erects no *per se* bar. A State may legitimately conclude that evidence about the victim and about the impact of the murder on the victim's family is relevant to the jury's decision as to whether or not the death penalty should be imposed. There is no reason to treat such evidence differently than other relevant evidence is treated.[37]

Justice O'Connor, concurring with the majority, wrote that the grisly facts of the case impacted the jury more than the evidence from the grandmother:

> That line was not crossed in this case. The State called as a witness Mary Zvolanek, Nicholas' grandmother. Her testimony was brief. She explained that Nicholas cried for his mother and baby sister and could not understand why they did not come home. I do not doubt that the jurors were moved by this testimony—who would not have been? But surely this brief statement did not inflame their passions more than did the facts of the crime: Charisse Christopher was stabbed 41 times with a butcher knife and bled to death; her 2-year-old daughter Lacie was killed by repeated thrusts of that same knife; and 3-year-old Nicholas, despite stab wounds that penetrated completely through his body from front to back, survived—only to witness the brutal murders of his mother and baby sister. In light of the jury's unavoidable familiarity with the facts of Payne's vicious attack, I cannot conclude that the additional information provided by Mary Zvolanek's testimony deprived petitioner of due process.[38]

Dissenting, Justice Stevens lamented that the Court's decision was a sharp break with long-existing law:

---

[36] *Id.* at 816.
[37] *Id.* at 827.
[38] *Id.* at 831–32.

Our cases provide no support whatsoever for the majority's conclusion that the prosecutor may introduce evidence that sheds no light on the defendant's guilt or moral culpability, and thus serves no purpose other than to encourage jurors to decide in favor of death rather than life on the basis of their emotions rather than their reason.[39]

Justice Stevens found that victim impact evidence only appealed to the jury's sympathies, and he offered the example of a victim of questionable moral character to demonstrate the point:

Until today our capital punishment jurisprudence has required that any decision to impose the death penalty be based solely on evidence that tends to inform the jury about the character of the offense and the character of the defendant. Evidence that serves no purpose other than to appeal to the sympathies or emotions of the jurors has never been considered admissible. Thus, if a defendant, who had murdered a convenience store clerk in cold blood in the course of an armed robbery, offered evidence unknown to him at the time of the crime about the immoral character of his victim, all would recognize immediately that the evidence was irrelevant and inadmissible. Evenhanded justice requires that the same constraint be imposed on the advocate of the death penalty.[40]

Noncourtroom examples of appeals to sympathy can be found in President Clinton's memoranda in opposition to impeachment.

The President's lawyers sought to portray him as contrite and deserving of sympathy:

The President has acknowledged misleading his family, staff and the country about the nature of his relationship with Ms. Lewinsky, and he has apologized and asked for forgiveness. However, this personal failing does not constitute a criminal abuse of power.[41]

. . . .

On August 17, 1998, the President expressed regret to the grand jury and, later, to the country, that what began as a friendship came to include this conduct, and he took full responsibility. He has frequently, to different audiences, made similar expressions of regret and apology.[42] (ellipses added).

---

[39]*Id.* at 856.
[40]*Id.* at 856–57.
[41]CHICAGO TRIBUNE, Sept. 13, 1998, at 32.
[42]*Id.* at 33.

Casting the Special Prosecutor as an ogre, the President's lawyers sought sympathy for those who had to pay their own legal bills: "The OIC, however, refused to allow the White House lawyers to represent even the most junior, uninvolved witnesses. Thus all White House officials, from the most senior to the most junior, were required to obtain private counsel."[43]

President Clinton was depicted as the victim, pursued by a relentless adversary: "The President has admitted he had an improper relationship with Ms. Lewinsky. He has apologized. The wrongfulness of that relationship is not in dispute. And yet that relationship is the relentless focus of virtually every page of the OIC's Referral."[44]

And, as if his actions weren't bad enough, the President suffered the scorn of public humiliation: "In his grand jury testimony on August 17, 1998, the President acknowledged having had an improperly intimate relationship with Ms. Lewinsky. This is enormously difficult for any person to do even in private, much less in public."[45]

---

[43] *Id.* at 32.
[44] *Id.* at 40.
[45] *Id.* at 33.

CHAPTER FIFTEEN

Hurling Epithets

A popular epithet directed by some members of society, including some members of Congress, toward the judiciary involves the denunciation of "activist judges." Generally the definition of an "activist judge" is one who decides the outcome of a controversy before him according to personal conviction, even one sincerely held, as opposed to the dictates of the law as constrained by legal precedent and, ultimately, our constitution.

Schiavo v. Schiavo, 404 F.3d 1270, 1271 (11th Cir. 2005)
(Birch, J., specially concurring).

AN EPITHET IS A WORD or phrase that emotionally suggests a fact that is yet to be proven. Epithets (also known by such names as *ad lapidem*, "mud slinging, name calling, . . . loaded words, . . . controversial phrases, verbal suggestion, emotive language,"[1] question begging epithets,[2] loaded epithets, and colored words) concisely describe their intended target, often in unfavorable terms, often begging the question. Because epithets evoke strong emotions, they obscure the issues the parties are addressing, and they contribute nothing to understanding the facts. Frequently, epithets are aimed at people, as in the case of ad hominem attacks (abusive and circumstantial), but entities and concepts are also fair game.

A courtroom defense to an epithet may involve a First Amendment claim that a party is being punished for his or her speech. Another courtroom defense could involve an assertion that a party's due process rights were violated if the other side improperly used an epithet. Defending

---

[1] S. MORRIS ENGEL, WITH GOOD REASON: AN INTRODUCTION TO INFORMAL FALLACIES 165 (Bedford/St. Martins, 6th ed. 2000).
[2] *Id.*

against an epithet outside the courtroom is considerably more difficult, as there are few legal options except, perhaps, where libel or slander actions may be filed. Once an epithet has attached itself, the burden has shifted to disprove the accusations inherent in the epithet.

In the quotation above, the epithet "activist judges" evokes a negative reaction: those judges who do not follow the dictates of the law but, instead, inject their own beliefs into their decisions. It is a label customarily hurled by conservatives at judges (i.e., "liberal" judges) whose decisions do not comport with conservative views of the law. Ironically, in the *Schiavo* case, many of the judges who upheld the removal of Terry Schiavo's feeding tube were appointed by conservative presidents.

Types of Lies

In legal circles, a frequent epithet is the word "lie," or a derivative, such as "liar." Then, too, there are different types of lies, e.g., "bald-faced" lies, or "preposterous" lies, or "outright" lies. During closing arguments at the 2006 Enron trial "a prosecutor urged jurors to 'hold them (defendants Ken Lay and Jeff Skilling) accountable for the lies that they told.'"[3] Other epithets appeared in the prosecution's closing argument: "accounting tricks, hocus pocus, fiction, and outright lies."[4]

The Ninth Circuit has ruled on the proper and improper use of the word "lie":

> During opening and rebuttal arguments, the government used some derivative of the word "lie" to describe (the defendant's) story at least eight times. We have held, however, that it "is neither unusual nor improper for a prosecutor to voice doubt about the veracity of a defendant who has taken the stand." Prosecutors may "argue reasonable inferences based on the evidence," including, in a case turning on "which of two conflicting stories is true . . ., that one of the two sides is lying." There is thus no prejudice merely from using a derivative of the word "lie" in summation; to show misconduct, the defendant must establish that the prosecutor's use of the word "lie" was not founded upon a reasonable inference from the evidence.[5] (parentheses added; ellipses in original; citations omitted).

Certain epithets may be used as evidence of a defendant's motive:

---

[3]http://www.washingtonpost.com/wp-dyn/content/article/2006/5/16AR2006051600795.html (May 16, 2006).
[4]*Id.*
[5]U.S.A. v. Velarde-Gomez, 224 F.3d 1062, 1073 (9th Cir. 2000).

> The trial court did not abuse its discretion in refusing to exclude defendant's racial epithets. Contrary to defendant's conclusion, his use of the epithets was not irrelevant. Defendant used them to describe the victim specifically in two instances and to describe members of the victim's race generally in the third instance . . . Expressions of racial animus by a defendant towards the victim and the victim's race, like any other expression of enmity by an accused murderer towards the victim, is relevant evidence in a murder or murder conspiracy case. Among other things, it is evidence of the defendant's prior attitude toward the victim, a relevant factor in deciding whether the murder was deliberate and premeditated because it goes to the defendant's motive.[6] (ellipses added; citations omitted).

Both former House Majority Leader Tom DeLay and former President Clinton denounced the prosecutors investigating their actions. DeLay labeled the prosecutor a "rogue" district attorney, and charged the indictment was "reckless."[7] Additional epithets criticized the indictment: "baseless" indictments, "sham," "zealots," and "hollow" investigation.[8]

President Clinton's attorneys employed numerous variations of the epithet "overreaching" to characterize the Special Prosecutor's (Office of Independent Counsel's) Referral (epithets in bold added):

> The OIC's very allegation that the President committed perjury by re-explaining his belief and interpretation to the grand jury is yet another indication of the extent of the OIC's **overreaching**.[9]

> The document is at bottom **overreaching in an extravagant effort** to find a case where there is none.[10]

> The Referral quickly emerges as a portrait of biased recounting, skewed analysis, and **unconscionable overreaching**.[11]

> The OIC's claims are wrong and again, the product of **extraordinary overreaching** and pejorative conjecture—a transparent attempt to draw the most negative inference possible about lawful conduct.[12]

> Indeed, because of the Independent Counsel's **unorthodox overreaching**, Senator Hatch vowed to seek legislation to enact the type

---

[6] People v. Quartermain, 941 P.2d 788, 804–05 (Cal. 1997).
[7] NEW YORK TIMES, http://www.nytimes.com/2005/09/28/politics/28text-delay.html.
[8] Id.
[9] CHICAGO TRIBUNE, Sept. 13, 1998, at 38.
[10] Id.
[11] Id.
[12] Id. at 40.

of limited privilege asserted by the Secret Service in response to the Independent Counsel's sweeping actions.[13]

Again, the OIC has **wholly overreached** to make baseless allegations of criminal conduct.[14]

Instead, from press reports, if true, it appears that the OIC has **dangerously overreached** to describe in the most dramatic of terms conduct that not only is not criminal but is actually proper and lawful.[15]

Additionally, the President's lawyers wielded other epithets against the Special Prosecutor and his findings:

Oddly enough, the OIC finds abuse of power both in the assertion of the privilege and its withdrawal—surely evidence of an **overwrought imagination** or of **a conceit** that any legal position other than the OIC's is presumptively obstructive.[16]

The OIC has **wandered aimlessly** down more alleys and byways than any federal prosecutor would appropriately do.[17]

This means that the OIC report is left with nothing but the details of a private sexual relationship told in graphic details with the intent to embarrass. Given the **flimsy and unsubstantiated basis** for the accusations, there is a complete lack of any credible evidence to initiate an impeachment inquiry concerning the President.[18]

The "talking points" were the basis of **thinly veiled smears**, **groundless speculation**, and allegations against President Clinton, White House aides and others close to the president.[19]

Any charge the OIC might make that the President has abused the powers of this office through the assertion of privileges—privileges that were asserted at the initiation and recommendation of the Counsel's Office, not by the President himself—is **utterly baseless**.[20]

In its fifth allegation, the OIC contends that President Clinton obstructed justice by concealing gifts he had given to Ms. Lewinsky. This claim is **wholly unfounded** and **simply absurd**.[21]

---

[13] *Id.* at 35.
[14] *Id.* at 40.
[15] *Id.* at 32.
[16] *Id.* at 40.
[17] *Id.* at 35.
[18] *Id.* at 32.
[19] *Id.* at 34.
[20] *Id.* at 35.
[21] *Id.* at 39.

The Monica Lewinsky investigation is the most recent phase of an **amorphous, languorous, expensive,** and **seemingly interminable** investigation into the affairs of a small Arkansas real estate firm, Whitewater Development Company, Inc.[22]

Florida's Supreme Court was assailed by then-Governor George W. Bush in the aftermath of the 2000 presidential election when it ruled that the vote count could continue. In his brief seeking cert., the Governor referred to the Florida Supreme Court as having "embarked on an **ad hoc, standardless,** and **lawless** exercise of judicial power, which appears designed **to thwart** the will of the electorate" (epithets in bold added):

> Petitioner George W. Bush, the candidate of the Republican party for the office of President of the United States, respectfully prays that a writ of certiorari be issued to review the judgment of the Supreme Court of Florida in this case. In plain contravention of the requirements of the Constitution of the United States and federal law, the state supreme court has embarked on an ad hoc, standardless, and lawless exercise of judicial power, which appears designed to thwart the will of the electorate as well as the considered judgments of Florida's executive and legislative branches. Because the selection of presidential electors is governed directly by the Constitution and congressional enactments, as well as by state law, the court's decision involves issues of the utmost federal importance.[23]

Improper Epithets

May a prosecutor deprecate a defendant with epithets? The Supreme Court of California allows the use of epithets when they amount "to fair comment on the evidence, which can include reasonable inferences, or deductions to be drawn therefrom."[24] A California prosecutor referred, "in his closing argument, to the occupants of the van from which the fatal shots were fired as 'a pack of laughing hyenas.'"[25] On appeal, the court concluded this epithet was not improper: "the prosecutor's 'laughing hyenas' epithet does not seem beyond the pale, in light of evidence that the occupants of the van were laughing and joking about doing injury to the victim just prior to this death."[26] (ellipses added).

---

[22] *Id.* at 33.
[23] http://supreme.lp.findlaw.com/supreme_court/briefs/00-836/00-836.pet.aa.html (11-22-00).
[24] People v. Williams, 940 P.2d 710, 756 (Cal. 1997).
[25] *Id.* at 755.
[26] *Id.* at 756.

The court also considered, and rejected, a claim that the epithet had racial overtones:

> We find unpersuasive defendant's suggestion that the prosecutor's reference to "hyenas" appealed to jurors' "racial animus and biases" because the hyena, assertedly, is an African animal. A fundamental factual premise of the suggestion is mistaken; some species of hyena are native to India and other parts of southern Asia, as well as Africa. Moreover, we agree with the People the prosecutor's reference apparently was just to the popular understanding of hyenas, which includes the notion that they "laugh."[27] (citation omitted).

Additionally, the defendants argued that their counsel should have objected to the epithet:

> The epithet was not misconduct; hence, trial counsel was not ineffective for failing to object.[28]

In a Ninth Circuit case involving a conviction for first degree murder and rape, the defendant likewise claimed his counsel should have objected to the prosecutor's epithets in closing arguments:

> But to get up here and get on the stand and look at you people and tell you the story that he told you in front of the family, this piece of garbage, making up every little bit of it, he's the biggest liar you've ever encountered. He's worse than that. I'm not going to tell you. You can imagine some of the things I could tell you what he really is. I'm not going to tell you, because you know. You know in your hearts what else.[29]

The Ninth Circuit noted that the epithets did not refer to the defendant, personally, but even if they did, defense counsel was not ineffective in failing to object:

> Both the California Court of Appeal and the district court found that the "piece of garbage" reference, when read in context, referred to [defendant's] story, not to [defendant] himself. We see no reason to disagree. Furthermore, even assuming that 'piece of garbage' referred to [defendant], we would not conclude that trial counsel fell below the [ineffective assistance of counsel] standard by not objecting.[30] (brackets added; citations omitted).

---

[27]*Id.*
[28]*Id.*
[29]Dubria v. Smith, 224 F.3d 995, 1003 (9th Cir. 2000).
[30]*Id.* at 1004.

In another Ninth Circuit case, a defendant argued that the prosecutor "called him 'stupid' four times, and once referred to defense counsel's argument as 'trash.'"[31] The court declined to find any improprieties:

> Stupidity is among the least negative characteristics that might be attributed to (the defendant), and might even be claimed as a mitigating characteristic, as it often is in sentencing arguments. We cannot see how it could unfairly have prejudiced him. Calling an argument on his behalf "trash" cannot be characterized as improper. He did not say the man was "trash"; he said the argument was. A lawyer is entitled to characterize an argument with an epithet as well as a rebuttal.[32] (parentheses and citations omitted).

A defendant claimed the prosecutor committed misconduct by referring to him as "the monster that is sitting before us."[33] The trial court overruled the defendant's objection and, on appeal, the California Supreme Court held there was no basis for a new trial:

> A "prosecutor is allowed to make vigorous arguments and may even use such epithets as are warranted by the evidence, as long as these arguments are not inflammatory and principally aimed at arousing the passion or prejudice of the jury." In this case, even assuming that the reference to defendant as a "monster" exceeded the bounds of "vigorous yet fair argument", no prejudice is shown, in light of the record as a whole.[34] (citations omitted).

The defendant, convicted of mail fraud and money laundering, argued on appeal that

> ... his conviction was tainted by prosecutor misconduct in labeling him a "con man" in opening statement, and in asserting in closing argument that he "exhibits all the signs of a liar" and "is still making false representations to [the jury] today."[35] (brackets in original).

As no contemporaneous objection was lodged, the Eighth Circuit reviewed the case only for "plain error":

> The prosecutor's opening was limited to describing what the government would attempt to prove. The use of colorful pejoratives is not improper. Likewise, the prosecutor's closing was carefully limited to

---

[31]Williams v. Borg, 139 F.3d 737, 744 (9th Cir. 1998).
[32]Id. at 744–45.
[33]People v. Sanders, 905 P.2d 420, 447 (Cal. 1995).
[34]Id.
[35]United States v. Shoff, 151 F.3d 889, 893 (8th Cir. 1998).

arguing what the evidence had proved, rather than improperly expressing the prosecutor's personal opinion. There was no misconduct.[36] (citations omitted).

The appellation, "Dragon Lady," appeared in a Florida prosecutor's argument:

> The loquacious psychiatrist, who testified for the defendant, volunteered an irrelevant statement by his wife that the appellant reminded her of "a very sophisticated, highly-styled, fashionable Dragon Lady in ancient comics."
>
> In commenting upon that statement, the prosecutor argued: "Her own doctor, Dr. Stillman, typified her as the Dragon Lady, beautiful, cunning and evil. That's a Dragon Lady."[37]

Florida courts are not predisposed to prosecutors using epithets to describe defendants:

> The "typifications" of the appellant were not the testimony of the witness but rather were the prosecutor's own prejudicial characterizations. It is improper in the prosecution of persons charged with a crime for the representative of the state to apply offensive epithets to defendants or their witnesses, and to engage in vituperative characterizations of them. There is no reason, under any circumstances, at any time for a prosecuting attorney to be rude to a person on trial; it is a mark of incompetency to do so.[38] (citations omitted).

The Appeals Court reversed the conviction for grand larceny, based on these remarks, and other errors.[39]

Catalog of Offenses

Convicted of wire fraud, money laundering, and conspiracy, defendants claimed the prosecutor's epithets (a veritable catalog) denied them a fair trial:

> The defendants first allege that the prosecutor's opening statement was peppered with inflammatory jingles such as "scam," "Ponzi Scheme," "gibberish," "victim," "outlandish," "charlatan," "con," "deceit," "misrepresentation," "falsehoods," "fool's mission," "fictitious business entity," "store front office," and "front person." They acknowledge that each statement itself may have been harmless, but

---

[36] Id.
[37] Green v. State, 427 So. 2d 1036, 1038 (Fla. App. 3 Dist. 1983).
[38] Id.
[39] Id.

suggest that their cumulative effect crossed the line between permissible oratorical tactics and comments calculated to incite jury prejudice. They maintain that this prejudicial conduct persisted throughout the trial, including the prosecution's statements in closing argument. They suggest the prosecutors referred to the defendants as "crooks" or "evil" at least eleven times; used terms or phrases such as "con man," "charlatans," "trolling around for victims" "lie," "lies," or "lied" over 90 times; and also used words such as "Ponzi Scheme," "practicing their craft," "perfecting their craft," and "victim."[40]

According to the Ninth Circuit, the truth was an absolute defense, and the prosecutor's comments did not emulate the case name (*United States v. Rude*): "Viewed in their entirety and in the context of the month-long trial below, the government's choice of terms and phrases was not overly repetitious, and in fact reasonably described the practices of defendants."[41]

Defendants are not the only ones subject to epithets; judges are, too. Attorney Stephen Yagman was brought up on bar charges after submitting comments about a Federal District Court Judge to the Almanac of the Federal Judiciary. The relevant segment of the ad hominem (abusive) attacks in Yagman's letter to the Almanac reads:

> It is outrageous that the Judge wants his profile redone because he thinks it to be inaccurately harsh in portraying him in a poor light. It is an understatement to characterize the Judge as "the **worst judge** in the central district." It would be fairer to say that he is **ignorant, dishonest, ill-tempered**, and **a bully**, and probably is one of the **worst** judges in the United States. If television cameras ever were permitted in his courtroom, the other federal judges in the Country would be so embarrassed by this **buffoon** that they would run for cover. One might believe that some of the reasons for this **sub-standard human** is the recent **acrimonious** divorce through which he recently went, but talking to attorneys who knew him years ago indicates that, if anything, he has mellowed. One other comment: his girlfriend . . ., like the Judge, is a **right-wing fanatic**.[42] (bold added; ellipses in original).

The Ninth Circuit dismissed the charges, with the following analysis:

> When considered in context, however, Yagman's statement cannot reasonably be interpreted as accusing Judge . . . of criminal misconduct.

---

[40]United States V. Rude, 88 F.3d 1538, 1547–48 (9th Cir. 1996).
[41]*Id.*
[42]Standing Committee v. Yagman, 55 F.3d 1430, 1434 n.4 (9th Cir. 1995).

> The term "dishonest" was one in a string of colorful adjectives Yagman used to convey the low esteem in which he held Judge . . . . The other terms he used—"ignorant," "ill-tempered," "buffoon," "sub-standard human," "right-wing fanatic," "a bully," "one of the worst judges in the United States"—all speak to competence and temperament rather than corruption; together they convey nothing more substantive than Yagman's contempt for Judge . . . Viewed in context these "lusty and imaginative expression[s]" cannot reasonably be construed as suggesting that Judge . . . had committed specific illegal acts.[43] (Judge's name omitted; citations omitted; brackets in original).

Courts Under Criticism

Courts come in for their share of criticism, as when a prosecutor referred "to the Psychiatric Institute, which is a branch of the Circuit Court of Cook County, as the 'armpit' of the courts."[44] The Illinois court hearing the case deemed the epithet not worthy of comment: "Second, calling a branch of this State's courts an 'armpit' does not deserve comment."[45]

U.S. Supreme Court Justices frequently punctuate their decisions with epithets. Justices Blackmun and Kennedy disagreed as to the correct approach to deciding whether religious symbols are appropriately displayed on public property, in *Allegheny County v. Greater Pittsburgh ACLU*.[46] Justice Blackmun labeled Justice Kennedy's opinion as "unprincipled":

> Contrary to Justice Kennedy's assertion, the Court's decision in *Lynch* does not foreclose this conclusion. *Lynch* certainly is not "dispositive of [a] claim," regarding the government's display of a creche bearing an explicitly proselytizing sign (like "Let's all rejoice in Jesus Christ, the Redeemer of the world.") As much as Justice Kennedy tries, there is no hiding behind the fiction that *Lynch* decides the constitutionality of every possible government creche display. Once stripped of this fiction, Justice Kennedy's opinion transparently **lacks a principled basis**, consistent with our precedents, for asserting that the creche display here must be held constitutional.[47] (bold added; citations omitted).

---

[43]*Id.* at 1440.
[44]People v. Stack, 613 N.E.2d 1175, 1185 (Ill. App. 1 Dist. 1993).
[45]*Id.*
[46]492 U.S. 573 (1989).
[47]*Id.* at 609–10 n.57.

Justice Kennedy, in turn, criticized the majority for adopting a standard which produces a "bizarre result": "For the reasons expressed below, I submit that the endorsement test is flawed in its fundamentals and unworkable in practice. The uncritical adoption of this standard is every bit as troubling as the **bizarre result** it produces in the cases before us."[48] (bold added).

Among the more notable epithets employed by Justice Kennedy in criticizing the majority are: "obsessive, implacable resistance" and "Orwellian rewriting of history":

> The approach adopted by the majority contradicts important values embodied in the Clause. **Obsessive, implacable resistance** to all but the most carefully scripted and secularized forms of accommodation requires this Court to act as a censor, issuing national decrees as to what is orthodox and what is not. What is orthodox, in this context, means what is secular; the only Christmas the State can acknowledge is one in which references to religion have been held to a minimum. The Court thus lends its assistance to an **Orwellian rewriting of history** as many understand it. I can conceive of no judicial function more antithetical to the First Amendment.[49]

Dissenting in *Dickerson v. United States*,[50] where the Court considered the constitutional underpinnings of *Miranda*, Justice Scalia invoked the epithet "Orwellian":

> Those who understand the judicial process will appreciate that today's decision is not a reaffirmation of *Miranda*, but a **radical revision** of the most significant element of *Miranda* (as of all cases): the rationale that gives it a permanent place in our jurisprudence.
>
> . . . .
>
> Despite the Court's **Orwellian** assertion to the contrary, it is undeniable that later cases have "undermined [*Miranda's*] doctrinal underpinnings," denying constitutional violation and thus stripping the holding of its only constitutionally legitimate support. *Miranda's* critics and supporters alike have long made this point.[51] (parentheses in original; citations omitted; bold and ellipses added).

---

[48] *Id.* at 669.
[49] *Id.* at 676–78.
[50] 530 U.S. 428 (2000).
[51] *Id.* at 445, 461–62.

In *Hill v. Colorado*,[52] Justice Scalia dissented from the majority's holding that an eight-foot, no-communication perimeter around a health care facility is a permissible restriction on speech:

> None of these remarkable conclusions should come as a surprise. What is before us, after all, is a speech regulation directed against the opponents of abortion, and it therefore enjoys the benefit of the **"ad hoc nullification machine"** that the Court has set in motion to push aside whatever doctrines of constitutional law stand in the way of that highly favored practice. Having **deprived** abortion opponents of the **political right** to persuade the electorate that abortion should be restricted by law, the Court today continues and expands its **assault** upon their individual right to persuade women contemplating abortion that what they are doing is wrong. Because, like the rest of our abortion jurisprudence, today's decision is in stark contradiction of the constitutional principles we apply in all other contexts, I dissent.[53] (bold added; citation omitted).

Justice Blackmun's use of epithets in *Webster v. Reproductive Health Services*[54] comes to the fore in this excerpt from his dissent:

> At the outset, I note that in its **haste** to limit abortion rights, the plurality compounds the errors of its analysis by **needlessly reaching out** to address constitutional questions that are not actually presented. The conflict between 188.029 and *Roe*'s trimester framework, which purportedly drives the plurality to reconsider our past decisions, is a **contrived conflict**: the product of an **aggressive misreading** of the viability-testing requirement and a **needlessly wooden application** of the *Roe* framework.[55] (bold added).

"Vandalizing" is the epithet Justice Scalia employed in his dissent in *J.E.B. v. United States*:[56]

> In order, it seems to me, not to eliminate any real denial of equal protection, but simply to pay conspicuous obeisance to the equality of the sexes, the Court imperils a practice that has been considered an essential part of fair jury trial since the dawn of the common law. The Constitution of the United States neither requires nor permits this **vandalizing** of our people's traditions.[57] (bold added).

---

[52] 530 U.S. 703 (2000).
[53] *Id.* at 741–42.
[54] 492 U.S. 490 (1989).
[55] *Id.* at 542.
[56] 511 U.S. 127 (1994).
[57] *Id.* at 163.

In *Alden v. Maine*,[58] Justice Souter's dissent offers a defense to an epithet: appeal to authority—in this case, George Washington.

> Finally, the Court calls Wilson's view "a **radical nationalist vision** of the constitutional design," apparently in an attempt to discount it. But while Wilson's view of sovereignty was indeed radical in its deviation from older conceptions, this hardly distanced him from the American mainstream, and in October 1787, Washington himself called Wilson "as able, candid, & honest a member as any in Convention."[59] (citations omitted; bold added).

Unwarranted Hyperbole

Another defense to an epithet is to label it "unwarranted hyperbole," as Chief Justice Burger, dissenting, wrote in *Furman v. Georgia*,[60] the case reinstating the death penalty:

> Counsel for petitioners rely on a different body of empirical evidence. They argue, in effect, that the number of cases in which the death penalty is imposed, as compared with the number of cases in which it is statutorily available, reflects a general revulsion toward the penalty that would lead to its repeal if only it were more generally and widely enforced. It cannot be gainsaid that by the choice of juries—and sometimes judges—the death penalty is imposed in far fewer than half the cases in which it is available. To go further and characterize the rate of imposition as "**freakishly rare**," as petitioners insist, is **unwarranted hyperbole**. And regardless of its characterization, the rate of imposition does not impel the conclusion that capital punishment is now regarded as intolerably cruel or uncivilized.[61] (footnotes omitted; bold added).

---

[58] 527 U.S. 706 (1999).
[59] *Id.* at 776 n.16.
[60] 408 U.S. 238 (1972).
[61] *Id.* at 386–87.

CHAPTER SIXTEEN

Humor and Ridicule

Judge: Are you trying to show contempt for the court?
Flower Belle Lee: No, I'm doing my best to hide it.

W. C. Fields and Mae West in the film *My Little Chickadee*[1]

HUMOR AND ITS CAUSTIC COUSIN—ridicule—swiftly deliver their messages without explicitly presenting all the facts. A kernel of truth can be found in the message, but it is usually submerged in the levity or sarcasm. Humor and ridicule are often targeted at an individual's character—ad hominem (abusive); epithets frequently convey that humor and ridicule. Little can be done, inside or outside the courtroom, to respond to successful humor or ridicule, as the audience (judge or jury, for example) will likely consider the humor or ridicule as having trumped any factual claim or argument. A quick reply with a counter example of humor or ridicule is the best response, but quick-wittedness at critical moments is a hit-or-miss proposition.

Self-deprecating humor can effectively diffuse a tense situation, by diverting attention from the causes of that tension to the advocate. Former U.S. House of Representatives Majority Leader Tom DeLay, on September 28, 2005, began his response to the indictment handed down that day with self-deprecating humor:

DeLay: How are you doing? You got any news today?
QUESTION: A little.

---

[1] LAWYER'S WIT AND WISDOM, 153 (Bruce Nash and Allan Zullo eds., 1995).

(LAUGHTER)

DeLay: Just another day at the office.[2]

DeLay assuredly knew that his indictment was front and center in the news that day, yet he broke the ice by asking if the media reporters had heard any news.

One of the most devastating and effective uses of sarcasm occurred during President Clinton's first term. He nominated a little-known law professor from the University of Pennsylvania to head the Justice Department's Civil Rights Division.[3] The professor had been friends of the Clintons' since the 1970s, when they all attended Yale Law School.[4] Her nomination was destined never to reach the Senate floor. In substantial part, Lani Guinier's nomination was the victim of a Republican effort to portray her as favoring the "segregati[on] of black voters into black-majority districts."[5] An appellation suggestive of her views on segregation conveyed the sarcastic message:

> Another media tactic against Guinier was to dub her a "quota queen," a phrase first used in a *Wall Street Journal* op-ed (4/30/93) by Clint Bolick, a Reagan-era Justice Department official. The racially loaded term combines the "welfare queen" stereotype with the dreaded "quota," a buzzword that almost killed the 1991 Civil Rights Act.[6] (parentheses in original).

Once the "quota queen" title was affixed to Guinier, the President withdrew her nomination, without a Senate fight.

Although the humor/ridicule cannot be tied to the result as easily as in Guinier's case, an example by Sen. John McCain (R-AZ) qualifies for honorable mention. During the debate on an energy bill, late in the 2003 congressional session, Sen. McCain took to the floor of the Senate to decry the legislation as the "hooters and polluters" bill. The "polluters" reference is, "an allusion to the bill's rollback of environmental law.[7] The reference to "Hooters" is described on Sen. McCain's website:

> There are also four proposals known as green bonds that will cost taxpayers $227 million to finance approximately $2 billion in private

---

[2]NEW YORK TIMES, http://www.nytimes.com/2005/09/28/politics/28text-delay.html (9/28/05).
[3]NEWSWEEK, June 14, 1993, at 26.
[4]*Id.* at 27.
[5]http://www.fair.org/extra/best-of-extra/guinier-queen.htm (July 4, 2007).
[6]*Id.*
[7]WASHINGTON POST, Nov. 23, 2003, at B.06.

bonds. One of my favorite green bond proposals is a $150 million riverfront area in Shreveport, LA. This riverwalk has about 50 stores, a movie theater, and a bowling alley. One of the new tenants in the Louisiana riverwalk is a Hooters restaurant. Yes, my friends, an Energy bill subsidizing Hooters and polluters, probably giving new meaning to the phrase "budget busters." Although I am sure there is a great deal of energy expended at Hooters, I have never been present. Perhaps something has been missing in my life.[8]

Whether a judge's instruction to the jury to disregard certain evidence is effective is the subject of continuing debate. The Fifth Circuit used an analogy to describe the impact of a judge's cautionary instructions:

> Furthermore, the cleansing effect of the cautionary instructions in this case is dubious for, as the trial judge himself observed during the trial, "(y)ou can throw a skunk into the jury box and instruct the jurors not to smell it, but it doesn't do any good." Stated another way, the bench and bar are both aware that cautionary instructions are effective only up to a certain point. There must be a line drawn in any trial where, after repeated exposure of a jury to prejudicial information, a judge realizes that cautionary instructions will have little, if any, effect in eliminating the prejudicial harm. It is at this point that a motion for a mistrial should be granted.[9] (parentheses in original).

The prosecutor's disparagement of defense counsel, in a sexual assault case, produced a droll—even a slightly risqué—exchange:

> During the course of trial Oakes repeatedly made disparaging and uncalled-for remarks pertaining to defense counsel's ability to carry out the required functions of an attorney. For example, during Oakes's direct examination of the victim, Oakes asked her if appellant had an erection at the time of the assault. The witness answered, "I guess he did." Defense counsel then objected and moved to strike the answer, apparently on the ground the "guess" constituted speculation. In response to defense counsel's seemingly legitimate objection, Oakes then said: "How do you strike an erection?"[10]

A defendant, accused of embezzling and obtaining money under false pretenses, alleged the prosecutor impermissibly disparaged his case: "Mr. Lane (prosecutor) argued twice during final argument that if the jury believed the defendants' testimony or defense theory, then he

---

[8]http://mccain.senate.gov/press_office/view_article (July 13, 2007).
[9]O'Rear v. Fruehauf Corp., 554 F.2d 1304, 1309 (5th Cir. 1977).
[10]McGuire v. State, 677 P.2d 1060, 1063–64 (Nev. 1984).

had 'some ocean front property in Tonopah' that he wanted to sell."[11] (parentheses added).

Although the Nevada Supreme Court concluded that the disparagement was not a basis for reversing the conviction, the court noted that the prosecutor's remarks were improper: "Mr. Lane's statements were also a violation of a district attorney's duty not to ridicule or belittle the defendant or his case."[12]

Exceeding Boundaries

A different approach to disparagement is taken in California. On appeal, a defendant argued that the prosecutor's attack on his (defense) expert exceeded permissible boundaries:

> Defendant complains of the prosecutor's vigorous attack on the testimony of the defense expert, Dr. Globus, who opined that defendant suffered from organic brain damage. Among other things, the prosecutor accused Dr. Globus of misapplying the results of brain scans performed on defendant. In this regard, the prosecutor suggested that Dr. Globus's job was "to save [defendant's] life, now. He's part of a forensic team." The prosecutor claimed he "[did] not fault the defense team for doing anything to save their client's life." However, he asked, "Where's the beef, Doctor? Where's the evidence of it? See, it doesn't exist. It's not in his tests. All the possibilities in the world could happen, but they didn't. No. Doctor Globus, go some place else and sell your tonic water to another forum."[13] (brackets in original).

The court explained that ridicule of a party's expert is not improper per se:

> [C]ounsel may mount colorful attacks on the credibility of opposing lay and expert witnesses.

> Such an attack is not improper simply because it includes epithets intended to ridicule the witness's testimony. Thus, where counsel claims that an expert's conclusions are illogical, he may illustrate the point by describing them in such derisive terms as "tonic water." Nor is counsel prohibited from mentioning the witness's possible bias or interest supported by the evidence. Accordingly, it is not wrong to argue that an expert's conclusions are so implausible as to suggest a lack of impartiality. And counsel is not precluded from reminding the

---

[11]Barron v. State, 783 P.2d 444, 452 (Nev. 1989).
[12]*Id.*
[13]People v. Arias, 51 Cal. Rptr. 770, 828 (Cal. 1996).

jurors that the expert's findings support the goals of the party who called him, and may therefore not be objective.[14] (citation omitted).

In a case arising in the Fifth Circuit, the prosecutor used a common expression to belittle the defense.

During the second day of trial, defense counsel objected repeatedly to the testimony of Officer Rob Maddalozzo. In response to these objections Assistant U.S. Attorney Constantine Georges argued to the trial court in this manner:

> Your Honor, the issue is very simple and Mr. Ashley wants to make a mountain out of a molehill. The issue is very simple.[15]

The prosecution's remarks were weighed under the court's test for reversible error:

> Randall asserts that the prosecutorial comment was highly prejudicial because it told the jury that Randall's defense was insignificant and unimportant. Even if we were to find that these comments constituted error, under the test set forth by this court, they do not constitute reversible error. First, the prejudicial effect of such a comment was trivial; second, the two cautionary instructions would easily cure any remaining prejudicial effect; and third, the evidence of Randall's guilt was overwhelming.[16] (citation omitted).

During the 2006 Enron trial, the prosecution ridiculed the defense with epithets.

The prosecution also sought to disarm the defense by mocking its central arguments, including the theory that Enron collapsed during a market panic fueled by skeptical news reports and investors called short sellers, who bet that a company's stock price will drop. Calling the defense rhetoric a "diversionary tactic," Ruemmler said: "It's absurd. It's ridiculous. Don't buy it."[17]

Ridicule is not confined to the lower courts. Quite frequently, the Justices on the U.S. Supreme Court express their written displeasure with their colleagues. In *Allegheny County v. Greater Pittsburgh ACLU*,[18] Justice Blackmun, writing for the majority, employed a mathematical analysis to ridicule Justice Kennedy's test for unconstitutional religious preference:

---

[14] *Id.*
[15] United States v. Randall, 887 F.2d 1262, 1269 (5th Cir. 1989).
[16] *Id.*
[17] http://www.washingtonpost.com/wp-dyn/content/article/2006/5/16/AR2006051600795.html.
[18] 492 U.S. 573 (1989).

If one wished to be "uncharitable" to Justice Kennedy, one could say that his methodology requires counting the number of days during which the government displays Christian symbols and subtracting from this the number of days during which non-Christian symbols are displayed, divided by the number of different non-Christian religions represented in these displays, and then somehow factoring into this equation the prominence of the display's location and the degree to which each symbol possesses an inherently proselytizing quality. Justice Kennedy, of course, could defend his position by pointing to the inevitably fact-specific nature of the question whether a particular governmental practice signals the government's unconstitutional preference for a specific religious faith.[19] (citation omitted).

Justice Brennan, who concurred in part and dissented in part, disassembled the words, "Christmas tree," to make his point:

> Thus, while acknowledging the religious origins of the Christmas tree, Justices Blackmun and O'Connor dismiss their significance. In my view, this attempt to take the "Christmas" out of the Christmas tree is unconvincing. That the tree may, without controversy, be deemed a secular symbol if found alone does not mean that it will be so seen when combined with other symbols or objects. Indeed, Justice Blackmun admits that "the tree is capable of taking on a religious significance if it is decorated with religious symbols."[20] (citations omitted).

He also used an analogy to describe Justice Blackmun's Establishment Clause analysis:

> I would not, however, presume to say that my interpretation of the tree's significance is the "correct" one, or the one shared by most visitors to the City-County Building. I do not know how we can decide whether it was the tree that stripped the religious connotations from the menorah, or the menorah that laid bare the religious origins of the tree. Both are reasonable interpretations of the scene the city presented, and thus both, I think, should satisfy Justice Blackmun's requirement that the display "be judged according to the standard of a 'reasonable observer.'" I shudder to think that the only "reasonable observer" is one who shares the particular views on perspective, spacing, and accent expressed in Justice Blackmun's opinion, thus making analysis under the Establishment Clause look more like an exam in Art 101 than an inquiry into constitutional law.[21] (citations omitted).

---

[19] *Id.* at 607–08.
[20] *Id.* at 639.
[21] *Id.* at 642–43.

Allegheny County involved the placement of a menorah and a Christmas tree on county property and whether the two symbols represented state sponsorship of religion. Justice Brennan's analysis included the juxtaposition of other symbols:

> If it is not religious pluralism that the display signifies, then I do not know what kind of "pluralism" Justice O'Connor has in mind. Perhaps she means the cultural pluralism that results from recognition of many different holidays, religious and nonreligious. In that case, however, the display of a menorah next to a giant firecracker, symbolic of the Fourth of July, would seem to be equally representative of this pluralism, yet I do not sense that this display would pass muster under Justice O'Connor's view. If, instead, Justice O'Connor means to approve the pluralistic message associated with a symbolic display that may stand for either the secular or religious aspects of a given holiday, then this view would logically entail the conclusion that the display of a Latin cross next to an Easter bunny in the springtime would be valid under the Establishment Clause; again, however, I sense that such a conclusion would not comport with Justice O'Connor's views. The final possibility, and the one that seems most consonant with the views outlined in her opinion, is that the pluralism that Justice O'Connor perceives in Pittsburgh's display arises from the recognition that there are many different ways to celebrate "the winter holiday season." But winter is "the holiday season" to Christians, not to Jews, and the implicit message that it, rather than autumn, is the time for pluralism sends an impermissible signal that only holidays stemming from Christianity, not those arising from other religions, favorably dispose the government towards "pluralism."[22] (citations omitted).

"Happy Speech"

Justice Scalia, dissenting in *Hill v. Colorado*,[23] ridiculed the majority's content-based First Amendment analysis by proposing a "happy speech" limitation:

> Imagine, for instance, special place-and-manner restrictions on all speech except that which "conveys a sense of contentment or happiness." This "happy speech" limitation would not be "viewpoint-based"—citizens would be able to express their joy in equal measure at either the rise or fall of the NASDAQ, at either the success or the failure of the Republican Party—and would not discriminate on the basis of subject matter, since gratification could be expressed

---

[22] *Id.* at 640 n.*.
[23] 530 U.S. 703 (2000).

about anything at all. Or consider a law restricting the writing or recitation of poetry—neither viewpoint-based nor limited to any particular subject matter. Surely this Court would consider such regulations to be "content-based" and deserving of the most exacting scrutiny.[24] (footnote omitted).

Also, in his dissent, Justice Scalia commented on the disagreement between the State of Colorado and the Court, and suggested a mock funeral for the judicial doctrine of narrow tailoring in the context of the First Amendment:

> This requires us to determine, first, what is the significant interest the State seeks to advance? Here there appears to be a bit of a disagreement between the State of Colorado (which should know) and the Court (which is eager to speculate).
>
> . . . .
>
> I scarcely know how to respond to such an unabashed repudiation of our First Amendment doctrine. Prophylaxis is the antithesis of narrow tailoring, as the previously quoted passage from *Button* makes clear ("Broad prophylactic rules in the area of free expression are suspect. . . . Precision of regulation must be the touchstone in an area so closely touching our most precious freedoms." If the Court were going to make this concession, it could simply have dispensed with its earlier (unpersuasive) attempt to show that the statute was narrowly tailored. So one can add to the casualties of our whatever-it-takes proabortion jurisprudence the First Amendment doctrine of narrow tailoring and overbreadth. R. I. P.[25] (parentheses and ellipses in original; citations omitted).

In *Atkins v. Virginia*,[26] a case where the murder defendant was mentally retarded, Justice Scalia dissented, and suggested that a prize be awarded:

> But the Prize for the Court's Most Feeble Effort to fabricate "national consensus" must go to its appeal (deservedly relegated to a footnote) to the views of assorted professional and religious organizations, members of the so-called "world community," and respondents to opinion polls. I agree with the Chief Justice, (dissenting opinion), that the views of professional and religious organizations and the results

---

[24]*Id.* at 743.
[25]*Id.* at 749, 762.
[26]536 U.S. 304 (2002).

of opinion polls are irrelevant. Equally irrelevant are the practices of the world community, whose notions of justice are (thankfully) not always those of our people. We must never forget that it is a Constitution for the United States of America that we are expounding. . . . [W]here there is not first a settled consensus among our own people, the views of other nations, however enlightened the Justices of this Court may think them to be, cannot be imposed upon Americans through the Constitution.[27] (brackets, parentheses, and ellipses in original; citations omitted).

Combining an appeal to authority, with begging the question, Justice Scalia ridiculed the majority opinion in *Rogers v. Tennessee*:[28]

Today's opinion produces, moreover, a curious constitution that only a judge could love. One in which (by virtue of the *Ex Post Facto* Clause) the elected representatives of all the people cannot retroactively make murder what was not murder when the act was committed; but in which unelected judges can do precisely that. One in which the predictability of parliamentary lawmaking cannot validate the retroactive creation of crimes, but the predictability of judicial lawmaking can do so. I do not believe this is the system that the Framers envisioned—or, for that matter, that any reasonable person would imagine.[29] (parentheses in original).

Justice Ginsburg, dissenting in *Muscarello v. United States*,[30] humorously cited films and television productions in support of her argument about the meaning of the word "carry":

Popular films and television productions provide corroborative illustrations. In "The Magnificent Seven," for example, O'Reilly (played by Charles Bronson) says: "You think I am brave because I carry a gun; well, your fathers are much braver because they carry responsibility, for you, your brothers, your sisters, and your mothers." And in the television series "M*A*S*H," Hawkeye Pierce (played by Alan Alda) presciently proclaims: "I will not carry a gun. . . . I'll carry your books, I'll carry a torch, I'll carry a tune, I'll carry on, carry over, carry forward, Cary Grant, cash and carry, carry me back to Old Virginia, I'll even 'harikari' if you show me how, but I will not carry a gun!"[31] (parentheses and ellipses in original; citations omitted).

---

[27] *Id.* at 347–48.
[28] 532 U.S. 451 (2001).
[29] *Id.* at 468.
[30] 524 U.S. 125 (1998).
[31] *Id.* at 144 n.6.

Eleventh Amendment Cases

A number of cases involving the meaning of the Eleventh Amendment have come before the Supreme Court in recent years. Justice Souter, in *Alden v. Maine*,[32] derided the majority's analysis by arguing that its newfound rationale could have saved much effort in deciding a previous case:

> In thus complementing its earlier decision, the Court of course confronts the fact that the state forum renders the Eleventh Amendment beside the point, and it has responded by discerning a simpler and more straightforward theory of state sovereign immunity than it found in *Seminole Tribe*: a State's sovereign immunity from all individual suits is a "fundamental aspect" of state sovereignty "confirm[ed]" by the Tenth Amendment. As a consequence, *Seminole Tribe*'s contorted reliance on the Eleventh Amendment and its background was presumably unnecessary; the Tenth would have done the work with an economy that the majority in *Seminole Tribe* would have welcomed. Indeed, if the Court's current reasoning is correct, the Eleventh Amendment itself was unnecessary. Whatever Article III may originally have said about the federal judicial power, the embarrassment to the State of Georgia occasioned by attempts in federal court to enforce the State's war debt could easily have been avoided if only the Court that decided *Chisholm v. Georgia*, had understood a State's inherent, Tenth Amendment right to be free of any judicial power, whether the court be state or federal, and whether the cause of action arise under state or federal law.[33] (citations omitted).

In another Eleventh Amendment case, *College Savings v. Fla. Prepaid Postsecondary Education*,[34] Justice Scalia, writing for the majority, tongue-in-cheek credited Justice Breyer's judicial brevity for saving paper:

> The principal thrust of Justice Breyer's dissent is an attack upon the very legitimacy of state sovereign immunity itself. In this regard, Justice Breyer and the other dissenters proclaim that they are "not *yet* ready," to adhere to the still-warm precedent of *Seminole Tribe* and to the 110-year-old decision in *Hans* that supports it. Accordingly, Justice Breyer reiterates (but only in outline form, thankfully) the now-fashionable revisionist accounts of the Eleventh Amendment set forth in other opinions in a degree of repetitive detail that has despoiled our

---

[32] 527 U.S. 706 (1999).
[33] *Id.* at 760–61.
[34] 527 U.S. 666 (1999).

northern woods.³⁵ (citations and footnote omitted; parentheses and italics in original).

Dissenting in *Ramdass v. Angelone*,³⁶ Justice Stevens tendered a complex description of a hypothetical:

> The plurality offers no evidence whatsoever that this possibility—an "if only" wrapped in a "might have" inside of a "possibly so"—is at all more likely to occur than the "hypothetical future developments" that *Simmons* itself refused to countenance. Why is that possibility of setting aside the verdict any more likely than the fanciful scenarios dismissed in *Simmons*?³⁷

Justice Scalia's dissent in *Lawrence v. Texas*,³⁸ asked the reader to imagine the circumstances under which a search warrant could be obtained in connection with consensual sodomy:

> Next the Court makes the claim, again unsupported by any citations, that "[l]aws prohibiting sodomy do not seem to have been enforced against consenting adults acting in private." The key qualifier here is "acting in private"—since the Court admits that sodomy laws were enforced against consenting adults (although the Court contends that prosecutions were "infrequen[t].")*.* I do not know what "acting in private" means; surely consensual sodomy, like heterosexual intercourse, is rarely performed on stage. If all the Court means by "acting in private" is "on private premises, with the doors closed and windows covered," it is entirely unsurprising that evidence of enforcement would be hard to come by. (Imagine the circumstances that would enable a search warrant to be obtained for a residence on the ground that there was probable cause to believe that consensual sodomy was then and there occurring.)³⁹ (brackets and parentheses in original; citations omitted).

*Hein v. Freedom from Religion Foundation, Inc.*⁴⁰ involved a challenge under the Establishment Clause to the creation of certain entities by the Executive Branch. Justice Scalia, concurring in the judgment, derided the majority's *deus ex machina*:

---

³⁵ *Id.* at 687–88.
³⁶ 530 U.S. 156 (2000).
³⁷ *Id.* at 203.
³⁸ 539 U.S. 558 (2003).
³⁹ *Id.* at 597.
⁴⁰ 127 S. Ct. 2553 (2007).

But that created a problem: If the taxpayers in *Flast* have standing based on Psychic Injury, and without regard to the effect of the litigation on their ultimate tax liability, why did not the taxpayers in *Doremus and Frothingham* have standing on a similar basis? Enter the magical two-pronged nexus test. It has often been pointed out, and never refuted, that the criteria in *Flast's* two-part test are *entirely unrelated* to the purported goal of ensuring that the plaintiff has a sufficient "stake in the outcome of the controversy." In truth, the test was designed for a quite different goal.[41] (citations omitted; italics in original).

Later in his opinion, Justice Scalia drew upon a sports analogy:

In distinguishing between the Spending Clause and the Property Clause, *Valley Forge* achieved the seemingly impossible: It surpassed the high bar for irrationality set by *Flast's* distinguishing of *Doremus and Frothingham*. Like the dissenters in *Valley Forge*, I cannot fathom why Article III standing should turn on whether the government enables a religious organization to obtain real estate by giving it a check drawn from general tax revenues or instead by buying the property itself and then transferring title.[42] (citations omitted).

Chief Justice Roberts's majority opinion in *Federal Election Commission v. Wisconsin Right to Life*,[43] (where the Bipartisan Campaign Reform Act of 2002, previously found to be facially valid, was challenged "as applied"), according to Justice Souter, involved "magic words":

This refusal to see and hear what any listener to WRTL's ads would actually consider produces a rule no different in practice from the one adopted by the District Court, which decline to look beyond the "four corners" of the ads themselves. Although the Chief Justice ostensibly stops short of categorically foreclosing consideration of context, the application of his test here makes it difficult to see how relevant contextual evidence could ever be taken into account the way it was in *McConnell,* and it is hard to imagine The Chief Justice would ever find an ad to be "susceptible of no reasonable interpretation other than as an appeal to vote for or against a specific candidate," unless it contained words of express advocacy. The Chief Justice thus effectively reinstates the same toothless "magical words" criterion of regulable electioneering that led Congress to enact BCRA in the first place.[44] (citation omitted).

---

[41] *Id.* at 2576–77.
[42] *Id.* at 2578.
[43] 127 S. Ct. 2652 (2007).
[44] *Id.* at 2702.

The extent to which high school students have First Amendment rights was the subject of *Morse v. Frederick*,[45] where a student, during a school-sponsored event, unfurled a 14-foot banner that read: "BONG HITS 4 JESUS." Justice Stevens's dissent offered two variations on the banner:

> A significant fact barely mentioned by the Court sheds a revelatory light on the motives of both the students and the principal of Juneau-Douglas High School (JDHS). On January 24, 2002, the Olympic Torch Relay gave those Alaska residents a rare chance to appear on national television. As Joseph Frederick repeatedly explained, he did not address the curious message—"BONG HITS 4 JESUS"—to his fellow students. He just wanted to get the camera crews' attention. Moreover, concern about a nationwide evaluation of the conduct of the JDHS student body would have justified the principal's decision to remove an attention-grabbing 14-foot banner, even if it had merely proclaimed "Glaciers Melt!"
>
> . . . .
>
> Consider, too, that the school district's rule draws no distinction between alcohol and marijuana, but applies evenhandedly to all "substances that are illegal to minors." Given the tragic consequences of teenage alcohol consumption—drinking causes far more fatal accidents than the misuse of marijuana—the school district's interest in deterring teenage alcohol use is at least comparable to its interest in preventing marijuana use. Under the court's reasoning, must the First Amendment give way whenever a school seeks to punish a student for any speech mentioning beer, or indeed anything else that might be deemed risky to teenagers? While I find it hard to believe the Court would support punishing Frederick for flying a "WINE SIPS 4 JESUS" banner —which could quite reasonably be construed either as a protected religious message or as a pro-alcohol message—the breathtaking sweep of its opinion suggests it would.[46] (cites omitted; ellipses added).

---

[45]127 S. Ct. 2618 (2007).
[46]*Id.* at 2643, 2650.

CHAPTER SEVENTEEN

Appealing to the Mob

> *A[n] [impermissible] conscience of the community argument "extends to all impassioned and prejudicial pleas intended to evoke a sense of community law through common duty and expectation."*
>
> Airport Rent-A-Car, Inc. v. Lewis, 701 So. 2d 893, 896 (Fla. App. 4 Dist. 1997). (brackets added).

AN ATTEMPT TO GAIN ACCEPTANCE of an argument through an appeal to crowd instincts is known in Latin as *argumentum ad populum* (appeal to the people). Other names for this informal fallacy are: "appeal to the gallery, appeal to the majority, appeal to what is popular, appeal to popular prejudice, appeal to the multitude, and appeal to mob instinct."[1] This emotional catchall technique involves

> arguing in order to arouse an emotional, popular acceptance of an idea without presenting a logical justification of the idea. An appeal is made to such things as biases, prejudices, feelings, enthusiasms, and attitudes of the multitude in order to evoke assent rather than to rationally support the idea."[2]

Collective Interests

Attorneys frequently importune juries, in opening and closing arguments, to side with their clients by appealing to the members' collective

---

[1] PETER A. ANGELES, THE HARPERCOLLINS DICTIONARY OF PHILOSOPHY, 106 (HarperCollins 2nd ed. 1992).
[2] *Id.*

interests. Appeals may be made to the jurors as taxpayers, as patriots, as soldiers in the war on drugs, as insurance premium payers, as residents of the local community (in contrast to "outsiders"), as the conscience of the community, as the "ears" of the community, or as the "voice" of the community. These and other mob appeals are discussed below.

At the close of arguments in the 2006 Enron trial, prosecutor Sean Berkowitz appealed to jurors to consider the investors who lost their money from Enron's collapse, people just like them:

> Berkowitz reminded the jury that Enron's investors consisted of people just like them: dairy farmers and teachers, personnel administrators and retired engineers, teachers, clerks and dental hygienists. Some of the jurors nodded as Berkowitz clicked off each of their professions, one by one.

The people who bought Enron's stock, Berkowitz said, "weren't entitled to much, but they were entitled to honesty." After he finished, deliberations began.[3]

Appeals to Regionalism

In the first of two appeals to sectionalism, plaintiff's counsel twice emphasized the situs of the trial, and reminded the hometown jurors that the defendant was a "national corporation":

> *"[A]s a little old lawyer down here in Mississippi, to take on a national corporation*, I knew I had to bring in the best experienced person in security that I knew"; and "[n]ow when I, as a lawyer *here in Mississippi*, bring a legal action against a *national corporation*—having done this a few years—they are tough cases."[4] (italics in original).

The same message was communicated in the second appeal, only this time the location of the defendant's corporate headquarters was emphasized, rather than the jurors' locale:

> The problem is—*way up there in Troy, Michigan*—*way up there* in *Troy, Michigan*, where they decide to write a two or three inch thick loss prevention manual, they don't think about the customers' safety and security in the parking lot. Because they are more concerned about profits and not people.[5] (italics in original).

---

[3]http://www.usatoday.com/money/industries/energy/2006-05-17-enron-jury_x.htm.
[4]Whitehead v. Food Max of Miss., Inc., 163 F.3d 265, 276 (5th Cir. 1998).
[5]*Id.*

The Fifth Circuit overturned the jury's damages verdict in favor of the plaintiff,[6] and remarked: "That this blatant appeal to sectionalism would be made in a federal court in this day and time is nothing short of amazing."[7]

A widow, whose husband was killed when he rented a plane, argued on appeal that the defendant's counsel improperly appealed to regionalism: "Specifically, she complains that counsel exhorted the jury during closing argument, not to 'send her counsel back to New York with a croker sack full of money.'"[8]

The court rejected her argument:

> Such trial strategy is at a minimum impolite and arguably unprofessional. But even had the issue been properly preserved for our review, which it was not, we do not believe that it was so inflammatory as to have blinded the jury to the eight days of evidence which was otherwise competently presented.[9]

During closing argument and voir dire, a prosecutor pointed out that the defense counsel was from out of town, that jurors would be setting the standard for community justice, that relatives and children of the jury would have to live with their verdict, and that the jurors should do their duty as the representatives of their community—all appeals to regionalism:

> (1) "Unlike Mr. Murray [out-of town defense counsel], I have to live in this community with you . . .";
>
> (2) "It's not easy to be where you are at, but what you are doing is just as important as what the soldiers did in our World Wars and in Viet Nam. You are setting the standard of justice in Trumbull County.";
>
> (3) ". . . I agree with Defense counsel that you will live with that in the future. You will live with that not only for yourselves but for your parents, for your children and for your grandchildren . . ."; and
>
> (4) "[I] ask you only to . . . do your duty as a collective group representing a community. . . ."[10] (brackets and ellipses in original; citations omitted).

---

[6]*Id.* at 282.
[7]*Id.* at 276.
[8]Cohen v. Lowe Aviation Co., Inc., 470 S.E.2d 813, 815 (Ga. App. 1996).
[9]*Id.* at 815–16.
[10]Lorraine v. Coyle, 291 F.3d 416 (6th Cir. 2002).

The Sixth Circuit found that there was overwhelming evidence of guilt, and that the remarks were "permissible appeals to community sentiment."[11]

One measure that an attorney has improperly appealed to regionalism is the size of the jury award: "[A]ppeals to local bias against an outsider are prejudicial, and a large verdict accompanied by such appeals leads us to conclude they had an influential impact on the jury's deliberations."[12] (brackets added).

Send a Message

Juries are often asked to "send a message," by appealing to their sense of community and their ability to make a difference through their verdict. Counsel for a stepson, who was being sued by his stepfather for conversion, failed to object to the following exhortation to "send a message," during closing argument:

> If all this is so right and so good, why did Tom Murphy have to slide into town unannounced, go into the apartment, park his car down the way? And he said he lied as to why he was here. If this was so right, why lie about it? Why be a sneak about it? Why be a thief about it?
>
> He went over to the bank, that's his business, his dirty business, he went over to the bank, got in the safety box and cleaned it out.
>
> On May 20th, 1991, Mr. John Murphy was robbed, unfortunately, by his own son. Now, what I would like to have us do is send a message. The message is this: That I want John Murphy to know that justice does prevail, that he will get justice here today, after what has been done to him. Also, I want to send a message to the community, to anyone else that has that kind of depraved mind, so they won't think they can get away with stealing some elderly folks monies. This is what I'm looking for on behalf of Mr. Murphy, for damages.[13]

Despite the lack of a contemporaneous objection, the verdict in favor of the stepfather was reversed:

> We are cognizant of the glamorization of the "cowboy" litigator. We believe, however, that a trial jury should not resemble a "Shoot-out at the OK Corral." What we believe is of course irrelevant, we are pleased it is also the law.

---

[11]*Id.* at 445.
[12]Westbrook v. General Tire and Rubber Co., 754 F.2d 1233, 1241 (5th Cir. 1985).
[13]Murphy v. Murphy, 622 So. 2d 99, 101–02 (Fla. App. 2 Dist. 1993).

APPEALING TO THE MOB

. . . .

> We conclude the conduct of counsel for John deprived the parties of a fair and dispassionate trial by jury.[14] (ellipses added).

Trials involving odious or abhorrent crimes are susceptible to mob appeals for vengeance or revenge. A prosecutor's concluding remarks to the jury sought to exact a measure of revenge for the defendant's crimes by asking to even the score:

> So I'll say this: Show them sympathy. If you feel that way, be sympathetic. Exhibit the same sympathy that was exhibited by these men on January 3rd, 1980. No more. No more.
>
> I want you to remember this: We have a death penalty for a reason. Right now, the score is John Lesko and Michael Travaglia two, society nothing. When will it stop? When is it going to stop? Who is going to make it stop? That's your duty.[15] (citations omitted).

The Third Circuit had no difficulty reversing the jury's verdict for the death penalty:[16]

> We believe that the conclusion of the prosecutor's closing argument was improper in two important respects. First, the prosecutor's comments were "directed to passion and prejudice rather than to an understanding of the facts and of the law." . . . [T]he prosecutor exceeded the bounds of permissible advocacy by imploring the jury to make its death penalty determination in the cruel and malevolent manner shown by the defendants when they tortured and drowned William Nicholls and shot Leonard Miller.[17] (ellipses and brackets added).

Some retribution may be urged in a closing argument, but it must not be the central theme of a prosecutor: "Isolated, brief references to retribution or community vengeance . . ., although potentially inflammatory, do not constitute misconduct so long as such arguments do not form the principal basis for advocating the imposition of the death penalty."[18] (ellipses in original).

A rather lengthy closing argument festooned with religious references, and pleas "'to make a statement,' to do 'the right thing,' and restore 'confidence' in the criminal justice system by returning a verdict

---

[14]*Id.* at 102.
[15]Lesco v. Lehman, 925 F.2d 1527, 1540–41 (3d Cir. 1991).
[16]*Id.* at 1546, 1554.
[17]*Id.* at 1545.
[18]People v. Ghent, 239 Cal. Rptr. 82, 103 (Cal. 1987), *cited in* People v. Wash, 24 Cal. Rptr. 2d 421, 450 (Cal. 1993).

of death,"[19] did not require overturning the conviction because they were "not particularly inflammatory, nor did they constitute the principal basis" of the prosecutor's argument for the death penalty.[20]

When the judicial system allows a defendant who committed a crime to be free, and that individual commits a serious crime, may the prosecutor beseech the jury to become the representatives of the criminal justice system by voting for the death penalty?

> He [Williams] had advantages from the system and he took advantage of the system. *The system failed William and Alice Nail once* because we didn't hold him in custody so he couldn't commit the unspeakable. Do not let the system fail them again. When we failed them in the first instance it cost them their lives. *Should we fail in this instance it will take away the meaning and dignity of their lives.*[21] (italics and brackets in original).

The Nevada Supreme Court found nothing wrong with the prosecutor's argument:

> Williams argues that the prosecutor implied that the system's failure cost the Nails their lives, and that the jury carried the burden of ensuring proper functioning of the criminal justice system in its sentencing of Williams. Williams interprets the prosecutor's remarks as equating failure of the criminal justice system with returning less than a death penalty.
>
> . . . a prosecutor in a death penalty case properly may ask the jury, through its verdict, to set a standard or make a statement to the community.[22] (ellipses added).

Rally Round the Flag

Patriotic appeals may be made at any time, but they take on special significance during time of war, when the "rally around the flag" arguments are their most effective. When the men and women of the armed forces are fighting in foreign lands, few individuals want to break ranks to say or do anything that would undermine the support for our troops. (Support for a particular war may be a different issue.) During World War II, a registration statement was required of agents of foreign principals. In a case involving a defendant who willfully omitted a material

---

[19] *People v. Wash,* id.
[20] *Id.*
[21] Williams v. State, 945 P.2d 438, 445 (Nev. 1997).
[22] *Id.*

fact on a registration form filed with the Secretary of State, the prosecutor made an impassioned plea to patriotism:

> In closing, let me remind you, ladies and gentlemen, that this is war. This is war, harsh, cruel, murderous war. There are those who, right at this very moment, are plotting your death and my death; plotting our death and the death of our families because we have committed no other crime than that we do not agree with their ideas of persecution and concentration camps.
>
> This is war. It is a fight to the death. The American people are relying upon you ladies and gentlemen for their protection against this sort of crime, just as much as they are relying upon the protection of the men who man the guns in Bataan Peninsula, and everywhere else. They are relying upon you ladies and gentlemen for their protection. We are at war. You have a duty to perform here.
>
> As a representative of your Government I am calling upon every one of you to do your duty.[23]

The U.S. Supreme Court termed the remarks "highly prejudicial," and found they constituted "an appeal wholly irrelevant to any facts or issues in the case, the purpose and effect of which could only have been to arouse passion and prejudice."[24]

A modern-day appeal to patriotism occurred when a prosecutor argued to the jury:

> It's not easy to be where you are at, but what you are doing is just as important as what the soldiers did in our World Wars and in Viet Nam. You are setting the standard of justice in Trumbull County.[25]

The Sixth Circuit held this, and other related arguments, to be permissible appeals to community sentiment.[26]

Not all appeals to patriotism involve the Armed Forces. Americans have cherished freedoms, not the least of which, according to one writer, is the freedom to use a cell phone while driving a vehicle: "Numerous mundane distractions can contribute to automobile accidents, but cell phones figure among the least of these. Until the government can prove otherwise, Americans ought to be free to use their cell phones how and where they please."[27]

---

[23] Viereck v. United States, 318 U.S. 236, 247–48 n.3 (1943).
[24] *Id.* at 247–48.
[25] *Lorraine v. Coyle, supra* at 445 (6th Cir. 2002).
[26] *Id.*
[27] Helen Chaney, *Drive to limit cell phones based on bad information*, MILWAUKEE JOURNAL SENTINEL, July 1, 2001, at 02J.

No one wants to be laughed at or made a fool of; it is part of human nature to want to be accepted. A prosecutor played to that emotion in a rebuttal argument to the jury:

> And this, of course, would be the biggest day of all for him, if you were to, in the face of this mountain of evidence against him, ignore it and let him skate free. Let him ride. Let him go. This would be a huge day. This would be the biggest day.
>
> And as the saying goes, it may be inappropriate in this case, he would be laughing at you. He would be laughing all the way to the bank.[28]

The defendant argued that this argument foisted "onto the jury the extra-judicial consequences of a not-guilty verdict," when the jury should only have been considering the guilt or innocence of the defendant.[29] Rejecting that argument, the First Circuit concluded that the prosecutor's "ill-advised rhetoric or pained attempt at humor" did not require reversal of the conviction.[30]

The Second Circuit, while finding that a similar argument was improper, nevertheless concluded that the prosecutor's rebuttal did not warrant reversing the conviction:

> I submit to you that the Government has proven the proof. It has proven the charges in this case beyond every doubt. The proof is very clear. Don't let (the defendant) walk out of this room laughing at you.[31] (parentheses added).

During closing argument, a prosecutor reminded jurors of the increasing number of car thefts (potentially impacting them as car owners):

> [T]he case is not trivial. At a time when the number of cars which are being stolen are increasing—
>
> . . . .
>
> At a time when more security devices are being put on individual cars than you sometimes find on a Brinks truck because of thefts.[32] (brackets and ellipses in original).

The defendant was not denied a fair trial, the Seventh Circuit held, because the prosecutor's argument (pointing out the increasing number

---

[28]United States v. Auch, 187 F.3d 125, 132 n.13 (1st Cir. 1999).
[29]*Id.*
[30]*Id.*
[31]United States v. Modica, 663 F.2d 1173, 1180 (2nd Cir. 1981).
[32]United States v. Shirley, 435 F.2d 1076, 1079 (7th Cir. 1970).

of car thefts) did not constitute "an emotional appeal to the juror's self interest designed to arouse their prejudice against the defendant."[33]

Overcrowded Courtrooms

A woman injured at an amusement park brought a personal injury action against the park's owner. The attorney for the amusement park argued that lawsuits like this one caused overcrowding in the nation's courtrooms:

> Now, I don't mean to insult your intelligence and please excuse me if I do. [Referring to plaintiff's chart which summarized possible damages and which was left in the courtroom.] This adds up to $48,300.00 and it is absolutely ridiculous. This is why we're here. This is why our courtrooms are crowded and this is why we read articles in the newspaper, because of things like that.[34] (brackets in original).

The woman's attorney contemporaneously objected to these remarks, and at the end of the closing argument, again, asked for a curative instruction and a mistrial. Both objections were overruled and the jury found that the amusement park was not negligent. On appeal, the Florida appeals court held:

> The reference to problems of overcrowded courtrooms is clearly an attempt to appeal to the conscience of the community and matters far afield from the evidence admitted in the case. As such it was highly improper and may have been grounds for a new trial even absent objection.[35]

Pecuniary Interests

Appeals to the pecuniary interests of jurors can take many forms. A minor who was hit in the eye with a baseball while watching a game at a local park sued the town. The town's attorney drew a contemporaneous objection during closing argument when he stated:

> But here's the problem. If juries start awarding verdicts against coaches, against schools or against towns that have the fields, there's

---

[33] Id.
[34] Stokes v. Wet 'N Wild, Inc., 523 So. 2d 181, 182 (Fla. App. 5 Dist. 1988).
[35] Id.

no question that you're not going to have any injuries, but you're not going to have sports or competitive sports.[36]

In the absence of a curative instruction, the appeals court reversed the verdict in favor of the town, reasoning as follows:

> Here, defense counsel introduced or suggested for consideration the financial burdens that towns like Stratford suffer from personal injury suits. Counsel also suggested that the jurors' decision could adversely impact town parks and recreation programs. In doing so, he appealed to not only whatever civic sympathies they might harbor but also their self-interest as taxpayers and patrons of parks and recreation programs. This form of argument was highly improper and clearly inappropriate.[37]

During closing argument, counsel for the defendant stated that the plaintiff was "suit happy," and was looking for a "hand out."[38] Counsel also asked the jury to

> [s]end a message to the public by not granting or rewarding dollars to this plaintiff so that we won't have this type of activity. We say this type of lawsuit must stop. We say this type of conduct must stop. All of you have wages. You have to earn them. Please do not award her any damages.[39]

The trial court set aside the verdict in favor of the defendant, and the appeals court affirmed. One of the arguments held to be improper was the appeal to the jurors' interest as wage earners, in contrast to those who receive public assistance:

> These comments in closing argument must be viewed in light of the lack of any evidence that the plaintiff's claim was fraudulent, that she was a person who had brought many lawsuits or that she was looking for a "hand out." These comments plus the statement that the jurors had to "earn" their wages must also be viewed in light of the evidence before the jury that the plaintiff was a recipient of state assistance. It is difficult to imagine how the defense argument could be construed as anything other than appeal to the jury to decide the case based on passion or prejudice; especially in view of the continuing public discourse over the cost of public assistance, and the amount and type of litigation in our courts.[40]

---

[36] Fonk v. Town of Stratford, 584 A.2d 1198, 1199 (Conn. App. 1991).
[37] *Id.* at 1199–1200.
[38] McKee v. Erikson, 654 A.2d 1263, 1267 (Conn. App. 1995).
[39] *Id.*
[40] *Id.*

A Wisconsin circuit court decided that, as a condition of probation, a man who intentionally failed to support his nine children can be required to avoid having another child, unless he demonstrates he could support all of his children. Wisconsin Supreme Court Justice Bablitch concurred with the majority that such a stricture on the man's ability to have future children was lawful:

> I conclude that the harm to others who cannot protect themselves is so overwhelmingly apparent and egregious here that there is no room for question. Here is a man who has shown himself time and again to be totally and completely irresponsible. He lives only for himself and the moment, with no regard to the consequences of his actions and taking no responsibility for them. He intentionally refuses to pay support and has been convicted of that felony. The harm that he has done to his nine living children by failing to support them is patent and egregious. He has abused at least one of them. Under certain conditions, it is overwhelmingly obvious that any child he fathers in the future is doomed to a future of neglect, abuse, or worse. That as yet unborn child is a victim from the day it is born.[41]

Passing references to a "defendant's life in a 'citizen supported California institution' and 'society's obligation to expend time and vast amounts of resources' on him . . ." did not deprive the defendant of a fair trial.[42] Even if the remarks constituted "improper comment on the costs of punishment," the failure to object and ask for a curative instruction doomed the appeal.[43]

Biblical Authority

Attorneys often appeal to the jurors' religious beliefs in an attempt to win the case for their clients. During closing argument, a prosecutor referred to two of the Ten Commandments:

> He is a wolf in sheep's clothing, and you know it. And so is James Mason. Wolves in sheep's clothing, they were masquerading and parading in our society as pillars of the community, and this is why we have so many problems in dealing with drugs. This is why we cannot educate our children to have respect when members of the community who are pillars are aiding and abetting the sales of this product that is destroying our communities whether they are in public housing or whether they are in upscale neighborhoods.

---

[41]State v. Oakley, 629 N.W.2d 200, 215 (Wis. 2001).
[42]People v. Morris, 807 P.2d 949, 991 n.17 (1991).
[43]*Id.*

> He has violated laws of ages. Thou shalt not covet. Thou shalt not kill.
>
> He has violated the law of the United States. James Mason has violated the law of the United States.[44]

The Eleventh Circuit found that the prosecutor "may have gone a bit overboard" with the religious references, but in light of the evidence against the defendants, they were not denied a fair trial.[45]

Seeking the death penalty for a defendant convicted of four murders, a prosecutor invoked biblical authority in his final argument to the jury:

> Mr. Applebaum [defendant's counsel] says don't play God. Let every person be in subjection to the governing authorities for there is no authority except from God and those which are established by God. Therefore, he who resists authority has opposed the ordinance of God, and they who have opposed will receive condemnations upon themselves for rulers are not a cause of fear for good behavior, but for evil. Do you want to have no fear or authority? Do what is good and you will have praise for the same for it is a minister of God to you for good. But if you do what is evil, be afraid for it does not bear the sword for nothing for it is a minister of God an Avenger who brings wrath upon one who practices evil.
>
> You are not playing God. You are doing what God says. This might be the only opportunity to wake him up. God will destroy the body to save the soul. Make him get himself right. . . .
>
> . . . Let him have the opportunity to get his soul right. That's the only way to get his attention. You are not playing God. God ordains authority.[46] (brackets added; ellipses in original).

The defendant claimed that the prosecutor's argument, quoted above, violated several of his rights: "his rights to due process, a fair trial, separation of church and state and freedom from cruel and unusual punishment . . ."[47] The court found that the quotation "was a paraphrase of Romans 13:1–7 and that such reliance on biblical authority to advocate imposition of the death penalty (was) improper."[48]

By invoking biblical authority as justification for the death penalty, the prosecutor ignored the state statute's mandate to only consider the

---

[44] United States v. Tokars, 95 F.3d 1520, 1540–41 n.21 (11th Cir. 1996).
[45] *Id.* at 1540–41.
[46] People v. Sandoval, 14 Cal. Rptr. 2d 342, 363 (Cal. 1992).
[47] *Id.* at 362.
[48] *Id.*

factors listed in the statute. Though the prosecutor engaged in misconduct, the court did not reverse the penalty phase determination because it concluded the jury would not have reached a different verdict had the misconduct not occurred.[49]

After a recitation of "biblical references to the death penalty," a prosecutor argued that capital punishment was sanctioned by the Bible and by God:

> [I]t is important that you understand that what I'm going to ask you to do is totally in keeping with religious principles. It is totally in keeping with the Spirit of Christ or God or whatever beliefs you have.
>
> . . . .
>
> God recognized there'd be people like [defendant]. That's why those commandments were delivered. . . . Who must be punished for what they have done and if they have done things like he's doing they must forfeit their lives . . . ."[50] (brackets in original; first ellipses added).

Notwithstanding the improper appeal, the California Supreme Court declined to reverse the death penalty determination, finding that the jury would have reached the same outcome, in any case.[51]

War on Drugs

Enlisting juries in the war on drugs is a frequent theme of prosecutors' arguments. When the jury is asked to decide the case, not on the facts, but on the larger issue of the menace posed by drugs, the potential for reversal of a conviction is likely.

"Throughout his closing argument the prosecutor urged the jury to view this case as a battle in the war against drugs, and the defendants as enemy soldiers":[52]

> When the captain . . . and the rest of the defendants departed Colombia they knew what was inside the boat. They knew that the boat was full with bales of marijuana, and they had no concern for the youth. They had no concern for the people that would have used the marijuana. They had no concern for the people that would have been addicted by the use of marijuana.

---

[49] *Id.* at 364.
[50] *People v. Wash, supra,* at 449.
[51] *Id.* at 450.
[52] Arrieta-Agressot v. United States, 3 F.3d 525, 527 (1st Cir. 1993).

....

> Nobody has the right to poison the people and poison our children . . . And we are here today because we want to say no to drugs. We want to say no to what is corrupting and disrupting the society, because marijuana not only disrupts and corrupts our society but it also corrupts and disrupts any society in the world.
>
> ....
>
> That is why, ladies and gentlemen of the jury, they [the U.S. Coast Guard] were in the drug interdiction. To save you all from the evil of drugs. Because the defendants are not soldiers in the army of good. They are soldiers in the army of evil, in the army which only purpose [sic] is to poison, to disrupt, to corrupt.[53] (ellipses and first brackets added).

The First Circuit vacated the convictions, based on the "plain error" rule, inasmuch as defense counsel did not object to any of the argument.[54] At the core of the court's holding, that the argument exceeded the proper bounds, was the following:

> It is hard enough for a jury to remain dispassionate and objective amidst the tensions and turmoil of a criminal trial, and this is not the occasion for superheated rhetoric from the government urging jurors to enlist in the war on drugs.[55]

A defendant's counsel raised a timely objection to this prosecutorial rebuttal argument:

> [Y]ou heard in his closing defense counsel make a lot about truth and justice and the Pledge of Allegiance. Well, ladies and gentlemen, justice does not have one eye; it's got two eyes. Justice protects not only the person who is accused, but it also protects persons like those individuals who—those 400-plus individuals that the crack cocaine were intended for. That is another person justice is intended to serve.[56]

The D.C. Circuit, reviewing for harmless error, upheld the conviction, but concluded the argument was impermissible: "On its face, the prosecutor's argument in this case improperly suggested that the jury should convict the defendant in order to protect others from drugs."[57]

---

[53] *Id.*
[54] *Id.*
[55] *Id.*
[56] United States v. Johnson, 231 F.3d 43, 46 (D.C. Cir. 2000).
[57] *Id.* at 47.

A defendant argued on appeal that the prosecutor's repeated references to the "war on drugs" in his closing argument warranted reversal of her conviction:

> **[The Prosecutor:]** I want to say a few words about—and I know you've heard it and I've heard it—war on drugs, war on drugs. You've heard it. You hear it all the time. And this is a war. This is just—this is just another battle in that war. It's a battle to save folks from being enslave [sic] by crack cocaine. That's what, that's what this battle's about. Now I've got a place in that war. You've got a place in that war. The judge has got a place. Those defendants over there all have a place in it.
>
> **Defense Counsel:** Judge, I object to [the prosecutor] saying that these people have a place in a war against—
>
> **THE COURT:** I sustain that.
>
> **Defense Counsel:** That's not right these people—
>
> **THE COURT:** No. You are neutral, you are impartial, and so is the judge. So am I. I'm neutral.
>
> . . . .
>
> **[The Prosecutor:]** And for profiteers like (defendant) to do that to—not just his—not just Esau Street. It's not just Esau Street. It's all over the country. And people, there's another John Christopher out there somewhere—
>
> **Defense Counsel:** Judge, I object to this line of questioning. They are not engaged in the war against crime. They are to decide this case, not anywhere else in the country, and I object to it—
>
> **THE COURT:** Again ... ladies and gentlemen of the jury, you are supposed to be fair and impartial. You are neutral. You are not engaged in any war. And neither is the court.[58] (brackets and ellipses in original; parentheses added).

The Eleventh Circuit noted that the prosecutor's closing argument "made references to war and employed war-related terminology to draw an analogy between the participants in a war and the participants in defendants' drug organization and in the law enforcement agencies that investigated the organization."[59] Although the Eleventh Circuit found the comments to be improper, it did not reverse the conviction, because of the district court's curative instructions, and in the context of the entire trial, the remarks were not prejudicial.[60]

---

[58] United States v. Beasley, 2 F.3d 1551, 1559–60 (11th Cir. 1993).
[59] *Id.* at 1559.
[60] *Id.* at 1559.

Conscience of the Community

The quote at the beginning of this chapter refers to "conscience of the community" arguments, arguments intended to cause jurors to decide cases based on their sense of what the community would do, rather than what they, as individuals, would do, based on the evidence presented to them. It is difficult to predict whether these arguments, in any particular case, impermissibly cross the line by "inflam[ing] the jurors' emotions."[61] The best guidance comes from decisions where the courts have concluded that specific arguments did not trespass onto forbidden ground.

During closing argument involving a defendant accused of selling cocaine, the prosecutor remarked:

> [**Assistant U.S. Attorney**]: *What you're listening to is a wholesale distributor of narcotics, cocaine discuss her business affairs* and complain about her busy schedule, the lack of good product and the trouble she's having getting this stuff up here now. And I'd submit to you folks, that *she's been caught now. And I'm asking you to tell her and all of the other drug dealers like her*—(defense counsel's objection and the Court's response omitted)—*[t]hat we don't want that stuff in Northern* Kentucky and that anybody who brings that stuff in Northern Kentucky and . . ."[62] (italics, ellipses, parentheses, and brackets in original).

The Sixth Circuit found that the prosecutor's statements asked the jury to solve their community's drug problem by convicting the defendant:

> In the case before us, the effect of the prosecutor's comments was to suggest to the jury that, because of defendant's participation in the drug trade in northern Kentucky, the drug problem facing the jurors' community would continue if they did not convict her. It is error for a prosecutor to direct the jurors' desire to end a social problem toward convicting a particular defendant.[63]

The court also held that the prosecutor impermissibly cobbled a "conscience of the community" argument with a War on Drugs plea:

> Here, defendant's constitutional right to a fair trial was violated because the appeal to the community conscience in the context of the War on Drugs prejudicially impacted on her. The fear surround-

---

[61]United States v. Solivan, 937 F.2d 1146, 1153 (6th Cir. 1991).
[62]*Id.* at 1148.
[63]*Id.* at 1153.

ing the War on Drugs undoubtedly influenced the jury by diverting its attention away from its task to weigh the evidence and submit a reasoned decision finding defendant guilty or innocent of the crimes with which she was charged. The substance of the statements made by the prosecutor in this case were designed, both in purpose and effect, to arouse passion and prejudice and to inflame the jurors' emotions regarding the War on Drugs by urging them to send a message and strike a blow to the drug problem.[64]

Finding that the prosecutor engaged in "egregious prosecutorial conduct," and that it was not a constitutionally harmless error, the Sixth Circuit reversed the conviction.[65]

By way of contrast, the Sixth Circuit concluded that the following prosecution argument was not an impermissible appeal to the "conscience of the community":

> You, the jurors, are called upon in this case to be the world conscience of the community. And I'm calling on this jury to speak out for the community and let the John Alloways know that this type of conduct will not be tolerated, that we're not going to tolerate [armed robbery] . . .[66] (brackets added; ellipses in original).

The videotaping of Rodney King's beating at the hands of law enforcement personnel attracted nationwide media attention. At the trial of the police officers involved, the prosecutor presented a "conscience of the community" argument to the jury:

> Judge Davies will give you your break, and then he'll instruct you in the law, and you will walk into the jury room to deliberate, and you will leave this courtroom, and convinced and confident with the truth, and you will leave with your collective good common sense, because ladies and gentlemen of the jury, *you're the conscience of the community. You decide what conduct is acceptable by your police. And what conduct violates the law.* Defendant Koon and the other defendants beat a man who was not combative, who was not an aggressor until he begged for mercy, knowing it was wrong. . . . *There are some countries where people can be beaten by the police until they beg the police to stop, but not in this country. Not now, not 200 years ago when this Constitution was written, and with your decision, not ever.*[67] (italics and ellipses in original; citation omitted).

---

[64]*Id.*
[65]*Id.* at 1157.
[66]United States v. Alloway, 397 F.2d 105, 113 (6th Cir. 1968).
[67]United States v. Koon, 34 F.3d 1416, 1444 n.24 (9th Cir. 1994).

The Ninth Circuit found that the prosecutor's argument was not improper:

> An appeal to the jury to be the conscience of the community is not impermissible unless it is "specifically designed to inflame the jury." In this case, when the prosecutor's statement is considered in context, it is clear that it was not designed to inflame the jury, but rather to explain to jurors that they were in the position to determine whether the charged conduct comported with community standards of reasonableness. The reference was not accompanied by any suggestion of the consequences of a particular verdict, nor did the prosecutor suggest to the jury that it had a direct stake in the outcome of the case. The comment did not cross the line "demarcating permissible oratorical flourish from impermissible comment calculated to incite the jury against the accused."[68] (citations omitted).

The attorney for a fair patron injured on a slide argued that the jurors were the "conscience of the community":

> I'll leave you with two thoughts. The fair is coming back to Jacksonville, bringing the amusement back. You folks, as you sit here in Duval County Florida you become the conscience of the community. It is you who will tell the fair what kind of standard and what kind of protection you want for the citizens of this town by your verdict; that you aren't going to tolerate this type of thing where they invite people to use their amusements and don't safeguard them properly and hurt the people in Jacksonville, Florida. You are the conscience of the community.[69]

The Florida Appellate Court concluded the remarks were improper, but not "so egregious as to constitute fundamental error."[70]

A motorist who was injured in a collision with a taxicab sued the owner and driver of the taxicab. By asking for punitive damages in his closing argument, the attorney for the motorist shoved his "conscience of the community" argument out of bounds:

> Tomorrow you get to go home and tell everyone about this case that you sat on and I want you to tell them what you get in Broward County if a taxi driver runs a red light and injures somebody. . . . I wish you could punish them, but you can't.[71] (ellipses in original).

---

[68] *Id.* at 1444.
[69] Blue Grass Shows, Inc. v. Collins, 614 So. 2d 626, 627 n.1 (Fla. App. 1 Dist. 1993).
[70] *Id.* at 629.
[71] *Airport Rent-A-Car, Inc., supra,* at 896.

It did not matter that the attorney phrased his comments negatively:

> We hold this comment constituted an impermissible conscience of the community argument. A conscience of the community argument "extends to all impassioned and prejudicial pleas intended to evoke a sense of community law through common duty and expectation."

> Generally, where an argument is not otherwise inflammatory or egregious, an isolated statement is only harmful if coupled with an argument for punitive damages. Counsel's caveat to the jury, "I wish you could punish [appellants], but you can't," did not mitigate the prejudicial impact of his statement. Rather, we conclude that counsel's statement planted the seed to motivate the jury to include a punitive aspect in the damage award.[72] (citations omitted; brackets in original).

The Florida court reversed the decision in favor of the motorist, finding that the owner and driver of the taxicab were denied a fair trial.[73]

To pass legal muster in Texas and North Carolina, an argument has to involve the correct part of a juror's anatomy. Such an issue arose when a prosecutor attempted to impress on the jury the importance of its role in the criminal justice system with the following remarks:

> This defendant displayed a heartless evil, callous disregard for the victim. He was without conscience, he was without pity. His was a wicked and vile act, Ladies and Gentlemen of the Jury, and when you hear of such acts, you say, "Gee somebody ought to do something about that." You know something, Ladies and Gentlemen of the Jury, today you are the somebody that everybody talks about, and justice is in your lap. The officers can't do any more. The State can't do anymore. You speak for all the people of the State of North Carolina as to this bloody murder in the first degree.[74]

The North Carolina Supreme Court held that the prosecutor's entreaty involved the correct parts of the jurors' anatomy:

> Defendant contends that these remarks improperly inform the jury that community or public sentiment urges the death penalty and that the jury is effectively an arm of the State in the prosecution of the defendant. These would be improper suggestions. The State must not ask the jury "to lend a[n] ear to the community rather than a voice."

---

[72] Id.
[73] Id. at 897.
[74] State v. Brown, 358 S.E.2d 1, 18 (N.C. 1987).

But these suggestions do not arise from this argument, which does no more than remind the jurors that "the buck stops here" and that for purposes of defendant's trial, they are the voice and conscience of the community.[75] (citations omitted).

A Texas jury found the defendant guilty of aggravated robbery and assessed a punishment of 10 years' confinement. The prosecutor, at the punishment stage of the trial, argued that probation was not appropriate:

> Do you feel like you owe (the defendant) something? Do you, or do you feel like you've already given him what you owe him? That's a fair trial. That's all anybody's entitled to. He's the only person that stands between this young man and the penitentiary. Well, there are twelve of you and him. That makes thirteen and me and everybody else in the community. There are over a million people that stand between him and the penitentiary. They'd want him to go there if they knew what he did. Not just Mr. Topek.
>
> **MR. TOPEK:** I object to the prosecutor telling the jury what other people might want in this case. That's not proper.
> **The COURT:** Overruled.[76] (parentheses added).

Lend Me Your Ears

The Texas Court of Appeals reversed the judgment in this case (based on an appeal to the jurors' ears), and remanded to the lower court, where the prosecutor stated:

> The State contends that the argument merely was "telling the jury that they were the voice and conscience of the community."
>
> [I]n this case there was a statement made as to the desires of the citizens, and there was a demand for a punishment of confinement because of the citizens' desires. The State was asking the jury to lend an ear to the community rather than a voice.[77] (citations omitted; brackets added).

Anatomy also played a role in this prosecutor's argument to the jury when he remarked:

> I'm sure you've probably made the comment or heard folks say, "And why doesn't somebody do something" when you hear about a bad

---
[75] *Id.*
[76] Prado v. State, 626 S.W.2d 775, 776 (Tex. Crim. App. 1982).
[77] *Id.*

crime. Well, the buck stops right there today. Right here. Go back, deliberate, and come back with a verdict. "Verdict" means "truth." That's the gist of what it means in Latin. Go back and deliver a verdict that you can be proud of tonight, tomorrow, a week from now, a month from now, a year from now. This case deserves a verdict of "guilty," and as a spokesman on behalf of the State, we demand a verdict of "guilty."[78]

The North Carolina Supreme Court held:

Defendant argues that the prosecutor improperly urged the jury to "lend its ear" to anticrime sentiment in the community and to convict defendant in order to "do something" about crime.

"[P]rosecutorial argument encouraging 'the jury to lend an ear to the community rather than a voice' is improper." However, we have repeatedly stated that it is proper to urge the jury to act as the voice and conscience of the community.

. . . .

In the present case the prosecutor did not suggest that the jury should punish defendant based on community sentiment against murder rather than evidence presented. The prosecutor's argument merely referred to community sentiment and urged the jury to render a verdict justified by the evidence and the law. Accordingly, we conclude that the argument at issue was proper.[79] (citations omitted; ellipses added).

---

[78]State v. Bishop, 488 S.E.2d 769, 785 (N.C. 1997).
[79]Id. at 785–86.

CHAPTER EIGHTEEN

Slippery Slope

We are not asking the Court to unravel the fabric of unenumerated and privacy rights . . . which this Court has woven in cases like Meyer *and* Pierce *and* Moore *and* Griswold. *Rather, we are asking the Court to pull this one thread.*

Charles Fried, Oral argument before Supreme Court in *Webster v. Reproductive Health Services,* 26 April 1989, quoted in *New York Times,* 27 April 1989, at B12.[1] (ellipses in original).

I think the Solicitor General's [Charles Fried's] submission . . . is somewhat disingenuous when he suggests to this Court that he does not seek to unravel the whole cloth of procreational rights, but merely to pull a thread. It has always been my personal experience that when I pull a thread, my sleeve falls off. There is no stopping.

Frank Susman, Oral argument before Supreme Court in *Webster v. Reproductive Health Services,* 26 April 1989, quoted in *New York Times,* 27 April 1989, at B13.[2] (brackets and ellipses in original).

ALL OF THE NAMES for the slippery slope fallacy—including nose in the tent, foot in the door, thin edge of the wedge, fall like dominoes—suggest that a particular decision is but the first step in a process that will inevitably lead to unwanted consequences. In other words, the issue is shifted from the merits to the consequences of a particular decision, as they impact other cases. The most effective slippery slope arguments

---

[1] FRED R. SHAPIRO, THE OXFORD DICTIONARY OF AMERICAN LEGAL QUOTATIONS 3 (Oxford University Press 1993).
[2] *Id.*

occur when a decision is novel or when a credible argument can be made that the decision rests outside the jurisprudential mainstream. Mainstream decisions offer fewer opportunities to claim that extraordinary consequences will naturally follow.

Stick to the Issues

There are two primary refutations of a slippery slope argument. First, everyone's attention must be redirected to the issues, because the slippery slope argument focuses on the consequences of the decision, not on the merits of the case. It must be asked, "Should a case's outcome be decided on the facts and the law, or on the ruling's consequences?" If the latter is the choice, what does that say about the integrity of the law? Perhaps the adjudicator(s) should also be asked, "If you are the litigant, how would you want your case decided?" Second, refuting a slippery slope argument often requires a demonstration that there is no inevitability of consequences flowing from the decision.

A close relative of the slippery slope argument is the reductio ad absurdum argument, discussed in the next chapter. The latter argument exaggerates the consequences of a decision by describing the decision in its most extreme application. At times, a single argument can be both a slippery slope argument and a reductio ad absurdum argument, as when it is suggested a decision will inevitably lead to a preposterous construct.

One way to separate these two arguments is to think of them as examples of "affect" and "effect." The slippery slope argument will affect other decisions; the reductio ad absurdum argument describes the effect of a decision, albeit in exaggerated terms. Another way to separate these two fallacies is to consider the slippery slope argument as the journey (down the slippery slope), and the reductio ad absurdum as the destination (an absurd result).

Solicitor Fried, in the first quotation above, suggested that it was possible to pull a lone thread out of the fabric of procreational rights, but Frank Susman argued that the removal of a single thread would unravel the entire fabric, a slippery slope argument. Even though the Supreme Court modified *Roe v. Wade*,[3] its decision in *Webster v. Reproductive Health Services*[4] has not (yet?) proven to be the undoing of individual procreational rights.

---

[3] 410 U.S. 113 (1973).
[4] 492 U.S. 490 (1989).

Darrow on Evolution

In his opening remarks at the Scopes trial, in Dayton, Tennessee, in 1925, Clarence Darrow presented one of the most memorable slippery slope arguments:

> If today you can take a thing like evolution and make it a crime to teach it in the public school, tomorrow you can make it a crime to teach it in the private school, and the next year you can make it a crime to teach it from the hustings or in the church. At the next session you may ban books and the newspapers. Soon you may set Catholic against Protestant and Protestant against Protestant, and try to foist your own religion upon the minds of men. If you can do one you can do the other. Ignorance and fanaticism is ever busy and needs feeding. Always it is feeding and gloating for more. Today it is the public-school teachers, tomorrow the private. The next day the preachers and the lecturers, the magazines, the books, the newspapers. After a while, Your Honor, it is setting of man against man and creed against creed until, with flying banners and beating drums, we are marching backward to the glorious ages of the sixteenth century when bigots lighted fagots to burn the men who dared to bring intelligence and enlightenment and culture to the human mind.[5]

Darrow's detailed and vivid depiction of the consequences of banning the teaching of evolution in the public schools has a much more dramatic and enduring effect than if he just said to the jury, "Ladies and gentlemen. Your decision could put the teaching of evolution in the public schools on a slippery slope that would require other school districts to bar its teaching."

Justice Harlan's dissent in *Plessy v. Ferguson*,[6] which upheld Louisiana's law requiring rail carriers to provide separate coaches for blacks and whites, employed questions to promote an effective slippery slope argument:

> If a state can prescribe, as a rule of civil conduct, that whites and blacks shall not travel as passengers in the same railroad coach, why may it not so regulate the use of the streets of its cities and towns to compel white citizens to keep on one side of a street and black citizens to keep on the other? Why may it not, upon like grounds, punish whites and blacks who ride together in street cars or in open vehicles on a public road or street? Why may it not require sheriffs to assign whites to one side of a court-room and blacks to the other? And why

---

[5]ATTORNEY FOR THE DAMNED—CLARENCE DARROW IN THE COURTROOM 187–88 (Arthur Weinberg ed., University of Chicago Press 1989).
[6]163 U.S. 537 (1896).

may it not also prohibit the commingling of the two races in the galleries of legislative halls or in public assemblages convened for the consideration of the political questions of the day?[7]

Ordinarily, one side to a controversy will offer a slippery slope argument, fearing the consequences of an adverse decision. But in *Hamdan v. Rumsfeld*,[8] a 2006 end-of-term decision by the U.S. Supreme Court, both sides to the case presented a slippery slope argument. In *Hamdan*, a 5-3 majority of the Court found that the military commissions established by the President lacked the appropriate structures and procedures. (Chief Justice Roberts did not participate in the consideration or decision.)

During oral argument, Hamdan's attorney argued that acceptance of the government's position would allow the government to proceed with 75 commission cases that do not meet due process requirements:

> Hamdan's attorney, Neal Katyal, told the justices, "If you adopt the government's reading here, they have said they want to try 75 military commission cases or so in the first wave, you then will be left with 75 trials that take place without even the most basic question of what the parameters are that these commissions are operating under."[9]

On the other side of the issue, Justice Scalia, dissenting, contended that the Court's willingness to assert jurisdiction in the face of the Detainee Treatment Act of 2005 (DTA), an Act he viewed as divesting the Court of jurisdiction in any Guantanamo case, would create unjustifiable work for the courts:

> A final but powerful indication of the fact that the Court has made a mess of this statute is the nature of the consequences that ensue. Though this case concerns a habeas application challenging a trial by military commission DTA §1005(e)(1) strips the courts of jurisdiction to hear or consider *any* "application for a writ of habeas corpus filed by or on behalf of an alien detained by the Department of Defense at Guantanamo Bay, Cuba." The vast majority of pending petitions, no doubt, do not relate to military commissions at all, but to more commonly challenged aspects of "detention" such as the terms and conditions of confinement. The Solicitor General represents that "[h]abeas petitions have been filed on behalf of a purported 600 [Guantanamo Bay] detainees, "including one that "seek[s] relief on behalf of every Guantanamo detainee who has not already filed an

---

[7]*Id.* at 557–58.
[8]548 U.S. 557 (2006).
[9]http://www.cnn.com/2006/LAW/06/29/scotus.tribunals/index.html.

action, ..." The Court's interpretation transforms a provision abolishing jurisdiction over *all* Guantanamo-related habeas petitions into a provision that retains jurisdiction over cases sufficiently numerous to keep the courts busy for years to come.[10] (italics and brackets in original; citations omitted; ellipses added).

Justice Thomas, also dissenting, presented a slippery slope argument when he argued that the Court's decision impedes the President's ability to fight terrorism:

> Though the charge against Hamdan easily satisfied even the plurality's manufactured rule, the plurality's inflexible approach has dangerous implications for the Executive's ability to discharge his duties as Commander in Chief in future cases.[11] (citation omitted).

The Nose of the Camel

A dispute over the definition of an "emission standard" produced a 5-4 U.S. Supreme Court decision in *Adamo Wrecking Co. v. United States*.[12] Justice Potter Stewart's dissent described the majority's opinion as allowing the camel to come into the tent:

> Finally, the Court provides no real guidance as to which aspects of an emission standard are so critical that they fall outside the scope of the exclusive judicial review procedure provided by Congress. For example, §112 requires that an emission standard relate to a "hazardous air pollutant," and that it be set so as to provide "an ample margin of safety to protect the public health." Such express congressional mandates would seem at least as important in determining whether a regulation is a statutorily authorized emission standard as the supposed requirement that the regulation be numerical in form. Are issues such as these, therefore, now to be subject to review in trial court enforcement proceedings? The Court today has allowed the camel's nose into the tent, and I fear that the rest of the camel is almost certain to follow.[13]

Justice Breyer invoked the "camel" analogy in *Zelman v. Simmons-Harris*,[14] a case involving the legality of school vouchers in the private schools:

---

[10] *Hamden, supra* note 8, at 669.
[11] *Id.* at 691.
[12] 434 U.S. 275 (1978).
[13] *Id.* at 292–93.
[14] 536 U.S. 639 (2002).

Vouchers also differ in *degree*. The aid programs recently upheld by the Court involved limited amounts of aid to religion. But the majority's analysis here appears to permit a considerable shift of taxpayer dollars from public secular schools to private religious schools. That fact, combined with the use to which these dollars will be put, exacerbates the conflict problem. State aid that takes the form of peripheral secular items, with prohibitions against diversion of funds to religious teaching, holds significantly less potential for social division. In this respect as well, the secular aid upheld in *Mitchell* differs dramatically from the present case. Although it was conceivable that minor amounts of money could have, contrary to the statute, found their way to the religious activities of the recipients, that case is at worst the camel's nose, while the litigation before us is the camel itself.[15] (italics in original).

The author of an article entitled, "The Nose of the Camel: Extending the Public Policy Exception Beyond the Wrongful Discharge Context,"[16] argues that the judicial exceptions to the employment at-will doctrine have gone too far, and should be strictly limited:

> Given the substantial increase in litigation that an expansion of the public policy tort portends, and given the protection which employees are already afforded by the myriad of employment discrimination laws in existence, the better approach would be to halt any further encroachment of the public policy exception to at-will employment on the rights of employers to make legitimate business decisions. If any further expansion of this tort is permitted, it should be in the area of wrongful demotion or transfer, rather than the context of wrongful failure to hire or promote . . .[17] (ellipses added).

"Portends" in the preceding quotation, and "harbinger" in the next, are tip-offs to a slippery slope argument. Justice Thurgood Marshall's critique of Justice O'Connor's concurring opinion in *Duckworth v. Eagan*,[18] a case involving the appropriate scope of *Miranda* warnings, intimates she is willing to undermine habeas corpus law:

> Today, however, Justice O'Connor seeks to extend *Stone* beyond the Fourth Amendment even though this issue was not raised by petitioner Duckworth below or in his petition for certiorari. Her concurring opinion evinces such a palpable distaste for collateral review

---

[15]*Id.* at 727.
[16]Lab. Law. 371 (ABA 1997).
[17]*Id.* at 390–91.
[18]492 U.S. 195 (1989).

of state-court judgments that it can only be viewed as a harbinger of future assaults on federal habeas corpus.[19] (footnote omitted).

Decrying lawsuits against tobacco companies for selling legal products, the Deputy General Counsel of the R.J. Reynolds Tobacco Co., writing in the ABA Journal, advanced a slippery slope argument that the manufacturers of other legal products could fall victim to debilitating lawsuits:

> The States should also give notice to the manufacturers of other consumer products that the rules have changed, and the manufacturers of alcoholic beverages, motorcycles, fatty foods, to name a few, may find themselves the next object of their attention. Just recall the words of Dexter Douglas, general counsel to Gov. Lawton Chiles, who, at the state of Florida's Feb. 21, 1995, press conference to announce its Medicaid suit, responded to a question whether this kind of suit could be brought against the alcoholic beverage industry:
>
> "At this point we don't have the statistics to proceed in that regard. We're only proceeding against tobacco. You gotta take 'em one at a time. I don't believe anybody in the world could handle all those industries at once."
>
> Like tobacco, the widespread awareness of the risks of products from those industries also stems back decades to centuries.[20]

Legal Floodgates

Several states filed amicus briefs in support of the Florida Supreme Court, in *Bush v. Gore*,[21] arguing that the U.S. Supreme Court's failure to uphold the Florida court's decision would open the legal floodgates to due process claims.

> If this Court were to hold that the Florida Supreme Court's interpretation of Florida law constituted a retroactive "change" in the law, rather than an explanation of what the law had always been, this Court would be opening the door to a flood of due process claims. Whenever a court adopted a new interpretation of a statute, or answered a question of statutory interpretation of a statute, or answered a question of statutory interpretation for the first time, individuals adversely affected by the decision could claim a violation of due process rights. Whenever the courts were required to interpret statutes with civil or

---

[19]*Id.* at 221.
[20]A.B.A. J. 56 (Jan. 1997).
[21]531 U.S. 98 (2000).

criminal penalties, such as consumer fraud statutes, to apply to new factual situations, adversely affected parties could claim a violation of due process rights. Any new interpretation of a criminal statute could lead to claims of *ex post facto* laws in violation of Article I, section 10 of the Constitution. Indeed, this Court itself engages in statutory construction of federal statutes. Litigants could very well claim that new interpretations of federal statutes by this Court, or other federal courts, give rise to claims that their due process rights were violated.[22]

On Justice Thurgood Marshall's last day on the U.S. Supreme Court, a 5-4 majority, in *Payne v. Tennessee*,[23] overruled two recent decisions, *Booth v. Maryland*[24] and *South Carolina v. Gathers*,[25] thereby permitting the introduction of victim impact statements in criminal trials. Justice Marshall directed his ire at the consequences for *stare decisis*, and argued the Court was on a slippery slope:

> In dispatching *Booth* and *Gathers* to their graves, today's majority ominously suggests that an even more extensive upheaval of this Court's precedents may be in store. Renouncing this Court's historical commitment to a conception of "the judiciary as a source of impersonal and reasoned judgments," the majority declares itself free to discard any principle of constitutional liberty which was recognized or reaffirmed over the dissenting votes of four Justices and with which five or more Justices *now* disagree. The implications of this radical new exception to the doctrine of *stare decisis* are staggering. The majority today sends a clear signal that scores of established constitutional liberties are now ripe for reconsideration, thereby inviting the very type of open defiance of our precedents that the majority rewards in this case. Because I believe that this Court owes more to its constitutional precedents in general and to *Booth* and *Gathers* in particular, I dissent.[26] (citations omitted).

Not only does Justice Marshall utilize a slippery slope argument (e.g., "scores of established constitutional liberties are now ripe for reconsideration"), he also presents a reductio ad absurdum argument ("the majority declares itself free to discard *any principle* of constitutional liberty"). (italics added). As discussed in the next chapter, Marshall's

---

[22]http://frwebgate.access.gopo.gov/supremecourt/amicuscuriaebriefofiowa.pdf (2000).
[23]501 U.S. 808 (1991).
[24]482 U.S. 496 (1987).
[25]490 U.S. 805 (1989).
[26]*Payne, supra* note 23, at 844–45.

declaration that "any" principle is open to reconsideration is an exaggeration of the Court's holding.

Justice Scalia, a majority participant in *Payne*, became a dissenter in *Rogers v. Tennessee*,[27] where the Court eliminated the requirement that a victim's death must occur within a year and a day of the fatal injury in order to establish proximate cause. Instead of referring to "constitutional liberties . . . ripe for reconsideration," Justice Scalia refers to "outdated relics (of the common law) subject to judicial rescission"—the identical argument Justice Marshall made in *Payne*:

> Even if I agreed with the Court that the Due Process Clause is violated only when there is lack of "fair warning" of the impending retroactive change, I would not find such fair warning here. It is not clear to me, in fact, what the Court believes the fair warning consisted of. Was it the mere fact that "[t]he year and a day rule is widely viewed as an outdated relic of the common law"? So are many of the elements of common-law crimes, such as breaking the close as an element of burglary, or "asportation" as an element of larceny. Are all of these "outdated relics" subject to retroactive judicial rescission?[28] (brackets in original; citations omitted).

Two years later, in *Lawrence v. Texas*,[29] Justice Scalia, in dissent, again presents the identical argument, when he argues that the majority's decision calls into question every single state law mentioned below:

> State Laws against bigamy, same-sex marriage, adult incest, prostitution, masturbation, adultery, fornication, bestiality, and obscenity are likewise sustainable only in light of *Bowers'* validation of laws based on moral choices. Every single one of these laws is called into question by today's decision; the Court makes no effort to cabin the scope of its decision to exclude them from its holding.[30]

Rejecting this slippery slope argument, Justice Kennedy draws attention to the facts of the case to illustrate why the decision will not lead to unwanted consequences:

> The present case does not involve minors. It does not involve persons who might be injured or coerced or who are situated in relationships where consent might not easily be refused. It does not involve public conduct or prostitution. It does not involve whether the government must give formal recognition to any relationship that homosexual

---

[27] 532 U.S. 451 (2001).
[28] *Id.* at 478–79.
[29] 539 U.S. 558 (2003).
[30] *Id.* at 590.

persons seek to enter. The case does involve two adults who, with full and mutual consent from each other, engaged in sexual practices common to a homosexual lifestyle. The petitioners are entitled to respect for their private lives. The State cannot demean their existence or control their destiny by making their private sexual conduct a crime. Their right to liberty under the Due Process Clause gives them the full right to engage in their conduct without intervention of the government. "It is a promise of the Constitution that there is a realm of personal liberty which the government may not enter."[31] (citation omitted).

Justice Kennedy attempted to head off a slippery slope debate, in *Allegheny County v. Greater Pittsburgh ACLU*,[32] by citation to existing case law:

> There is no realistic risk that the creche and the menorah represent an effort to proselytize or are otherwise the first step down the road to an establishment of religion. *Lynch* is dispositive of this claim with respect to the creche, and I find no reason for reaching a different result with respect to the menorah. Both are the traditional symbols of religious holidays that over time have acquired a secular component. Without ambiguity, *Lynch* instructs that "the focus of our inquiry must be on the [religious symbol] in the context of the [holiday] season." In that context, religious displays that serve "to celebrate the Holiday and to depict the origins of that Holiday" give rise to no Establishment Clause concern. If Congress and the state legislatures do not run afoul of the Establishment Clause when they begin each day with a state-sponsored prayer for divine guidance offered by a chaplain whose salary is paid at government expense, I cannot comprehend how a menorah or a creche, displayed in the limited context of the holiday season, can be invalid.[33] (brackets in original; footnotes and citations omitted).

Point/Counterpoint

A point/counterpoint exchange occurred in *Webster v. Reproductive Health Services*,[34] between Justice Blackmun and Chief Justice Rehnquist. The plurality's decision, according to Justice Blackmun, would inevitably lead to more restrictions on abortion laws:

---

[31]*Id.* at 578.
[32]492 U.S. 573 (1989).
[33]*Id.* at 664–65.
[34]*Webster, supra* at 556.

It is impossible to read the plurality opinion and especially its final paragraph, without recognizing its implicit invitation to every State to enact more and more restrictive abortion laws, and to assert their interest in potential life as of the moment of conception. All these laws will satisfy the plurality's nonscrutiny, until sometime, a new regime of old dissenters and new appointees will declare what the plurality intends: that *Roe* is no longer good law.[35] (footnote omitted).

Responding, Chief Justice Rehnquist proffered a reductio ad absurdum argument (exaggeration: "Dark Ages") and explained why the asserted consequences were not inevitable (his faith in the state legislators and those who elect them):

The goal of constitutional adjudication is to hold true the balance between that which the Constitution puts beyond the reach of the democratic process and that which it does not. We think we have done that today. Justice Blackmun's suggestion, that legislative bodies, in a Nation where more than half of our population is women, will treat our decision today as an invitation to enact abortion regulation reminiscent of the Dark Ages not only misreads our views but does scant justice to those who serve in such bodies and the people who elect them.[36] (citation omitted).

A similar argument to that of the Chief Justice, that undesirable forfeitures are not inevitable—because of faith in the States and the political branches of the Federal Government—was put forth by Justice Scalia in *Bennis v. Michigan*:[37]

Improperly used, forfeiture could become more like a roulette wheel employed to raise revenue from innocent but hapless owners whose property is unforeseeably misused, or a tool wielded to punish those who associate with criminals, than a component of a system of justice. When the property sought to be forfeited has been entrusted by its owner to one who uses it for crime, however, the Constitution apparently assigns to the States and to the political branches of the Federal Government the primary responsibility for avoiding that result.[38]

The Supreme Court's rejoinder to the petitioner's slippery slope argument, in *Buckhannon v. West Virginia*[39] (that plaintiffs would be deterred from filing meritorious claims), was to note the lack of empirical evidence to support such deterrence (appeal to ignorance):

---

[35] *Id.* at 556.
[36] *Id.* at 521.
[37] 516 U.S. 442 (1996).
[38] *Id.* at 456–57.
[39] 532 U.S. 598 (2001).

Petitioners finally assert that the "catalyst theory" is necessary to prevent defendants from unilaterally mooting an action before judgment in an effort to avoid an award of attorney's fees. They also claim that the rejection of the "catalyst theory" will deter plaintiffs with meritorious but expensive cases from bringing suit. We are skeptical of these assertions, which are entirely speculative and unsupported by any empirical evidence . . .[40] (ellipses added).

For many years, beginning in the late 1800s through the mid-1930s, the U.S. Supreme Court frequently invalidated social legislation based on substantive due process grounds. The lack of standards to evaluate legislation under this legal theory created many problems. Once the Court heads down the path to widespread use of substantive due process, there may be no stopping. The Court, itself, acknowledged this potential and provided reasons to avoid this slippery slope, reasons that transcend the substantive due process debate:

But we "ha[ve] always been reluctant to expand the concept of substantive due process because guideposts for responsible decisionmaking in this unchartered area are scarce and open ended." By extending constitutional protection to an asserted right or liberty interest, we, to a great extent, place the matter outside the arena of public debate and legislative action. We must therefore "exercise the utmost care whenever we are asked to break new ground in this field," lest the liberty protected by the Due Process Clause be subtly transformed into the policy preferences of the members of this Court.[41] (citations omitted; brackets in original).

Similarly, in *Ramdass v. Angelone*,[42] the U.S. Supreme Court refused the defendant's request to extend the Court's ruling in *Simmons v. South Carolina*,[43] to cover his case:

Ramdass contends the Virginia Supreme Court nevertheless was bound to extend *Simmons* to cover his circumstances. He urges us to ignore the legal rules dictating his parole eligibility under state law in favor of what he calls a functional approach, under which, it seems, a court evaluates whether it looks like the defendant will turn out to be parole ineligible. We do not agree that the extension of *Simmons* is either necessary or workable; and we are confident in saying

---

[40] *Id.* at 608.
[41] Washington v. Glucksberg, 521 U.S. 702 (1997).
[42] 530 U.S. 156 (2000).
[43] 512 U.S. 154 (1994).

that the Virginia Supreme Court was not unreasonable in refusing the requested extension.[44]

Arguments against expanding the law, because of a lack of standards or because they are simply unworkable, are not confined to majority opinions. Justice Stevens, dissenting in *Boy Scouts of America v. Dale*,[45] advances the same argument:

> If this Court were to defer to whatever position an organization is prepared to assert in its briefs, there would be no way to mark the proper boundary between genuine exercises of the right to associate, on the one hand, and sham claims that are simply attempts to insulate nonexpressive private discrimination, on the other hand. Shielding a litigant's claim from judicial scrutiny would, in turn, render civil rights legislation a nullity, and turn this important constitutional right into a farce. Accordingly, the Court's prescription of total deference will not do.[46]

---

[44]*Id.* at 169.
[45]530 U.S. 640 (2000).
[46]*Id.* at 687.

CHAPTER NINETEEN

Reductio Ad Absurdum

> *The process of Constitutional adjudication does not thrive on conjuring up horrible possibilities that never happen in the real world and devising doctrines sufficiently comprehensive in detail to cover the remotest contingency.*
>
> Justice Felix Frankfurter, *New York v. United States*, 326 U.S. 572, 583 (1946).

THE PREVIOUS CHAPTER considered arguments that suggested unwanted consequences would flow from a particular decision. This chapter explores arguments that present a decision in its most extreme form, with the expectation that the decision will be rejected, because no "reasonable" person would conclude those exaggerated consequences are acceptable. Here, too, the argument is shifted from the merits, but in this case—"reductio ad absurdum" or "blow out of proportion" fallacy—the decision is described in its most absurd application. Often, these arguments can be recognized by their use of superlatives or absolutes, such as: any, all, none, no, only, the end of. Outlandish examples describing the consequences of a decision should also be suspect.

As is the case with the slippery slope argument, defending against this fallacy requires a re-direction of the argument to the facts of the case, and questioning whether the case should be decided on its merits—or on its most extreme construct. Justice Frankfurter's quote above suggests two other defenses to this fallacy: (1) the real world consequences are so unlikely to happen that the exaggerated consequences can be discounted or ignored, and (2) laws cannot be written to cover all the remotest contingencies, and extremism should not be the measure of legislation.

President Clinton's attorneys described the Special Prosecutor's (Office of Independent Counsel's) allegation of abuse of power in the following terms:

> The OIC begins with the charge that the President's false denial that he had an improper relationship with Ms. Lewinsky—something that he has now admitted and apologized for—was itself an abuse of power because it served to deceive the American people.[1]

Using words such as "any" (three times in one sentence) and "no," the President's lawyers then defended against the allegation with a reductio ad absurdum argument:

> Implicit in this charge is the notion that **any** official, in **any** branch of the government, who makes a public statement about his own conduct, or indeed **any** other matter, that is not true may be removed from office. It would follow, therefore, that **no** official could mount a defense to impeachment, or to ethics charges, or to a criminal investigation while remaining in office, for anything other than an immediate admission of guilt will necessarily be misleading.[2] (bold added).

Exaggerated Terms

Another technique is to propound a question that exaggerates the consequences, as in this refutation of the abuse of power allegation:

> Last, the OIC charges that it was an abuse of power for the President, at a time when both his personal and official interests were in the balance, not to testify before the grand jury until August—surely a claim that must astound lawyers and laymen alike. Could the OIC truly be taking the position that **any** government official who is the subject of a criminal investigation must immediately come forward and testify at a prosecutor's whim or risk impeachment? To state the question is to answer it.[3]

The final sentence identifies a different fallacy posed by the query: begging the question, because the conclusion is but a restatement of the proof.

Describing the implications of the abuse of power allegation, in exaggerated terms, is another technique that can be employed:

---

[1] CHICAGO TRIBUNE, Sept. 13, 1998, at 40.
[2] Id.
[3] Id.

Implicit in the allegation is the notion that **any** official, in **any** branch of the government, who makes a statement about his own conduct, or indeed **any** other matter, that is not absolutely true is liable for misusing his office for so long as he fails to admit wrongdoing, for the official's staff will inevitably repeat his explanation in any number of forums. It would follow, therefore, according to what appears to be the OIC's reasoning, that **no** official could mount a defense to impeachment, or to ethics charges, or to a criminal investigation while remaining in office, for anything other than an admission of guilt will be treated as an abuse of his official powers.[4]

Justice Thurgood Marshall similarly attacked the implications of the majority's decision for *stare decisis*, in *Payne v. Tennessee*[5]:

Carried to its logical conclusion, the majority's debilitated conception of *stare decisis* would destroy the Court's very capacity to resolve authoritatively the abiding conflicts between those with power and those without. If this Court shows so little respect for its own precedents, it can hardly expect them to be treated more respectfully by the state actors whom these decisions are supposed to bind.[6] (citations omitted).

In the previous chapter, Justice Marshall's quote from *Payne v. Tennessee* was described as a reductio ad absurdum argument:

[T]he majority declares itself free to discard **any** principle of constitutional liberty which was recognized or reaffirmed over the dissenting votes of four Justices and with which five or more Justices now disagree. The implications of this radical new exception to the doctrine of stare decisis are staggering.[7] (bold added).

The word "any" describes the implications of the majority's opinion and suggests there is no immutable principle of constitutional liberty.

Like Justice Marshall in *Payne v. Tennessee*, Justice Scalia attacked the implications of the majority's decision in *J.E.B. v. Alabama*,[8] involving peremptory challenges based solely on sex:

The irrationality of today's strike-by-strike approach to equal protection is evident from the consequences of extending it to its logical conclusion. If a fair and impartial trial is a prosecutor's only legitimate goal; if adversarial trial stratagems must be tested against that goal in

---

[4]*Id.* at 35.
[5]501 U.S. 808 (1991).
[6]*Id.* at 853.
[7]*Id.* at 845.
[8]511 U.S. 127 (1994).

abstraction from their role within the system as a whole; and if, so tested, sex-based stratagems do not survive heightened scrutiny—then the prosecutor presumably violates the Constitution when he selects a male or female police officer to testify because he believes one or the other sex might be more convincing in the context of the particular case, or because he believes one or the other might be more appealing to a predominantly male or female jury. A decision to stress one line of argument or present certain witnesses before a mostly female jury—for example, to stress that the defendant victimized women—becomes, under the Court's reasoning, intentional discrimination by a state actor on the basis of gender.[9]

To rebut the charge that President Clinton tampered with witnesses, his lawyers exaggerated the consequences of the charge, again by using the word "any":

> In fact, the President simply repeated to aides substantially the same statement he made to the whole country. There was no action here intended specifically to influence the grand jury through the testimony of presidential aides. Under the OIC's theory, it could have subpoenaed to the grand jury **any** citizen who heard the President's denial and thus have created a new violation of law.[10] (bold added).

Exaggeration was the technique employed by Justice Scalia to attack Justice O'Connor's opinion in *Webster v. Reproductive Health Services*[11]:

> Similarly irrational is the new concept that Justice O'Connor introduces into the law in order to achieve her result, the notion of a State's "interest in potential life when viability is possible." Since "viability" means the mere possibility (not the certainty) of survivability outside the womb, "possible viability" must mean the possibility of a possibility of survivability outside the womb. Perhaps our next opinion will expand the third trimester into the second even further, by approving state action designed to take account of "the chance of possible viability."[12] (citations omitted; parentheses in original).

Extreme Examples

A common reductio ad absurdum technique entails an overstated example to illustrate the application of a particular decision.

---

[9] *Id.* at 163.
[10] CHICAGO TRIBUNE, Sept. 13, 1998, at 35.
[11] 492 U.S. 490 (1989) (Scalia, J., concurring).
[12] *Id.* at 536–37 n.*.

In *Hill v. Colorado*,[13] the majority described the issue before the Court as:

> At issue is the constitutionality of a 1993 Colorado statute that regulates speech-related conduct within 100 feet of the entrance to any health care facility. The specific section of the statute that is challenged, makes it unlawful within the regulated areas for any person to "knowingly approach" within eight feet of another person, without that person's consent, "for the purpose of passing a leaflet or handbill to, displaying a sign to, or engaging in oral protest, education, or counseling with such other person."[14] (citation and footnote omitted).

Justices on both sides of the issue noted extreme examples that they contended would constitute the natural fallout of the decision. Justice Stevens, writing for the majority, cited two examples from the petitioner's brief to the Court:

> [S]uppose two women march along a sidewalk within 100 feet of a health care facility, deliberately approaching within 8 feet of a man headed to the facility to have a disfiguring wart removed. Without obtaining consent, one says, "Good morning," while the second tells passersby, "Natural is best, don't put plastic surgery to the test." The second woman would be violating Colorado law (if permission is not obtained), but not the first woman—yet the only difference is the content of the message.

> Or suppose two lab technicians on a coffee break while working at a community hospital are walking over to a smokers' hospitality zone and, while within 100 feet of the entrance to the hospital they deliberately approach within 8 feet of a third person. Without first asking consent, one man recites a few lines of *Jabberwocky* by Lewis Carroll, and the second declares, "I object to the hospital board's penurious treatment of staff." The second man would be guilty of uttering an oral protest, while the first man presumably would not.[15]

Both examples play to the argument that the majority is regulating the content of speech in the protected zone around a health care facility. Justice Scalia argued, by way of reductio ad absurdum, that "the vice . . . is not that it is always used for invidious thought-control purposes, but that it lends itself to use for those purposes."[16] (ellipses added).

---

[13] 530 U.S. 703 (2000).
[14] *Id.* at 707.
[15] *Id.* at 720, n.28. http://supreme.lp.findlaw.com/supreme_court/briefs/98-1856/98-1856.mer.aa.pdf. Brief for Petitioners, at 40–41.
[16] *Id.* at 743.

The majority countered this argument by minimizing the likelihood the Court would become embroiled in a dispute over what someone says:

> Petitioners contend that an individual near a health care facility who knowingly approaches a pedestrian to say "good morning" or to randomly recite lines from a novel would not be subject to the statute's restrictions. Because the content of the oral statements made by an approaching speaker must sometimes be examined to determine whether the knowing approach is covered by the statute, petitioners argue that the law is "content-based" under our reasoning in *Carey v. Brown*.[17] (citation omitted).
>
> . . . .
>
> We have never held, or suggested, that it is improper to look at the content of an oral or written statement in order to determine whether a rule of law applies to a course of conduct. With respect to the conduct that is the focus of the Colorado statute, it is unlikely that there would often be any need to know exactly what words were spoken in order to determine whether "sidewalk counselors" are engaging in "oral protest, education, or counseling" rather than pure social or random conversation.[18] (ellipses added).

Considerable Overstatement

Another defense offered by the majority was to label the dissent's reductio ad absurdum argument "considerable overstatement," followed by an explanation why this was so:

> Justice Kennedy, however, argues that the statute leaves petitioners without adequate means of communication. This is a considerable overstatement. The statute seeks to protect those who wish to enter health care facilities, many of whom may be under special physical or emotional stress, from close physical approaches by demonstrators. In doing so, the statute takes a prophylactic approach; it forbids all unwelcome demonstrators to come closer than eight feet. We recognize that by doing so, it will sometimes inhibit a demonstrator whose approach in fact would have proved harmless. But the statute's prophylactic aspect is justified by the great difficulty of protecting, say, a pregnant woman from physical harassment with legal rules that focus exclusively on the individual impact of each instance of behavior,

---

[17]*Id.* at 720.
[18]*Id.* at 721.

demanding in each case an accurate characterization (as harassing or not harassing) of each individual movement within the 8-foot boundary. Such individualized characterization of each individual movement is often difficult to make accurately. A bright-line prophylactic rule may be the best way to provide protection, and, at the same time, by offering clear guidance and avoiding subjectivity, to protect speech itself.[19] (citation omitted; parentheses in original).

Not to be outdone, the majority then presents its own reductio ad absurdum example, applying the statute to those who are most unlikely to offer their message at a health care facility:

The Colorado statute's regulation of the location of protests, education, and counseling is easily distinguishable from *Carey*. It places no restrictions on—and clearly does not prohibit—either a particular viewpoint or any subject matter that may be discussed by a speaker. Rather, it simply establishes a minor place restriction on an extremely broad category of communications with unwilling listeners. Instead of drawing distinctions based on the subject that the approaching speaker may wish to address, the statute applies equally to used car salesmen, animal rights activists, fundraisers, environmentalists, and missionaries. Each can attempt to educate unwilling listeners on any subject, but without consent may not approach within eight feet to do so.[20]

Justice Scalia quoted French novelist Anatole France, noted for an expression of similar import: "The law, in its majestic equality, forbids the rich as well as the poor to sleep under bridges, to get in the streets, and to steal bread."[21]

The petitioners in *Hill v. Colorado* argued in their brief that the Colorado statute was vague because the examples they tendered were not specifically defined by the statute:

Moreover, although the statute restricts "knowingly approaching" others, the statute does not indicate whether approaches are measured from the body or from the limbs or from personal property in the physical possession of the speaker, such as signs, leaflets, or pamphlets. Will the stretching outward of an arm constitute "approaching"? Will the tendency of an orator to rock forward on the balls of his feet as he speaks transform otherwise protected expression into a crime? . . . The statute does not clarify in a constitutionally sufficient manner whether the motion of a hand, intentionally extended toward another

---

[19] *Id.* at 729.
[20] *Id.* at 723.
[21] *Id.* at 744 (quoting J. BARTLETT, FAMILIAR QUOTATIONS 550 (16th ed. 1992)).

person while the pamphleteer stands *still*, violates the statute.[22] (ellipses added; italics in original).

Justice Stevens defended against these reductio ad absurdum arguments, by noting that language does not share the precision of mathematics, and that the statute is sufficiently specific in the majority of its applications:

> Petitioners proffer hypertechnical theories as to what the statute covers, such as whether an outstretched arm constitutes "approaching." And while "[t]here is little doubt that imagination can conjure up hypothetical cases in which the meaning of these terms will be in nice question," because we are "[c]ondemned to the use of words, we can never expect mathematical certainty from our language," *Grayned v. City of Rockford*. For these reasons, we rejected similar vagueness challenges to the injunctions at issue in *Schenck*, and *Madsen*. We thus conclude that "it is clear what the ordinance as a whole prohibits." *Grayned*. More importantly, speculation about possible vagueness in hypothetical situations not before the Court will not support a facial attack on a statute when it is surely valid "in the vast majority of its intended applications."[23] (footnotes and citations omitted; brackets in original).

Not all reductio ad absurdum arguments depend on extreme examples for their success. Justice Kennedy, dissenting in *Hill v. Colorado*, makes use of common examples (asking for the time, the weather forecast, or directions) in a way that makes them seem absurd in light of the majority's decision:

> To say that one citizen can approach another to ask the time or the weather forecast or the directions to Main Street but not to initiate discussion on one of the most basic moral and political issues in all of contemporary discourse, a question touching profound ideas in philosophy and theology, is an astonishing view of the First Amendment. For the majority to examine the statute under rules applicable to content-neutral regulations is an affront to First Amendment teachings.[24]

Humor and Ridicule

Another dissenter in *Hill v. Colorado*, Justice Scalia, combined a reductio ad absurdum argument with humor/ridicule. He argued that the major-

---

[22]http://supreme.lp.findlaw.com/supreme_court/briefs/98-1856/98-1856mo1/brief/brief30.html. Petitioners' Brief at 48.
[23]*Id.* at 733.
[24]*Id.* at 768.

ity's decision renders the First Amendment "a dead letter," and he burlesqued "narrow tailoring":

> Suffice it to say that if protecting people from unwelcome communications (the governmental interest the Court posits) is a compelling state interest, the **First Amendment is a dead letter.** And if (as I shall discuss at greater length below) forbidding peaceful, nonthreatening, but uninvited speech from a distance closer than eight feet is a "narrowly tailored" means of preventing the obstruction of entrance to medical facilities (the governmental interest the State asserts) **narrow tailoring must refer not to the standards of Versace, but to those of Omar the tentmaker.**[25] (parentheses in original; bold added).

In *J.E.B. v. Alabama*,[26] Justice Scalia maintained the majority's opinion placed "all" peremptory strikes at risk, if based on "any" group characteristic, but, nevertheless, allowed selective stereotyping:

> That places *all* peremptory strikes based on *any* group characteristic at risk, since they can all be denominated "stereotypes." Perhaps, however (though I do not see why it should be so), only the stereotyping of groups entitled to heightened or strict scrutiny constitutes "the very stereotype the law condemns"—so that other stereotyping (e.g., wide-eyed blondes and football players are dumb) remains OK. Or perhaps when the Court refers to "impermissible stereotypes," it means the adjective to be limiting, rather than descriptive—so that we can expect to learn from the Court's peremptory/stereotyping jurisprudence in the future which stereotypes the Constitution frowns upon and which it does not.[27] (parentheses and italics in original; citation omitted).

A car was forfeited to the State of Michigan when a husband used the vehicle to carry out an illicit tryst, in *Bennis v. Michigan*[28] Justice Stevens argued that the majority's approval of the forfeiture would set the stage for even more extreme confiscations:

> The logic of the Court's analysis would permit the States to exercise virtually unbridled power to confiscate vast amounts of property where professional criminals have engaged in illegal acts. Some airline passengers have marijuana cigarettes in their luggage; some hotel guests are thieves; some spectators at professional sports events carry concealed weapons; and some hitchhikers are prostitutes. The State

---

[25] *Id.* at 748–49.
[26] *Supra* note 8.
[27] *Id.* at 161.
[28] 516 U.S. 442 (1996).

surely may impose strict obligations on the owners of airlines, hotels, stadiums, and vehicles to exercise a high degree of care to prevent others from making illegal use of their property, but neither logic nor history supports the Court's apparent assumption that their complete innocence imposes no constitutional impediment to the seizure of their property simply because it provided the locus for a criminal transaction.[29]

Two conservatives complained to President Bush about a Department of Justice plan to use local law enforcement to enforce immigration laws. As in a previous example, above, a question can serve as a vehicle for a reductio ad absurdum argument:

> Two leading conservatives have joined a chorus of police officials and immigrant rights advocates in opposing a Justice Department proposal to allow state and local law enforcement agencies to track down illegal immigrants as a way to fight terrorism.
>
> The two conservatives, . . . , wrote President Bush on Friday to complain that the plan under review by Attorney General John Ashcroft would set a dangerous precedent by empowering local jurisdictions to enforce many federal laws.
>
> "If local police are to enforce our immigration laws, will they soon be required to seek out and apprehend those who violate our environmental laws, or the Americans with Disabilities Act as well?" the letter said.[30] (ellipses added).

Name-calling epithets can instantly transform an ordinary argument into a reductio ad absurdum argument. When the Patriot Act was up for renewal, one commentator invoked the opprobrious name of the former East German secret police in connection with the government's surveillance powers:

> Against the backdrop of wide public support for repealing the Patriot Act, Congress now has an obligation to revisit the Patriot Act and at least remove some [of] its more egregious elements.
>
> It should block efforts by the Justice Department to amass even greater surveillance powers. Turning the nation's librarians, bankers and internet service providers into East German Stasi-like snoops for the FBI is as un-American as it is absurd.[31] (brackets added).

---

[29]*Id.* at 458–59.
[30]http://www.nytimes.com/2002/06/02/politics/02ENFO.html.
[31]MILWAUKEE JOURNAL SENTINEL, Nov. 9, 2003, at 5J.

Harsh Penalties

The invocation of disproportionately harsh penalties to deter certain conduct is a common reductio ad absurdum technique. Justice Blackmun suggested the majority's abortion position, in *Webster v. Reproductive Health Services*,[32] could be accommodated, among other means, by a tax or criminal penalty:

> The "permissibly furthers" standard completely disregards the irreducible minimum of *Roe*: the Court's recognition that a woman has a limited fundamental constitutional right to decide whether to terminate a pregnancy. That right receives no meaningful recognition in the plurality's written opinion. Since, in the plurality's view, the State's interest in potential life is compelling as of the moment of conception, and is therefore served only if abortion is abolished, every hindrance to a woman's ability to obtain an abortion must be "permissible." Indeed, the more severe the hindrance, the more effectively (and permissibly) the State's interest would be furthered. A tax on abortions or a criminal prohibition would both satisfy the plurality's standard. So, for that matter, would a requirement that a pregnant woman memorize and recite today's plurality opinion before seeking an abortion.[33] (parentheses in original).

The Eighth Amendment's prohibition of "cruel and unusual punishments" has generated considerable disagreement on the U.S. Supreme Court. Justice Stevens, writing for the majority in *Atkins v. Virginia*,[34] which involved execution of the mentally retarded, concluded this excerpt with the hypothetical example of disproportionate punishment: someone confined to prison for having a common cold:

> The Eighth Amendment succinctly prohibits "[e]xcessive sanctions." It provides: Excessive bail shall not be required, nor excessive fines imposed, nor cruel and unusual punishments inflicted. In *Weems v. United States*, we held that a punishment of 12 years jailed in irons at hard and painful labor for the crime of falsifying records was excessive. We explained that it is a precept of justice that punishment for crime should be graduated and proportioned to the offense. We have repeatedly applied this proportionality precept in later cases interpreting the Eighth Amendment. See *Harmelin v. Michigan*. Thus, even though "imprisonment for ninety days is not, in the abstract, a punishment which is either cruel or unusual," it may not be imposed as a penalty

---

[32] 492 U.S. 490 (1989).
[33] *Id.* at 555–56.
[34] 536 U.S. 304 (2002).

for the status of narcotic addiction, *Robinson v. California*, because such a sanction would be excessive. As Justice Stewart explained in *Robinson*: "Even one day in prison would be a cruel and unusual punishment for 'the crime' of having a common cold."[35] (brackets in original; footnote and citations omitted).

Justice Powell, dissenting in *Rummel v. Estelle*,[36] argued that the Eighth Amendment, indeed, contained a "disproportionality" component, and cited an example of extreme punishment for an overtime parking violation:

> The scope of the Cruel and Unusual Punishments Clause extends not only to barbarous methods of punishment, but also to punishments that are grossly disproportionate. Disproportionality analysis measures the relationship between the nature and number of offenses committed and the severity of the punishment inflicted upon the offender. The inquiry focuses on whether a person deserves such punishment, not simply on whether punishment would serve a utilitarian goal. A statute that levied a mandatory life sentence for overtime parking might well deter vehicular lawlessness, but it would offend our felt sense of justice. The Court concedes today that the principle of disproportionality plays a role in the review of sentences imposing the death penalty, but suggests that the principle may be less applicable when a noncapital sentence is challenged. Such a limitation finds no support in the history of Eighth Amendment jurisprudence.[37]

Signaling the End

Predictions that a decision will signal "the end of" something constitute an extreme declaration that leaves no room for interpretation. Justice Scalia declared the majority opinion in *Lawrence v. Texas*,[38] marked "the end of all morals legislation," and punctuated his statement with "none" (referring to laws that could survive rational-basis review):

> The Texas statute undeniably seeks to further the belief of its citizens that certain forms of sexual behavior are "immoral and unacceptable," *Bowers*—the same interest furthered by criminal laws against fornication, bigamy, adultery, adult incest, bestiality, and obscenity. *Bowers* held that this was a legitimate state interest. The Court today reaches the opposite conclusion. The Texas statute, it says, "*furthers*

---

[35]*Id.* at 311.
[36]445 U.S. 263 (1980).
[37]*Id.* at 288.
[38]539 U.S. 558 (2003).

no legitimate state interest which can justify its intrusion into the personal and private life of the individual." The Court embraces instead Justice Stevens' declaration in his *Bowers* dissent, that "the fact that the governing majority in a State has traditionally viewed a particular practice as immoral is not a sufficient reason for upholding a law prohibiting the practice." This effectively decrees **the end of** all morals legislation. If, as the Court asserts, the promotion of majoritarian sexual morality is not even a legitimate state interest, **none** of the above-mentioned laws can survive rational-basis review.[39] (bold added; italics in original; citations omitted).

In 2000, Microsoft criticized the government's proposed settlement of the pending lawsuit, by combining an appeal to the public (a setback for consumers), with a reductio ad absurdum argument (prohibit improvements and new features):

> The government proposal would flatly ban any improvements to Internet Explorer. It would, for all practical purposes, prohibit the addition of any significant new features to Windows for up to 10 years. This would be a major setback not only for Microsoft, but for consumers; our efforts to create a new generation of PCs that easily recognize speech, handwriting and even gestures would be effectively shut down for a decade.[40]

The U.S. Supreme Court, in *Dickerson v. United States*,[41] was called upon to decide whether *Miranda* warnings are constitutional guarantees or whether Congress can legislate restrictions on these rights. Justice Scalia argued that the warnings were not constitutionally guaranteed, and contended the majority had created a "new" Constitution:

> Since there is in fact no other principle that can reconcile today's judgment with the post-*Miranda* cases that the Court refuses to abandon, what today's decision will stand for, whether the Justices can bring themselves to say it or not, is the power of the Supreme Court to write a prophylactic, extraconstitutional Constitution, binding on Congress and the States.[42]

---

[39] *Id.* at 599.
[40] NEWSWEEK, May 22, 2000, at 42.
[41] 530 U.S. 428 (2000).
[42] *Id.* at 461.

CHAPTER TWENTY

Two Wrongs Rarely Make a Right

Lex Talionis

"An eye for an eye, a tooth for a tooth"

Exodus 21:22–23.

IN THE LEGAL SYSTEM, "wrongs" have consequences that could result in forfeitures, penalties, or punishments. A "two wrongs make a right" argument seeks to avoid any adverse consequences for committing a wrong, by citing a previous example of a wrong (related or unrelated) for which there were no adverse consequences. Another version of this argument suggests that there should be no repercussions for committing a wrong, because the "ends justify the means"; that is, a wrong may have been committed, but it was in the pursuit of a proper end or goal or outcome. Both versions depend on a form of moral justification to avoid the consequences of the wrong.

Justice Brandeis, dissenting in *Olmstead v. United States*,[1] a case deciding whether wiretapped evidence violated the Fourth and Fifth Amendments, argued eloquently against the evils of "two wrongs make a right" and the "ends justify the means," in the context of the government engaging in crimes to obtain criminal convictions:

> Decency, security and liberty alike demand that government officials shall be subjected to the same rules of conduct that are commands to the citizen. In a government of laws, existence of the government will be imperiled if it fails to observe the law scrupulously. Our

---
[1] 277 U.S. 438 (1928).

> Government is the potent, the omnipresent teacher. For good or for ill, it teaches the whole people by its example. Crime is contagious. If the Government becomes a lawbreaker, it breeds contempt for law; it invites every man to become a law onto himself; it invites anarchy. To declare that in the administration of the criminal law the end justifies the means—to declare that the Government may commit crimes in order to secure the conviction of a private criminal—would bring terrible retribution. Against that pernicious doctrine this Court should resolutely set its face.[2]

In a tu quoque argument, the proponent is attacked for saying one thing, and doing another—the justification for the argument is the proponent's own conduct. In a "two wrongs make a right" argument, the justification for the second wrong is not limited to a specific person's conduct. Of course, the defense to a "two wrongs make a right" argument is that the second wrong stands on its own as far as any consequence is concerned. The justification, however, may play a role in mitigating the consequences of the wrong.

Under "lex talionis," the victim is permitted to inflict the same injurious conduct that the assailant has inflicted. That may result in a measure of gratification, but does that justify the revenge? Apparently, that theory had (and may still have) a certain following. Although "cruel and unusual" punishments are prohibited by the Constitution (banning the removal of an eye or tooth), capital punishment is left to the states. Some would argue that capital punishment is "an eye for an eye" form of justice.

As discussed in the first chapter, Deputy District Attorney Ann Rundle, who prosecuted actress Winona Ryder, presented a top ten list of things the law doesn't say, including: "8. If you sell $200 hair bows, you deserve to get ripped off." Rundle was denigrating the argument that if a store charges outrageous prices (a wrong), shoplifting (a second wrong) is justifiable. Legally, the only response to a store's charging excessive costs is to refuse to buy the items.

Does the End Justify the Means?

Two significant areas where a "two wrongs make a right" argument come into play are legal ethics and the "invited response" rule. Attorneys charged with violating state ethics codes often respond that their

---
[2] *Id.* at 485.

conduct was justified by the ends they sought to achieve, even if the means were not always proper. Under the "invited response" rule, an attorney is permitted, within limits, to respond to the opposing side's arguments in a manner that, standing alone, would be improper.

On June 8, 1998, Mark Pautler, Chief Deputy District Attorney, was summoned to a Colorado crime scene where police were on the telephone with William Neal, accused of three brutal murders. While talking to police, Neal said he wanted to speak to a Public Defender before he would turn himself in. After making unsuccessful efforts to secure defense counsel and a Public Defender, Pautler posed as a Public Defender in order to get Neal to give himself up. Neal eventually surrendered. Later the Public Defender's office learned of Pautler's deception, and lodged a complaint with the Colorado Bar Association.

Pautler raised a "two wrongs make a right" defense at the hearing before the Colorado Disciplinary Board:

> Pautler contends, however, that the circumstances existing at the time of his conduct, namely, the fear that Neal might harm or kill others, the fact that law enforcement agents did not know Neal's location, and the particularly brutal nature of Neal's crimes, justified his actions and constituted a defense to the charges against him.
>
> . . . .
>
> Pautler also argues that "justification" should be a defense to the professional misconduct charges advanced in the Complaint.[3] (footnote omitted; ellipses added).

The majority of the Board concluded that Pautler's conduct, no matter how noble, did not excuse violating the Colorado disciplinary code:

> While (Pautler's) motives and the erroneous belief of other public prosecutors that (Pautler's) conduct was ethical do not excuse these violations of the Code of Professional Responsibility, they are mitigating factors to be taken into account in assessing the appropriate discipline.[4]

The majority also rejected the "two wrongs" argument:

> The ends do not justify the means. Justification does not present a defense to an alleged violation of (Colorado disciplinary rules). To the extent evidence of justification, or motive, may be considered at all in

---

[3] www.coloradosupremecourt.us/pdj/opinions and summaries/pautler,opinionNo .00PDJ016,4.02.01.PDF.

[4] *Id.* (citing People v. Reichman, 819 P.2d 1035, 1038 (Colo. 1991)).

a disciplinary proceeding against an attorney, it is limited to a consideration of mitigation for the misconduct undertaken.[5]

The lone dissenter found that Pautler's motives should have provided a defense to the ethics charges:

> Because I do not find that the aggravating factor of a selfish or dishonest motive has been established, I also find that most of the cases cited by the majority are not applicable here. In each of those cases in which a substantial sanction was imposed, the violation was committed for reasons of personal gain, sloth, or to skew the legal process to gain a tactical advantage. There are very few cases in which it was found that the attorney had a "good" motive underlying his violation.
>
> In these cases, the most serious sanction was public censure. To the extent that prior cases should influence the imposition of a sanction, I find that these cases are more persuasive.[6] (citations omitted).

The Colorado Supreme Court affirmed the Hearing Board, and rejected "Pautler's assertion that his deception of Neal was 'justified' under the circumstances . . . ."[7] His motive for impersonating a Public Defender, nevertheless, was considered significant in determining the appropriate discipline:

> We stress, however, that the reasons behind Pautler's conduct are not inconsequential. "While the respondent's motives and the erroneous belief of other public prosecutors that the respondent's conduct was ethical do not excuse these violations of the Code of Professional Responsibility, they are mitigating factors to be taken into account in assessing the appropriate discipline."[8] (citation omitted).

Pautler was suspended for three months, which was stayed during 12 months of probation, during which he was required to fulfill various ethics obligations.[9]

An inmate in New York was severely beaten by several corrections officers. Only one officer was willing to come forward, in defiance of the "code of silence" among fellow officers, to state that he had witnessed the unprovoked attack. To protect the identity of this officer, the Inspector General of the New York State Department of Correctional

---

[5] *Pautler, id.*
[6] *Id.*
[7] *In re* Mark C. Pautler, 47 P.3d 1175, 1179 (Colo. 2002).
[8] *Id.* at 1180.
[9] *Id.* at 1183-84.

Services, an attorney, "instructed the officer to testify falsely under oath at one point during the investigation."[10]

Before taking statements from the five implicated officers, the Inspector General met with the officer breaking ranks, in order to determine his credibility. The meeting took place away from the correctional facility, and the officer provided a "true" statement of the beating, afterward condoned by the Commissioner of the Department of Correctional Services to keep the officer's identity secret. When the Inspector General later interviewed the six officers under oath, at the correctional facility, they all denied using undue force, including the officer breaking ranks. His "false" testimony was at the direction of the Inspector General.

Three of the five officers were charged with "the use of undue force and giving false testimony."[11] They filed grievances over their discharges, and on the first day of the arbitration hearing, the officer breaking ranks testified that he provided two contradictory affidavits at the behest of the Inspector General. No one would have known the officer's identity if there had not been an arbitration hearing.

After the arbitration hearing, the Inspector General was charged with violating New York's disciplinary rules "in that 'he counseled and instructed a witness to give contradictory, misleading and inconsistent testimony and attempted to mislead and deceive a party or parties.'"[12]

A referee found that the Inspector General engaged in "conduct involving deceit and misrepresentation."[13]

The Inspector General argued that he did nothing unethical because he was motivated by a desire to protect the identity of the officer. Both the referee and the Appeals Court rejected that argument as "a contention that the end justifies the means."[14]

The two Appeals Court dissenters argued that the ". . . truth rather than being subverted has been augmented,"[15] and

> [d]eceptive behavior by an attorney warrants condemnation when it obscures truth or contravenes the due administration of justice. But not every deception merits punishment for occasions do arise when

---

[10]*In re* Brian F. Malone, 480 N.Y.S.2d 603, 604 (A.D. 3 Dept. 1984).
[11]*Id.* at 605.
[12]*Id.*
[13]*Id.*
[14]*Id.*
[15]*Id.* at 608.

the only practicable law enforcement technique is deceit.[16] (citations omitted).

In other words, the dissenters believed that it was permissible to engage in deception (submitting a false affidavit) in order to right the previous wrong (get the truth about the beating). They even cited Chief Justice Warren:

> There are some situations when the law could not adequately be enforced without the employment of some guile or misrepresentation of identity . . . . It blinks the realities of sophisticated, modern-day criminal activity and legitimate law enforcement practices to argue the contrary.[17] (ellipses in original).

The Chief Justice happened to be a dissenter in that case.

Finally, the dissenters countered the majority's "two wrongs are still wrong" argument with a reductio ad absurdum argument: Corrupt conduct will go unpunished if attorneys are censured for similar actions:

> [w]e believe it worthy of mention that the practical but unwholesome effect of censuring (the Inspector General) may well be the cessation of meaningful investigations of corrupt conduct by similarly engaged lawyers, prosecutors and judges.[18] (citation omitted; parentheses added).

The "Invited Response" Rule

The "invited response" rule is rooted firmly in the U.S. Supreme Court's decision in *United States v. Young*,[19] where the defendant, vice president and general manager of Compton Petroleum Corporation in Abilene, Texas, was charged, among other things, with making false statements to the government and mail fraud. Young's corporation contracted to deliver crude oil to a refinery. More than half of the delivered oil consisted of fuel oil, a refined product not as valuable as crude oil. Young concocted a scheme to have another company purchase fuel oil and sell it to Compton under a false certification, for which he paid the other firm 10 cents a barrel as a fee for "recertification."

Before delivering the fuel oil to the refinery, Young disguised it by adding condensate, a liquid from natural gas wells. (He testified that he thought the mixture could be legitimately certified to be the equivalent

---

[16]*Id.*
[17]*Id.* (citing Hoffa v. United States, 385 U.S. 293, 315 (1966)).
[18]*Malone, supra,* at 609.
[19]470 U.S. 1 (1985).

of crude oil.) Testing by the refinery led to the discovery that fuel oil had been mixed with condensate. The FBI was contacted and a criminal trial followed.

The Court described the defense counsel's closing argument, which followed the prosecutor's:

> Defense counsel began his own summation by arguing that the case against (the defendant) "has been presented unfairly by the prosecution," and that "[f]rom the beginning" to "this very moment the [prosecution's] statements have been made to poison your minds unfairly." He intimated that the prosecution deliberately withheld exculpatory evidence, and proceeded to charge the prosecution with "reprehensible" conduct in purportedly attempting to cast a false light on (the defendant's) activities. Defense counsel also pointed directly at the prosecutor's table and stated: "I submit to you that there's not a person in this courtroom including those sitting at this table who think that Billy Young intended to defraud Apco." Finally, defense counsel stated that (the defendant) had been "the only one in this whole affair that has acted with honor and with integrity" and that "[t]hese complex [Department of Energy] regulations should not have any place in an effort to put someone away."[20] (brackets in original; parentheses added; citation omitted).

No objection was raised to the defendant's argument; instead, the prosecutor responded to the defendant's remarks:

> I think [defense counsel] said that not anyone sitting at this table thinks that Mr. Young intended to defraud Apco. Well, I was sitting there and I think he was. I think he got 85 cents a barrel for every one of those 117,250.91 barrels he hauled and every bit of the money they made on that he got one percent of. So, I think he did. If we are allowed to give out personal impressions *since it was asked of me.*
>
> I don't know what you call that, I call it fraud.
>
> You can look at the evidence and you can remember the testimony, you remember what [the witnesses] said and what (defendant) admitted they said. I think it's a fraud.[21] (brackets and italics in original; citations omitted).

Lastly, the prosecutor answered the assertion that the defendant had acted with honor and integrity:

> I don't know whether you call it honor and integrity, I don't call it that [defense counsel] does. If you feel you should acquit him for that

---

[20] *Id.* at 4–5.
[21] *Id.* at 5.

it's your pleasure. I don't think you're doing your job as jurors in finding facts as opposed to the law that this Judge is going to instruct you, you think that's honor and integrity then stand up here in Oklahoma courtroom and say that's honor and integrity; I don't believe it.[22] (brackets in original; citation omitted).

The majority was unwilling to characterize the prosecutor's remarks as "two wrongs make a right," choosing instead to define the issue as whether defense counsel's failure to object constituted "plain error":

The principal issue to be resolved is not whether the prosecutor's response to defense counsel's misconduct was appropriate, but whether it was "plain error" that a reviewing court could act on absent a timely objection. Our task is to decide whether the standard laid down in . . ., and codified in Federal Rule of Criminal Procedure 52(b) was correctly applied by the Court of Appeals.[23] (citation omitted).

As part of its analysis, the majority lamented the prevalent tit-for-tat responses:

The situation brought before the Court of Appeals was but one example of an all too common occurrence in criminal trials—the defense counsel argues improperly, provoking the prosecutor to respond in kind, and the trial judge takes no corrective action. Clearly two improper arguments—two apparent wrongs—do not make for a right result. Nevertheless, a criminal conviction is not to be lightly overturned on the basis of a prosecutor's comments standing alone, for the statements or conduct must be viewed in context, only by so doing can it be determined whether the prosecutor's conduct affected the fairness of the trial. To help resolve this problem, courts have invoked what is sometimes called the "invited response" or "invited reply" rule . . .[24] (citation omitted; ellipses added).

Accordingly, the majority set forth the test for determining the lawfulness of the prosecutor's argument:

[T]he remarks must be examined within the context of the trial to determine whether the prosecutor's behavior amounted to prejudicial error. In other words, the Court must consider the probable effect the prosecutor's response would have on the jury's ability to judge the evidence fairly. In this context, defense counsel's conduct, as well as the nature of the prosecutor's response, is relevant.[25] (citations omitted.)

---

[22] *Id.* at 5–6.
[23] *Id.* at 6–7.
[24] *Id.* at 11.
[25] *Id.* at 12.

The partial dissenters noted that the Government's petition for certiorari laid claim to a "two wrongs make a right" argument:

> Whether a prosecutor may rebut [improper] closing defense argument... by responsive argument that would be inappropriate in the absence of such provocation. The Government contends that we should recognize "a prosecutor's right to respond" to improper defense arguments and that, in light of this "right," we should hold that such responses "are not improper" even if standing alone they would be impermissible.[26] (brackets and ellipses in original; citations omitted).

The partial dissenters then took issue with the majority's "invited error" analysis: "The conclusion is that prosecutorial misconduct, if 'invited' by defense misconduct, will be excused if it 'did no more than respond substantially in order to 'right the scale.'"[27] (citations omitted).

As for the outcome of the case, the majority concluded the prosecutor's argument did no more than respond to defense counsel's argument, and the remarks did not prejudice the defendant. And so, the Court put its imprimatur on the "invited response" doctrine.

A defense lawyer tried to shift blame to a codefendant (Coleman), by referring to her as a "slick talking monster."[28] The prosecutor retorted that the defendant (Brown) was guilty "and that she was the monster who committed the crime."[29] Brown's conviction was upheld by the Ohio Supreme Court, with this finding: "We do not believe the prosecutor erred to the detriment of (Brown) because the comment was invited by defense counsel."[30]

Seventh Circuit Judge Richard Posner formulated this description of the "invited response" rule:

> Properly understood, that doctrine does not condone the prosecutor's descending to the level of defense counsel or enact the proposition that two wrongs make a right; it merely recognizes that the impact on the defendant from the prosecutor's [misstatements] may be less if the defendant's counsel aroused the jury against the prosecutor.[31] (brackets added).

---

[26] *Id.* at 23.
[27] *Id.* at 25.
[28] State v. Brown, 528 N.E.2d 523, 538 (Ohio 1988).
[29] *Id.*
[30] *Id.*
[31] United States v. Mazzonne, 782 F.2d 757, 763 (7th Cir. 1986) (citing United States v. Young, 470 U.S. 1, 12 (1985)).

And Judge Posner suggested alternatives available to the prosecution when a defense attorney steps out of the ring:

> The government argues that the prosecutor's comments were proper because invited by the defense lawyers, who in their five hours of closing argument accused the government of perjury, fraud, intimidation, and other improprieties in prosecuting their clients. We reject the argument. The federal government's lawyers may not fight fire with fire. If defense counsel exceed proper bounds in their closing arguments, the prosecutor can object; he can, if need be, ask that counsel be held in contempt for improper argument or questions (we sustained such a contempt judgment in *United States v. Lowery*; but he cannot respond in kind and violate ethical standards himself.[32] (citation omitted).

A prosecutor properly responded to a defense attorney's argument invoking facts not in evidence, by describing an alternative scenario:

> Here, defense counsel opened the door by suggesting that Lauretta had been left alone several times with a loaded gun, himself arguing facts that were not in evidence. To rebut this argument, the prosecutor suggested an alternative scenario—that Elisha took the shotgun shell with him into the store, leaving the unloaded gun behind. Viewing the prosecutor's statement in the entire context of the closing argument, it is clear to us that the government's argument was a legitimate response to the defense's speculative closing argument, and the government did not act egregiously or with the intent to deceive. We find no reversible error.[33]

In a conspiracy and multiple fraud case, defense counsel argued that a witness (Finn) who tape recorded the defendant was attempting to gather evidence against him:

> At trial, Finn testified that he surreptitiously tape recorded a telephone conversation that he had with defendant from Finn's attorney's office. During cross examination, defense counsel challenged Finn's motives in making this taped conversation. In summation, defense counsel returned to this testimony and pointed out to the jury that there were a number of questions that Finn did not ask in that taped conversation. Counsel argued that the absence of these questions indicated that Finn was really trying to gather evidence against defendant to then turn over to the Government as part of a plea bargain.

---

[32] *Id.* at 762–63.
[33] United States v. Jacobs, 244 F.3d 503, 508 (6th Cir. 2000).

Defense counsel argued that Finn's attempt to gather evidence failed because defendant was innocent.[34]

Responding to defense counsel's argument that Finn asked questions to incriminate the defendant, the prosecutor posed his own hypothetical questions, arguing that these unasked questions necessarily would have been part of an attempt to incriminate the defendant:

> Can you imagine what the questioning would have been if he was really trying to get evidence?
>
> Mickey what about the $9 million in WBL advances?
>
> Mickey, what about the $295 million [sic] of Phar-Mor money we ran through Jewelry 90?[35] (brackets in original).

The Sixth Circuit found that the prosecutor's hypothetical questions were justified by defense counsel's argument:

> [T]he prosecutor's hypothetical questions to the jury, was proper argument in response to defense counsel's interpretation of the taped conversation. It would take at least two inferential steps for the jury to move from these questions to draw an inference based on defendant's decision not to testify. Even if these comments were improper, we would find they were not flagrant error.[36]

"Plain Error" Rule

"Plain error" is not confined to criminal cases, although it is rare for civil cases to be reversed for this reason, because it requires a showing that the error "resulted in a miscarriage of justice or seriously affected the fairness, integrity or public reputation of the judicial proceedings."[37] Kmart sought to invoke the plain error rule in a case where its counsel, unsuccessfully, replied to the plaintiffs' improper argument with his own improper argument:

> We do not find such a miscarriage of justice in this case, where Kmart's own closing argument was nearly as improper as that of which it complains. Kmart repeatedly introduced emotional elements of its own into the jury's deliberations in response to plaintiffs' counsel's attempts

---

[34]United States v. Monus, 123 F.3d 376, 393–94 (6th Cir. 1997).
[35]*Id.* at 394.
[36]*Id.*
[37]Smith v. Kmart, 177 F.3d 19, 26 (1st Cir. 1999).

to paint Kmart as an uncaring villain. Kmart sought to demonize the plaintiffs when, under the guise of credibility arguments, defense counsel argued: (1) that Smith forgot she was supposed to be in pain until her lawyer reminded her; (2) that Orth was planning litigation rather than attending to his supposedly injured wife; and (3) that Orth claimed to have seen another person express shock at "what [they]'ve done to hide the fact that he caused the accident himself."[38] (brackets in original).

According to the First Circuit, Kmart could not complain when its "wrong" was unsuccessful:

> Both sides made emotional arguments in this case, sometimes proper, sometimes not. But it is hardly a miscarriage of justice when a party fails to object to improper argument by its opponent and chooses to retaliate with improper argument of its own, only to have this strategic decision backfire when the jury returns a substantial award against it.
>
> For all of these reasons, we find no reversible error either in plaintiffs' counsel's summation or in the district court's failure sua sponte to grant a new trial due to that summation.[39]

Consequently, Kmart's improper argument excused the previous improper argument by plaintiffs' counsel, a reversal of the standard "two wrongs make a right" argument, where the first wrong usually excuses the second.

Attempts to limit cell phone use while driving a car have occasionally been the subject of proposed legislation. An opponent of such legislation argues that other conduct, far more dangerous, is unregulated, so why regulate cell phone use?

> Lawmakers should not be involved in regulating what people do inside their cars. If fiddling with the car stereo is more dangerous than cell phone use, should legislators slap a ban on car radios and CD players as well?
>
> A number of different activities—adjustment of air conditioning, drinking coffee, arguing with a spouse, dealing with a rowdy child—can lead to wrecks and even fatal crashes. But there are no bans on these actions because Americans want the liberty to decide when and how they will take risks in favor of convenience or efficiency.[40]

---

[38] *Id.* at 28.

[39] *Id.*

[40] Helen Chaney, *Drive to Limit Cell Phones Based on Bad Information,* Milwaukee Journal Sentinel, July 1, 2001, at 02j.

Should legislators be precluded from enacting prohibitions on cell phone use while driving, when other distractions are not prohibited?

In *Dickerson v. United States*,[41] a case involving the constitutional basis for affording *Miranda* rights, Justice Scalia offered another expression of "two wrongs make a right":

> The foregoing demonstrates that, petitioner's and the United States' suggestions to the contrary notwithstanding, what the Court did in *Miranda* (assuming, as later cases hold, that *Miranda* went beyond what the Constitution actually requires) is in fact extraordinary. That the Court has, on rare and recent occasion, repeated the mistake does not transform error into truth, but illustrates the potential for future mischief that the error entails.[42] (parentheses in original).

Yet another formulation of the "two wrongs" fallacy, drawing upon an analogy, appears in the following: "[A] trespass by the defense [does not] give[] the prosecution a hunting license exempt from ethical restraints on advocacy."[43]

---

[41] 530 U.S. 428 (2000).
[42] *Id.* at 460.
[43] United States v. Capone, 683 F.2d 582, 586 (1st Cir. 1982)(quoting Patriarca v. United States, 402 F.2d 314, 321 (1st Cir. 1968)).

❧ CHAPTER TWENTY-ONE

Threats, Force, and Fear

> *The jury must act objectively, without fear or prejudice. They must determine the guilt or innocence of the defendant from the evidence and it is improper for the prosecutor to taint their judgment with suggestions of personal danger to them or their families if the defendant is acquitted.*
>
> State v. Raspberry, 452 S.W.2d 169, 172 (Mo. 1970).

APPEALS TO THREATS, force, or fear suggest that dire consequences will follow unless a specified argument is accepted. The dire consequences could include: physical harm, pecuniary ruin, character assassination. The Latin name for this fallacy is argumentum ad baculum, argument to the stick or rod. A successful ad baculum argument depends on two conditions: (1) the argument's proponent must make a credible threat or appeal to force; (2) the recipient must fear the consequences. If the threat or force appeals are not plausible or probable, the recipient has no reason to fear the consequences, and the argument loses its effectiveness.

Courtroom ad baculum appeals may emanate from the parties, witnesses, opposing attorneys, and even judges. Criminal trials are especially noteworthy for threats and appeals to force, because defendants are accused of wrongdoing to others (and the future holds a potential for more wrongdoing). Moreover, in criminal trials the individual stakes are high—possibly including the death penalty. Defending against ad baculum appeals in the courtroom may require a "prejudicial" objection, a jury instruction to disregard, or a request for a mistrial. Post-trial, Fourteenth Amendment due process concerns are the most favored appeal route to combat ad baculum appeals.

The quotation at the beginning of this chapter came from a murder case where the prosecutor argued:

> Let us make believers out of these vicious murderers. Let's put a stop to it. Not for a feather in my cap; for the sake of your children and for your wives, and for your families, for the sake of the people in the community.[1]

The prosecution's argument implied that if the jury did not convict the defendants, everyone in the community would be at risk for their lives. The Missouri Supreme Court concluded that the prosecutor's appeal to fear was improper, but the trial court did not abuse its authority by refusing to grant a mistrial.[2]

In a similar vein, another prosecutor urged the jury to convict a defendant accused of assaulting a little girl, by appealing to their fears that it could happen to a child they knew and cared about:

> Send this man to five years in the Pen. Don't let him out running around the streets 'cause if any of you have any daughters and if this defendant ever got the opportunity your daughter could be the next one, or your grandchild or something.[3]

The Missouri Supreme Court held that the prosecutor could, among other things, appeal to the "evil results" that would result from a failure to convict the defendant:

> The prosecuting attorney has the right and it is his duty to prosecute with vigor those cases wherein the evidence warrants him in so doing, as did the evidence in this case. And, in so doing, he properly may call the attention of the jury to the prevalence of crime, if such be the commonly known fact, the necessity of convicting those proved guilty of crime and the evil results that will flow to society from a failure of the jury to do its duty.[4]

What the prosecutor could not do, however, was to appeal to the jury's personal fears:

> But it is a different thing if the prosecuting attorney seeks by inflammatory appeals to arouse personal hostility of the jurors toward the defendant, especially by implanting fear in them that acquittal of defendant will endanger their own safety or the safety of some member of their family.

---

[1] *Id.*
[2] *Id.* at 173.
[3] State v. Groves, 295 S.W.2d 169, 173 (Mo. 1956).
[4] *Id.* at 174.

. . . .

> The argument made in the instant case was a direct effort to bring home to each juror (who had a daughter or granddaughter—and we may safely presume some did) the fear that if defendant be permitted to remain at large he might rape the daughter or granddaughter of that juror. Once such a fear entered the mind of a juror, he would find it difficult to consider his verdict with the objectivity required of an impartial juror. When the natural and probable consequence of such an appeal is apparent, as we think it is in this case, we must and do hold that the argument was prejudicial to the right of the defendant to a fair and impartial trial.[5] (parentheses in original; ellipses added).

Sons and their girlfriends were the subject of a California prosecutor's argument to the jury:

> Now, just a minute. Now, I want you to think, if your son happens to get the idea of buying a Triumph or a BSA or a Harley Davidson or anything, and wants to go out with his girl friend and friends and drive around, make sure, Ladies and Gentlemen, that he doesn't go in an area where this defendant is located, because apparently he's got a thing against this sort of thing, and he reacts and he reacts very seriously.[6]

Only the overwhelming evidence of the defendant's guilt saved the prosecution from having to retry this case:

> The prosecutor's remarks to the effect that the sons of the jurors and their girl friends dare not ride motorcycles into an area where the appellant is located, because he reacts seriously, were patently uncalled for, were a crude appeal to the fears and emotions of the jurors, and constituted misconduct. If the issue of guilt or innocence in this case was a close one on the facts, a reversal would be required. But the evidence of appellant's felonious attack on innocent persons, minding their own business, is so overwhelming and gross that a verdict of anything less than assault by means of force likely to produce great bodily injury, as returned by the jury, would have been a dereliction of its duty.[7]

Two prominent defense attorneys, Louis Nizer and William Kunstler, represented a defendant convicted of two counts of murder.[8] On

---

[5]*Id.*
[6]People v. Jones, 86 Cal. Rptr. 516, 518 (Cal. App. 5 Dist. 1970).
[7]*Id.* at 518–19.
[8]State v. Gold, 431 A.2d 501 (Conn. 1980).

appeal, the defendant argued that the conclusion of the State's Attorney's final argument was improper:

> Now, when Mr. Kunstler says to you you'll wake up screaming if you return the verdict of guilty, I say to you you'll wake up screaming if you return a verdict of not guilty, because to do good to the bad, the spirit of the bad, is to do evil to the good and make you responsible, you, yes, you, for all the acts this man may subsequently commit, because you let him go free. Thank you for your attention.[9] (footnote omitted).

The State's Attorney was responding to this remark: "But if you have a reasonable doubt, you must stand firm or you will wake up screaming some night."[10]

Citing the ABA's "Standards Relating to the Prosecution Function and the Defense Function," the Connecticut Supreme Court found that the State's Attorney improperly made "predictions of the consequences of the jury's verdict."[11] In addition,

> The State's Attorney improperly argued the necessity of preventing further injury to society by the defendant himself. A defendant is on trial for what has been done and not for what he or she might do. Also, by threatening that a verdict of not guilty would make "you responsible, you, yes, you, for all the acts this man may subsequently commit, because you let him go free," the State's Attorney even further diverted the jury from its duty to decide the case solely on the evidence.[12]

"Death for Dangerousness" Argument

Closely related to the "convict to protect" argument is the "death for dangerousness" argument. Prosecutors sometimes urge juries in capital cases to recommend the death penalty because that is the only deterrent to future dangerousness. A defendant charged with two counts of first-degree murder, and other serious crimes, contended the prosecutor's rhetorical questions improperly influenced the jury to return a death penalty verdict: "What is our only guarantee that this defendant will not rape again? What is our only guarantee that he will not kill again."[13]

---

[9]*Id.* at 520.
[10]*Id.* at 520 n.18.
[11]*Id.* at 520.
[12]*Id.*
[13]State v. Connor, 480 S.E.2d 626, 632 (N.C. 1997).

The North Carolina Supreme Court thought otherwise:

> Defendant contends that this specific-deterrence argument was improper and should not have been permitted. This court has overruled similar assignments of error in many cases, concluding that it is not improper for a prosecutor to urge the jury to recommend death out of concern for the future dangerousness of the defendant.[14]

In another "future dangerousness" challenge, a defendant asserted the prosecutor's guilt phase closing argument constituted misconduct:

> Ask yourself what exactly [defense counsel] are . . . saying in their closing argument. What are they telling you? Did they tell you he didn't do it? No, they didn't tell you that. They told you basically [the evidence does not show guilt] beyond a reasonable doubt, be afraid, be fearful beyond a reasonable doubt. Well, [the applicable standard is] not beyond any doubt. The judge is going to tell you that. Remember, it's not possible to be perfect. If you apply a perfect standard to imperfect evidence, everybody is going to be acquitted. No one ever will be convicted. This man will walk free. This man will be out there in the streets with you and I.[15] (ellipses and brackets in original).

The California court noted:

> Defendant first contends the prosecutor committed misconduct by urging the jury to consider his future dangerousness . . . The prosecutor reasonably relied on . . . in which the Court of Appeal, in rejecting the defendant's claim of prosecutorial misconduct, stated that "[s]uggesting that a defendant will commit a criminal act in the future is not an inappropriate comment when there is sufficient evidence in the record to support the statement." . . . In light of the unprovoked and vicious attack defendant perpetrated, there was sufficient evidence to support the prosecutor's argument.[16] (citations omitted; ellipses added).

Prosecution of cases where the defendant claims to have been insane when the crime was committed presents the problem of release from a mental institution. The ever-present danger is that a prosecutor may readily appeal to the jury's fear that an insane defendant may be prematurely released from the mental institution, and turned loose on society to commit additional crimes. For that reason, the argument goes, the jury should reject the insanity defense, and fittingly find the defendant guilty, to ensure a long jail sentence.

---

[14] *Id.* at 632–33.
[15] People v. Brown (Andrew), 3 Cal. Rptr. 3d 158, 180 (Cal. 2003).
[16] *Id.* at 181.

Over defense counsel's objection, a prosecutor questioned the state's expert about such a subject, where the defendant was accused of murdering his wife and two minor children:

> **Q:** If he were in fact sent to the state hospital, the state hospital at any time within their discretion could release him; is that not correct?
>
> **A:** That's right.
>
> **Q:** And in your experience you have seen cases where persons have been found not guilty by reason of insanity and have been back on the streets soon thereafter; haven't you?
>
> **A:** That's right.[17]

The Arizona Supreme Court noted that "[e]very jurisdiction which has passed upon a similar argument has held that it is erroneous misconduct on the part of the prosecuting attorney."[18]

In reversing the conviction, the court concluded the evidence of insanity was overwhelming, and pointed out that

> [t]he principal thrust of the prosecution's argument to the jury in both opening and closing was that [the defendant] was dangerous to other people and could be released and that he should be found guilty without regard to the issue of insanity. For example, the state concluded its closing argument with these statements:
>
> ". . . He is essentially dangerous to other people; he is very dangerous to himself. We can't afford—society can't afford to have [the defendant] take the life of any other innocent victims. Society can't afford that.
>
> "Those that have consciences can't afford that, ladies and gentlemen. Don't arrive at a verdict which will give [the defendant] the opportunity to kill again."[19] (brackets added; ellipses in original).

Using a slightly more subtle approach, a prosecutor asked the jury how they would feel if they found the defendant "not guilty by reason of insanity and heard about a murder in the future":

> [Y]ou know, the next time you are out on a nice, pretty, sunny afternoon, perhaps with your family, and you are driving along the roads or maybe you are at a picnic, your radio is on and you hear about a murder or something like that, or an aggravated assault, you think

---

[17]State v. Makal, 455 P.2d 450, 451 (Ariz. 1969).
[18]*Id.* at 452.
[19]*Id.*

back to this case. You are going to have to be able to say right then and there that you were convinced . . . that the evidence was clear and convincing that this man was insane. Not just paranoid schizophrenic, not mentally ill, not possibly mentally ill, but insane. Because you know, you go back there in your deliberation now and you are sitting there and you can't imagine that day, ladies and gentlemen, when you hear this on the report and you can't say, yes, I was clearly convinced, you know, that the defendant carried his burden.[20]

Defendant's counsel objected, but the objection was overruled. Counsel then asked for ten minutes of surrebuttal on the insanity defense, and that, too, was denied. A motion for a mistrial, after the jury instructions, similarly was denied.

The defendant argued that the prosecutor's remark "was a direct attempt to try and prejudice the jury, put the fear in them that if they acquit (the defendant), that number one, he'll probably get out of custody, and number two, he will be uncontrolled and he'll be violent."[21]

The trial judge, finding no error, likened the prosecution's argument to the

> "same argument that is often used in defense cases of, ladies and gentlemen, this is the only time you will ever be able to vote on the defendant being not guilty. You don't get to do it twice, you don't get to, someday down the road, it is the similar argument."[22]

The Arizona Supreme Court disagreed with the trial judge's analogy:

> The defense referred to by the trial court is a reminder to the jurors of the finality of their decision, it is not a suggestion that the jurors will feel responsible for future crimes unless they reject the insanity defense. Also, when defense counsel makes a "this is the only time" argument, the prosecutor gets the last word in rebuttal. Here, Defendant had the burden of proof on the insanity defense, but the State had the last word on it.[23]

And the court also rejected the state's argument:

> The State asserts that the prosecutor was referring to future crimes in general, not to future crimes by Defendant. We seriously doubt that this prosecutor was trying to walk that line. He referred to the same violent crimes that Defendant had committed, and he associated those

---

[20] State v. Hughes, 969 P.2d 1184, 1197 (Ariz. 1998).
[21] Id. at 1199.
[22] Id.
[23] Id.

future crimes with the consequence of finding Defendant not guilty by reason of insanity. The improper inference is clear, in a trial and an argument as permeated by prosecutorial misconduct as this one.[24]

Reversing the conviction, the court concluded the prosecution's argument was improper:

> It is improper, however, for a prosecutor to draw the jury's attention to the potential disposition of Defendant if found not guilty by reason of insanity.
>
> ... A prosecutor can certainly argue that Defendant has the burden of proving insanity by clear and convincing evidence, for that is the law. However, the comment about a future "murder or something like that" is an improper appeal to fear.[25] (ellipses added; citations omitted).

Although threats, force, and fear are generally synonymous forms of ad baculum appeals, there are circumstances where they are not interchangeable. Evidence that a defendant has threatened witnesses to alter their testimony is not always admissible, but witnesses may be asked if they are afraid to testify:

> We believe that the prosecutor did not act improperly in this instance. He asked the witness about fear, not threats. Although evidence that a defendant is threatening witnesses implies a consciousness of guilt and thus is highly prejudicial and admissible only if adequately substantiated, evidence that a witness is afraid to testify is relevant to the credibility of that witness and therefore admissible.[26] (citations omitted).

To explain inconsistencies in their testimony and a reluctance of witnesses to testify, a prosecutor intimated that a "mysterious third person" threatened them:

> You heard Mr. Amato state that the defendant, Mr. Modica had someone else with him at the time. You heard Mr. Miradoli say that, too. You heard Mr. Costanzo, who testified today, say that, too. There is only one person who didn't say that—
>
> Mr. Modica. And when these witnesses—again, talking about Mr. Miradoli, Mr. Costanzo, Mr. Amato, when they were asked about this other person, did you see their reaction? Did they look like they

---

[24]*Id.* at 1200.
[25]*Id.*
[26]People v. Warren, 754 P.2d 218, 224 (Cal. 1988).

were anxious, that they were trying to describe them? What did their faces look like? They were scared. I am telling you—.[27]

This argument was found to be improper because of the suggested threat by a third party:

> The statement seems to have been designed to explain Amato's testimonial inadequacies by associating [the defendant] with an unknown and threatening individual.
>
> The trial judge should have sustained the objection and taken corrective action. A prosecutor is free to comment upon the evidence, including demeanor. But he may not use the presence of an unknown individual, concerning whom no evidence was introduced, as a vehicle for suggesting that the defendant is associated with threatening people. Such a suggestion has a special potential for prejudice, moreover, when it is made by a prosecutor, who the jury may well think knows something about the defendant's mysterious associate that cannot be revealed, and who at the same time vouches for the truthfulness of the frightened witness's testimony.[28] (brackets added; citations omitted).

The Sixth Amendment affords a defendant the right "to have compulsory process for obtaining witnesses in his favor."[29] Prosecutors, at times, have been accused of improperly threatening defendants' witnesses, to the point the witnesses have refused to testify.

A defendant, as part of his claim of self-defense, subpoenaed an eyewitness to the killing.[30] The assistant U.S. attorney informed the witness that if he testified on behalf of the defendant, he would face charges of "carrying a dangerous weapon," "obstruction of justice," and being an accessory.[31] After consulting a public defender, the witness informed the judge he would not testify because "charges could be brought against me if I testify in this case."[32] Defendant's counsel then called the witness to the stand, and elicited the following:

> **Q:** Mr. Twitty, do you remember speaking to me yesterday afternoon at the conclusion of the day in Court?
>
> **A:** Yes, sir.

---

[27]United States v. Modica, 663 F.2d 1173, 1179 (2nd Cir. 1981).
[28]*Id.* at 1179–80.
[29]United States v. Blackwell, 694 F.2d 1325, 1333 (D.C. Cir. 1982), quoting Washington v. Texas, 388 U.S. 14, 19 (1967).
[30]United States v. Smith, 478 F.2d 976 (D.C. Cir. 1973).
[31]*Id.* at 978.
[32]*Id.*

Q: Do you remember the conversation that we had?
A: Yes, sir.

Q: Do you remember telling me, sir, that you had been told by the Assistant United States Attorney . . . in this matter, that if you testified, you were told this yesterday, that if you testified in this case you would be charged with CDW, obstruction of justice, and as a principal in a murder?
A: Your're (sic) right.

THE COURT: Did he say you could be or would be?
THE WITNESS: Would be.[33] (ellipses in original).

The D.C. Circuit found the prosecutor improperly threatened the witness, and reversed the conviction:

> We think the prosecutor's warning was plainly a threat that resulted in depriving the defendants of Twitty's testimony. The government argues in its brief that Twitty had a right to be advised that he might incriminate himself and be subject to prosecution if he elected to testify, and the government suggests that the prosecutor was only protecting Twitty's rights when he warned him. Even if the prosecutor's motives were impeccable, however, the implication of what he said was calculated to transform Twitty from a willing witness to one who would refuse to testify, and that in fact was the result. We therefore conclude that the prosecutor's remarks were prejudicial.[34]

Threats to witnesses are not limited to prosecutors. The U.S. Supreme Court, in *Webb v. Texas*,[35] considered whether a trial judge improperly threatened a witness, who was in jail at the time, by reminding the witness that, among other things, he could face additional jail time for lying on the witness stand.

The record shows that, after the prosecution had rested its case, the jury was temporarily excused. During this recess, the petitioner called his only witness, Leslie Max Mills, who had a prior criminal record and was then serving a prison sentence. At this point, the trial judge, on his own initiative, undertook to admonish the witness as follows:

> "Now you have been called down as a witness in this case by the Defendant. It is the Court's duty to admonish you that you don't have to testify, that anything you say can and will be used against you. If you take the witness stand and lie under oath, the Court will person-

---

[33] *Id.*
[34] *Id.* at 979.
[35] 409 U.S. 95 (1972).

ally see that your case goes to the grand jury and you will be indicted for perjury and the likelihood [sic] is that you would get convicted of perjury and that it would be stacked onto what you have already got, so that is the matter you have got to make up your mind on. If you get on the witness stand and lie, it is probably going to mean several years and at least more time that you are going to have to serve. It will also be held against you in the penitentiary when you're up for parole and the Court wants you to thoroughly understand the chances you're taking by getting on that witness stand under oath. You may tell the truth and if you do, that is all right, but if you lie you can get into real trouble. The court wants you to know that. You don't owe anybody anything to testify and it must be done freely and voluntarily and with the thorough understanding that you know the hazard you are taking."[36] (brackets in original).

After the judge's admonition, the witness refused to testify, prompting the Supreme Court to draw the inference that the admonition caused the refusal to testify:

> The fact that Mills was willing to come to court to testify in the petitioner's behalf, refusing to do so only after the judge's lengthy and intimidating warning, strongly suggests that the judge's comments were the cause of Mills' refusal to testify.[37]

Improper Conduct

The Court stated that even if the judge was incapable of carrying out all the threats, his conduct was improper:

> The trial judge gratuitously singled out this one witness for a lengthy admonition on the dangers of perjury. But the judge did not stop at warning the witness of his right to refuse to testify and of the necessity to tell the truth. Instead, the judge implied that he expected Mills to lie, and went on to assure him that if he lied, he would be prosecuted and probably convicted for perjury, that the sentence for that conviction would be added on to his present sentence, and that the result would be to impair his chances for parole. At least some of these threats may have been beyond the power of this judge to carry out. Yet, in light of the great disparity between the posture of the presiding judge and that of a witness in these circumstances, the unnecessarily strong terms used by the judge could well have exerted such

---

[36] *Id.* at 95–96.
[37] *Id.* at 97.

duress on the witness' mind as to preclude him from making a free and voluntary choice whether or not to testify.[38]

Relying on the Fourteenth Amendment, the Court held the judge deprived the defendant of his due process rights:

> In the circumstances of this case, we conclude that the judge's threatening remarks, directed only at the single witness for the defense, effectively drove that witness off the stand, and thus deprived the petitioner of due process of law under the Fourteenth Amendment.[39]

Not all reminders to a witness about the consequences of perjury violate the Fourteenth Amendment:

> Judges and prosecutors do not necessarily commit a *Webb* type violation merely by advising a witness of the possibility that he or she could face prosecution for perjury if his or her testimony differs from that he or she has given previously. In fact, the government has an obligation to warn unrepresented witnesses of the risk that the testimony they are going to give can be used against them. Where, however, the substance of what the prosecutor communicates to the witness is a threat over and above what the record indicates is necessary, and appropriate, the inference that the prosecutor sought to coerce a witness into silence is strong. . . . The defense must show that the contact substantially interfered with any free and unhampered determination the witness might have had as to whether to testify.[40] (citations omitted).

Self-Incrimination Privilege

Appeals to force involve entreaties to coercive conduct that leave the recipient little choice but to accept the intended proposition. An area of the law where this becomes an issue is the invocation of the privilege against self-incrimination.

The Fifth Amendment states that no person "shall be compelled in any criminal case to be a witness against himself."[41]

In *McKune v. Lile*,[42] the U.S. Supreme Court divided 5-4 over the interpretation of "compelled" in the context of the Fifth Amendment.

---

[38]*Id.* at 97–98.
[39]*Id.* at 98.
[40]United States v. Pierce, 62 F.3d 818, 832–33 (6th Cir. 1995).
[41]U.S. Const. amend. V.
[42]536 U.S. 24 (2002).

Lile, a convicted sex offender, was within a few years of completing his sentence. In contemplation of his release, the Kansas Department of Corrections ordered him to participate in a Sexual Abuse Treatment Program (SATP). The program required participating inmates to fill out and sign an "Admission of Responsibility" form, accepting responsibility for the crime for which they were serving time. In addition, participating inmates were required to complete a sexual history form, providing details of all previous sexual activities, even if they constituted uncharged criminal offenses. Inmates then underwent a polygraph examination to verify their sexual history.

None of the information provided by the inmates in the SATP was shielded from disclosure or future prosecution, and Lile refused to participate in the program, invoking his Fifth Amendment privilege against self-incrimination. Lile was told that if he refused to participate in the SATP he would suffer the following consequences (appeal to force):

> [H]is privilege status would be reduced from Level III to Level I. As part of this reduction, [Lile's] visitation rights, earnings, work opportunities, ability to send money to family, canteen expenditures, access to a personal television and other privileges automatically would be curtailed. In addition, [Lile] would be transferred to a maximum-security unit, where his movement would be more limited, he would be moved from a two-person to a four-person cell, and he would be in a potentially more dangerous environment.[43] (brackets added).

Justice Kennedy, writing for the plurality, found that the consequences for nonparticipation in the SATP were not significant, especially in the prison context:

> The consequences in question here—a transfer to another prison where television sets are not placed in each inmate's cell, where exercise facilities are not readily available, and where work and opportunities are more limited—are not ones that compel a prisoner to speak about his past crimes despite a desire to remain silent. The fact that these consequences are imposed on prisoners, rather than ordinary citizens, moreover, is important in weighing [Lile's] constitutional claim.[44] (brackets added).

Justice O'Connor, concurring in the plurality's judgment, wrote that "[t]he text of the Fifth Amendment does not prohibit all penalties levied in response to a person's refusal to incriminate himself or herself—it

---

[43] *Id.* at 30–31.
[44] *Id.* at 36.

prohibits only the compulsion of such testimony. Not all pressure necessarily 'compel[s]' incriminating statements."[45] (brackets in original).

She then noted "that certain types of penalties (appeals to force) are capable of coercing incriminating testimony": ". . . termination of employment, the loss of a professional license, ineligibility to receive government contracts, and the loss of the right to participate in political associations and to hold public office."[46] (citations omitted).

According to Justice O'Connor: "All of these penalties, however, are far more significant than those facing [Lile] here."[47]

Writing for the four dissenters, Justice Stevens concluded that the penalties for nonparticipation were coercive and that the penalties were the same as those for "the most serious violations of prison rules":

> The coerciveness of the penalty in this case must be measured not by comparing the quality of life in a prison environment with that in a free society, but rather by the contrast between the favored and disfavored classes of prisoners. It is obviously impossible to measure precisely the significance of the difference between being housed in a four-person, maximum-security cell in the most dangerous areas of the prison, on the one hand, and having a key to one's own room, the right to take a shower, and the ability to move freely within adjacent areas during certain hours, on the other—or to fully appreciate the importance of visitation privileges, being able to send more than $30 per pay period to family, having access to the yard for exercise, and the opportunity to participate in group activities. What is perfectly clear, however, is that it is the aggregate effect of those penalties that creates compulsion. Nor is it coincidental that petitioners have selected this same group of sanctions as the punishment to be imposed for the most serious violations of prison rules.[48]

---

[45] *Id.* at 49.
[46] *Id.* at 49.
[47] *Id.* at 50.
[48] *Id.* at 67–68.

CHAPTER TWENTY-TWO

Begging the Question

> *If what the statute says must be ignored, one would think we might settle at least for what the statute was meant to say; but alas, we are told, what the statute says prevents this.*
>
> Justice Scalia, dissenting, *USA v. X-Citement Video, Inc.*, 513 U.S. 64, 83 (1994).

CIRCULAR ARGUMENT, circular reasoning, petitio principii, vicious circle—each is another name for begging the question.

One way to recognize this argument is to focus on the proof for the asserted conclusion. Has independent evidence sufficient to establish the conclusion been demonstrated? Or, has there merely been a reassertion or restatement of the conclusion, using other words, presumed to be true, to describe the conclusion? Isolating the proof from the conclusion is not always a simple task.

Offensively, a beg-the-question argument can be used when there is little or no evidence to support the conclusion to be established. With a little luck, the opposing side will not connect the lack of evidence with the conclusion. Defensively, scrutiny should be given to arguments for which an attorney suspects there is little or no evidence to prove the conclusion.

Justice Scalia's statement above was probably written "tongue in cheek," but it, nevertheless, is an example of begging the question. The conclusion is that the statutory language in the case must be ignored; the proof consists of the statutory language itself, but it does not say the language should be ignored; it does not even give a clue to what the statute was meant to say. Therefore, according to Justice Scalia, the majority has no basis for concluding the statutory language must be ignored, because there is no proof.

Allegheny County v. Greater Pittsburgh ACLU,[1] involved the placement of a creche and a menorah on county grounds and whether doing so violated the First Amendment. Justice Blackmun, writing for the majority, noted that one of the county's arguments merely repeated the conclusion in another form:

> Finally, the county argues that it is sufficient to validate the display of the creche on the Grand Staircase that the display celebrates Christmas, and Christmas is a national holiday. This argument obviously proves too much. It would allow the celebration of the Eucharist inside a courthouse on Christmas Eve.[2]

The conclusion is that the display of the creche lawfully appears on the Grand Staircase, and the proof consists of the fact that the creche celebrates Christmas, deemed to be a secular holiday, not a religious one.

A similar instance of repeating the conclusion in another form is Justice Scalia's statement in *College Savings v. Florida Prepaid Postsecondary Education*,[3] where he discusses the doctrine of constructive waiver in the context of sovereign immunity jurisprudence:

> As further evidence that constructive waiver is little more than abrogation under another name, consider the revealing facts of this case: The statutory provision relied upon to demonstrate that Florida constructively waived its sovereign immunity is the very same provision that purported to abrogate it.[4]

According to Justice Scalia, one statutory provision was relied on to waive sovereign immunity and, at the same time, to eliminate it.

Is the conclusion established, or merely explained or defined in other terms? A California Appeals Court, struggling to come up with a definition of "unfair business practice" within the meaning of the Federal Trade Commission Act, described it in other terms:

> We conclude an "unfair" business practice occurs **when it offends an established public policy** or when the practice is **immoral,**

---

[1] 492 U.S. 573 (1989).
[2] *Id.* at 601.
[3] 527 U.S. 666 (1999).
[4] *Id.* at 684.

unethical, oppressive, unscrupulous or substantially injurious to consumers.[5] (bold added; footnote omitted).

Justice Potter Stewart, in what may be the best known legal example of begging the question, admitted he could not define "hard-core pornography," but declared he knew it when he saw it:

> It is possible to read the Court's opinion in *Roth v. United States* and *Alberts v. California*, in a variety of ways. In saying this, I imply no criticism of the Court, which in those cases was faced with the task of trying to define what may be indefinable. I have reached the conclusion, which I think is confirmed at least by negative implication in the Court's decisions since *Roth* and *Alberts*, that under the First and Fourteenth Amendments criminal laws in this area are constitutionally limited to hard-core pornography. I shall not today attempt further to define the kinds of material I understand to be embraced within that shorthand description; and perhaps I could never succeed in intelligibly doing so. But I know it when I see it, and the motion picture involved in this case is not that.[6] (footnotes omitted).

Of course, Justice Stewart's declaration concerning hard-core pornography did not help define it, or give guidance to the lower courts, but in fairness, no one else has provided a precise definition suitable for a legal conclusion.

Sometimes a mere declaration serves as evidence to support a conclusion, as argued by Justice Blackmun in *Webster v. Reproductive Health Services*[7]:

> Having set up the conflict between § 188.029 and the *Roe* trimester framework, the plurality summarily discards *Roe*'s analytic core as "'unsound in principle and unworkable in practice.'" This is so, the plurality claims, because the key elements of the framework do not appear in the text of the Constitution, because the framework more closely resembles a regulatory code than a body of constitutional doctrine, and because under the framework the State's interest in potential human life is considered compelling only after viability, when, in fact, that interest is equally compelling throughout pregnancy. The plurality does not bother to explain these alleged flaws in *Roe*. Bald

---

[5]People v. Casa Blanca Convalescent Homes, Inc., 206 Cal. Rptr. 164, 177 (Cal. App. 4 Dist. 1984).
[6]Jacobellis v. Ohio, 378 U.S. 184, 197 (1964).
[7]492 U.S. 490 (1989).

assertion masquerades as reasoning. The object, quite clearly, is not to persuade, but to prevail.[8] (citations omitted).

Mere declarations, without analytical support for the conclusion, is the argument Justice Scalia leveled at the majority in *Dickerson v. U.S.*[9]:

> The Court today insists that the decision in *Miranda* is a "constitutional" one: that it has "constitutional underpinnings"; a "constitutional basis" and a "constitutional origin"; that it was "constitutionally based"; and that it announced a "constitutional rule." It is fine to play these word games; but what makes a decision "constitutional" in the only sense relevant here—in the sense that renders it impervious to supersession by congressional legislation such as §3501—is the determination that the Constitution *requires* the result that the decision announces and the statute ignores.[10] (italics in original; citations omitted)

A related beg-the-question argument cites an authority as proof for the conclusion, as in this example where President Clinton's testimony is cited as evidence that he did not tamper with a witness:

> There was no witness tampering. Betty Curie was not supposed to be a witness in the Paula Jones case. If she was not called or going to be called, it was impossible for any conversations the President had with her to be witness tampering. The President testified that he did not in any way attempt to influence her recollection.[11]

In *Nevada Dept. of Human Resources v. Hibbs*,[12] involving alleged state discrimination in providing family leave, Justice Kennedy argued that the majority simply noted the problem, but failed to provide evidence for their conclusion:

> When the federal statute seeks to abrogate state sovereign immunity, the Court should be more careful to insist on adherence to the analytic requirements set forth in its own precedents. Persisting overall effects of gender-based discrimination at the workplace must not be ignored; but simply noting the problem is not a substitute for evidence which identifies some real discrimination the family leave rules are designed to prevent.[13]

---

[8]*Id.* at 546.
[9]530 U.S. 428 (2000).
[10]*Id.* at 454.
[11]CHICAGO TRIBUNE, Sept. 13, 1998, at 32.
[12]538 U.S. 721 (2003).
[13]*Id.* at 746.

Reasonable vs. Unreasonable

Certain words repeatedly found in legal arguments beg the question, because they assume a conclusion without providing evidence to support it. The word "reasonable," for example, suggests that the proponent has staked out a completely defensible position, while the opposing party's argument must be "unreasonable," because there is no other alternative to "reasonable." If the opposing argument is "unreasonable," it cannot have any merit, for that is the definition of "unreasonable." So, the alternatives are to agree with the proponent, thereby assuming the mantle of "reasonableness," or to disagree, and risk having your argument deemed "unreasonable," regardless of its merit.

It must be disheartening to have a U.S. Supreme Court practice. After a case has been litigated in the lower courts, and has been subject to scrutiny at various levels of the legal system, the Supreme Court gets the last word on the merits of the case. When a Supreme Court Justice in the majority writes that there is only one "reasonable" outcome, what does that say for the losing attorney or, for that matter, the minority Justices? Was there a great deal of time wasted in bringing such an "easily" resolvable case before the Supreme Court?

"Fair Reading"

In *Zelman v. Simmons-Harris*,[14] where the legality of school vouchers was at issue, Justice O'Connor suggested that Justice Souter's interpretation of a case was not a "fair reading":

> Justice Souter portrays this inquiry as a departure from *Everson*. A fair reading of the holding in that case suggests quite the opposite. Justice Black's opinion for the court held that the [First] Amendment requires the state to be a neutral in its relations with groups of religious believers and non-believers; it does not require the state to be their adversary.[15] (citations omitted; brackets in original).

"Fair reading" also appeared in Chief Justice Rehnquist's concurrence in *Bush v. Gore*[16]:

---

[14]536 U.S. 639 (2002).
[15]*Id.* at 669.
[16]531 U.S. 98 (2000).

Relying on *NAACP*, we concluded that the South Carolina Supreme Court's interpretation of a state penal statute had impermissibly broadened the scope of that statute beyond what a fair reading provided, in violation of due process. What we would do in the present case is precisely parallel: Hold that the Florida Supreme Court's interpretation of the Florida election laws impermissibly distorted them beyond what a fair reading required, in violation of Article II.[17] (citations omitted).

Justice Ginsburg, dissenting in *Buckhannon v. West Virginia*,[18] also used the question-begging phrase "fair reading":

Under a fair reading of the FHAA and ADA provisions in point, I would hold that a party "prevails" in "a true and proper sense," when she achieves, by instituting litigation, the practical relief sought in her complaint.[19] (citation omitted).

Likewise, "fair reading" is an expression used by Justices Kennedy and Scalia:

A fair reading of our opinion is that the defendant did not publish a falsification sufficient to sustain a finding of actual malice.[20]

A court would remain free to apply common-law criminal rules to new fact patterns, so long as that application is consistent with a fair reading of prior cases.[21] (citation omitted).

In his concurrence in *Gore v. Bush*,[22] the Chief Justice used the question-begging terms "plainly" and "reasonably be thought":

Moreover, the court's interpretation of "legal vote" and hence its decision to order a contest-period recount, plainly departed from the legislative scheme. Florida statutory law cannot reasonably be thought to *require* the counting of improperly marked ballots.[23] (italics in original).

He also invoked the "reasonable person" standard:

No reasonable person would call it "an error in the vote tabulation," or a "rejection of legal votes," when electronic or electromechanical equipment performs precisely in the manner designed, and fails

---

[17]*Id.* at 115.
[18]532 U.S. 598 (2001).
[19]*Id.* at 634.
[20]Masson v. New Yorker Magazine, Inc., 501 U.S. 496, 519 (1991).
[21]Rogers v. Tennessee, 532 U.S. 451, 481 (2001).
[22]531 U.S. 98 (2000).
[23]*Id.* at 118–19.

to count those ballots that are not marked in the manner that these voting instructions explicitly and prominently specify.[24] (citations omitted).

Use of the word "clear" also begs the question, as these quotes from different cases illustrate:

> Although it is clear that the Sixth Amendment right to counsel attaches only to charged offenses, we have recognized in other contexts that the definition of "offense" is not necessarily limited to the four corners of a charging instrument.[25] (citation omitted).

> Given the clear meaning of "prevailing party" in the fee-shifting statutes, we need not determine which way these various policy arguments cut.[26]

In *Bush v. Gore*, Justice Stevens, dissenting, employed the expression "perfectly clear":

> Wherever the term "legislature" is used in the Constitution it is necessary to consider the nature of the particular action in view. It is perfectly clear that the meaning of the words "Manner" and "legislature" as used in Article II, §1, parallels the usage in Article I, §4, rather than the language in Article V. As a result, petitioners' reliance on *Leser v. Garnett*, and *Hawke v. Smith (No. 1)*, is misplaced.[27] (citation omitted).

Justice Blackmun, writing for the majority in *Allegheny County v. Greater Pittsburgh ACLU*,[28] begged the question by his use of "reasonably":

> Furthermore, the creche sits on the Grand Staircase, the "main" and "most beautiful part" of the building that is the seat of county government. No viewer could reasonably think that it occupies this location without the support and approval of the government.[29] (citations and footnote omitted).

Arguing that the "year and a day rule" was a legal "relic," Justice O'Connor, in *Rogers v. Tennessee*,[30] employed the question-begging expression "without question":

---

[24]*Id.* at 119.
[25]Texas v. Cobb, 532 U.S. 162, 172–73 (2001).
[26]*Buckhannon*, 532 U.S. at 610.
[27]*Supra* at 123 n.1.
[28]*Supra* note 1.
[29]*Id.* at 599-600.
[30]532 U.S. 451 (2001).

> Petitioner does not even much as hint that good reasons exist for retaining the rule as practically every court recently to have considered the rule has noted, advances in medical and related science have so undermined the usefulness of the rule as to render it without question, obsolete.[31] (citations omitted).

In the same case, Justice Scalia countered that the Supreme Court should have deferred to the Tennessee Supreme Court's "reasonable reading":

> Though the Court spends some time questioning whether the year-and-a-day rule was ever truly established in Tennessee, the Supreme Court of Tennessee said it was, and this reasonable reading of state law by the States' highest court is binding upon us.[32] (citations omitted).

Justice Scalia arrived at the opposite conclusion in *Bush v. Gore*, when he joined in Chief Justice Rehnquist's concurring opinion. In *Bush*, according to the concurrence, the Florida Supreme Court's interpretation of the Florida election laws was not a "fair reading" of the statute, and was, therefore, not binding on the U.S. Supreme Court:

> What we would do in the present case is precisely parallel: Hold that the Florida Supreme Court's interpretation of the Florida election laws impermissibly distorted them beyond what a fair reading required, in violation of Article II.[33] (footnote omitted).

Chief Justice Rehnquist and Justice Scalia, in different cases, convey the same question-begging message by employing similar terms ("not fairly debatable" and "not at all arguable"):

> The clarity of Congress' intent here is not fairly debatable.[34]

> That is surely an arguable question, the question that reconsideration of *Roe v. Wade* entails. But what is not at all arguable, it seems to me, is that we should decide now and not insist that we be run into a corner before we grudgingly yield up our judgment.[35]

In *Ledbetter v. Goodyear Tire & Rubber Co.*,[36] Justice Alito contended that the majority applied the statute "as written," suggesting the minority was unwilling to do so:

---

[31] *Id.* at 462–63.
[32] *Id.* at 468–69.
[33] *Supra* at 115.
[34] *Nevada Dept. of Human Resources, supra* at 726.
[35] *Webster, supra* at 492 U.S. 536.
[36] 127 S. Ct. 2162 (2007).

Ledbetter's policy arguments for giving special treatment to pay claims find no support in the statute and are inconsistent with our precedents. We apply the statute as written, and this means that any unlawful employment practice, including those involving compensation, must be presented to the EEOC within the period prescribed by statute.[37] (footnote omitted).

Naming Names

In October 1999, Senator John McCain (R-AZ), who was seeking his party's nomination for the presidency, strongly advocated a campaign finance bill that bore his name, arguing that "soft money" was corrupting the political process. A Republican Senate colleague, Mitch McConnell (R-KY), zealously opposed the McCain-Feingold bill, and wielded a beg-the-question argument against Senator McCain. Senator McConnell argued that in order for "soft money" to corrupt members of Congress, there must be members who have been corrupted, and he challenged Senator McCain to name names on the Senate floor. Presumably, the failure to name senators who had been corrupted by "soft money" would demonstrate that there had been no corruption. Did Senator McCain take the bait?

> **Mr. McCONNELL:** By the way, I only quoted the Senator's comments and everything was quoted accurately. I raised the Senator's own words in the debate, words he has used as a justification for this bill that is currently before us.
>
> I ask the Senator from Arizona, how can it be corruption if no one is corrupt? That is like saying the gang is corrupt but none of the gangsters are (sic). If there is corruption, someone must be corrupt.
>
> On the Senator's web site, he names some projects that he specifically says are in these bills as a result of soft money contributions which, of course, as we all know, cannot be received by anybody who votes anyway; they are given to a party.
>
> I repeat my question to the Senator from Arizona. Who is corrupt?
>
> **Mr. McCAIN:** First of all, I have already responded to the Senator that I will not get into people's names. I will, indeed, repeat, again, to the Senator from the web site from which he is quoting. Here it is:
>
> For 10 years, Senator McCain has reviewed the annual appropriations bills to determine whether they contain items that are low priority,

---

[37] *Id.* at 2177.

unnecessary, or wasteful spending. In this process, he has used five objective criteria.

And I go on to list them. That is why—

Mr. McCONNELL: Does that equal corruption though?[38]

Senator McCain was unwilling to name names, but he continued to insist that soft money corrupted senators.

Brief writing, particularly topic headings and statements of the issues, provide fertile ground for begging-the-question arguments. Some attorneys prefer to use "neutral" statements of the issues, as in this example from Vice President Gore's brief to the U.S. Supreme Court, opposing certiorari, in *Bush v. Gore*:

> 1. Whether the Florida Supreme Court's interpretation of Florida Law presents a substantial federal question for this Court to review or instead a determination reserved to the States?[39]

The second question presented in the Vice President's brief, however, begs the question:

> 2. Whether the State of Florida's statutorily mandated manual recount process, **indistinguishable from the laws in other states and reflective of a process that has been applied throughout this country for centuries**, violates the U.S. Constitution?[40] (bold added).

The bold portion begs the question by assuming that because other states use the same process, and have done so for centuries, Florida's mandatory recount process must, therefore, pass constitutional muster.

Then-Governor Bush's brief to the U.S. Supreme Court, seeking certiorari, similarly begs the question in setting forth the issues:

> 3. Whether the state court's decision, **which cannot be reconciled with state statutes enacted before the election was held**, is inconsistent with Article II, Section 1, clause 2 of the Constitution, which provides that electors shall be appointed by each State "in such Manner as the Legislature thereof may direct."[41]

---

[38] 145 CONG. REC. S12585 (Oct. 14, 1999).
[39] http://supreme.lp.findlaw.com/supreme_court/briefs/00-836.resp.gore.html.
[40] *Id.*
[41] http://supreme.lp.findlaw.com/supreme_court/briefs/00-836.pet.aa.html.

BEGGING THE QUESTION

The bolded clause assumes that the Florida Supreme Court's decision is inconsistent with previously enacted statutes.

4. Whether the use of **arbitrary, standardless, and selective manual recounts** that threaten to overturn the results of the election for President of the United States violates the Equal Protection or Due Process Clauses, or the First Amendment.[42] (bold added).

In question number four, it is assumed that the manual recounts are arbitrary and standardless.

Justice Ginsburg, dissenting in *Bush v. Gore*, notes that the majority's argument begs the question:

> The Court assumes that time will not permit "orderly judicial review of any disputed matters that might arise." But no one has doubted the good faith and diligence with which Florida election officials, attorneys for all sides of this controversy, and the courts of law have performed their duties. Notably, the Florida Supreme Court has produced two substantial opinions within 29 hours of oral argument. In sum, the Court's conclusion that a constitutionally adequate recount is impractical is a prophecy the Court's own judgment will not allow to be tested.[43] (citation omitted).

Her response to this argument: "Such an untested prophecy should not decide the Presidency of the United States."[44]

Responding to the same majority argument, Justice Breyer notes there is no evidence to support the majority's conclusion that there is insufficient time for a recount:

> The majority justifies stopping the recount entirely on the ground that there is no more time. In particular, the majority relies on the lack of time for the Secretary to review and approve equipment needed to separate undervotes. But the majority reaches this conclusion in the absence of any record evidence that the recount could not have been completed in the time allowed by the Florida Supreme Court. The majority finds facts outside of the record on matters that state courts are in a far better position to address. Of course, it is too late for any such recount to take place by December 12, the date by which election disputes must be decided if a State is to take advantage of the

---

[42] *Id.*
[43] *Supra* at 144.
[44] *Id.*

safe harbor provisions of 3 U.S.C. §5. Whether there is time to conduct a recount prior to December 18, when the electors are scheduled to meet, is a matter for the state courts to determine. And whether, under Florida law, Florida could or could not take further action is obviously a matter for Florida courts, not this Court, to decide.[45] (citations omitted).

In *Ramdass v. Angelone*,[46] the U.S. Supreme Court considered whether the death penalty was appropriate when there was a question whether the defendant was parole ineligible. When the current jury considered the death sentence, the defendant had been found guilty of another crime, but the judgment on the conviction had not issued. Had the judgment been rendered when the jury considered the death penalty, the jury would have been informed that the defendant was parole ineligible, and perhaps would not have voted for the death penalty. Justice Kennedy, for the majority, argued that the uncertainty of the defendant's parole eligibility was established by the defendant's own testimony:

> Our conclusion is confirmed by a review of petitioner's conduct in this litigation. The current claim that it was certain at the time of trial that Ramdass would never be released on parole in the event the jury sentenced him to life is belied by the testimony his counsel elicited from him at sentencing. Ramdass' counsel asked him, "Are you going to spend the rest of your life in prison?" Despite the claim advanced now that parole would be impossible, the answer counsel elicited from Ramdass at trial was, "I don't know." We think Ramdass' answer at trial is an accurate assessment of the uncertainties that surrounded his parole and custody status at the time of trial.[47]

Justice Stevens, dissenting, contended that there was no question about the defendant's parole ineligibility when the jury considered the appropriate sentence, and therefore, the majority's argument begged the question:

> The plurality never tells us, for it simply declares, without support, elaboration, or explanation, that a verdict is more uncertain than a judgment is. The only reason it suggests for why the verdict here was uncertain is rather remarkable—that *Ramdass himself* said so. That is, the plurality relies upon the fact that a convicted murderer with minimal education and a history of drug experimentation including PCP and cocaine said, "I don't know" when asked if he could ever be

---

[45] *Id.* at 146.
[46] 530 U.S. 156 (2000).
[47] *Id.* at 176–77.

released from prison. This evidence is thinner than gossamer.⁴⁸ (citations omitted; italics in original).

Justice White argued in *Harmelin v. Michigan*⁴⁹ that the Eighth Amendment has a proportionality guarantee, and responded to Justice Scalia's beg-the-question argument—that extreme examples of punishment would not occur merely because they are easy to decide—by arguing that without a proportionality guarantee there would be no basis for considering those examples:

> Two dangers lurk in Justice Scalia's analysis. First, he provides no mechanism for addressing a situation such as that proposed in *Rummel*, in which a legislature makes overtime parking a felony punishable by life imprisonment. He concedes that "one can imagine extreme examples"—perhaps such as the one described in *Rummel*—"that no rational person, in no time or place, could accept," but attempts to offer reassurance by claiming that "for the same reason these examples are easy to decide, they are certain never to occur." This is cold comfort indeed, for absent a proportionality guarantee, there would be no basis for deciding such cases should they arise.⁵⁰ (citation omitted).

In *Webster v. Reproductive Health Services*,⁵¹ Justice Blackmun laments the majority's beg-the-question argument:

> Finally, the plurality asserts that the trimester framework cannot stand because the State's interest in potential life is compelling throughout pregnancy, not merely after viability. The opinion contains not one word of rationale for its view of the State's interest. This "it-is-so-because-we-say-so" jurisprudence constitutes nothing other than an attempted exercise of brute force; reason, much less persuasion, has no place.⁵² (citation omitted).

Justice O'Connor, in *Ewing v. California*,⁵³ argues that the statistical support for Justice Breyer's conclusion—before passage of California's "three strikes" law no repeat felon could have served more than 10 years in prison—begs the question. She asserts that enactment of the three-strikes law resulted from "the perceived lenity" in the sentencing of recidivist felons, and that is the true reason for the earlier dearth of cases with long sentences:

---

⁴⁸*Id.* at 203–04.
⁴⁹501 U.S. 957 (1991).
⁵⁰*Id.* at 1018.
⁵¹*Webster, supra* note 7.
⁵²*Id.* at 552.
⁵³538 U.S. 11 (2003).

It is hardly surprising that the statistics relied upon by Justice Breyer show that prior to the enactment of the three strikes law, "*no* one like Ewing could have served more than *10* years in prison." Profound disappointment with the perceived lenity of criminal sentencing (especially for repeat felons) led to passage of the three strikes laws in the first place.[54] (italics in original; citations omitted).

---

[54]*Id.* at 24 n.1.

CHAPTER TWENTY-THREE

The Complex Question

> *A browbeating lawyer was demanding that a witness answer a certain question in the negative or affirmative.*
>
> *"I cannot do it," said the witness. "There are some questions that cannot be answered by a 'yes' or a 'no,' as anyone knows."*
>
> *"I defy you to give an example to the court," thundered the lawyer.*
>
> *The retort came like a flash. "Are you still beating your wife?"*
>
> LEWIS COPELAND & FAYE COPELAND, 10,000 JOKES, TOASTS & STORIES 479 (1939).[1]

THE FALLACY OF THE COMPLEX QUESTION is known by various names: fallacy of the false question, fallacy of many questions, loaded question, and trick question. A complex question actually contains two questions: one asked; one unasked. The attorney propounding the complex question attempts to have the witness respond to the unasked question in the same manner as the asked question. In the joke above, the witness asks the attorney if he is still beating his wife. The unasked question is whether the attorney beats his wife; the asked question is whether the attorney still does so. If the answer is "No," does that mean the attorney stopped beating his wife? Or does it mean he never beat his wife? Without clarification—an answer to the unasked question, for example—it is impossible to determine the answer's meaning.

---

[1] FRED R. SHAPIRO, THE OXFORD DICTIONARY OF AMERICAN LEGAL QUOTATIONS 104 (Oxford University Press 1993).

Attorneys object to a complex question at trial by declaring: "The question assumes facts not in evidence." Another way of phrasing the objection is to object to the form of the question, as the question contains two questions, not one. "Argumentative" is yet another objection heard in response to a complex question. In objecting to a complex question, an attorney must ensure that the preliminary (unasked) question receives an appropriate response, before the response to the asked question.

McCormick on Evidence explains the vice in asking complex questions:

> [A] common vice is for the examiner to couch the question so that it assumes as true matters to which the witness has not testified, and which are in dispute between the parties. The danger here is two-fold. First, if the examiner is putting the question to a friendly witness, the recitation of the assumed fact may suggest the desired answer; and second, whether the witness is friendly or hostile, the answer is likely to be misleading. Oftentimes, the question will be so separate from the assumption that if the witness answers the question without mentioning the assumption, it is impossible to ascertain whether he ignored the assumption or affirmed it.[2] (brackets added; citation omitted).

Frequently, a complex question arises during an attorney's examination of a witness at a trial, but that is not the only circumstance where such a question arises. A complex question, framed rhetorically, may replace a declarative statement in a brief or other legal writing. President Clinton's attorneys employed this technique to attack the Office of the Independent Counsel's (OIC's) Report:

> 1) What were Linda Tripp's motives in seeking out the OIC in January, 1998? Did she articulate a fear of being prosecuted in Maryland under that State's anti-taping laws? Why did she request immunity from prosecution? Why was she given immunity?
>
> . . . .
>
> 4) What assessment has the OIC made of Ms. Tripp's ideological motivations? Was the OIC aware she had submitted an anti-Clinton book proposal to avowed Clinton hater Lucianne Goldberg? Was the OIC aware of Goldberg's role in Ms. Tripp's taping and arrangement for Ms. Lewinsky's use of a messenger service?

---

[2]McCormick on Evidence 14 (3d ed. 1984).

5) How many statements on the Tripp Lewinsky tapes are false or exaggerated? How many statements contradict assertions in the OIC's report?[3]

The questions may be analyzed as follows:

1) What were Linda Tripp's motives in seeking out the OIC in January 1998?

The question assumes that Linda Tripp had (improper!) motives, and was not a disinterested party merely reporting possible violations of law.

Did she articulate a fear of being prosecuted in Maryland under that state's anti-taping laws?

Linda Tripp is assumed to have illicit motives because of her own possible misconduct: improper tape recording of conversations.

Why did she request immunity from prosecution?

Requesting immunity suggests she had previously engaged in illegal conduct, and wanted to avoid her own prosecution, which motivated her to assist the OIC.

Why was she given immunity?

There would have been no need to grant immunity if she had not engaged in unlawful conduct. Besides assuming she engaged in illegal conduct, the question presupposes she was not going to be prosecuted in exchange for her testimony against the President.

4) What assessment has the OIC made of Ms. Tripp's ideological motivations?

The question assumes that Tripp's testimony against the President was motivated by political bias.

Was the OIC aware she had submitted an anti-Clinton book proposal to avowed Clinton hater Lucianne Goldberg?

Linda Tripp is assumed to be biased against the President because she submitted a critical book proposal. Also, because Lucianne Goldberg is believed to be an "avowed Clinton hater," Tripp is assumed to have the same feelings because she is "guilty by association."

---

[3]CHICAGO TRIBUNE, Sept. 13, 1998, at 33.

Was the OIC aware of Goldberg's role in Ms. Tripp's taping and arrangement for Ms. Lewinsky's use of a messenger service?

It is assumed that Goldberg played a role in these "nefarious" activities.

5) How many statements on the Tripp-Lewinsky tapes are false or exaggerated?

The question presupposes that the tapes contain "false or exaggerated" statements—and that there are many of them.

How many statements contradict assertions in the OIC's report?

It is assumed that there are contradictory assertions (presumably many of them), and that the report is untrustworthy as a consequence.

Criminal trials provide abundant grounds for appeal by defendants who argue their rights have been denied by complex questions that imply harmful facts. Rules have evolved to guide attorneys in their questioning of witnesses. For example, the California Supreme Court holds that a defendant's failure to raise a "timely and specific objection" to a complex question constitutes a waiver of a misconduct claim. The California Supreme Court's reasoning begins with the obligation of prosecutors:

> It is misconduct for a prosecutor to ask a witness a question that implies a fact harmful to a defendant unless the prosecutor has reasonable grounds to anticipate an answer confirming the implied fact or is prepared to prove the fact by any other means.[4] (citation omitted).

The court then explains the difficulty posed by the failure to raise a trial objection, and why this leads to waiver:

> [I]f the defense does not object, and the prosecutor is not asked to justify the question, a reviewing court is rarely able to determine whether this form of misconduct has occurred. Therefore, a claim of misconduct on this basis is waived absent a timely and specific objection during trial.[5] (citations omitted).

The court's statements about waiver appeared in a case involving over 44,000 pages of transcript, the largest appellate record in a death penalty case as of that date. Another appeal in that case resulted from

---

[4]People v. Price, 821 P.2d 610, 705 (Cal. 1991).
[5]*Id.*

THE COMPLEX QUESTION 311

the prosecutor's asking the defendant: "Why did you tell Rebecca Williams to lie about Jennings' .22 caliber semiautomatic pistol?"[6]

This question, the court held, did not violate the defendant's rights:

> Defense counsel objected that the question was argumentative and assumed facts not in evidence. Impliedly sustaining the objection, the trial court directed the prosecutor to ask defendant if he had told Williams to lie. Defendant denied that he had done so, but his answers effectively admitted that he had invented the false story that the gun was a gift from a grandfather and that he had urged Williams to use the story when she retrieved the gun from the gunsmith. The prosecutor asked a few more questions along this line, but defense counsel made no further objections.
>
> We find no evidence of prosecutorial misconduct in this incident. The trial court sustained the only objection raised by defense counsel, and defendant effectively admitted that he had indeed urged Williams to lie about the gun.[7]

Two years earlier, the California Supreme Court also found that a complex question did not affect the defendant's right to a fair trial.[8] In this case, the prosecutor's cross-examination of a witness included a question about whether he received a letter from the defendant before September 14, a date the witness acknowledged receiving a letter from the defendant: "Isn't it a fact, Mr. Shoopman, that he [defendant] wrote you about the rape and killing of a girl in the mountains before September 14?"[9] (brackets in original).

"Shoopman denied receiving such a letter and the prosecutor did not mention the matter further."[10] The question assumes the defendant sent a letter before September 14, and that it discussed the rape and killing of a girl.

The court explained that it was difficult to apply the rule that prosecutors must not ask

> questions that clearly suggested the existence of facts which would have been harmful to defendant, in the absence of a good faith belief by the prosecutor that the questions would be answered in the affirmative, or

---

[6] *Id.*
[7] *Id.*
[8] People v. Bittaker, 259 Cal. Rptr. 630 (Cal. 1989).
[9] *Id.* at 660.
[10] *Id.*

with a belief on his part that the facts could be proved, and a purpose to prove them, if their existence should be denied.[11]

According to the California Supreme Court:

> The problem in applying this rule is that it makes the issue turn on the prosecutor's good faith, and the record will rarely contain the evidence bearing on that matter. In the present case, there is evidence that Shoopman received letters from defendant which he destroyed, but we have no information as to the contents of those letters, or what the prosecutor knew of their contents. Neither can we determine whether the prosecutor, at the time he asked the question, intended to prove the fact at issue. One might infer lack of intent from the fact that the prosecutor did not introduce evidence to prove the content of the destroyed letter, but one can readily imagine that by the time he could offer rebuttal evidence the prosecutor might have concluded that such additional evidence was unnecessary. On the record before us, misconduct has not been demonstrated.[12]

In addition to raising an objection, opposing counsel would be well advised to request an admonition to the jury. A California prosecutor's cross-examination of the defendant drew numerous objections from defense counsel, as described by the California Supreme Court:

> A representative sample of the questions, with emphasis on specific portions to which defense counsel's objections were sustained, may give a sense of the tone of the proceedings.
>
> "Q. So how many people did you discuss the case with before *deciding* on what to testify to?
>
> . . . Q. So you were not being truthful when you talked to certain individuals in the jail on tape, but *all of a sudden* now you are being truthful, is that correct? . . . Q. Is that correct? . . . Q. Is there some reason for this *transformation*? . . . Q. You are afraid of being prosecuted for perjury? . . . Q. You were out of money but, *of course*, you were not trying to borrow money [from another friend]? . . . Q. Did [some T.V. dinners at Maria's house] just happen to appear there miraculously when you went there? . . . Q. You have been saying Maria and Carmen are lying, too? . . . Weren't you able to get enough letters to them? . . . Q. Well, you are a pretty proficient liar, aren't you?"[13] (ellipses, brackets, and italics in original).

---

[11] *Id.*
[12] *Id.*
[13] *People v. Carrera*, 777 P.2d 121, 136 n.20 (Cal. 1989).

THE COMPLEX QUESTION 313

Defense counsel objected repeatedly to the prosecutor's questions, and even requested a mistrial:

> The prosecutor's cross-examination of defendant was marked by multiple objections from defense counsel on the grounds that the questions were argumentative or based on prejudicial facts not in evidence. The trial court sustained defense objections to 28 questions, but denied counsel's motion for a mistrial. Defendant now contends that it was prejudicial misconduct for the prosecutor to belittle and harass defendant, and complains that the prosecutor improperly injected into the guilt phase of the trial the subject of the death penalty by asking defendant whether "a snitch jacket in prison [for blaming the killings on others] is worse than going to the gas chamber on these murders?"[14] (footnote omitted; brackets in original).
>
> Although the Court did not condone the prosecutor's questioning of defendant, it, nevertheless, held: "But the fact remains that defense counsel's objections were sustained. If counsel believed that a potential for prejudice remained, she should have requested a specific admonition to the jury."[15] (citation omitted).

In another California case, a defendant convicted of murder argued that the prosecutor asked multiple complex questions, but the court noted that defense counsel failed to request an admonition to the jury:

> Defendant asserts that the prosecutor committed misconduct on numerous occasions by asking questions that insinuated facts that the prosecutor knew the defendant would deny, even though the prosecutor had no intention of proving those facts by other means. [improper to examine a witness solely to imply or insinuate the truth of the facts about which questions are posed] ... At trial defendant objected on this ground (that is, that the question "assumed facts not in evidence" or "misstated the evidence") as follows:
>
> After defendant conceded he had caused Haverstick pain by "nudging" his foot to make him cry out, the prosecutor asked: "But you went ahead and caused him some more injury to the leg that had already been shot?" The trial court sustained an objection that the question assumed that the "nudging" had caused "injury" rather than "pain."
>
> After defendant testified that Sergeant Wolfley had been "making statements to me indicating the fact that I was through or ... something to that effect," the prosecutor asked: "Well, that's not how you

---

[14]*Id.* at 136–37.
[15]*Id.* at 137.

testified the other day, was it?" The trial court sustained a defense objection that this misstated the evidence.

> The prosecutor asked: "You indicated that you at some point pulled yourself up on the wall and looked over the wall and saw some officers around Sergeant Wolfley that was on the ground. Do you recall that?" In response to a defense objection and the trial court's inquiry whether the prosecutor was intimating that defendant had seen Sergeant Wolfley on the ground, the prosecutor rephrased the question.
>
> The prosecutor asked a series of questions about fences defendant had gone over or walked next to after leaving the Sunstone Apartments parking lot. At one point the prosecutor asked a question referring to the "south fence." Upon defense objection that the question assumed facts not in evidence, the prosecutor amended the question to refer to the "west fence."
>
> Referring to events behind the service station, the prosecutor asked: "Did you have to turn after you got possession of the gun to run eastbound because you were facing west when you shot Sergeant Wolfley?" Defense counsel objected that the question assumed facts not in evidence. The trial court sustained the objection on the ground that the question was argumentative because it assumed a fact—that defendant had shot Sergeant Wolfley—that defendant had expressly denied.
>
> In each instance, the trial court sustained the defense objection or the prosecutor voluntarily rephrased the question. In each instance, defendant made no request for an admonition. We do not find misconduct or prejudice based on these isolated and relatively insignificant incidents.[16] (citations omitted; brackets and parentheses in original; second ellipses in original).

A single complex question, properly objected to, which went unanswered, nonetheless prejudiced the defendant's rights, according to the Ninth Circuit:

> During cross-examination, the prosecutor asked the defendant the following question: "Can you explain to me Mr. Sanchez, why you have a reputation [for] being one of the largest drug dealers on the reservation but you don't have more than one source of supply?" The court sustained Sanchez's objection to the question. The Government admits that "this question perhaps went further than it should." It notes, however, that Sanchez was not required to answer the question and that the court in its closing instructions properly instructed the

---

[16]People v. Mayfield, 928 P.2d 485, 534–35 (Cal. 1997).

jury that "[s]tatements of counsel are not to be regarded as evidence." The Government also points out that this was the only attempt to ask Sanchez about his drug-dealing reputation.[17] (brackets in original).

In this case, the burden was shifted to the prosecution:

> The Government's responsive argument is unpersuasive. The question assumed facts not in evidence. No attempt was made by the prosecutor to show that he acted in good faith because he had witnesses available to prove the facts insinuated in the question. The question was not harmless to Sanchez's right to a fair trial because it suggested to the jury that the defendant had "a reputation for being one of the largest drug dealers on the reservation."[18]

An Illinois Appellate Court similarly reversed a conviction where a single complex question, properly objected to, went unanswered:

> **Q. [Assistant State's Attorney]:** Let me ask you this, Mr. Jackson. Were you present when the defendant's mother offered the victim $500 to drop the charges?
> **[Defendant's Counsel]:** Objection, Judge.
> **THE COURT:** Objection sustained.
> **[Defendant's Counsel]:** Move for a mistrial.
> **THE COURT:** Overruled.[19] (brackets in original).

Several defenses were raised by the state to the complex question suggesting bribery:

> The State contends any error resulting from the State's question was harmless because there was no response to the question as defendant's objection was immediately sustained and, therefore, evidence rebutting the insinuation was unnecessary since there was nothing to rebut. The State also argues that the question does not form a basis for reversal because the insinuation was ambiguous, thus not prejudicial, and, further, the question's purpose was only to establish Jackson's bias. Lastly, the State maintains that the overwhelming evidence of guilt minimized any prejudicial effect of the question.[20]

The court rejected all of the defenses:

> [W]e need here address only defendant's contention that it was error for the State to insinuate to the jury that defendant's mother had tried

---

[17] United States v. Sanchez, 176 F.3d 1214, 1223 (9th Cir. 1999).
[18] *Id.*
[19] People v. Braggs, 540 N.E.2d 767, 768 (Ill. App. 1 Dist. 1988).
[20] *Id.* at 769.

to bribe the complainant to forgo prosecution of defendant, because we conclude that reason is sufficient to require retrial.[21]

The court also noted:

> Further, we are not persuaded that the resulting insinuation was ambiguous or that the question merely pertained to Jackson's bias. A careful reading of the formulation of the initial question put to Jackson specifically implies, as fact, that defendant's mother offered complainant the $500 bribe; the actual inquiry being only whether or not Jackson was present at that time. The second formulation of the question, while not specific to the purported bribe, similarly inquires of Jackson only whether he was present during any time when defendant's mother talked to complainant. We conclude the effect of these questions was to establish, by insinuation, that a conversation concerning the bribe had in fact taken place, notwithstanding the State's claim that the question's intended purpose was to elicit Jackson's bias. We view that questioning as highly improper in the absence of rebuttal evidence to support the resulting insinuation. And, because of the nature of the questioning, we are not persuaded that the insinuation can be considered harmless.[22]

A defendant convicted of robbery was asked a complex question related to his "occupation":

> The defendant next contends that prejudicial error occurred when the State established that the defendant lived in a poor neighborhood and had a limited education, and then asked if he had "[a]ny occupation other than robbing people." The defendant asserts that the prejudice was compounded when Poladian identified him by stating that he was seated between "the two public defenders." The defendant says that the only inference to be drawn was that he was uneducated, poor, and could only obtain money by robbery.[23] (brackets in original).

The Illinois Appeals Court held that striking the question from the record was not sufficient to ameliorate the harm to the defendant's rights, and it reversed the conviction:

> The statement by the prosecutor was inexcusable. The resolution of the conflict between the testimony of the three witnesses for the State and the defendant revolved around their credibility. [S]uch prosecutorial misconduct "strongly tended to lessen the credibility of (the defendant), and striking it from the record could not eradicate it from

---

[21] Id.
[22] Id. at 769.
[23] People v. McCray, 377 N.E.2d 46, 48 (Ill. App. 1 Dist. 1978).

THE COMPLEX QUESTION 317

the minds of the jurors." We believe that the prosecutor's comments, characterizing the defendant as a professional robber, within the context of this trial, prevented the jury from dispassionately evaluating the defendant's testimony.[24] (citation omitted; parentheses in original; brackets added).

A Pennsylvania prosecutor opened his cross-examination of a defense witness by asking about his "occupation":

> Bonasorte, a bar owner, was called to contradict testimony that the alleged conspirators in the Sacco murder had held a meeting in his bar. The prosecutor opened his cross-examination by asking Bonasorte, "How's the drug business?" On objection by defense counsel, the court ordered the prosecutor to rephrase the question. The cross-examination then continued as follows:
>
> **Q:** The Judge asked me to rephrase the question, Mr. Bonasorte, so we will rephrase. Do you deal drugs from Eggie Prosdocimo?
>
> **A:** No.
>
> **Q:** Ever deal drugs?
>
> **A:** Look at my record, no.
>
> **Q:** I don't want to look at the record. Did you ever deal drugs?
>
> **A:** No.[25] (citation omitted).

The Pennsylvania Supreme Court concluded the prosecutor's questions were improper, and they warranted a new trial:[26] "Although drug dealing was relevant in this case as a backdrop, it was improper to impeach Bonasorte in that fashion, as there was no evidence of his involvement on his part in the drug business."[27]

During closing argument, a prosecutor misstated the import of a complex question, by assuming the unasked question established an unproven fact:

> The problem in this case began with a classic error in trial technique. The prosecutor asked what was in essence a compound question: "Mr. Thomas, you believe that you know Watson's girlfriend, Tyra Jackson, right?" In so doing, he effectively asked both whether the witness knew Ms. Jackson, and whether the witness knew her to be the

---

[24] *Id.*
[25] Commonwealth v. Bricker, 487 A.2d 346, 348 (Pa. 1985).
[26] *Id.* at 355.
[27] *Id.* at 350.

defendant's girlfriend. At that point, the equally classic "objection as to form" would have been in order. Defense counsel, however, did not make it. Instead, the cross-examination unfolded as follows:

> **Prosecutor:** Mr. Thomas, you believe that you know Watson's girlfriend, Tyra Jackson, right?
>
> **Thomas:** I never testified I knew her or not.
>
> **Prosecutor:** You believe that you may have met her once or twice, right?
>
> **Thomas:** Maybe.[28] (citation omitted).

Fact Not in Evidence

The D.C. Circuit reversed the conviction because the prosecutor relied on a fact not in evidence:

> The unfortunate sequence of events arose when the prosecutor cross-examined defense witness Raymond Thomas about whether Tyra Jackson, the registered owner of the Subaru where the drugs and contraband were found, was Watson's girlfriend. In asking the question, however, the prosecutor presented the witness with a compound question assuming a key fact not in evidence—namely, that Jackson was Watson's girlfriend—with the result that the witness's response was ambiguous on the critical point the prosecutor sought to establish. Yet in closing argument the prosecutor, purporting to quote the defense witness, told the jury that Jackson was Watson's girlfriend, thereby establishing a stronger connection of Watson to the Subaru than the disputed evidence regarding the Subaru key and the seven week old sales receipt from Shaw's jewelry store. Otherwise the Subaru had been connected only to Jackson as the owner and to Hawkins as the user of her car.[29]

A surefire way to ask a complex question is to begin with the words "Are you aware . . .":

> During cross-examination, the government's attorney asked Spencer Smith: "Are you aware that two weeks ago, your wife called Keisha and Meredith [and] asked if they would testify today that Josh Booty was at Kristenwood on January 23rd, as late as 8:00 o'clock?" Spencer Smith responded: "Yes." Because the question was asked in this form, it was impossible for the jury to determine whether Spencer Smith

---

[28]United States v. Watson, 171 F.3d 695, 704 (D.C. Cir. 1999).
[29]*Id.* at 698–99.

was testifying solely that the phone call occurred, or whether he also was confirming the government's allegation that the purpose of the call was to affect testimony. The defendant properly objected on the ground that this compound question assumed facts not in evidence, and the objection should have been sustained.[30] (brackets in original; citation and footnote omitted).

Two defenses were raised to the improper question: (1) later questioning eliminated the problem, and (2) the error was harmless:

> Nevertheless, the error was made harmless by subsequent questioning. Spencer Smith indicated in response to one question that he was aware his wife had made the calls, and in response to another that he thought she was merely "trying to get some answers." The error is also rendered harmless beyond a reasonable doubt by the overwhelming evidence of defendant's complicity in the arson, conspiracy, and subsequent cover-up. Much of the evidence comes in the form of her own tape recorded statements and therefore is highly reliable.[31] (citation and footnotes omitted).

The North Carolina Supreme Court, confronted with a question incorporating "aware," likewise found the question was not prejudicial:

> Defendant next argues that the trial court erred by permitting the prosecutor to ask defendant whether she was "aware that [the victim] also went to her attorney, Steve Barden, and expressed concern that you hadn't paid her." The trial court overruled defendant's objection, and defendant responded that she was not aware of this fact. Defendant argues that there was no evidence to suggest that the victim ever expressed a concern to her attorney that defendant had not paid her and argues that the objection should have been sustained on the ground that it assumed a fact not in evidence. Even if the trial court erred by failing to sustain defendant's objection, defendant cannot show that she was prejudiced by the court's ruling.[32] (citation omitted; brackets in original).

The California Supreme Court found that a prosecutor's question was improper, but it, too, was harmless:

> Next, defendant contends that the prosecutor at times asked questions of him that were argumentative, improperly leading, or harassing, or that assumed facts not in evidence, all in violation of state law and the federal Constitution. Having reviewed the record, we disagree

---

[30]United States v. Elizabeth Smith, 354 F.3d 390, 396 (5th Cir. 2003).
[31]*Id.* at 396.
[32]State v. Bishop, 488 S.E.2d 769, 783 (N.C. 1997).

that any misconduct occurred, with one exception. At one point this exchange regarding the beating of Norma C. occurred:

Q: Did you take anything from her?

A: No, I didn't.

Q: Besides her dignity, I mean.

Mr. Reese: Objection, your Honor.

The Court: Overruled.

Mr. Reese: It's not time for final argument at this time, your Honor.

Defendant calls the prosecutor's comment inflammatory. His remark was gratuitous, but his misconduct was also de minimis. The jury was well acquainted with defendant's crimes and their effect on Norma C. No prejudice appears as a matter of state law.[33]

A defendant appealed the trial judge's sustaining an objection intended to cast doubt on his guilt:

Defendant next argues that the trial court erred in sustaining an objection to his question to Detective Bishop. Defendant asked Detective Bishop during cross-examination whether James Jones was "still a suspect at that time." Defendant argues that this question falls within the category of evidence pointing directly to the guilt of one other than the defendant, admissible under prior case law. We disagree. The question assumes a fact not in evidence, *viz*, that Jones had previously been a suspect in the victim's murder; the State's objection was properly sustained on that ground alone. In addition, the question as phrased does not tend to establish that Jones committed the murder.[34] (citations omitted).

Expert witnesses are not exempt from complex questions. An Illinois prosecutor overstepped the boundary between proper and improper questioning by directing complex questions at the defendant's expert witness:

Defendant contends that he was denied a fair trial when the prosecutor assumed a highly prejudicial fact not in evidence during the cross-examination of defendant's expert and then later repeated the matter in closing argument. During cross-examination of Dr. Garvin, the prosecutor asked Dr. Garvin: "Of course, [Richard] didn't tell you that in July of 1979 he was arrested in a bar and he began punching patrons in the bar and he threatened to kill anyone who signed

---

[33]People v. Osband, 919 P.2d 640, 687 (Cal. 1996).
[34]State v. Simpson, 393 S.E.2d 771, 778 (N.C. 1990).

[a complaint]." Defendant's objection to this question was sustained. Later, during the prosecutor's rebuttal argument, the prosecutor stated: "1979. When he beat somebody up in a bar and then threatened to kill them if they signed a [complaint]." Defendant's objection to this comment was sustained.

We agree that the question and subsequent comment [during] closing argument were error. Error occurs when the State, on cross-examination, asks a defense witness questions, presuming facts not in evidence, as a precursor to impeachment of that witness, in the absence of rebuttal evidence to substantiate the injury. The danger inherent in such questioning is that the jury will ignore any denial, presume the accuracy of the questions' insinuation or innuendo, and substitute that presumption for proof.[35] (citations omitted; brackets in original).

The Illinois Appeals Court reversed the conviction, based on these, and other, errors.[36]

---

[35]People v. Stack, 613 N.E.2d 1175, 1184 (Ill. App. 1 Dist. 1993).
[36]*Id.* at 1188.

CHAPTER TWENTY-FOUR

False Cause

"Although chronology is important in determining causation,

. . . it is by no means dispositive . . . "

Public Citizen Health Research Group v. Young, 909 F.2d 546, 551 (D.C. Cir. 1990). (ellipses added).

THE FALSE CAUSE FALLACY assumes that if event A preceded event B, event A must have caused event B. Does this temporal sequence guarantee a cause and effect relationship? Legally, the answer is "no," as the quotation above suggests. This fallacy is also known as: non causa pro causa ("there is no cause of the sort that has been given as the cause"[1]), faulty causal generalization, and post hoc, ergo propter hoc (Latin: "after this, therefore because of this")

A false cause argument frequently appears in tort liability cases, when there is no direct evidence to establish the cause of an accident or other tort, and the injured party is left to argue causation based solely on timing. Another area of the law in which these arguments commonly arise is in employment discrimination cases, where adverse actions are preceded by statutorily protected activity, and only the employer possesses the evidence to establish the cause of the adverse action.

An attorney who champions a cause and effect relationship, based on propitious timing, may try to bring the facts within an appropriate legal presumption, thereby shifting the burden of proof to the opposing party. Another technique, when defending a temporal cause and effect

---

[1] PETER A. ANGELES, THE HARPERCOLLINS DICTIONARY OF PHILOSOPHY 108 (2d ed. 1992).

relationship, is to present evidence which rules out other possible causes, leaving but a single cause. If the timing between the events is relatively brief, it can be argued that there was no opportunity for any intervening causes.

In attacking a false cause argument, an attorney may contend that the timing of the two events was a mere coincidence, and that no conclusion can be drawn about the cause. A long time between the events opens the door to an argument that the number of alternative causes is so great that the opposing party cannot establish a single cause. Even if the time between events is short, other plausible causes should be presented. Procedurally, a summary judgment motion should be filed, arguing that even if true, the asserted facts—resting solely on a time-based cause and effect relationship—do not establish the necessary cause in the legal action. Employment discrimination cases lend themselves to the argument that the discriminatee, aside from timing, is unable to present the needed evidence of unlawful motive by a preponderance of the evidence.

A man walking along the street spots a police vehicle, and immediately runs the other direction. Does his flight give rise to a "reasonable suspicion" that criminal activity was the cause of the flight? Would the outcome be any different if this scenario occurred in an area of a city known for heavy narcotics trafficking?

In *Illinois v. Wardlow*,[2] the U.S. Supreme Court split 5-4 over the question whether police officers had a "reasonable suspicion," under *Terry v. Ohio*,[3] to stop a man who fled on foot when he saw "a four car caravan of police vehicles converging on an area of Chicago known for heavy narcotics trafficking."[4] The majority held that "it was not merely respondent's presence in an area of heavy narcotics trafficking that aroused the officers' suspicion, but his unprovoked flight upon noticing the police."[5]

Chief Justice Rehnquist, writing for the majority, observed that "[h]eadlong flight—wherever it occurs—is the consummate act of evasion: it is not necessarily indicative of wrongdoing, but it is certainly suggestive of such."[6]

Justice Stevens, writing for the dissenters, noted that the majority did not adopt a *per se* rule that the police may detain any individual

---

[2]528 U.S. 119 (2000).
[3]392 U.S. 1 (1968).
[4]*Wardlow*, 528 U.S. at 124.
[5]*Id.*
[6]*Id.* at 124.

FALSE CAUSE 325

who flees upon seeing a law enforcement officer. There may be many circumstances, wrote Justice Stevens, where flight may be innocently explained:

> The question in this case concerns "the degree of suspicion that attaches to" a person's flight—or, more precisely, what "commonsense conclusions" can be drawn respecting the motives behind that flight. A pedestrian may break into a run for a variety of reasons—to catch up with a friend a block or two away, to seek shelter from an impending storm, to arrive at a bus stop before the bus leaves, to get home in time for dinner, to resume jogging after a pause for rest, to avoid contact with a bore or a bully, or simply to answer the call of nature—any of which might coincide with the arrival of an officer in the vicinity.[7]

On the other hand, he noted, flight may be the manifestation of illegal conduct:

> A pedestrian might also run because he or she has just sighted one or more police officers. . . . the State properly points out "that the fleeing person may be, *inter alia*, (1) an escapee from jail; (2) wanted on a warrant, (3) in possession of contraband, (i.e. drugs, weapons, stolen goods, etc.); or (4) someone who has just committed another type of crime."[8] (ellipses added).

Whether illegal conduct causes the flight will depend on a number of factors:

Factors such as the time of day, the number of people in the area, the character of the neighborhood, whether the officer was in uniform, the way the runner was dressed, the direction and speed of the flight, and whether the person's behavior was otherwise unusual might be relevant in specific cases.[9]

President Clinton's lawyers argued that he did not obstruct justice or tamper with witnesses, by speaking to his secretary, Betty Currie, because certain actions had not yet taken place, so there could be no argument that the requisite temporal cause and effect relationship existed:

> The President's actions could not as a matter of law give rise to either charge because Ms. Currie was not a witness in any proceeding at the time he spoke with her: her name had not appeared on any of the Jones witness lists; she had not been named as a witness in the Jones

---

[7]*Id.* at 128–29.
[8]*Id.* at 129.
[9]*Id.* at 129–30.

case; there were just two weeks of discovery left in the case; and there was no reason to suspect she would play any role in that case. The President had no reason to suspect that the OIC had embarked on a wholly new phase of its four-year investigation, one in which Ms. Currie would later be called by the OIC as a witness. To obstruct a proceeding or tamper with a witness, there must be both a witness and a proceeding. Here, there was neither. Despite the OIC's far-fetched suggestion to the contrary, there was no reason the President should not have spoken with Ms. Currie about Ms. Lewinsky.[10]

Defending against the argument by the special counsel that the timing of Monica Lewinsky's affidavit was delayed so that she could secure a new job, President Clinton's attorneys argued that the delay was occasioned by her attorneys, and not by any action of the President:

> Questions have been raised about a connection between the timing of Ms. Lewinsky's affidavit (which was executed January 7 and filed January 16) and the timing of any job offer. There was no connection. Francis Carter, Esq., Ms. Lewinsky's attorney at the time she executed the affidavit, apparently has stated that Ms. Lewinsky never asked him to delay the filing of an affidavit until after she had secured a job in New York and never suggested when the affidavit should be filed. Indeed, Mr. Carter has reported that he himself delayed the filing of the affidavit while he attempted to persuade the Jones attorneys to withdraw the subpoena to Ms. Lewinsky.[11] (parentheses in original; citation omitted).

President Clinton's attorneys also disputed any connection between Lewinsky's testimony and a job offer, by arguing that the job assistance began before there was any reason to suspect her testimony could be influenced by that assistance:

> The President made certain efforts to try to assure that Ms. Lewinsky had a fair shot at a job other than her Pentagon position, where she was not happy, and he generally was aware of other efforts by his secretary Ms. Currie and his friend Mr. Jordan. These actions were totally appropriate. At no time did the President ask that Ms. Lewinsky be accorded specially favorable or unfavorable treatment because of his relationship with her or for any other reason. These actions began well before Ms. Lewinsky was ever named a witness in the Jones litigation, and they were in no way intended to influence Ms. Lewinsky to keep secret what was at that time an already terminated relationship. There is no evidence of any link whatsoever between

---

[10] CHICAGO TRIBUNE, Sept. 13, 1998, at 40.
[11] Id. at 34.

the President's actions and possible testimony by Ms. Lewinsky in the Jones case.[12]

A trial judge found that the unexpected and unexplained sinking of a wood-hull barge, on October 17, 1956, was caused by a collision on the preceding September 9.[13] The Fifth Circuit concluded, however, that

> [t]he causal relation between the wrong doing on September 9 and the sinking on October 17 is not clear enough to bring this case within the doctrine that when a ship is damaged but not sunk in a collision, and later is injured or lost, the presumption is that the collision caused the later injury or sinking.[14] (footnote omitted).

The passage of 39 days since the accident, according to the court, allowed for too many potential intervening causes to claim that the accident was the sole cause of the sinking:

> As we see it, the time interval between the initial accident and the sinking is so long and the range of alternative possible explanations is so great that a finding of causation does not necessarily follow as a matter of logical deduction from the known circumstantial evidence.[15]

Ruled out were potential causes that could have arisen from the September 9 accident:

> [W]e have given weight to the slight damage the barge suffered in the September 9 accident, the apparent lack of harm to its timbers, the effect of the survey, the fact that all repairs were made in accordance with the survey, and the later use of the barge for thirty-two days, indicating that foreseeable damage had been repaired.[16]

Noting the circumstances in this case, the Court held:

> When the facts are unascertainable or so meager as they are here and an effect may follow from one of several causes it is a false generalization to suppose that because a sinking follows a collision thirty-nine days later, the sinking necessarily was an effect of the collision.[17]
>
> . . . .
>
> We conclude that it is as plausible to infer that the vessel sank because of an intervening cause, perhaps unknown to the owner, or, that she

---

[12] *Id.*
[13] Dreijer v. Girod Motor Company, 294 F.2d 549 (5th Cir. 1961).
[14] *Id.* at 554.
[15] *Id.*
[16] *Id.* at 556.
[17] *Id.*

sank because of the owner's intervening negligence in failing to attend to a vessel known to leak, as it is to infer that the barge sank because of the collision on September 9.[18]

The court held that the burden of proof rested with the barge owner, and he did not meet his burden:

> Where the evidence of the party on whom rests the burden of proof is equally consistent with several different hypotheses no single one is proved.
>
> . . . .
>
> Where the facts proven show that there are several probable causes of an injury, for one or more of which the defendant was not responsible, and it is just as reasonable and probable that the injury was the result of one cause or the other, plaintiff cannot have a recovery, since he has failed to prove that the negligence of the defendant caused the injury.[19] (ellipses added; citations omitted).

Cause of Negligence

Some negligence law of the 1920s did not assume a relationship existed between a probable cause and a consequent effect. A tenant who walked down an unlighted hallway, after sunset, and was found dead at the bottom of the stairs could not establish that the lack of lights caused the fall:

> A fatal defect exists, however, in the case of the plaintiff in that, assuming the accident to have occurred after sunset and the hallway to have been unlighted, there is a total absence of proof of any causal connection between the accident and the absence of light. The deceased was shown to have entered the premises and was heard by tenants upon the stairs and in the hallway. Following a thud, also heard by tenants, he was found at the foot of the stairs. No one saw him fall. Without further proof it would be solely a conjecture for a jury to draw the conclusion that the deceased fell down the stairs because of the absence of light.[20]

Chief Judge Cardozo, in an earlier New York case, posited assumptions underlying negligence actions that were more favorable to plain-

---

[18]*Id.*
[19]*Id.*
[20]Wolf v. Kaufman, 227 A.D. 281, 282 (App. Div. 1929).

tiffs. An after-dark collision between a car and an unlighted buggy presented the question whether the lack of lights caused the collision:

> We think, however, that evidence of a collision occurring more than an hour after sundown between a car and an unseen buggy, proceeding without lights, is evidence from which a causal connection may be inferred between the collision and the lack of signals. If nothing else is shown to break the connection, we have a case, prima facie sufficient, of negligence contributing to the result.[21] (citations omitted).

The court noted that negligence and cause must not be confused:

> We must be on our guard, however, against confusing the question of negligence with that of the causal connection between the negligence and the injury. A defendant who travels without lights is not to pay damages for his fault, unless the absence of lights is the cause of the disaster. A plaintiff who travels without them is not to forfeit the right to damages, unless the absence of lights is at least a contributing cause of the disaster. To say that conduct is negligence is not to say that it is always contributory negligence. "Proof of negligence in the air, so to speak, will not do."[22] (citation omitted).

An employee who filed a charge of race and sex discrimination in August was discharged the following December. The Seventh Circuit rejected her argument that a cause and effect relationship existed between the two events:

> This takes us to the end of Wilson's employment in December. Wilson contends that TRC cashiered her in retaliation for a charge of race and sex discrimination she had filed that August. She offers nothing to tie the events together, however. As the district judge pointed out, supervisors complained about Wilson's performance from the beginning of her work in March 1993. Targets for business generation went unmet. Wilson blames her shortcomings on lack of training, but we've been over that ground. She also treats Holton's vocal outbursts as support for the charge of retaliation, but she does not say that the quantity of angry words increased after August. Holton may well be an unpleasant person to work for, berating employees without much reason. Targets of his rancor appear to be selected without regard to race, however; Wilson tells us that Holton yelled at his own daughter too. Post hoc ergo propter hoc is not enough to support a finding of retaliation—if it were, every employee would file a charge just to get a little unemployment insurance. Timing may be an important clue

---

[21]Martin v. Herzog, 126 N.E. 814, 816 (N.Y. 1920).
[22]*Id.*

to causation, but does not eliminate the need to show causation—and Wilson really has nothing but the post hoc ergo propter hoc "argument" to stand on.[23] (citations omitted).

In another Seventh Circuit decision, where the plaintiff claimed his employer retaliated against him within the meaning of Section 1983, the court held that he must first establish a prima facie case, by proving: "(1) that he engaged in statutorily protected activity, (2) that he suffered an adverse employment action, and (3) that there is a causal connection between the two events."[24] (citation omitted).

The plaintiff argued that he produced sufficient evidence to shift the burden to his employer, but the Circuit disagreed, and found that timing, alone, could not defeat a summary judgment motion:

> Mr. Pugh relies, in part, on this test for his Section 1983 retaliation claim; he contends that he has established a prima facie inference of retaliation and that the burden should shift to the City to establish an affirmative defense. To make the prima facie inference, he argues, he must show only that the protected activity and his termination were not "wholly unrelated." However, the only factor to which he refers in attempting to establish the requisite relatedness is the timing of his discharge. We have made clear that this factor, without more, is insufficient to establish the defendant's burden. [T]his court held that "absent other evidence of retaliation, a temporal relation is insufficient evidence to survive summary judgment" on a Title VII or ADA retaliation claim. Therefore, Mr. Pugh could not establish a prima facie case of retaliation under the ADA.[25] (brackets added; citations omitted).

An employee failed to demonstrate that he was discharged because of his national origin, but he defeated a summary judgment motion, based on a claim of retaliatory discharge.[26] To make a prima facie case of retaliation, he had to show (1) "that he engaged in a protected activity; (2) that he was discharged subsequent to or contemporaneously with such activity; and (3) that a causal link exists between the protected activity and the discharge."[27]

The Third Circuit held the employee met the prima facie burden, with timing (two days between the filing of the discrimination claim and the discharge) as a crucial fact:

---

[23]Bermudez v. TRC Holdings, Inc., 138 F.3d 1176, 1179 (7th Cir. 1998).
[24]Pugh v. City of Attica, 259 F.3d 619, 630 n.9 (7th Cir. 2001).
[25]*Id.*
[26]Jalil v. Avdel Corp., 873 F.2d 701 (3d Cir. 1989).
[27]*Id.* at 708.

We believe plaintiff succeeded in establishing all three elements. Jalil unquestionably engaged in a protected activity when he filed discrimination claims with the DCR and the EEOC. And, obviously, Jalil was discharged. He demonstrated the causal link between the two by the circumstance that the discharge followed rapidly, only two days later, upon Avdel's receipt of notice of Jalil's EEOC claim.[28] (citation omitted).

The employer contended Jalil was discharged for cause, based on his "insubordination in twice refusing to immediately remove his headset radio when so directed."[29] Having advanced "a legitimate, nondiscriminatory reason for discharging Jalil," the employer confronted one more hurdle: "To obtain summary judgment, then, Avdel needed to show that plaintiff could not raise an issue of fact regarding whether defendant's proffered explanation was pretextual."[30] (citation omitted).

Evidence of motivation, the court found, was subject to dispute, and thus was not appropriate for summary judgment:

> Moreover, the absence of a written rule against radio headsets and the presence of a dispute whether there was an unwritten rule could permit the inference, in light of the timing of the discharge, that Avdel was harassing Jalil, trying to induce his insubordination to have a pretext for firing him, or it could suggest the very real possibility that Avdel "seized upon this instance of insubordination to fire" Jalil.[31] (citation omitted).

Two days between the filing of a discrimination claim and the discharge established the causal link in the previous case, but would two years between the protected activity and the discharge turn the presumption on its head? The Third Circuit has held that the "mere passage of time is not legally conclusive proof against retaliation."[32] In a case where two years elapsed between the protected activity and the discharge, the plaintiff was able to prove an atypical fact—a continuing pattern of antagonism: "The temporal proximity noted in other cases is missing here and we might be hard pressed to uphold the trial judge's finding were it not for the intervening pattern of antagonism that SEPTA demonstrated."[33] (citations omitted).

---

[28] *Id.*
[29] *Id.*
[30] *Id.*
[31] *Id.* at 709.
[32] Robinson v. SEPTA, 982 F.2d 892, 894 (3d Cir. 1993).
[33] *Id.* at 895.

A different employer asserted there could not have been a causal connection between the filing of administrative complaints and the employee's discharge almost two years later, because it established a legitimate business justification

> that Woodson was terminated in a company-wide reduction program nearly two years after he filed his discrimination complaints and after Scott had already promoted him to the position he sought when he filed those complaints.[34]

Responding, Woodson asserted there was more than enough evidence for a jury to conclude that there was "a pattern of antagonism in the intervening period,"[35] including such conduct as

> "setting Woodson up to fail" by hiring him as a product system leader in the poorly performing napkin division and then refusing to provide him with adequate resources; Scott's failure to respond appropriately to racist graffiti in its plant, and Scott's termination of Woodson pursuant to a "sham" ranking process performed by individuals who were not familiar with his employment record, but only with his charges of discrimination.[36]

The Third Circuit, in finding a sufficient causal link between Woodson's complaints and his discharge, held that a court cannot look at "each piece of evidence alone . . . to support an inference of a pattern of antagonistic behavior,"[37] but must look at all the evidence, much as with a play:

> A play cannot be understood on the basis of some of its scenes, but only on its entire performance, and similarly, a discrimination analysis must concentrate not on individual incidents, but on the overall scenario.[38] (citation omitted).

Vesting Questions

Employees nearing retirement are often concerned with the vesting of their pensions and the maximization of benefits. Is there a cause and effect relationship between a pre-vesting discharge and significant cost savings to the employer? That question arose when a plaintiff filed an action for age discrimination (ADEA) and interference with pension

---

[34] Woodson v. Scott Paper Co., 109 F.3d 913, 921 (3d Cir. 1997).
[35] Id.
[36] Id.
[37] Id.
[38] Id., quoting Andrews v. City of Philadelphia, 895 F.2d 1469, 1481 (3d Cir. 1990).

benefits (ERISA).[39] The trial court found that the plaintiff was, indeed, discharged "in order to prevent her vesting of pension benefits."[40] Upholding that determination, the Second Circuit concluded that the plaintiff had established more than a "proximity to benefits" and "cost savings," by demonstrating an unlawful motive. As is often the case in employment discrimination cases, motivation was evinced by an employer's statement: An employer agent declared that he "wouldn't be at all surprised" if the employee was being harassed by the employer because of her imminent vesting.[41]

Perhaps one of the best known cases involving denial of pension benefits was *Gavalik v. Continental Can Co.*,[42] where the employer devised

> a 'liability avoidance' scheme under which Continental maximized savings during plant closings and layoffs of blue-collar union workers in part by discharging unvested workers. The scheme's existance was well-documented in Continental's internal records.[43] (citations omitted).

Proving that an employee's discharge was motivated by the employer's desire to prevent the employee from maximizing his or her pension benefits is a difficult proposition. Where there are only facts suggesting a coincidence of timing, no cause and effect relationship can be demonstrated:

> Although Lightfoot's complaint alleged a "pattern or practice of age discrimination in employment intended to deprive older . . . employees of opportunity to optimize the benefits available to them," he has come forward with no specific facts to support this allegation. He argues on appeal that pre-termination discrimination against him "must" have resulted from Carbide's desire to interfere with his pension benefits because it had that effect. This is a textbook illustration of the post hoc ergo propter hoc fallacy. . . . Where an employee's ERISA claim is based only on a claim that the employee has been deprived of the opportunity to accrue additional benefits through more years of employment, "a prima facie case requires some additional evidence suggesting that pension interference might have been a motivating factor." Lightfoot has presented no such evidence, and summary judgment was appropriate.[44] (second ellipses added; citations omitted).

---

[39] Reichman v. Bonsignore, Brignati & Mazzotta P.C., 818 F.2d 278 (2d Cir. 1987).
[40] *Id.* at 280.
[41] *Id.* at 281.
[42] 812 F.2d 834 (3d Cir. 1987).
[43] Dister v. Continental Group, Inc., 859 F.2d 1108, 1117 (2d Cir. 1988).
[44] Lightfoot v. Union Carbide Corp., 110 F.3d 898, 906 (2d Cir. 1997).

The Third Circuit, though denying an employee's claim that he was discharged to prevent the accrual of additional pension benefits, intimated what evidence need be produced to prevail:

> [W]e note that the record contains no evidence that the savings to the employer resulting from Turner's termination were of sufficient size that they may be realistically viewed as a motivating factor. Indeed, there is no evidence at all about the economic consequences to Shering that flowed from Turner's termination.[7]

---

[7]We do not rule out the possibility that an employee with a vested pension can establish a *prima facie* case by showing a pension reduction of such size that it might reasonably be considered to have motivated the discharge. This is not such a case.[45]

Certain Federal Rules of Evidence eliminate the possibility of raising a temporal cause and effect argument. For example, a party who undertakes remedial measures after an event cannot be assumed to have made those changes in response to the event:

> Rule 407. Subsequent Remedial Measures
>
> When, after an injury or harm allegedly caused by an event, measures are taken that, if taken previously, would have made the injury or harm less likely to occur, evidence of the subsequent measures is not admissible to prove negligence, culpable conduct, a defect in a product, a defense in a product's design, or a need for a warning or instruction. This rule does not require exclusion of evidence of subsequent measures when offered for another purpose, such as proving ownership, control, or feasibility of precautionary measures, if controverted, or impeachment.

An offer to pay medical expenses to an injured party, likewise, is not subject to the argument that the injury caused the payments:

> Rule 409. Payment of Medical and Similar Expenses
>
> Evidence of furnishing or offering or promising to pay medical, hospital, or similar expenses occasioned by an injury is not admissible to prove liability for the injury.

Many people believe that if the U.S. Supreme Court overturns *Roe v. Wade*,[46] abortion will no longer be legal anywhere in the United

---

[45]Turner v. Schering-Plough Corp., 901 F.2d 335, 348 (3d Cir. 1990).
[46]410 U.S. 113 (1973).

States. Such a cause and effect relationship is not correct, as Justice Scalia notes in *Lawrence v. Texas*[47]: "This falsely assumes that the consequence of overruling *Roe* would have been to make abortion unlawful. It would not; it would merely have permitted the States to do so."[48]

During the 2006 Enron trial, defense counsel for former CEO Kenneth Lay argued that the jury should reject what to many was an obvious temporal cause and effect relationship:

> Bruce Collins, a defense lawyer for Lay told the jury Tuesday afternoon that "the key takeaway is, do not assume the collapse of Enron means fraud. Put the government to their proof."[49]

The jury apparently was unable to accept this argument, based on the evidence in the case.

---

[47]539 U.S. 558 (2003).
[48]*Id.* at 591.
[49]http://www.washingtonpost.com/wp-dyn/content/article/2006/5/16AR2006051600795.html (May 16, 2006).

CHAPTER TWENTY-FIVE

False Analogy

> [T]he majority's attempt to analogize this forfeiture to the system of tort liability for automobile accidents is unpersuasive. Tort law is tied to the goal of compensation (punitive damages being the notable exception), while forfeitures are concededly punitive. The fundamental difference between these two regimes has long been established.
>
> Bennis v. Michigan, 516 U.S. 442, 469 n.13 (1996) (Stevens, J., dissenting).
> (parentheses in original; citation omitted; brackets added).

AN ANALOGY INVOLVES the comparison of two or more similar cases, ideas, things, concepts, or individuals. Analogies may be implicit (simile), where the comparison is stated in terms such as "like" or "as," or explicit (metaphor), where the comparison is often stated with the word "is." A successful analogy convincingly draws relevant comparisons, and minimizes distinctions. False analogies succumb to claims that the relevant distinctions are critical, so that no successful comparison can be made. Analogies are useful because they compare unknowns or lesser-knowns to well-knowns, which enable the intended audience to draw upon their knowledge to understand the unknowns or lesser-knowns.

Outside the courtroom, attorneys defeat analogies by noting, for example, what facts, characteristics, or traits are relied upon to establish the analogy, and by minimizing their importance or relevance. Non-relevant facts, even if they are commonly shared, do not create a valid analogy. Emphasizing relevant dissimilarities is another method of creating a false or inappropriate analogy. In the courtroom, an attorney may argue that the comparison is not based on facts in evidence, that the comparison is unfair and prejudicial, or that the comparison runs afoul of the ethical obligations imposed on attorneys. A counter analogy may also diminish the effectiveness of the original analogy. In defense of an analogy, an attorney may argue that the analogy responds to an argument presented by opposing counsel (invited response), or constitutes harmless error.

Prosecutors have often compared defendants to notorious convicted criminals. A prosecutor in a federal murder trial, during the sentencing phase argument, drew an analogy between the defendant and Gary Gilmore: "Gary Gilmore, if your Honor please, will never kill anyone else again."[1]

The Eleventh Circuit concluded the prosecutor (Huff) did not encourage an inappropriate analogy:

> It would have been completely proper for Huff to have argued "If Henry Drake is executed, he will never kill again." Such a comment would have been acceptable as a reference to the specific deterrence (or incapacitation) effect of the death penalty. The remark is such a tautology that it could hardly be seen as potentially prejudicial. Referring to Gilmore, a man executed near in time to Drake's trial, was not improper. Read in context, the argument did not invite an unfair comparison between the two men.[2] (parentheses in original).

An Alabama prosecutor's closing argument compared the defendant to Jeffrey Dahmer:

> "Some of you may think, you know, he's in here wearing a shirt, wearing a tie, he doesn't look like what I would think a child sex abuser would look. He's been neat, nicely dressed and he doesn't look perhaps like a child molester.
>
> ". . . .
>
> "Do you think that the children who were abused by Jeffrey Dahmer knew when they saw Jeffrey Dahmer that—[3] (ellipses and dash in original).

At that point, the defendant's counsel objected:

> **"Mr. Huddleston [defense counsel]:** Your Honor, this is a very inflammatory bullying argument to which I object. I think that comparing Phillip Allen to Jeffrey Dahmer in the closing argument here is outrageous and would ask the Court fix it.[4] (brackets in original).

---

[1]Drake v. Kemp, 762 F.2d 1449, 1460 (11th Cir. 1985).
[2]*Id.*
[3]Allen v. State, 659 So. 2d 135, 141–42 (Ala. Crim. App. 1994).
[4]*Id.* at 142.

The reviewing court rejected the analogy, but nonetheless, upheld a 20-year prison sentence for first degree sexual assault:

> Jeffrey Dahmer is an infamous serial killer who distinguished himself by consuming the flesh of some of his victims. We find the prosecutor's remark in this case unwarranted.[5] (citation omitted).

The Alabama Court of Appeals cited a previous case, where the prosecutor argued:

> **Ms. Brooks [Prosecutor]:** . . . and they want you to say not guilty because of the nature of the crime. *That's like saying Raymond Eugene Brown who butchered somebody to death is not guilty*—(italics, ellipses, dash, and brackets in original).[6]

Although the court upheld the defendant's sentence, the prosecutor's remark elicited a stinging ethical rebuke for the false analogy:

> The comment by the prosecutor, without *any* question, crossed the line of permissible conduct established by the ethical rules of the legal profession. *ABA Standards for Criminal Justice* 3-5.8(B) (2d ed. 1980). Her behavior is particularly egregious and perhaps even reprehensible. Not only was the prosecutor's comment totally irrelevant to the issues before the trial court, but the prosecutor's comparison of appellants, who are on trial for the charge of arson in the first degree, to a capital murderer is a completely unwarranted and disproportionate analogy.[7] (italics in original).
>
> . . . .
>
> Our review of the record, in its entirety, reveals an overwhelming amount of circumstantial evidence supporting appellants' convictions. Although we view the prosecutor's comment as egregious, opprobrious, and condemnable, in light of the overwhelming evidence, the absolute absurdity of the analogy, and the sure probability that the jury used its common sense and disregarded the comment, we cannot say that the prosecutor's comment and the trial court's inaction so undermined the fairness of appellants' trial as to amount to a miscarriage of justice. Rather, we find that, beyond a reasonable doubt, the comment did not influence the jury's decision; there is no likelihood that a new trial would change the result of the trial.[8] (ellipses added).

In this case, the court noted the analogy broke down based on the nature of the criminal conduct: arson versus capital murder.

---

[5] *Id.* at 143.
[6] Sattari v. State, 577 So. 2d 535, 536–37 (Ala. Crim. App. 1990).
[7] *Id.* at 537.
[8] *Id.* at 540.

Defendant Henry H. Jones Jr. was convicted of one count of first degree murder in connection with the death of 15-year-old Vernon L. Guledge.[9] Jones appealed his conviction based on the prosecutor's closing and rebuttal arguments referring to insanity defenses raised by famous defendants in other cases. In his closing argument, the prosecutor stated:

> "You can read the paper in the big cases and it always is there, isn't it, Sirhan Sirhan, Jack Ruby, Ammidown, Timm and Caldwell, when they were caught red-handed in front of an audience or bevies of people, they turn to insanity because that is their only hope."
>
> . . . .
>
> "Now, oh, he is dangerous, he is a murderer. But he is not mentally ill. Sirhan Sirhan and Jack Ruby and Ammidown, they didn't fool anybody, nor does he, has he?"
>
> . . . .
>
> ". . . He is not crazy, ladies and gentlemen, or insane, you know somebody passed me in the hall a moment ago and said you'll never get first degree murder—
>
> **"THE COURT:** Wait a minute let's don't talk about things like that.
>
> **"Mr. Robinson:** I[t] was going to be an anology [sic], Your Honor.
>
> **"THE COURT:** No, you cannot make that analogy and the jury will disregard it.[10] (brackets, ellipses, and dash in original).

Citing a well-known case in the area, defense counsel moved for a mistrial after the prosecutor's closing argument. The court denied the motion.[11]

Not only were the prosecutor's arguments improper, but they were so prejudicial that the D.C. Circuit reversed the conviction:

> Here, as in *United States v. Clinton L. Phillips*, the same Government attorney resorted to arguments clearly designed to arouse the passion and prejudice of the jury. When a defendant's sole defense is insanity, a prosecutor cannot be permitted to compare that defense to other infamous crimes where that defense has been raised and rejected.[12] (footnote omitted).

---

[9]United States v. Hawkins, 480 F.2d 1151 (D.C. Cir. 1973).
[10]*Id.* at 1153.
[11]*Id.*
[12]*Id.* at 1154.

Infamous Individuals

Analogies involving infamous individuals need not be limited to U.S. citizens. A California prosecutor sought to draw a contrast between a defendant's modest demeanor in the courtroom and his demeanor when engaged in criminal acts:

> "You notice the quality of his testimony on the stand, a holiness, the empty shell of a man, a man who is motivated by some grotesque purpose, a man who like Marquis de Sade said was a sadist, a man who reveled in hearing human outcry, becoming powerful by torture and this is just typical, I submit, from the evidence in this case, of a person who is a devotee of Marquis de Sade, a practitioner of sadism."[13]

Defense counsel interposed no objection, but the prosecutor, "perhaps fearing that his rhetoric had carried him beyond the bounds of permissible argument,"[14] stated that the analogy was not evidence and was not his personal opinion, but was based on the evidence in the case.

The court rejected the defendant's claim that the analogy to the Marquis de Sade was inapplicable:

> We do not consider that the prosecutor's allusion was inappropriate in view of the evidence in this case. The prosecutor certainly had a right to point out to the jury that modest behavior at one time and place, i.e., in the courtroom, is not inconsistent with depraved conduct under other circumstances, and his recourse to history and literature to make this point was not improper in the circumstances. Moreover, as indicated above, defendant failed to object to the allusion in question.[15]

A California prosecutor suggested that the defendant "may have shared the same genocidal theories as Adolph Hitler":[16]

> "Nothing unusual about this [selective breeding] theory. A lot of people have had it. Hitler, good old Hitler. Hitler wrote poetry. You know, wrote a couple of other things too, and he had some real interesting theories on selective—selection and genetics breeding."[17] (brackets in original).

---

[13] People v. Thornton, 523 P.2d 267, 283 (Cal. 1974).
[14] Id.
[15] Id.
[16] People v. Hovey, 749 P.2d 776 (Cal. 1988).
[17] Id. at 797.

The California Supreme Court held that the prosecutor's remarks responded to arguments raised by the defense, and concluded there was no basis for reversing the verdict:

> The record indicates that the foregoing remarks were made in response to defense evidence indicating that defendant was a serious student and poet, and referred to extensive prosecution evidence revealing that defendant had expressed strong views on genetic engineering ("selectively breeding for intelligence"), including the necessity of "kill[ing] off the people to begin a new race." Thus, the prosecutor's remarks were not entirely inappropriate or unlinked to the evidence . . .[18] (parentheses and brackets in original; ellipses added).

In the same case, the prosecutor analogized the defendant's crime to an abstraction: "the 'worst possible' or the most 'incredibly horrible' crime one might commit."[19] This prosecutorial comment, too, was held not to be prejudicial:

> [D]efendant points to repeated statements by the prosecutor that defendant's crime was the "worst possible" or the most "incredibly horrible" crime one might commit. Defendant acknowledges that the prosecutor is entitled to comment on the gravity of the offense in penalty arguments, but he contends that in the present case the prosecutor went further and "implied a benchmark for comparison that was not in evidence," supposedly based on her experience as a prosecutor. We disagree. The prosecutor's hyperbole suggesting that defendant's crime was the "worst possible" crime one might commit did not purport to be based on any secret information known only to the prosecutor. Moreover, under the circumstances of the present case, the prosecutor's remark constituted a reasonably fair comment on the evidence. We also note that defendant failed to object to the comment or seek an appropriate admonition.[20] (brackets added; citations omitted).

Two defendants were found guilty of conspiracy and of having the intent to import cocaine into the U.S.[21] The First Circuit considered three of the prosecutor's analogies alleged to have violated the defendants' rights.

In the first analogy, the prosecutor compared one of the defendants to "a person who throws a stone into a crowd, injuring a particular individual, then denies having the 'intention of hitting that man in par-

---

[18]*Id.* at 797.
[19]*Id.* at 796.
[20]*Id.* at 796–97.
[21]United States v. Giry, 818 F.2d 120 (1st Cir. 1987).

ticular' . . . ."²² Because no contemporaneous objection was raised, and because the court did not believe that this analogy came within the "plain error exception," it did not consider this argument.²³

Defendant's counsel objected to the second analogy at the close of the prosecutor's argument. This analogy

> compared the appellants to two individuals who "agree to kill the Judge," with one furnishing money for a gun, the other purchasing the gun, and both lying in wait until the Judge appears: then, if "when you fire, the weapon is no good because it was defective, that doesn't mean there was no conspiracy." (citation omitted).²⁴

The court concluded the prosecutor offered a false analogy: "The prosecutor's reference to a plot on the judge's life improperly likened the appellants' conduct to a violent attack upon the court."²⁵

Even though no contemporaneous objection was interposed to the prosecutor's "reference to Peter's denial of Christ," the Court stated that the third analogy merited further consideration.²⁶ After due consideration, the court concluded:

> The prosecutor's reference to Peter's denial of Christ constituted an irrelevant and inflammatory appeal to the jurors' private, religious beliefs.²⁷
>
> . . . .
>
> Here, the prosecutor's improper statements appear to have been deliberate. They were relatively isolated incidents, but they were wholly unprovoked. The complete irrelevance of the reference to Peter's denial of Christ suggests that its sole purpose was to inflame the jury's passions.²⁸ (ellipses added).

Despite the improper arguments, however, the court upheld the convictions:

> In sum, the judge's instructions were sufficiently strong and explicit to have significantly reduced the prejudicial impact of the prosecutor's misstatements. It is possible that the instructions did not entirely neutralize the prejudice. But given the unambiguous evidence of the appellants' intent to supply a large quantity of cocaine to ostensible

---

²²*Id.* at 133.
²³*Id.*
²⁴*Id.*
²⁵*Id.*
²⁶*Id.*
²⁷*Id.*
²⁸*Id.* at 134.

domestic importers, we do not find that any surviving prejudice could have affected the outcome of the trial.[29]

Apples and Oranges

Comparing a proffered analogy to "apples and oranges" is a sure sign that someone believes a false analogy has been used, as this commentary about the government's antitrust case against Microsoft proclaims:

> While the government has tried to point to the AT&T divestiture to support its breakup proposal, the two situations are **apples and oranges**. AT&T was a government-regulated monopoly that agreed to a voluntary breakup in order to end decades of heavy government regulation. Microsoft and the broader personal-computer industry have created tremendous value for consumers without any government regulation; now the government is proposing an unprecedented breakup and unprecedented regulation affecting America's most competitive industry.[30] (bold added).

Chief Justice Rehnquist, writing for the majority, in *Payne v. Tennessee*,[31] rejected the dissent's argument that victim impact evidence places before the jury a comparison of the worthiness of the victims:

> *Payne* echoes the concern voiced in *Booth*'s case that the admission of victim impact evidence permits a jury to find that defendants whose victims were assets to their community are more deserving of punishment than those whose victims are perceived to be less worthy. As a general matter, however, victim impact evidence is not offered to encourage comparative judgments of this kind—for instance, that the killer of a hardworking, devoted parent deserves the death penalty, but that the murderer of a reprobate does not. It is designed to show instead each victim's "uniqueness as an individual human being," whatever the jury might think the loss to the community resulting from his death might be. The facts of *Gathers* are an excellent illustration of this: The evidence showed that the victim was an out of work, mentally handicapped individual, perhaps not, in the eyes of most, a significant contributor to society, but nonetheless a murdered human being.[32] (citation omitted).

---

[29]*Id.*
[30]Newsweek, May 22, 2000, at 42.
[31]501 U.S. 808 (1991).
[32]*Id.* at 823–24.

Attempting to justify a creche display on county grounds, in *Allegheny County v. Greater Pittsburgh ACLU*,[33] Justice Kennedy analogized the display to references to God on U.S. currency and in the Pledge of Allegiance. Justice Blackmun, writing for the majority, rejected those analogies, based on "obvious distinction(s)":

> In *Marsh*, the Court relied specifically on the fact that Congress authorized legislative prayer at the same time that it produced the Bill of Rights. Justice Kennedy, however, argues that *Marsh* legitimates all "practices with no greater potential for an establishment of religion" than those "accepted traditions dating back to the Founding." Otherwise, the Justice asserts, such practices as our national motto ("In God We Trust") and our Pledge of Allegiance (with the phrase "under God," added in 1954), are in danger of invalidity.
>
> Our previous opinions have considered in dicta the motto and the pledge, characterizing them as consistent with the proposition that government may not communicate an endorsement of religious belief. We need not return to the subject of "ceremonial deism," because there is an obvious distinction between creche displays and references to God in the motto and the pledge. However history may affect the constitutionality of nonsectarian references to religion by the government, history cannot legitimate practices that demonstrate the government's allegiance to a particular sect or creed.[34] (citations omitted).

In turn, Justice Kennedy, dissenting in part, accused the majority of relying on a false analogy in its analysis of Establishment Clause jurisprudence:

> Contrary to the majority's discussion, the relevant historical practices are those conducted by governmental units which were subject to the constraints of the Establishment Clause. Acts of "official discrimination against non-Christians" perpetrated in the 18th and 19th centuries by States and municipalities are of course irrelevant to this inquiry, but the practices of past Congresses and Presidents are highly informative.[35] (citations omitted).

Justice Scalia, dissenting in *Hill v. Colorado*,[36] argued that the majority's decision improperly "elevates the abortion clinic to the status of the home":

---

[33] 492 U.S. 573 (1989).
[34] *Id.* at 602–03.
[35] *Id.* at 670 n.7.
[36] 530 U.S. 703 (2003).

The limitation on a speaker's right to bombard the home with unwanted messages which we approved in *Frisby*—and in *Rowan v. Post Office Dept.*, upon which the Court also relies—was predicated on the fact that "'we are often 'captives' *outside* the sanctuary of the home and subject to objectionable speech.'" As the universally understood state of First Amendment law is described in a leading treatise: "Outside the home, the burden is generally on the observer or listener to avert his eyes or plug his ears against the verbal assaults, lurid advertisements, tawdry books and magazines, and other 'offensive' intrusions which increasingly attend urban life." The Court today elevates the abortion clinic to the status of the home.[37] (citations and footnote omitted; italics in original).

In *United States v. Russell*,[38] the defendant in a drug prosecution case argued that the U.S. Supreme Court should reconsider the entrapment defense—to bar any prosecution—"because of the police involvement in criminal activity."[39] Chief Justice Rehnquist, writing for the majority, rejected the defendant's analogy to the exclusionary rule and confessions without counsel, noting the dissimilarities in government conduct:

In the instant case, respondent asks us to reconsider the theory of the entrapment defense as it is set forth in the majority opinions in *Sorrells* and *Sherman*. His principal contention is that the defense should rest on constitutional grounds. He argues that the level of Shapiro's involvement in the manufacture of the methamphetamine was so high that a criminal prosecution for the drug's manufacture violates the fundamental principles of due process. The respondent contends that the same factors that led this Court to apply the exclusionary rule to illegal searches and seizures, and confessions, should be considered here. But he would have the Court go further in deterring undesirable official conduct by requiring that any prosecution be barred absolutely because of the police involvement in criminal activity. The analogy is imperfect in any event, for the principal reason behind the adoption of the exclusionary rule was the Government's "failure to observe its own laws." Unlike the situations giving rise to the holdings in *Mapp* and *Miranda*, the Government's conduct here violated no independent constitutional right of the respondent. Nor did Shapiro violate any federal statute or rule or commit any crime in infiltrating the respondent's drug enterprise.[40] (citations omitted).

---

[37] *Id.* at 752–53.
[38] 411 U.S. 423 (1973).
[39] *Id.* at 430.
[40] *Id.* at 430.

Reliance on Foreign Law

The U.S. Supreme Court's reliance upon the laws of other countries to determine rights under the U.S. Constitution has generated intense controversy. Chief Justice Rehnquist decried the majority's analogy to foreign law involving the execution of the mentally retarded, in *Atkins v. Virginia*.[41] He began his analysis with an appeal to ignorance, and then asserted the majority lacked a justification for relying on foreign law:

> In reaching its conclusion today, the Court does not take notice of the fact that neither petitioner nor his amici have adduced any comprehensive statistics that would conclusively prove (or disprove) whether juries routinely consider death a disproportionate punishment for mentally retarded offenders like petitioner. Instead, it adverts to the fact that other countries have disapproved imposition of the death penalty for crimes committed by mentally retarded offenders. I fail to see, however, how the views of other countries regarding the punishment of their citizens provide any support for the Court's ultimate determination. While it is true that some of our prior opinions have looked to the climate of international opinion to reinforce a conclusion regarding evolving standards of decency we have since explicitly rejected the idea that the sentencing practices of other countries could "serve to establish the first Eighth Amendment prerequisite, that [a] practice is accepted among our people." (emphasizing that *American* conceptions of decency are . . . dispositive).[42] (italics, ellipses, brackets, and parentheses in original; citations omitted).

One method of countering a false analogy is to propose a different analogy, as Justice Breyer, dissenting in *Texas v. Cobb*,[43] did:

> The test has emerged as a tool in an area of our jurisprudence that The Chief Justice has described as "a veritable Sargasso Sea which could not fail to challenge the most intrepid judicial navigator." Yet the Court now asks, not the lawyers and judges who ordinarily work with double jeopardy law, but police officers in the field, to navigate *Blockburger* when they question suspects. Some will apply the test successfully; some will not. Legal challenges are inevitable. The result, I believe, will resemble not so much the Sargasso Sea as the criminal law equivalent of Milton's "Serbonian Bog . . . Where Armies whole have sunk."[44] (ellipses in original; citations omitted).

---

[41]536 U.S. 304 (2002).
[42]*Id.* at 324–25.
[43]532 U.S. 162 (2001).
[44]*Id.* at 185–86.

Another technique to counter a false analogy is to make a reductio ad absurdum argument, as Justice Souter proposed in *Zelman v. Simmons-Harris*,[45] where school vouchers were at issue:

> The majority's argument that public school students within the program direct almost twice as much state funding to their chosen school as do program students who receive a scholarship and attend a private school, was decisively rejected in *Committee for Public Ed. & Religious Liberty v. Nyquist*.
>
> We do not agree with the suggestion . . . that tuition grants are an analogous endeavor to provide comparable benefits to all parents of schoolchildren whether enrolled in public or nonpublic schools. The grants to parents of private school children are given in addition to the right that they have to send their children to public schools "totally at state expense." And in any event, the argument proves too much, for it would also provide a basis for approving through tuition grants the *complete subsidization* of all religious schools on the ground that such action is necessary if the State is fully to equalize the position of parents who elect such schools—a result wholly at variance with the Establishment Clause.[46] (ellipses and italics in original; citation omitted).

The last sentence is a reductio ad absurdum argument because it characterizes the majority's position as providing a basis for the "subsidization of all religious schools."

Justice Ginsburg invoked popular culture (*Sesame Street* reference) to confute the majority's analogies in *Muscarello v. United States*:[47]

> The Government points to numerous federal statutes that authorize law enforcement officers to "carry firearms" and notes that, in those authorizing provisions, "carry" of course means "both on the person and in a vehicle." Quite right. But as viewers of "Sesame Street" will quickly recognize, "one of these things [a statute *authorizing* conduct] is not like the other [a statute *criminalizing* conduct]." The authorizing statutes in question are properly accorded a construction compatible with the clear purpose of the legislation to aid federal law enforcers in the performance of their official duties. It is fundamental, however, that a penal statute is not to be construed generously in the Government's favor.[48] (citations omitted; italics and brackets in original).

---

[45]536 U.S. 639 (2002).
[46]*Id.* at 698 n.7.
[47]524 U.S. 125 (1998).
[48]*Id.* at 147 n.11.

Justice Ginsburg, in *Bush v. Gore*,⁴⁹ argued that Chief Justice Rehnquist relied on cases that were distinguishable because of their "historical contexts":

> Rarely has this Court rejected outright an interpretation of state law by a state high court. *Fairfax's Devisee* v. *Hunter's Lessee*, 7 Cranch 603 (1813), *NAACP* v. *Alabama ex rel. Patterson*, 357 U.S. 449 (1958), and *Bouie* v. *City of Columbia*, 378 U.S. 347 (1964), cited by the Chief Justice, are three such rare instances. But those cases are embedded in historical contexts hardly comparable to the situation here.⁵⁰ (citation omitted).

Attorneys routinely distinguish "analogous" cases cited by opposing counsel, often pointing out the factual differences between the cases. Judges, too, rely on the facts of each case to find false analogies:

> The dissent's misuse of *Sailors* relies on a false analogy. In *Sailors*, voters challenged the selection of county school board members who had been appointed by delegates chosen from popularly elected local school boards. In the case at hand, the voters challenge the selection of members of the legislative delegations, who, the dissent concedes, are popularly "elected rather than appointed." Rather than analogizing the popularly elected legislative delegation members to the popularly elected local school board members in *Sailors*, the dissent attempts to analogize them to the *delegates* who had been selected by the local school boards to appoint the county board. Indisputably, these delegates were *not* popularly elected.⁵¹ (citation omitted).

---

⁴⁹531 U.S. 98 (2000).
⁵⁰*Id.* at 139–40.
⁵¹Vander Linden v. Hodges, 193 F.3d 268, 280 n.8 (4th Cir. 1999).

CHAPTER TWENTY-SIX

Either/Or: Hobson's Choice

> *As here, the inmate in Woodard claimed to face a Hobson's choice: He would damage his case for clemency no matter whether he spoke and incriminated himself, or remained silent and the clemency board construed that silence against him. Unlike here, the Court nevertheless concluded that the pressure the inmate felt to speak to improve his chances of clemency did not constitute unconstitutional compulsion.*
>
> McKune v. Lile, 536 U.S. 24, 43 (2002).

THE EITHER/OR INFORMAL FALLACY is known by many names: black and white fallacy, false dilemma, false dichotomy, and bifurcation. Legal writers frequently cite the expression "Hobson's choice" to represent this informal fallacy. Often, as in the quotation above, this expression is used incorrectly to depict two undesirable outcomes, akin to finding oneself "between a rock and a hard place." In its correct sense, Hobson's choice is the epitome of the either/or fallacy, because it denotes not only two options, but the exclusion of any alternatives, when, in fact, there are other alternatives.

Tobias (Thomas) Hobson operated a stable that rented horses to students at Cambridge University.[1] The students tended to select only certain horses, leaving to Hobson the task of exercising the others. To correct this problem, Hobson

> instituted a strict rotation system for his steeds. The most recently ridden were housed at the back of the stable, the most rested at the front, and only the horse nearest the door was available for hire. Any patron who objected to Hobson's system was, of course, free to walk

---

[1] http://www.word-detective.com/121800.html.

(also humorously known as "taking Shank's mare," the "shank" being one's own leg).² (parentheses in original).

Thus, students at Cambridge were limited to two alternatives—take the horse at the door or walk. The remainder of the stabled horses could not be selected, even though there was nothing wrong with them.

In a legal argument, where the issue is framed as either one alternative or another, the counter-argument requires pointing out (and demonstrating the relevance of) the omitted alternative(s). Another rejoinder may entail a challenge to the validity of the alternatives; perhaps they are not relevant to the issue at all. Alternatively, it may be possible to accept both choices because they are not mutually exclusive.

As the proponent of an either/or argument, an attorney seeks to control the parameters of the debate. Effectively limiting the issue to two outcomes forces the opposition to respond to those arguments, with little opportunity to advance unrelated arguments. The most obvious formulation of an either/or argument employs the terms "either" and "or":

> Either the endorsement test must invalidate scores of traditional practices recognizing the place religion holds in our culture, or it must be twisted and stretched to avoid inconsistency with practices we know to have been permitted in the past, while condemning similar practices with no greater endorsement effect simply by reason of their lack of historical antecedent. Neither result is acceptable.³ (footnote omitted).

Chief Justice Rehnquist, dissenting in *Atkins v. Virginia*,⁴ posed an either/or argument by limiting the alternatives to two sources:

> In my view, these two sources—the work product of legislatures and sentencing jury determinations—ought to be the sole indicators by which courts ascertain the contemporary American conceptions of decency for purposes of the Eighth Amendment. They are the only objective indicia of contemporary values firmly supported by our precedents.⁵

President Clinton's attorneys defined impeachable conduct in terms of "political offenses," involving "injury to the state":

> In our Preliminary Memorandum, we set forth at some length the various ways in which impeachable "high Crimes and Misdemean-

---

²*Id.*
³Allegheny County v. Greater Pittsburgh ACLU, 492 U.S. 573, 674 (1989).
⁴536 U.S. 304 (2002).
⁵*Id.* at 324.

ors" have been defined. Nothing in the Referral even approximates such conduct. In the English practice from which the Framers borrowed the phrase, "High Crimes and Misdemeanors" denoted political offenses, the critical element of which was injury to the state. Impeachment was intended to redress public offenses committed by public officials in violation of the public trust and duties.[6] (citation omitted).

The alternatives were that the President either committed a public offense, meriting impeachment, or he did not. By framing the debate in terms of "public offenses," the President's attorneys sought to exclude his "private conduct" from consideration. As an additional limiting measure, his attorneys argued, "nothing" the special prosecutor presented met the high impeachment standards.

The declaration that something is so "as a matter of law" may effectively delimit the options to those proposed:

> In sum, the President's statements to his aides could not have obstructed justice as a matter of law. Their legal duty was to answer the prosecutor's questions and to tell the truth honestly as they knew it, and the President's comments in no conceivable way affected that duty. The OIC suggests that the President's delay in acknowledging a relationship with Ms. Lewinsky somehow contributed to an obstruction of justice because it affected how the prosecutors would conduct the investigation. This claim is unfounded, as a matter of law. The President had no legal obligation to appear before the grand jury absent compulsion and every reason not to do so, given the OIC's tactics, illegal leaking, and manifest intent to cause him damage.[7]

"As a matter of law" may suggest a settled proposition, leaving no room for argument—or other options:

> The President has admitted he had an improper sexual relationship with Ms. Lewinsky. In a civil deposition, he gave narrow answers to ambiguous questions. As a matter of law, those answers could not give rise to a criminal charge of perjury. In the face of the President's admission of his relationship, the disclosure of lurid and salacious allegations can only be intended to humiliate the President and force him from office.[8]

A prosecutor's closing argument to the jury referred to the defendant's future dangerousness; at the same time, the prosecutor sought to

---

[6]CHICAGO TRIBUNE, Sept. 13, 1998, at 38.
[7]*Id.* at 40.
[8]*Id.* at 40.

preclude the jury from learning that the defendant was parole ineligible. The defendant had previously pleaded guilty to "first degree burglary and two counts of criminal sexual conduct in connection with two prior assaults on elderly women."[9] The guilty pleas "rendered (the defendant) ineligible for parole if convicted for any subsequent violent offense . . ."[10] (ellipses added).

At the penalty phase of the trial, the defense offered evidence of neglect and abuse. The prosecution argued that the defendant's "future dangerousness was a factor for the jury to consider when fixing the appropriate punishment," and asked what should be done with the defendant "now that he is in our midst."[11]

Urging the jury to return the death penalty, the prosecutor asserted that it would be "a response of society to someone who is a threat. Your verdict will be an act of self-defense."[12]

The trial judge instructed the jury not to consider parole, but the South Carolina Supreme Court, nevertheless, held that the defendant's due process rights were compromised:

> But even if the trial court's instruction successfully prevented the jury from considering parole, petitioner's due process rights still were not honored. Because petitioner's future dangerousness was at issue, he was entitled to inform the jury of his parole ineligibility. An instruction directing the jury not to consider the defendant's likely conduct in prison would not have satisfied due process and, for the same reasons, the instruction issued by the trial court in this case does not satisfy due process.[13] (citation omitted).

According to the court, the prosecutor's argument improperly created a "false dilemma":

> The State may not create a false dilemma by advancing generalized arguments regarding the defendant's future dangerousness while at the same time, preventing the jury from learning that the defendant never will be released on parole.[14]

Legal "dilemmas" have prompted courts to search for alternatives, to avoid sacrificing constitutional rights. In *Jones v. United States*,[15]

---

[9] Simmons v. South Carolina, 512 U.S. 154, 156 (1994).
[10] *Id.*
[11] *Id.* at 157.
[12] *Id.*
[13] *Id.* at 171.
[14] *Id.*
[15] 362 U.S. 257, 263 (1960).

the petitioner had been arrested in a friend's apartment and was charged with possession of narcotics found there. [The U.S. Supreme Court] was troubled about the "dilemma" that would be created by requiring the petitioner, in order to secure suppression of the narcotics, to swear that they were taken from his possession, thus confessing his guilt of the very offense charged against him. To avoid this situation the Court held that petitioner could make his motion to suppress without swearing to possession, either because of the dilemma itself or because as a guest in the apartment he had the "legally requisite interest in the premises."[16] (brackets added).

Although dilemmas are usually associated with only two alternatives—finding one's self on the horns of a dilemma, for example—"two" is not a magic number. In *Brogan v. United States*,[17] federal agents asked a union official whether he had ever received cash or gifts from an employer whose employees he represented. He answered, "No." Consequently, he was charged with unlawfully making a false statement, under 18 U.S.C. § 1001, which provided:

> Whoever, in any matter within the jurisdiction of any department or agency of the United States knowingly and willfully falsifies, conceals or covers up by any trick, scheme, or device a material fact, or makes any false, fictitious or fraudulent statements or representations, or makes or uses any false writing or document knowing the same to contain any false, fictitious or fraudulent statement or entry, shall be fined not more than $10,000 or imprisoned not more than five years, or both."[18]

The defendant admitted that his denial came within a "literal reading" of the statute, but he argued that a departure from a literal interpretation was appropriate, because a number of circuit courts excluded the so-called "exculpatory no" from the scope of the statute. As described by Justice Scalia: "The central feature of this doctrine ('exculpatory no') is that a simple denial of guilt does not come within the statute."[19] (parentheses added).

As part of his defense, the defendant argued that the statute created a "cruel trilemma," an argument rejected by Justice Scalia, writing for the majority:

> The second line of defense that petitioner invokes for the "exculpatory no" doctrine is inspired by the Fifth Amendment. He argues that

---

[16] Mancusi v. Deforte, 392 U.S. 364, 375 (1968).
[17] 522 U.S. 398 (1998).
[18] *Id.* at 400.
[19] *Id.* at 401.

a literal reading of §1001 violates the "spirit" of the Fifth Amendment because it places a "cornered suspect" in the "cruel trilemma" of admitting guilt, remaining silent, or falsely denying guilt. This "trilemma" is wholly of the guilty suspect's own making, of course. An innocent person will not find himself in a similar quandary (as one commentator has put it, the innocent person lacks even a "lemma"). And even the honest and contrite guilty person will not regard the third prong of the "trilemma" (the blatant lie) as an available option. The *bon mot* "cruel trilemma" first appeared in Justice Goldberg's opinion for the Court in *Murphy v. Waterfront Comm'n of N. Y. Harbor*, where it was used to explain the importance of a suspect's Fifth Amendment right to remain silent when subpoenaed to testify in an official inquiry. Without that right, the opinion said, he would be exposed "to the cruel trilemma of self-accusation, perjury or contempt." In order to validate the "exculpatory no," the elements of this "cruel trilemma" have now been altered—ratcheted up, as it were, so that the right to remain silent, which was the *liberation* from the original trilemma, is now *itself* a cruelty. We are not disposed to write into our law this species of compassion inflation.[20] (italics in original; citations omitted; parentheses in original).

Responding to either/or arguments takes many forms. Justice Blackmun, in *Allegheny County v. Greater Pittsburgh ACLU*,[21] pointed out the alternatives to Justice Kennedy's argument:

> Although Justice Kennedy repeatedly accuses the Court of harboring a "latent hostility" or "callous indifference" toward religion, nothing could be further from the truth, and the accusations could be said to be as offensive as they are absurd. Justice Kennedy apparently has misperceived a respect for religious pluralism, a respect commanded by the Constitution, as hostility or indifference to religion. No misperception could be more antithetical to the values embodied in the Establishment Clause.[22]
>
> . . . .
>
> It is thus incontrovertible that the Court's decision today, premised on the determination that the creche display on the Grand Staircase demonstrates the county's endorsement of Christianity, does not represent a hostility or indifference to religion but, instead, the respect for religious diversity that the Constitution requires.[23] (citation and footnote omitted; ellipses added).

---

[20] *Id.* at 404.
[21] 492 U.S. 573 (1989).
[22] *Id.* at 610.
[23] *Id.* at 612–13.

Justice Stevens, in the same case, likewise, argued that Justice Kennedy's alternatives are not exclusive:

> The suggestion that the only alternative to governmental support of religion is governmental hostility to it represents a giant step backward in our Religion Clause jurisprudence. Indeed in its first contemporary examination of the Establishment Clause, the Court, while differing on how to apply the principle, unanimously agreed that government could not require believers or nonbelievers to support religions.[24]

Third Alternative

A third alternative may be suggested as "more reasonable" than the alternatives in the either/or argument:

> Finally, the swiftness and near unanimity with which the Eleventh Amendment was adopted suggest "either that the Court had not captured the original understanding, or that the country had changed its collective mind most rapidly." The more reasonable interpretation, of course, is that regardless of the views of four Justices in *Chisholm*, the country as a whole—which had adopted the Constitution just five years earlier—had not understood the document to strip the States of their immunity from private suits. ("It is plain that just about everybody in Congress agreed the Supreme Court had misread the Constitution").[25] (citations omitted; parentheses in original).

The alternatives may be portrayed as extremes, lending themselves to moderate alternatives:

> The general principle deducible from the First Amendment and all that has been said by the Court is this: that we will not tolerate either governmentally established religion or governmental interference with religion. Short of those expressly proscribed governmental acts there is room for play in the joints productive of a benevolent neutrality which will permit religious exercise to exist without sponsorship and without interference.[26] (citations omitted).

In *Illinois v. Wardlow*,[27] the parties asked the U.S. Supreme Court to create rigid rules to determine whether an individual who takes flight at

---

[24]*Id.* at 652 n.11.
[25]Alden v. Maine, 527 U.S. 706, 724 (1999).
[26]*Allegheny County*, 492 U.S. at 661–62 (Kennedy, J., dissenting in part, quoting former Chief Justice Burger writing for the Court in *Walz* (*Walz v. Tax Commission of City of New York*, 397 U.S. 664 (1970))).
[27]528 U.S. 119 (2000).

the sight of law enforcement authorities may be stopped on suspicion of criminal activity. Justice Stevens noted the Court rejected these extreme views:

> The State of Illinois asks this Court to announce a "bright-line rule" authorizing the temporary detention of anyone who flees at the mere sight of a police officer. Respondent counters by asking us to adopt the opposite per se rule—that the fact that a person flees upon seeing the police can never, by itself, be sufficient to justify a temporary investigative stop of the kind authorized by *Terry v. Ohio*.
>
> The Court today wisely endorses neither *per se* rule. Instead, it rejects the proposition that "flight is . . . necessarily indicative of ongoing criminal activity," adhering to the view that "[t]he concept of reasonable suspicion . . . is not readily, or even usefully, reduced to a neat set of legal rules," but must be determined by looking to "the totality of the circumstances—the whole picture."[28] (parentheses and ellipses in original; citations omitted).

A simple rejection of both alternatives may suffice, as an example presented earlier in this chapter, now with the response, illustrates:

> Either the endorsement test must invalidate scores of traditional practices recognizing the place religion holds in our culture, or it must be twisted and stretched to avoid inconsistency with practices we know to have been permitted in the past, while condemning similar practices with no greater endorsement effect simply by reason of their lack of historical antecedent. Neither result is acceptable.[29]

Justice Stevens similarly dismissed the plurality's alternatives, in *Ramdass v. Angelone*,[30] labeling them "an illusion":

> The plurality's reasoning either draws an arbitrary line between these types of procedures, or it accepts that all of these possibilities make Simmons inapplicable, in which case that due process right is eviscerated entirely. It is abundantly clear that the proclaimed "workable" rule the plurality claims to be following is an illusion.[31] (citation and footnote omitted).

When neither alternative suggested is appropriate, an argument can be made that the proponent offered a false dichotomy:

> The dissenting opinion seeks to reopen these precedents, contending that state sovereign immunity must derive either from the common

---

[28] *Id.* at 126–27.
[29] *Allegheny County*, 492 U.S. at 674.
[30] 530 U.S. 165 (2000).
[31] *Id.* at 206.

law (in which case the dissent contends it is defeasible by statute) or from natural law (in which case the dissent believes it cannot bar a federal claim). As should be obvious to all, this is a false dichotomy. The text and the structure of the Constitution protect various rights and principles. Many of these, such as the right to trial by jury and the prohibition on unreasonable searches and seizures, derive from the common law. The common-law lineage of these rights does not mean they are defeasible by statute or remain mere common-law rights, however. They are, rather, constitutional rights, and form the fundamental law of the land.[32] (parentheses in original; citation omitted).

The Constitution may be cited as the authority to spurn the proposed alternatives:

Justice Blackmun and Justice O'Connor defend the majority's test by suggesting that the approach followed in *Lynch* would require equally difficult line drawing. It is true that the *Lynch* test may involve courts in difficult line-drawing in the unusual case where a municipality insists on such extreme use of religious speech that an establishment of religion is threatened. Only adoption of the absolutist views that either all government involvement with religion is permissible, or that *none* is, can provide a bright line in all cases. That price for clarity is neither exacted nor permitted by the Constitution.[33] (italics in original; citations omitted).

Ridicule and reductio ad absurdum arguments have been employed to reject an either/or argument:

The plurality claims that its treatment of *Roe*, and a woman's right to decide whether to terminate a pregnancy, "hold[s] true the balance between that which the Constitution puts beyond the reach of the democratic process and that which it does not." This is unadulterated nonsense. The plurality's balance matches a lead weight (the State's allegedly compelling interest in fetal life as of the moment of conception) against a feather (a "liberty interest" of the pregnant woman that the plurality barely mentions, much less describes). The plurality's balance—no balance at all—places nothing, or virtually nothing, beyond the reach of the democratic process.[34] (citations omitted; parentheses in original).

A counter-either/or example diverts attention from the original alternatives to new ones. A father of nine children refused to pay child

---

[32] *Alden*, 527 U.S. at 733.
[33] *Allegheny County*, 492 U.S. at 675 n.11.
[34] Webster v. Reproductive Health Services, 492 U.S. 490, 556 n.11 (1989).

support, and was required to avoid having more children, unless he could demonstrate he could support his existing children.[35] Wisconsin Supreme Court Justice Bradley, dissenting, wrote:

> If the tables are turned to the present case where the probationer is a man, a similar risk arises. Because the condition is triggered only upon the birth of a child, the risk of imprisonment creates a strong incentive for a man in Oakley's position to demand from the woman the termination of her pregnancy. It places the woman in an untenable position: have an abortion or be responsible for Oakley going to prison for eight years. Creating an incentive to procure an abortion in order to comply with conditions of probation is a result that I am not prepared to foster.[36]

Citing *Black's Law Dictionary*

When it comes to the meaning of terms contained in legislation, a frequently cited source is *Black's Law Dictionary*. Citing *Black's* creates an either/or argument—an ascribed meaning is supported, or it is not. Justice Ginsburg, in *Buckhannon v. West Virginia*,[37] contended that a third alternative should be adopted: a contextual reading.

> One can entirely agree with Black's Law Dictionary that a party "in whose favor a judgment is rendered" prevails, and at the same time resist, as most Courts of Appeals have, any implication that *only* such a party may prevail. In prior cases, we have not treated Black's Law Dictionary as preclusively definitive; instead, we have accorded statutory terms, including legal "term[s] of art," a contextual reading.[38] (brackets and italics in original; citations omitted).

Another way to express an either/or argument, in legal terms, is to refer to a "black-letter" rule or a "bright line" rule, that divides conduct into clear alternatives. The antithesis of such rules is a case-by-case analysis:

> The absence of a black-letter rule does not disable judges from exercising their discretion in construing the outer limits on sentencing authority that the Eighth Amendment imposes. After all, judges are "constantly called upon to draw . . . lines in a variety of contexts,"

---

[35] State v. Oakley, 629 N.W.2d 200 (Wis. 2000).
[36] *Id.* at 219.
[37] 532 U.S. 598 (2001).
[38] *Id.* at 628–29.

and to exercise their judgment to give meaning to the Constitution's broadly phrased protections. For example, the Due Process Clause directs judges to employ proportionality review in assessing the constitutionality of punitive damages awards on a case-by-case basis. Also, although the Sixth Amendment guarantees criminal defendants the right to a speedy trial, the courts often are asked to determine on a case-by-case basis whether a particular delay is constitutionally permissible or not.[39] (citations and footnote omitted; ellipses in original).

Justice Stevens, dissenting in *Good News Club v. Milford Central School*,[40] noted bright lines are not always definitive:

> A perceptive observer sees a material difference between the light of day and the dark of night, and knows that difference to be a reality even though the two are separated not by a bright line but by a zone of twilight.[41] (citation omitted).

Line drawing, by itself, does not end the discussion about what conduct falls into which category, as Justice Breyer notes in *Ewing v. California*[42]:

> I can find no such special criminal justice concerns that might justify this sentence. The most obvious potential justification for bringing Ewing's theft within the ambit of the statute is administrative. California must draw some kind of workable line between conduct that will trigger, and conduct that will not trigger, a "three strikes" sentence. "But the fact that a line has to be drawn somewhere does not justify its being drawn anywhere." The statute's administrative objective would seem to be one of separating more serious, from less serious, triggering criminal conduct. Yet the statute does not do that job particularly well.[43] (citation omitted).

. . . .

> I concede that a bright-line rule would give legislators and sentencing judges more guidance. But application of the Eighth Amendment to a sentence of a term of years requires a case-by-case approach. And, in my view, like that of the plurality, meaningful enforcement of the

---

[39] Ewing v. California, 538 U.S. 11, 33–34 (2003).
[40] 533 U.S. 98 (2001).
[41] *Id.* at 133 n.2.
[42] 538 U.S. 11 (2003).
[43] *Id.* at 48.

Eighth Amendment demands that application—even if only at sentencing's outer bounds.[44] (ellipses added).

Bright-Line Approach

Chief Justice Rehnquist rejected a case-by-case analysis when applying *Miranda* warnings, arguing that a bright-line approach is the most workable:

> The disadvantage of the *Miranda* rule is that statements which may be by no means involuntary, made by a defendant who is aware of his "rights," may nonetheless be excluded and a guilty defendant go free as a result. But experience suggests that the totality-of-the-circumstances test which §3501 seeks to revive is more difficult than *Miranda* for law enforcement officers to conform to, and for courts to apply in a consistent manner. ("The line between proper and permissible police conduct and techniques and methods offensive to due process is, at best, a difficult one to draw").[45] (parentheses in original; citation omitted).

Justice Scalia disagreed with the Chief Justice, and quoted Justice O'Connor's rejection of this argument in another case:

> *Miranda*, for all its alleged brightness, is not without its difficulties; and voluntariness is not without its strengths.... *Miranda* creates as many close questions as it resolves. The task of determining whether a defendant is in "custody" has proved to be "a slippery one." And the supposedly "bright" lines that separate interrogation from spontaneous declaration, the exercise of a right from waiver, and the adequate warning from the inadequate, likewise have turned out to be rather dim and ill defined. The totality-of-the-circumstances approach, on the other hand, permits each fact to be taken into account without resort to formal and dispositive labels. By dispensing with the difficulty of producing a yes-or-no answer to questions that are often better answered in shades and degrees, *the voluntariness inquiry often can make judicial decisionmaking easier rather than more onerous.*[46] (parentheses, italics, and ellipses in original; citations omitted).

President Clinton's attorneys reacted to the Special Prosecutor's either/or arguments by claiming that insufficient information was disclosed to appropriately respond:

---

[44]*Id.* at 52.
[45]Dickerson v. United States, 530 U.S. 428, 444 (2000).
[46]*Id.* at 463–64.

The real critique can occur only with access to the materials on which the prosecutors have ostensibly relied. Only at that time can contradictory evidence be identified and the context and consistency (or lack thereof) of the cited evidence be ascertained. Since we have not been given access to the transcripts and other materials compiled by the OIC, our inquiry is therefore necessarily limited. But even with this limited access, our preliminary review reaffirms how little this highly intrusive and disruptive investigation has in fact yielded. In instance after instance, the OIC's allegations fail to withstand scrutiny either as a factual matter, or a legal matter, or both. The Referral quickly emerges as a portrait of biased recounting, skewed analysis, and unconscionable overreaching.[47]

President George W. Bush, in a radio address about immigration, suggested that two alternatives need not be mutually exclusive:

In his weekly radio address on Saturday, Mr. Bush acknowledged the difficulty that lawmakers faced. "This is an emotional debate," he said. "America does not have to choose between being a welcoming society and being a lawful society. We can be both at the same time."[48]

Justice White employed an analogy to disagree with an either/or argument offered by Justice Scalia, in *Harmelin v. Michigan*[49]:

Under that view, capital punishment—a mode of punishment—would either be completely barred or left to the discretion of the legislature. Yet neither is true. The death penalty is appropriate in some cases and not in others. The same should be true of punishment by imprisonment.[50]

---

[47]CHICAGO TRIBUNE, Sept. 13, 1998, at 38.
[48]http://www.nytimes.com/2006/03/26/politics/26cornyn.html?hp&ex=1143349200&en=98246cf34f49f705&ei=5094&partner=homepage (Mar. 26, 2006).
[49]501 U.S. 957 (1991).
[50]*Id.* at 1014.

CHAPTER TWENTY-SEVEN
Genetic: Attacking the Origin

> *Inquiring into a law's original reasonableness was perhaps tantamount to questioning whether it existed at all. "In holding the origin to have been unreasonable, the Court nearly always doubts or denies the actual origin and continuance of the custom in fact."*
>
> Rogers v. Tennessee, 532 U.S. 451, 473 n.1 (2001) (Scalia, J., dissenting)[1] (roman in original).

AN ATTACK UPON AN ARGUMENT'S GENESIS, origin, or source is known as a genetic fallacy.[2] Two other names for this fallacy are the nothing-but fallacy or the reductive fallacy.[3] The underlying assumption of this fallacy is that an argument's validity depends on its source: a bad source equates to a bad argument. In reality, the validity of an argument depends not on its derivation, but on its merits.

The quotation above typifies a genetic fallacy by examining the source of a law to determine whether it was valid *ab initio*. If the origin was unreasonable, the law stood little chance of surviving a judicial challenge.

Challenges to the genesis of an argument or law often implicate other informal fallacies. An attorney may attack the proponent of an argument, either as having a bad character (ad hominem (abusive)) or being biased (ad hominem (circumstantial)) to demonstrate that the argument should not be accepted because the source is not trustworthy.

---

[1]Quoting C. ALLEN, LAW IN THE MAKING 140 (3d ed. 1939).
[2]PETER A. ANGELES, THE HARPERCOLLINS DICTIONARY OF PHILOSOPHY 110 (2d ed. 1992).
[3]*Id.*

Epithets, such as "novel," are sometimes used to describe legal decisions of recent origin, and to disparage their acceptance for lack of an approved pedigree.

A prosecutor argued to the jury that the "defendants' closing arguments were "smoke screens floated your way by defense counsel . . . [who are] very able people here."[4] (ellipses and brackets in original).

The defendants asserted on appeal that the prosecutor's statement "sought to convince the jury that the arguments of defense counsel were . . . manufactured by able lawyers seeking to hide the truth from the jury."[5] (ellipses in original).

Recognizing a genetic fallacy and noting the proper line of attack, the First Circuit stated:

> We agree that the prosecutor should have focused on the merits of the defendants' arguments rather than their source. Again, defense counsel failed to object to the statement at trial, and we have little trouble in holding that this isolated misstep did not rise to the level of plain error.[6]

Should a statute be declared unconstitutional because it was enacted by partisans? Justice Stevens rejected that idea, suggested by Justice Kennedy, in *Hill v. Colorado*[7]:

> Similarly, the contention that a statute is "viewpoint based" simply because its enactment was motivated by the conduct of the partisans on one side of a debate is without support. The antipicketing ordinance upheld in *Frisby v. Schultz*, a decision in which both of today's dissenters joined, was obviously enacted in response to the activities of antiabortion protesters who wanted to protest at the home of a particular doctor to persuade him and others that they viewed his practice of performing abortions to be murder. We nonetheless summarily concluded that the statute was content neutral.[8] (citations omitted).

By noting that the Court's dissenters previously upheld a statute's constitutionality when antiabortion protesters were the moving force, Justice Stevens responded with a tu quoque argument.

In the same case, Justice Scalia opined that the Court would find the legislation providing a *cordon-sanitaire* about an abortion clinic to be

---

[4]United States v. Whiting, 28 F.3d 1296, 1302 (1st Cir. 1994).
[5]*Id.*
[6]*Id.* at 1302–03.
[7]530 U.S. 703 (2000).
[8]*Id.* at 724–25.

"content-based," if the source of the law were something other than abortion-related:

> I have no doubt that this regulation would be deemed content-based *in an instant* if the case before us involved antiwar protesters, or union members seeking to "educate" the public about the reasons for their strike. "[I]t is," we would say, "the content of the speech that determines whether it is within or without the statute's blunt prohibition." But the jurisprudence of this Court has a way of changing when abortion is involved.[9] (italics and brackets in original; citation omitted).

In *Payne v. Tennessee*,[10] Justice Stevens criticized Justice Scalia's reliance on the voice of a nationwide "victims' rights" movement:

> In his concurring opinion today, Justice Scalia again relies on the popular opinion that has "found voice in a nationwide 'victims' rights' movement." His view that the exclusion of evidence about "a crime's unanticipated consequences" "significantly harms our criminal justice system," rests on the untenable premise that the strength of that system is to be measured by the number of death sentences that may be returned on the basis of such evidence. Because the word "arbitrary" is not to be found in the constitutional text, he apparently can find no reason to object to the arbitrary imposition of capital punishment.[11] (citations omitted).

Unwilling to acknowledge the "special place" *Miranda* rights hold for the general public, Justice Scalia dissented in *Dickerson v. United States*,[12] concluding that the Constitution does not give expression to those rights:

> Finally, I am not convinced by petitioner's argument that *Miranda* should be preserved because the decision occupies a special place in the "public's consciousness." As far as I am aware, the public is not under the illusion that we are infallible. I see little harm in admitting that we made a mistake in taking away from the people the ability to decide for themselves what protections (beyond those required by the Constitution) are reasonably affordable in the criminal investigatory process. And I see much to be gained by reaffirming for the people the wonderful reality that they govern themselves—which means that "[t]he powers not delegated to the United States by the Constitution" that the people adopted, "nor prohibited—to the States" by that Con-

---

[9] *Id.* at 742.
[10] 501 U.S. 808 (1991).
[11] *Id.* at 859 n.1.
[12] 530 U.S. 428 (2000).

stitution, "are reserved to the States respectively, or to the people."[13] (parentheses and brackets in original; citation omitted).

It could be said that anytime a court strikes down legislation as unconstitutional it is the court—not the representative of the people (i.e., the legislature)—that is the source of the law. Justice Scalia, in *Lawrence v. Texas*,[14] argued that the Court majority usurped the State legislature's role as the appropriate source of legislation:

> I would no more *require* a State to criminalize homosexual acts—or, for that matter, display any moral disapprobation of them—than I would forbid it to do so. What Texas has chosen to do is well within the range of traditional democratic action, and its hand should not be stayed through the invention of a brand-new "constitutional right" by a Court that is impatient of democratic change. It is indeed true that "later generations can see that laws once thought necessary and proper in fact serve only to oppress," and when that happens, later generations can repeal those laws. But it is the premise of our system that those judgments are to be made by the people, and not imposed by a governing caste that knows best.[15] (italics in original; citation omitted).

A judicial opinion may be in serious jeopardy if it was decided by a narrow majority, over "spirited dissent." This is especially so, if appointments to the Court establish a new majority, as happened in *Payne v. Tennessee*:[16]

> *Booth* and *Gathers* were decided by the narrowest of margins, over spirited dissents challenging the basic underpinnings of those decisions. They have been questioned by Members of the Court in later decisions and have defied consistent application by the lower courts. ("The fact that the majority and two dissenters in this case all interpret the opinions and footnotes in *Booth* and *Gathers* differently demonstrates the uncertainty of the law in this area"). Reconsidering these decisions now, we conclude, for the reasons heretofore stated, that they were wrongly decided and should be, and now are, overruled. We accordingly affirm the judgment of the Supreme Court of Tennessee.[17] (citations omitted).

---

[13]*Id.* at 464–65.
[14]539 U.S. 558 (2003).
[15]*Id.* at 603–04.
[16]*Supra* at 501 U.S. 808.
[17]*Id.* at 828–30.

GENETIC: ATTACKING THE ORIGIN 369

Justice Scalia, who went from dissenter in *Booth* to majority in *Payne*, charged there was no legal basis for the previous decision:

> The response to Justice Marshall's strenuous defense of the virtues of *stare decisis* can be found in the writings of Justice Marshall himself. That doctrine, he has reminded us, "is not 'an imprisonment of reason.'" If there was ever a case that defied reason, it was *Booth v. Maryland*, imposing a constitutional rule that had absolutely no basis in constitutional text, in historical practice, or in logic.[18]

As a dissenter in *Booth*, Justice Scalia used comparable language to attack the lack of an appropriate source:

> In sum, the principle upon which the Court's opinion rests—that the imposition of capital punishment is to be determined solely on the basis of moral guilt—does not exist, neither in the text of the Constitution, nor in the historic practices of our society, nor even in the opinions of this Court.[19]

Similar language was employed by Justice Ginsburg, in *Buckhannon v. West Virginia*[20], to describe legally valid sources for an opinion, none of which supported the majority's ruling:

> In my view, the "catalyst rule," as applied by the clear majority of Federal Circuits, is a key component of the fee-shifting statutes Congress adopted to advance enforcement of civil rights. Nothing in history, precedent, or plain English warrants the anemic construction of the term "prevailing party" the Court today imposes.[21]

When should stare decisis be honored and when may it be disregarded? According to Justice Thurgood Marshall, in *Payne*, the principles of stare decisis are inviolate, and not dependent on the nature of the law involved. He faulted the majority for adopting an improper sliding scale approach to stare decisis, depending on the source of the law:

> "Considerations in favor of *stare decisis* are at their acme," the majority explains, "in cases involving property and contract rights, where reliance interests are involved[;] the opposite is true in cases such as the present one involving procedural and evidentiary rules."[22] (citations omitted; brackets in original).

---

[18] *Id.* at 833–34.
[19] 482 U.S. at 520.
[20] 532 U.S. 598 (2001).
[21] *Id.* at 623.
[22] 501 U.S. at 850–51.

Justice Marshall also invoked a reductio ad absurdum argument to disparage the sources of law for the majority's disregard of stare decisis:

> This truncation of the Court's duty to stand by its own precedents is astonishing. By limiting full protection of the doctrine of *stare decisis* to "cases involving property and contract rights," the majority sends a clear signal that essentially *all* decisions implementing the personal liberties protected by the Bill of Rights and the Fourteenth Amendment are open to reexamination. Taking into account the majority's additional criterion for overruling—that a case either was decided or reaffirmed by a 5-4 margin "over spirited dissen[t],"—the continued vitality of literally scores of decisions must be understood to depend on nothing more than the proclivities of the individuals who *now* comprise a majority of this Court.[23] (italics in original; citations omitted; brackets in original).

Weighing in on the stare decisis doctrine, Justice Kennedy, in *Allegheny County v. Greater Pittsburgh ACLU*,[24] chides the majority for adopting a concurring opinion's rationale, as opposed to the plurality's opinion:

> The majority invalidates display of the creche, not because it disagrees with the interpretation of *Lynch* applied above, but because it chooses to discard the reasoning of the *Lynch* majority opinion in favor of Justice O'Connor's concurring opinion in that case. It has never been my understanding that a concurring opinion "suggest[ing] a clarification of our . . . doctrine," could take precedence over an opinion joined in its entirety by five Members of the Court. As a general rule, the principle of *stare decisis* directs us to adhere not only to the holdings of our prior cases, but also to their explications of the governing rules of law. Since the majority does not state its intent to overrule *Lynch*, I find its refusal to apply the reasoning of that decision quite confusing.[25] (citations and footnotes omitted; brackets and ellipses in original).

Dissenters often criticize the majority of adopting a "novel" approach, implying that "newness" does not deserve the respect of "long-standing." In *Bush v. Gore*,[26] Justice Stevens asserted that the majority's opinion was based on a previously unchallenged principle:

> Nor are petitioners correct in asserting that the failure of the Florida Supreme Court to specify in detail the precise manner in which the "intent of the voter," is to be determined rises to the level of a consti-

---

[23] *Id.* at 851.
[24] 492 U.S. 573 (1989).
[25] *Id.* at 668.
[26] 531 U.S. 98 (2000).

tutional violation. We found such a violation when individual votes within the same State were weighted unequally, but we have never before called into question the substantive standard by which a State determines that a vote has been legally cast. And there is no reason to think that the guidance provided to the factfinders, specifically the various canvassing boards, by the "intent of the voter" standard is any less sufficient—or will lead to results any less uniform—than, for example, the "beyond a reasonable doubt" standard employed everyday by ordinary citizens in courtrooms across this country.[27] (citations and footnote omitted).

Justice Scalia combines a slippery slope argument ("far-reaching implications") with a genetic attack ("unheard-of form") on the majority's opinion in *Lawrence v. Texas*[28]:

> Thus, while overruling the *outcome* of *Bowers*, the Court leaves strangely untouched its central legal conclusion: "[R]espondent would have us announce . . . a fundamental right to engage in homosexual sodomy. This we are quite unwilling to do." Instead the Court simply describes petitioners' conduct as "an exercise of their liberty"—which it undoubtedly is—and proceeds to apply an unheard-of form of rational-basis review that will have far-reaching implications beyond this case.[29] (ellipses and brackets in original; citations omitted).

Also from the *Lawrence* decision, Justice Scalia argues that "fundamental rights" must be "deeply rooted in this Nation's history and tradition[s]":

> Realizing that fact, the Court instead says: "[W]e think that our laws and traditions in the past half century are of most relevance here. These references show an emerging awareness that liberty gives substantial protection to adult persons in deciding how to conduct their private lives *in matters pertaining to sex*." Apart from the fact that such an "emerging awareness" does not establish a "fundamental right," the statement is factually false.
>
> . . . .
>
> In any event, an "emerging awareness" is by definition not "deeply rooted in this Nation's history and tradition[s]," as we have said "fundamental right" status requires. Constitutional entitlements do not spring into existence because some States choose to lessen or eliminate criminal sanctions on certain behavior. Much less do they spring

---

[27]*Id.* at 124–25.
[28]*Supra* at 539 U.S. 558 (2003).
[29]*Id.* at 586.

into existence, as the Court seems to believe, because *foreign nations* decriminalize conduct.[30] (italics and brackets in original).

In *Atkins v. Virginia*,[31] Justice Scalia wrote that the majority's decision is based on short-standing principles:

> Moreover, a major factor that the Court entirely disregards is that the legislation of all 18 States it relies on is still in its infancy. The oldest of the statutes is only 14 years old; five were enacted last year; over half were enacted within the past eight years. Few, if any, of the States have had sufficient experience with these laws to know whether they are sensible in the long term. "It is myopic to base sweeping constitutional principles upon the narrow experience of [a few] years."[32] (citations and footnotes omitted; brackets in original).

Combining a genetic attack with a reductio ad absurdum argument, Justice Scalia argued in *Dickerson v. United States*,[33] that the majority not only created a "significant new" constitutional principle, but usurped power that previously did not exist:

> And so, to justify today's agreed-upon result, the Court must adopt a significant *new*, if not entirely comprehensible, principle of constitutional law. As the Court chooses to describe that principle, statutes of Congress can be disregarded, not only when what they prescribe violates the Constitution, but when what they prescribe contradicts a decision of this Court that "announced a constitutional rule." As I shall discuss in some detail, the only thing that can possibly mean in the context of this case is that this Court has the power, not merely to apply the Constitution but to expand it, imposing what it regards as useful "prophylactic" restrictions upon Congress and the States. That is an immense and frightening antidemocratic power, and it does not exist.[34] (italics in original; citation omitted).

A bit further in his dissent, Justice Scalia wrote that the majority's source for *Miranda* rights was misplaced:

> In my view, our continued application of the *Miranda* code to the States despite our consistent statements that running afoul of its dictates does not necessarily—or even usually—result in an actual con-

---

[30] *Id.* at 597–98.
[31] 536 U.S. 304 (2002).
[32] *Id.* at 344.
[33] *Supra* at 530 U.S. 428.
[34] *Id.* at 445–46.

stitutional violation, represents not the source of *Miranda*'s salvation but rather evidence of its ultimate illegitimacy.[35] (citations omitted).

A "Novel" Theory

Sometimes a dissenter just applies the term "novel" to the majority's rationale, as did Justice Kennedy, in *Allegheny County v. Greater Pittsburgh ACLU*[36]:

> The endorsement test has been criticized by some scholars in the field. Only one opinion for the Court has purported to apply it in full, but the majority's opinion in these cases suggests that this novel theory is fast becoming a permanent accretion to the law.[37] (citations omitted).

Justice Scalia not only refers to the majority's decision in *Rogers v. Tennessee*, as "novel," but asserts that its genesis is "almost-valid arguments":

> I reiterate that the only "fair warning" discussed in our precedents, and the only "fair warning" relevant to the issue before us here, is fair warning of *what the law is*. That warning, unlike the new one that today's opinion invents, goes well beyond merely safeguarding defendants against *unjustified and unpredictable* breaks with prior law. It safeguards them against *changes in the law after the fact*. But even accepting the Courts novel substitute, the opinion's conclusion that this watered-down standard has been met seems to me to proceed on the principle that a large number of almost-valid arguments makes a solid case. As far as I can tell, petitioner had nothing that could fairly be called a warning that the Supreme Court of Tennessee would retroactively eliminate one of the elements of the crime of murder.[38] (citation omitted; italics in original).

The epithet "proabortion novelties" was used by Justice Scalia to signal his displeasure with the majority's opinion in *Hill v. Colorado*[39]:

> Does the deck seem stacked? You bet. As I have suggested throughout this opinion, today's decision is not an isolated distortion of our

---

[35] *Id.* at 456.
[36] *Supra* at 492 U.S. 573.
[37] *Id.* at 669.
[38] *Supra* at 532 U.S. 480.
[39] *Supra* at 530 U.S. 703.

traditional constitutional principles, but is one of many aggressively proabortion novelties announced by the Court in recent years.[40] (citations omitted).

Next, Justice Scalia criticized what he believed to be an unheard-of right:

> Today's distortions, however, are particularly blatant. Restrictive views of the First Amendment that have been in dissent since the 1930's suddenly find themselves in the majority. "Uninhibited, robust, and wide open" debate is replaced by the power of the state to protect an unheard-of "right to be let alone" on the public streets.[41]

A clear opponent of *Roe v. Wade*,[42] Justice Scalia wields humor/ridicule, in *Webster v. Reproductive Health Services*,[43] to describe what the U.S. Supreme Court would require to overrule that decision, a decision he believes was "constructed overnight":

> It was an arguable question today whether 188.029 of the Missouri law contravened this Court's understanding of *Roe v. Wade*, and I would have examined *Roe* rather than examining the contravention. Given the Court's newly contracted abstemiousness, what will it take, one must wonder, to permit us to reach that fundamental question? The result of our vote today is that we will not reconsider that prior opinion, even if most of the Justices think it is wrong, unless we have before us a statute that in fact contradicts it—and even then (under our newly discovered "no-broader-than-necessary" requirement) only minor problematical aspects of *Roe* will be reconsidered, unless one expects state legislatures to adopt provisions whose compliance with *Roe* cannot even be argued with a straight face. It thus appears that the mansion of constitutionalized abortion law, constructed overnight in *Roe v. Wade*, must be disassembled doorjamb by doorjamb, and never entirely brought down, no matter how wrong it may be.[44] (parentheses in original).

A "new" approach to common law decision making is derided, in *Rogers v. Tennessee*,[45] by Justice Scalia, who would adhere to the "original" approach taken by the framers:

---

[40] *Id.* at 764.
[41] *Id.* at 765.
[42] 410 U.S. 113 (1973).
[43] 492 U.S. 490 (1989).
[44] *Id.* at 536–37.
[45] *Supra* at 532 U.S. 451.

The Court's opinion considers the judgment at issue here "a routine exercise of common law decisionmaking," whereby the Tennessee court "brought the law into conformity with reason and common sense," by "laying to rest an archaic and outdated rule." This is an accurate enough description of what modern "common law decisionmaking" consists of—but it is not an accurate description of the theoretical model of common-law decisionmaking accepted by those who adopted the Due Process Clause. At the time of the framing, common-law jurists believed (in the words of Sir Francis Bacon) that the judge's "office is *jus dicere*, and not *jus dare*; to interpret law, and not to make law, or give law." Or as described by Blackstone, whose Commentaries were widely read and accepted [by the framing generation] as the most satisfactory exposition of the common law of England, judicial decisions are the principal and most authoritative *evidence*, that can be given, of the existence of such a custom as shall form a part of the common law.[46] (italics, parentheses, and brackets in original; citations omitted).

In *Boy Scouts of America v. Dale*,[47] Justice Stevens argued that the majority's rationale sprung up overnight:

In fact, until today, we have never once found a claimed right to associate in the selection of members to prevail in the face of a State's antidiscrimination law. To the contrary, we have squarely held that a State's antidiscrimination law does not violate a group's right to associate simply because the law conflicts with that group's exclusionary membership policy.[48]

Justice Ginsburg ridiculed the majority, in *Buckhannon v. West Virginia*,[49] for detecting the "clear meaning" of a term, based on *Black's Law Dictionary*, when a large majority of courts failed to reach the same conclusion:

The Court today detects a "clear meaning" of the term prevailing party, that has heretofore eluded the large majority of courts construing those words. "Prevailing party," today's opinion announces, means "one who has been awarded some relief by the court." The Court derives this "clear meaning" principally from Black's Law Dictionary, which defines a "prevailing party," in critical part, as one "in whose favor a judgment is rendered."[50] (citations omitted).

---

[46] *Id.* at 472.
[47] 530 U.S. 640 (2000).
[48] *Id.* at 679.
[49] *Supra* at 532 U.S. 598.
[50] *Id.* at 628.

Justices who write majority opinions use a variety of tactics in response to genetic attacks. When the dissent, in *Lawrence v. Texas*[51] argued that laws providing punishment for private conduct had "ancient roots," and deserved not to be overruled, Justice Kennedy explained that these laws were of recent vintage:

> The policy of punishing consenting adults for private acts was not much discussed in the early legal literature. We can infer that one reason for this was the very private nature of the conduct. Despite the absence of prosecutions, there may have been periods in which there was public criticism of homosexuals as such and an insistence that the criminal laws be enforced to discourage their practices. But far from possessing "ancient roots," American laws targeting same-sex couples did not develop until the last third of the 20th century.[52] (citation omitted).

In *Payne v. Tennessee*, where the U.S. Supreme Court overturned existing precedent, Justice Stevens argued that the majority opinions in *Booth* and *Gathers* were rooted more firmly in the nation's history than the dissenting opinions, which formed the basis for the new majority's decision:

> Our decision in *Booth* was entirely consistent with the practices that had been followed "both before and since the American colonies became a nation." Our holding was mandated by our capital punishment jurisprudence, which requires any decision to impose the death penalty to be based on reason rather than caprice or emotion. The dissenting opinions in *Booth* and in *Gathers* can be searched in vain for any judicial precedent sanctioning the use of evidence unrelated to the character of the offense or the character of the offender in the sentencing process. Today, however, relying on nothing more than those dissenting opinions, the Court abandons rules of relevance that are older than the Nation itself and ventures into uncharted seas of irrelevance.[53] (citations omitted).

A law that had a reasonable origin, but becomes unreasonable, should still be given effect by the courts, argued Justice Scalia, in *Rogers v. Tennessee*. The task of overturning the law should be left to the legislature:

> By way of example, Blackstone pointed to the seemingly unreasonable rule that one cannot inherit the estate of one's half-brother.

---

[51] *Supra* at 539 U.S. 558.
[52] *Id.* at 570.
[53] *Supra* at 501 U.S. 858–59.

Though he accepted that the feudal reason behind the law was no longer obvious, he wrote "yet it is not *in [a common law judge's]* power to alter it." Moreover, "the unreasonableness of a custom in modern circumstances will not affect its validity if the Court is satisfied of a reasonable origin." "A custom once reasonable and tolerable, if after it become grievous, and not answerable to the reason, whereupon it was grounded, yet is to be . . . taken away by act of parliament."[54] (italics, brackets, and ellipses in original; citations omitted).

This view of the law contrasts with that of Justice Kennedy, for whom a genetic pedigree is important:

> In summary, the historical grounds relied upon in *Bowers* are more complex than the majority opinion and the concurring opinion by Chief Justice Burger indicate. Their historical premises are not without doubt and, at the very least, are overstated.[55]

Long-Standing Practices

In defense of a new principle of law, in *Ewing v. California*,[56] Justice O'Connor argued that the principle was intimately associated with another principle, one of long standing. She then cited a number of cases in support of the long-standing principle:

> Though three strikes laws may be relatively new, our tradition of deferring to state legislatures in making and implementing such important policy decisions is longstanding. *Weems, Gore v. United States; Payne v. Tennessee; Rummel; Solem; Harmelin*.[57] (footnote and citations omitted).

It is permissible to overturn existing law, and establish new principles, according to Justice Kennedy, in *Lawrence v. Texas*,[58] where detrimental reliance on the old law cannot be demonstrated:

> In *Casey* we noted that when a Court is asked to overrule a precedent recognizing a constitutional liberty interest, individual or societal reliance on the existence of that liberty cautions with particular strength against reversing course. ("Liberty finds no refuge in a jurisprudence of doubt"). The holding in *Bowers*, however, has not induced detrimental reliance comparable to some instances where

---

[54] *Supra* at 532 U.S. 473.
[55] *Lawrence v. Texas*, 539 U.S. 558 (2003).
[56] 538 U.S. 11 (2003).
[57] *Id.* at 24–25.
[58] *Supra* at 539 U.S. 558.

recognized individual rights are involved. Indeed, there has been no individual or societal reliance on *Bowers* of the sort that could counsel against overturning its holding once there are compelling reasons to do so. *Bowers* itself causes uncertainty, for the precedents before and after its issuance contradict its central holding.[59] (parentheses in original; citations omitted).

Even practices that are long standing do not deserve deference, argued Justice O'Connor, in *Allegheny County v. Greater Pittsburgh ACLU*,[60] unless they are accompanied with sufficient rationale to merit their continuation. She defended her view of the "endorsement test" by citing the purposes served in observing certain historical "religious" practices:

> Justice Kennedy submits that the endorsement test is inconsistent with our precedents and traditions because, in his words, if it were "applied without artificial exceptions for historical practice," it would invalidate many traditional practices recognizing the role of religion in our society. This criticism shortchanges both the endorsement test itself and my explanation of the reason why certain longstanding government acknowledgments of religion do not, under that test, convey a message of endorsement. Practices such as legislative prayers or opening Court sessions with "God save the United States and this honorable Court" serve the secular purposes of "solemnizing public occasions" and "expressing confidence in the future." These examples of ceremonial deism do not survive Establishment Clause scrutiny simply by virtue of their historical longevity alone. Historical acceptance of a practice does not in itself validate that practice under the Establishment Clause if the practice violates the values protected by that Clause, just as historical acceptance of racial or gender based discrimination does not immunize such practices from scrutiny under the Fourteenth Amendment. As we recognized in *Walz v. Tax Comm'n of New York City*: "[N]o one acquires a vested or protected right in violation of the Constitution by long use, even when that span of time covers our entire national existence and indeed predates it."[61] (citations omitted; brackets in original).

---

[59] *Id.* at 577.
[60] *Supra* at 492 U.S. 573.
[61] *Id.* at 630.

❧ CHAPTER TWENTY-EIGHT

Red Herrings

A prosecutor may not urge jurors to convict a criminal defendant in order to protect community values, preserve civil order, or to deter future lawbreaking. The evil lurking in such prosecutorial appeals is that the defendant will be convicted for reasons wholly irrelevant to his own guilt or innocence. Jurors may be persuaded by such appeals to believe that, by convicting a defendant, they will assist in the solution of some pressing social problem. The amelioration of society's woes is far too heavy a burden for the individual criminal defendant to bear.

United States v. Monaghan, 741 F.2d 1434, 1441 (D.C. Cir. 1983). (footnote omitted).

THIS CHAPTER AND THE FOLLOWING ONE ("Straw Man") examine the infusion of irrelevant arguments into the case or controversy, which may divert attention from the issues, and improperly influence the outcome. Unlike the straw man fallacy (where the proponent attempts to defeat a related issue), the red herring fallacy consists of the introduction of an unrelated issue. Various names are given to this fallacy: "irrelevant conclusion, ignoring the issue, befogging the issue, diversion,"[1] fallacy of distraction, irrelevant thesis, smoke screen, and wild goose chase. The name "red herring"

> derives from the fact that prison escapees have been known to smear themselves with a herring (which turns brown or red when it spoils) in order to throw dogs off their track. To sway a red herring in an

---

[1] S. MORRIS ENGEL, WITH GOOD REASON: AN INTRODUCTION TO INFORMAL FALLACIES 190 (Bedford/St. Martins, 6th ed. 2000).

argument is to try to throw the audience off the right track onto something not relevant to the issue at hand.[2] (parentheses in original).

Effective red herring arguments may use any number of informal fallacies. For example, appeals to sympathy, appeals to fear, and ad hominem attacks may effectively divert attention from the issues. Outside the courtroom, there are few restraints on the use of red herring arguments. Answering a red herring argument outside the courtroom requires a reminder to the audience of the issues, and how the red herring is unrelated to those issues. In the courtroom, a "relevance" objection usually prompts an explanation of the relatedness of any red herring argument—followed by more argument. There are several defenses that may be used to defend a red herring argument: the remarks were "invited" by the opposing attorney; they were responsive to the opposing attorney's arguments; the judge gave curative instructions; a timely objection was not interposed; and there was overwhelming evidence in support of the verdict.

Red herring evidence, as opposed to argument, is subject to the rules of evidence. Nevertheless, these rules may also prove beneficial when contesting a red herring argument:

> Rule 401. Definition of "Relevant Evidence"
>
> "Relevant evidence" means evidence having any tendency to make the existence of any fact that is of consequence to the determination of the action more probable or less probable than it would be without the evidence.
>
> Rule 402. Relevant Evidence Generally Admissible; Irrelevant Evidence Inadmissible
>
> All relevant evidence is admissible . . . Evidence which is not relevant is not admissible.[3]

In 1989, the February *ABA Journal*[4] posed the following question:

PARDONING OLLIE NORTH
Was Reagan wrong not to grant a pretrial pardon? Then-Senator George Mitchell (D-ME) answered, "No." Then-Congressman Henry Hyde (R-IL) answered, "Yes."

---

[2] *Id.*
[3] FED. R. EVID. 401 and 402.
[4] A.B.A. J. 42 (Feb. 1989).

RED HERRINGS

Senator Mitchell addressed his arguments to the pretrial pardon issue:

> It would be a mockery for this administration, after adopting stricter regulations for pardons of all other citizens—permitting only those already convicted of crimes and then only after a substantial waiting period to petition for a pardon—to consider pretrial pardons for those who worked in or closely with the White House.
>
> A pretrial pardon would be a striking misuse of the presidential power to pardon.
>
> . . . .
>
> The private "act of grace" theory of the pardon power was transformed by the Supreme Court over 60 years ago, when Justice Holmes made clear that the pardon power is to be wielded only so as to benefit the public, "not [as] a private act of grace from an individual happening to possess power."
>
> . . . .
>
> The granting of pretrial pardons to the Iran-Contra defendants would have the adverse effect of confirming the widespread belief that a dual standard of justice exists in our society, one for the powerful, another for all other citizens.
>
> . . . .
>
> These pardons, if offered, would come in the twilight of the Reagan presidency, when the constitutional remedy, electoral disapproval, would be unavailable. But the potential damage to the integrity of the rule of law could linger for years.[5] (ellipses added).

Congressman Hyde weighted his arguments with sympathy (red herring) for the defendants:

> There is something grotesque about a private citizen forced to confront a vast array of top legal talent, government investigators and a virtually unlimited expense account to defend oneself. More than $10 million has been spent so far in the prosecutions of Lt. Col. Oliver North and Adm. John Poindexter. The very real financial problems confronting the defendants should trouble those who demand these long and complicated trials go forward.
>
> It is no answer to say this disadvantage faces every defendant prosecuted by the government. Of course it does. But in the cases of North

---

[5]*Id.* at 43.

and Poindexter, is justice really served by requiring them to impoverish themselves and their families and then rely on passing a tin cup to defend themselves?

And North and Poindexter are not your ordinary defendants. Before our judicial system sends two men to prison in disgrace for trying to serve the president, however unwisely, I believe the totality of their services to our country needs to be weighed in the balance, and on a scale no jury would be permitted to measure.

. . . .

While North, after graduating from Annapolis, class of '68, was getting ready to fight in Vietnam, the anti-war movement was in full swing at home. It wasn't the best of times to walk around city streets in a Marine uniform. North was rushed into combat, where he earned a bronze star, a silver star and a purple heart. He was twice wounded in action and anyone interested in duty, honor and country ought to read the citations accompanying North's combat awards. Anyone interested in rare physical courage ought to read them.

Many have forgotten the sort of reception our military received upon their homecoming from Vietnam. Cries of "murderers" and thrown tomatoes were not unusual. Then, in 1977, President Carter granted amnesty to draft evaders, raising them to the level of "moral purists," in James Webb's phrase.

. . . .

I believe fervently that we owe the men and women who fought in Vietnam a great debt. And yes, their sacrifices were different from those of us who fought in World War II—we were appreciated, not denigrated.[6] (ellipses added).

There is certainly nothing "wrong" with Congressman Hyde's arguments, although there were those who ardently disagreed with his point of view. His arguments, no doubt, reflected a heartfelt sympathy for Col. North and Adm. Poindexter, but were those arguments relevant to the issue: "Was Reagan wrong not to grant a pretrial pardon?"

Of course, a similar issue surfaced in the summer of 2007, with the conviction of "Scooter" Libby, former chief-of-staff to Vice President Cheney. President Bush, under pressure from conservatives to pardon Libby before he was to be sent off to jail, commuted his sentence to eliminate any time in jail. Libby was, however, required to pay the fine imposed by the court.

---

[6]*Id.* at 42.

A defendant, found guilty by a jury of transporting stolen vehicles across state lines, asserted that the prosecutor presented an irrelevant and improper argument:

> [T]he case is not trivial. At a time when the number of cars which are being stolen are increasing—.
>
> . . . .
>
> At a time when more security devices are being put on individual cars than you sometimes find on a Brinks truck because of thefts.[7] (brackets and ellipses in original).

The Seventh Circuit upheld the conviction, but noted the prosecutor's remarks were irrelevant:

> While we agree with the defendant that these statements were not particularly relevant and had no bearing on the guilt or innocence of the defendant, we do not find them an emotional appeal to the jurors' self interest designed to arouse their prejudice against the defendant.[8]

Juries must not be led to believe that they do not have the responsibility for imposing the death penalty.[9] An "eye for an eye" argument is also impermissible. A defendant sentenced to death contended that the following remarks, in the prosecutor's closing argument, violated these prohibitions:

> Phil Skiff and Inez Skiff didn't get due process of law. This man got a fair trial. He got two attorneys. He got resources, he got the benefit, everything that our system gives to a defendant, everything, and he got a fair trial and he will get more than that. He will get appeals, you name it, because that is our system and this system has treated him fairly. Something that he didn't do—he killed unmercifully, but our system gives him due process of law so don't think that you're killing him because you're giving him the law and you're giving him justice.[10]

The Ninth Circuit disagreed with the defendant's contentions, and upheld the sentence:

> [The defendant's] arguments are not persuasive. The prosecutor's passing reference to Jeffries' right to appeal did not indicate to the jury

---

[7] United States v. Shirley, 435 F.2d 1076, 1079 (7th Cir. 1970).
[8] *Id.*
[9] Caldwell v. Mississippi, 472 U.S. 320 (1985).
[10] Jeffries v. Blodgett, 5 F.3d 1180, 1192 (9th Cir. 1993).

that it was relieved of its responsibility for determining the appropriateness of the death penalty. Jurors know that cases can be appealed. Moreover, the penalty phase instruction made clear to the jury that the responsibility lay with it. Finally, the statement does not suggest that the jury ignore its legal responsibility impartially to weigh all of the evidence and to impose a death sentence as a matter of retribution.[11] (brackets added).

Religious arguments, offered by the prosecution and defense, figured prominently in a defendant's appeal before the Fourth Circuit. According to the defendant, the prosecution's

> religiously-loaded sentencing arguments were "inflammatory, irrelevant, and grossly prejudicial," hence violated his due process rights.[12]

In closing argument, the prosecution remarked:

> Some will say that society shouldn't take a life because that's murder also. That's not true. Vengeance is mine saith the Lord, but later when he covered the Earth with water and left only Noah and his family and some animals to survive, when he saw the damage what [sic] had been done to the Earth, God said "I'll never do that again" and handed that sword of justice to Noah.
>
> Noah is now the Government. Noah will make the decision who dies. "Thou shall [sic] not kill" is a prescription [sic] against an individual; it is not against Government. Because Government has a duty to protect its citizens.[13] (brackets in original).

Defense counsel responded with his own religious argument, on behalf of the defendant:

> Mr. Watson [the Commonwealth's attorney] has told you that vengeance is mine saith the Lord, and I submit to you that is true because Ronnie will answer for this to someone far greater than this jury, and I would submit to you that the ultimate power of punishment belongs not with this jury, and the concept we have long since discarded of an eye for an eye or tooth for a tooth, that has been replaced since the Sermon on the Mount, and the message we as Christians have been brought up with is even as the only perfect person in the world, as I understand it, hung on the cross between other murderers. The message then, as it still was [sic], was "Father forgive them," do not punish

---

[11]*Id.*
[12]Bennett v. Angelone, 92 F.3d 1336, 1345 (4th Cir. 1996).
[13]*Id.* at 1346.

these people for what they do to me. That is the message of a faith.[14] (brackets in original; citations omitted).

Having the last word, the prosecutor again returned to his religious theme:

> Our Government has decided that the death penalty is legitimate and is morally right. The law says for a wantonly, outrageous, or vile murder, a person may be put to death. When Jesus was being tormented by the Roman soldiers before his death, they asked him jokingly, is it lawful to pay tribute unto Caesar? Jesus said give those things that are Caesar's unto Caesar, and those things that are God's to God. The moral being follow the law and leave the rest to Heaven.[15] (citation omitted).

The Fourth Circuit noted that religious arguments are "universally condemned":

> Federal and state courts have universally condemned such religiously charged arguments as confusing, unnecessary, and inflammatory.[16] (citations omitted).

The court then concluded the prosecution's argument was impermissible:

> Here, the Commonwealth's attorney improperly drew on his reading of biblical law to justify the morality of the state's death penalty. Such statements, worthy of the profoundest respect in proper contexts, have no place in our non-ecclesiastical courts and may not be tolerated there.[17]

Although impermissible, the prosecution's remarks must be balanced against other considerations:

> Nevertheless, we must bear in mind that not every improper trial argument amounts to a denial of due process. And, as objectionable and unwarranted as was this argument, we are convinced that, viewed in the total context of the trial, it was not sufficiently egregious to render (the defendant's) trial fundamentally unfair. First, the evidence of (the defendant's) guilt was powerful, and there is little doubt that the murder of which he was convicted was a particularly vile one. Next, immediately before the sentencing arguments, the trial court

---

[14] *Id.* at 1346 n.9.
[15] *Id.*
[16] *Id.*
[17] *Id.*

gave the standard instruction, "What the lawyers say is not evidence. You heard the evidence. You decide what the evidence is." Thus, we ultimately are convinced that the Commonwealth's improper arguments—though clearly such—did not so infect the sentencing proceedings as to render them constitutionally unfair.[18] (citations omitted; parentheses added).

Irrelevant issues are also raised in civil cases. On appeal, the plaintiff in an auto accident case challenged certain remarks from defendants' counsel, invoking comments made by a judge in another case:

> I then spent some time listening today, spent time listening to an economist project future wage loss of $707,000. Well, God bless America. Now, [plaintiff's counsel] tells you, well, that is not what he really meant to say. When I gave you that shocking or, as she phrased it, obscene figure in the opening statement that was a figure apparently that I made up. And Dr. Latham wasn't going to say that. Well, ladies and gentlemen of the jury, didn't he? Didn't he project $707,000 wage loss? I'm going to come back to that in a second.
>
> Judge Latchum of the Federal District Court—if you head out this door and go south, you'll run across the United States District Court—in a case called *Belardinelli* versus *Carroll*, a case issued within the last year, made a reference to just this kind of case when he said that a personal injury action is not like winning a lottery ticket. Ladies and gentlemen of the jury, that is what this case is about. It's about winning a lottery ticket.[19] (brackets in original).

The reviewing court concluded there were three reasons why the remarks were irrelevant:

> To attempt to present to the jury decisions or rulings of law in cases other than the one under consideration not only permits consideration of irrelevant evidence but serves as well to confuse the jury. The comments of counsel in this case violated these restrictions in at least three important respects. First, referring approvingly to a comment made by another judge in another case distracts the jury's focus from the instructions to be given in the present case. Since the trial judge in this case did not, and could not, use the lottery metaphor in the jury instructions, any such reference as the law of the case is materially misleading. Second, it is improper to identify any legal authority, other than the trial judge, and to suggest that the comments of a Federal Judge are entitled to special deference. Finally the lottery

---

[18]*Id.* at 1346–47.
[19]Deangelis v. Harrison, 628 A.2d 77, 79 (Del. Super. Ct. 1993).

reference attributed to Judge Latchum was not part of a jury instruction but a quotation from an opinion of the Third Circuit Court of Appeals dealing with review of excessive jury verdicts . . .[20] (citations omitted; ellipses added).

Defendants' counsel argued that the "truth is a defense," a position the court rejected:

> The contention of defendants' counsel that he correctly quoted Judge Latchum's comments misses the point. Irrelevant and misleading comments in jury summations are not judged on the basis of truth or falsity, *per se*, but whether they distract the jury from the task at hand—the individualized determination of the factual merit of a specific claim. The purpose of an award of damages in a tort action is just and full compensation, with the focus on the plaintiff's injury and loss. Generalized statements comparing a claim for personal injuries to a game of chance have no place in that process whether or not such remarks originate with judges.[21] (citation omitted).

The court reversed the verdict in favor of the defendants, finding that

> [t]he objectionable aspect of counsel's comments in this case is not simply that it attempted to convert argument into evidence. The argument was itself misleading and improper to the extent it attempted to present to the jury, in indirect fashion, judicial commentary on the sole question the jury was called upon to decide—the award of damages where liability was conceded.[22]

Can the prosecution permissibly comment on whether defense counsel believes in the innocence of his client?

> During his rebuttal argument the prosecutor remarked that defense counsel had spent some time on the special circumstances issues, "and for a man who says that his client didn't commit the crime, that must be a waste of time. But, on the other hand, he might be worried that he did commit it."[23]

The California Supreme Court found that "[i]t is improper for a prosecutor to argue to the jury as an analysis of the defense argument or strategy that defense counsel believes his client is guilty."[24]

---

[20] *Id.* at 80–81.
[21] *Id.* at 81.
[22] *Id.*
[23] People v. Bell, 778 P.2d 129, 149 (Cal. 1989).
[24] *Id.*

Seeking to bring the remarks out from under the rule, the prosecution asserted

> that the remark was not improper here since the prosecutor was not making a factual statement of defense counsel's belief, but was simply pointing out the "internal disharmony" between the defense theories that the crimes were not premeditated and that the charge against defendant involved mistaken identity. A similar argument was rejected in . . . and is equally unavailing here.[25] (citation omitted).

Rejecting that argument, the court concluded that the views of counsel are irrelevant:

> There is no inconsistency in denying that an accused was the perpetrator of an offense while simultaneously arguing that no matter who committed it the crime was not premeditated. We note also that while comment on apparent inconsistencies in argument is permissible, defense counsel's personal belief in his client's guilt or innocence is no more relevant than the belief of the prosecutor. Inviting the jury to speculate about such belief is misconduct.[26] (citations omitted).

A prosecutor, during his closing argument in a murder case, commented on the defendant's lack of remorse:

> [T]he prosecutor referred to a letter that defendant wrote in prison to his sister. Adverting to its contents, the prosecutor observed, "And I would have to admit that if this letter were full of compassion and recognition for the wrong he had done there'd be some meaning in here, something you'd really have to consider. . . . [p] No remorse for his crimes. They are not mentioned at all. There is no compassion for the victims' family. They are not mentioned at all."[27] (ellipses and brackets in original).

The California Supreme Court drew a distinction between an aggravating and a mitigating factor:

> Defendant claims that the prosecutor's comments improperly invoked defendant's lack of remorse as an aggravating factor. Such an argument would have been improper. However, as the comments themselves make clear, the prosecutor was merely observing that the letter provides no evidence in mitigation, that there was no "meaning," "nothing to consider," in the letter. It is proper to argue that remorse

---

[25] *Id.*
[26] *Id.*
[27] People v. Wash, 861 P.2 1107, 1138–39 (Cal. 1993).

is lacking as a circumstance in mitigation. That is precisely what occurred here.[28] (citations omitted).

Prosecutors often appeal to juries to "do something" about the drug problem, and advise them that their communities are counting on them "to convict and thereby to help rid the streets of drug dealers."[29] A defendant convicted of narcotic violations argued the prosecutor stepped out of bounds with these remarks:

> You know that there are people who live in that area who don't like that, people who call up and complain about it. They have a right to. They are not here. More or less, I am representing them.
>
> If they were here, they would say that they believe presumably what I would say, that "[w]e don't need drug dealers; we don't need people selling Preludin in our neighborhood. We can't do anything about it. The DA's office and the police should do something about it."
>
> We did something about it. All we can do is bring it to you and turn it over in your hands.[30] (citation omitted; brackets in original).

The D.C. Circuit concluded reversal was not justified, even if the remarks were improper, because of the relative strength of the case against the defendant, and the judge's curative admonition.[31]

A short passage in the prosecution's closing argument to the jury referred to the public's perception of drinking and driving:

> Now, we often hear, we often read in the paper or hear on television or anything else, something that happens, there's a lot of public sentiment at this point against driving and drinking, causing accidents on the highway. And you know, you read these things and you hear these things and you think to yourself, "My God, they ought to do something about that." . . .
>
> . . . .
>
> Well, ladies and gentlemen, the buck stops here. You twelve judges in Cumberland County have become the "they." (ellipses in original).[32]

The North Carolina Supreme Court reversed the conviction based on these irrelevant arguments:

---

[28]*Id.* at 1139.
[29]United States v. Hawkins, 595 F.2d 751, 754 (D.C. Cir. 1979).
[30]*Id.* at 754 n.10.
[31]*Id.* at 755.
[32]State v. Scott, 333 S.E.2d 296, 297 (N.C. 1985).

The prosecutor fell into improper argument, however, when he emphasized to the jury that "there's a lot of public sentiment at this point against driving and drinking, causing accidents on the highway." This argument was improper because it went outside the record and appealed to the jury to convict the defendant because impaired drivers had caused other accidents.[33]

Booth v. Maryland,[34] later overturned in *Payne v. Tennessee*,[35] generated spirited debate over the use of victim impact statements (VIS). Justice Powell, writing for the majority in *Booth*, concluded that victim impact statements were irrelevant to a capital sentencing decision:

> The VIS in this case provided the jury with two types of information. First, it described the personal characteristics of the victims and the emotional impact of the crimes on the family. Second, it set forth the family members' opinions and characterizations of the crimes and the defendant. For the reasons stated below, we find that this information is irrelevant to a capital sentencing decision, and that its admission creates a constitutionally unacceptable risk that the jury may impose the death penalty in an arbitrary and capricious manner.[36]

He then discussed the purpose of a capital sentencing hearing:

> While the full range of foreseeable consequences of a defendant's actions may be relevant in other criminal and civil contexts, we cannot agree that it is relevant in the unique circumstance of a capital sentencing hearing. In such a case, it is the function of the sentencing jury to "express the conscience of the community on the ultimate question of life or death." When carrying out this task the jury is required to focus on the defendant as a "uniquely individual human bein[g]." The focus of a VIS, however, is not on the defendant, but on the character and reputation of the victim and the effect on his family. These factors may be wholly unrelated to the blameworthiness of a particular defendant.[37] (citations omitted: brackets in original).

According to Justice Powell, use of a VIS could produce a death sentence for irrelevant reasons:

> As our cases have shown, the defendant often will not know the victim, and therefore will have no knowledge about the existence or characteristics of the victim's family. Moreover, defendants rarely

---

[33] *Id.* at 298.
[34] 482 U.S. 496 (1987).
[35] 501 U.S. 808 (1991).
[36] Booth, 482 U.S. at 502–03.
[37] *Id.* at 504.

select their victims based on whether the murder will have an effect on anyone other than the person murdered. Allowing the jury to rely on a VIS therefore could result in imposing the death sentence because of factors about which the defendant was unaware, and that were irrelevant to the decision to kill. This evidence thus could divert the jury's attention away from the defendant's background and record, and the circumstances of the crime.[38]

Divert Jury's Attention

There was a danger, argued Justice Powell, that the VIS would divert the jury's attention from the issues in the case:

> We also note that it would be difficult—if not impossible—to provide a fair opportunity to rebut such evidence without shifting the focus of the sentencing hearing away from the defendant. A threshold problem is that victim impact information is not easily susceptible to rebuttal. Presumably the defendant would have the right to cross-examine the declarants, but he rarely would be able to show that the family members have exaggerated the degree of sleeplessness, depression, or emotional trauma suffered. Moreover, if the state is permitted to introduce evidence of the victim's personal qualities, it cannot be doubted that the defendant also must be given the chance to rebut this evidence.[39] (citations and footnote omitted).

Justice White dissented, and responded to Justice Powell's argument that the VIS would divert the jury's attention:

> The supposed problems arising from a defendant's rebuttal of victim impact statements are speculative and unconnected to the facts of this case. No doubt a capital defendant must be allowed to introduce relevant evidence in rebuttal to a victim impact statement, but Maryland has in no wise limited the right of defendants in this regard. Petitioner introduced no such rebuttal evidence, probably because he considered, wisely, that it was not in his best interest to do so.[3] At bottom, the Court's view seems to be that it is somehow unfair to confront a defendant with an account of the loss his deliberate act has caused the victim's family and society. I do not share that view, but even if I did I would be unwilling to impose it on States that see matters differently.[40]

---

[38] *Id.* at 504–05.
[39] *Id.* at 506–07.
[40] *Id.* at 518.

³The possibility that the jury would be distracted by rebuttal evidence is purely hypothetical, since petitioner introduced no such evidence. It is also unclear how distracting (as opposed to offending) the jury would disadvantage the defendant, and why, if there were some disadvantage to the defendant in pressing too hard a rebuttal to a victim impact statement, he should be heard to complain of the consequences of his tactical decisions.[41] (parentheses in original).

---

[41] *Id.* at 518 n.3.

CHAPTER TWENTY-NINE

Straw Man

> *I submit to you that if you can't take this evidence and find these defendants guilty on this evidence that we might as well open all the banks and say, "Come on and get the money, boys, because we'll never be able to convict them."*
>
> Prosecutor's closing argument, United States v. Barker, 553 F.2d 1013, 1025 (6th Cir. 1977).

THIS CHAPTER AND THE PRECEDING ONE (red herring) examine the introduction of irrelevant issues into a dispute. When the irrelevant argument is related to the issue in the controversy, the proponent creates a straw man; when the irrelevant argument is unrelated, the proponent introduces a red herring:

> The straw man fallacy is an argument that so alters a position that the result is easier to attack than the original and yet claims that it has provided grounds for attacking the original. The name of this fallacy is particularly revealing of what it accomplishes. In effect, it sets up a "straw," which is easy to blow over. Of course, the "straw" is not the original argument at all. But that's the whole point. The original was much harder to assail than the straw. Having set up the straw, the arguer is then in a position to "blow it over." And if we're not more careful, we may erroneously conclude that the original argument has been demolished.[1] (italics in original).

It is not always an easy task to determine whether the introduction of an irrelevant argument is closely related to the dispute, or whether it is

---

[1] BARRY AND SOCCIO, PRACTICAL LOGIC 104 (Holt, Rinehart, and Winston, 3d ed. 1976).

an entirely new argument. In either case, however, the important point to remember is that it is irrelevant to the issues in the controversy.

One way to recognize a straw man argument is to ask yourself, "Is this an argument responding to one that I am making or have made?" If the answer to that question is "no," and the answer to the second question—"Is the argument related to the dispute?"—is "yes," then the opposition has presented a straw man argument. A typical response will note the irrelevancy of the argument, and reiterate the disputed issue.

The defendant in the case quoted at the beginning of this chapter was accused, and ultimately convicted of, bank robbery. The prosecutor's argument to the jury importuned them to convict, not because of the evidence in the case, but because if they didn't, the community would have to open all the banks. "Opening all the banks" was not relevant to the conviction, but it was an easily defeatable argument. The Sixth Circuit found:

> We have also permitted some reference, when accompanied immediately by a limiting instruction by the trial judge, to the community need to convict people who are guilty of crimes such as the one charged. However, it is beyond the bounds of propriety for a prosecutor to suggest that unless this defendant is convicted it will be impossible to maintain "law and order" in the jurors' community.[2] (citations omitted).

Impose Martial Law

In a case arising in the D.C. Circuit, the defendant was convicted of assaulting a police officer with a dangerous weapon.[3] The prosecutor argued that the defendant had to be convicted in order to maintain "law and order," otherwise "martial law" was the only recourse:

> But no matter how you twist it, no matter how you turn it, and no matter how you argue, the fact comes out that the defendant assaulted, opposed and impeded this police officer who was acting in the District of Columbia in the performance of his duties, and without any justifiable and excusable cause, whatsoever.
>
> Unless we reach that conclusion, ladies and gentlemen of the jury, then this city must have martial law.
>
> . . . .

---

[2]553 F.2d at 1025.
[3]Brown v. United States, 370 F.3d 242 (D.C. Cir. 1966).

> Now, ladies and gentlemen, when I said in the closing argument, "If you wished to come to that conclusion, you might as well have martial law," I meant exactly what I said. If this is what the police officers in the District of Columbia, in a given set of circumstances, must contend with, then you, who live here and have to protect yourselves, you might as well have martial law.
>
> You make the choice.
>
> You live with it.[4] (ellipses in original).

The issue was whether the defendant assaulted a police officer, not whether martial law should be imposed. The prosecutor posed an either/or argument for the jury's consideration—convict the defendant or impose martial law. In a democracy, martial law is a last resort, and most people would say that it is inappropriate, except under the most dire of circumstances. By knocking over the "straw man"—imposition of martial law—the prosecutor hoped the jury would convict the defendant of assaulting a police officer. Reversing the conviction, the court held that

> [w]hile such an argument is always to be condemned as "an appeal wholly irrelevant to any facts or issues in the case," and as a dereliction of the prosecutor's high duty to prosecute fairly in the context of current events, raising the spectre of martial law was an especially flagrant and reprehensible appeal to passion and prejudice.[5] (citations omitted).

Chief Justice Rehnquist, in the aftermath of the 2000 presidential election, wrote in *Bush v. Gore*:[6]

> Yet in the late afternoon of December 8th—four days before this deadline—the Supreme Court of Florida ordered recounts of tens of thousands of so-called "undervotes" spread through 64 of the State's 67 counties. This was done in a search for elusive—perhaps delusive—certainty as to the exact count of 6 million votes. But no one claims that these ballots have not previously been tabulated; they were initially read by voting machines at the time of the election, and thereafter reread by virtue of Florida's automatic recount provision. No one claims there was any fraud in the election. The Supreme Court of Florida ordered this additional recount under the provision of the

---

[4] *Id.* at 246 n.11.
[5] *Id.* at 246.
[6] 531 U.S. 98 (2000).

election code giving the circuit judge the authority to provide relief that is "appropriate under such circumstances."[7]

The Chief Justice asserted that all the Florida ballots were "tabulated," read by voting machines, and "reread by virtue of Florida's automatic recount provision." Vice President Gore did not contest the fact that the Florida ballots were "tabulated" and "read by voting machines." He maintained that tens of thousands of ballots were not "counted" because the voting machines did not—for various reasons—register a vote for president. In this case, the Chief Justice utilized "tabulated" in the sense of "numerically counted," not "counted" in the sense of recording the intent of the voter to choose a presidential candidate. By arguing that the ballots were "tabulated," the Chief Justice sought to lay to rest the Vice President's argument that the ballots should be individually reviewed to determine which candidate the voter intended to choose.

Justice Blackmun, in *Allegheny County v. Greater Pittsburgh ACLU*,[8] posed a hypothetical as a straw man:

> Justice Kennedy is clever but mistaken in asserting that the description of the menorah, purports to turn the Court into a "national theology board." Any inquiry concerning the government's use of a religious object to determine whether that use results in an unconstitutional religious preference requires a review of the factual record concerning the religious object—even if the inquiry is conducted pursuant to Justice Kennedy's "proselytization" test. Surely, Justice Kennedy cannot mean that this Court must keep itself in ignorance of the symbol's conventional use and decide the constitutional question knowing only what it knew before the case was filed. This prescription of ignorance obviously would bias this Court according to the religious and cultural backgrounds of its Members, a condition much more intolerable than any which results from the Court's efforts to become familiar with the relevant facts.[9] (citations omitted).

The straw man consists of the argument that Justice Kennedy surely could not

> mean that this Court must keep itself in ignorance of the symbol's conventional use and decide the constitutional question knowing only what it knew before the case was filed.[10]

---

[7]*Id.* at 121.
[8]492 U.S. 573 (1989).
[9]*Id.* at 614 n.60.
[10]*Id.*

Knocking down the straw man, Justice Blackmun contended:

> This prescription of ignorance obviously would bias this Court according to the religious and cultural backgrounds of its Members, a condition much more intolerable than any which results from the Court's efforts to become familiar with the relevant facts.[11]

In the same case, Justice Kennedy constructed a straw man argument, using an example:

> One can imagine a case in which the use of passive symbols to acknowledge religious holidays could present this danger. For example, if a city chose to recognize, through religious displays, every significant Christian holiday while ignoring the holidays of all other faiths, the argument that the city was simply recognizing certain holidays celebrated by its citizens without establishing an official faith or applying pressure to obtain adherents would be much more difficult to maintain. On the facts of these cases, no such unmistakable and continual preference for one faith has been demonstrated or alleged.[12]

The straw man involves the assertion that if a city chose to recognize "every significant Christian holiday," but ignored every non-Christian holiday, it could not argue that it had not established "an official faith or [apply] pressure to obtain adherents."[13] Because the facts of this particular case did not match those of the example, Justice Kennedy argued a preference for a particular faith was not established.

Colorado enacted a statute in 1993 regulating "speech-related conduct within 100 feet of the entrance to any health care facility."[14] The constitutionally challenged section of the statute made

> it unlawful within the regulated areas for any person to "knowingly approach" within eight feet of another person, without that person's consent, "for the purpose of passing a leaflet or handbill to, displaying a sign to, or engaging in oral protest, education, or counseling with such other person . . ."[15] (footnote omitted; ellipses in original).

The majority of the U.S. Supreme Court found the challenged statute passed constitutional muster.

Justice Scalia, dissenting, asserted that the majority based its holding on a "straw interest," a position Colorado did not advocate on behalf of the statute's constitutionality:

---

[11] *Id.*
[12] *Id.* at 664–65 n.3.
[13] *Id.*
[14] Hill v. Colorado, 530 U.S. 703 (2000).
[15] *Id.* at 707.

Indeed, the situation is even more bizarre than that. The interest that the Court makes the linchpin of its analysis was not only unasserted by the State; it is not only completely *different* from the interest that the statute specifically sets forth; it was explicitly *disclaimed* by the State in its brief before this Court, and characterized as a "straw interest" *petitioners* served up in the hope of discrediting the State's case. We may thus add to the lengthening list of "firsts" generated by this Court's relentlessly proabortion jurisprudence, the first case in which, in order to sustain a statute, the Court has relied upon a governmental interest not only unasserted by the State, but positively repudiated.[16] (citation omitted; italics in original).

Colorado's brief to the Court argued that

[t]he statute is expressly designed to safeguard access to medical care. The legislative debate also reveals other goals: protecting public safety and order, assuring freedom of movement on sidewalks and streets, preventing violent confrontations, and improving enforcement of existing laws against assault.[19]

---

[19] Petitioners, instead of addressing the government interests shown on the face of the statute and in the legislative history, have chosen to invent "straw interests" to knock down (protection from "offensive or controversial" speech, right to be left alone on public sidewalks), or to claim that no "valid," "conceivable," or "legitimate" government interest underlies the statute.[17] (citations omitted; parentheses in original).

In an earlier dissent, involving the Virginia Military Institute (VMI), Justice Scalia also contended the majority relied on an argument no one advocated:

In the face of these findings by two courts below, amply supported by the evidence, and resulting in the conclusion that VMI would be fundamentally altered if it admitted women, this Court simply pronounces that "[t]he notion that admission of women would downgrade VMI's stature, destroy the adversative system and, with it, even the school, is a judgment hardly proved." The point about "downgrad[ing] VMI's stature" is a strawman; no one has made any such claim.[18] (citation omitted; brackets in original).

---

[16]*Id.* at 750.
[17]Respondent's brief at 25 n.19. http://supreme.lp.findlaw.com/supreme_court/briefs/98-1856mo2/brief.pdf.
[18]United States v. Virginia et al., 518 U.S. 515, 588-89 (1996).

Cell Phone Laws

Driving a vehicle while talking on a handheld cell phone has generated intense controversy. Supporters of such a practice argue that it is no different from talking to passengers inside the vehicle. Opponents argue that if drivers must talk on the phone while driving, they should use hands-free technology. If handheld cell phones cause accidents (although by a smaller percentage than other accident causes), should the straw man argument—that legislatures should ban these other more likely accident causes first—carry the day? That is the argument raised in the following newspaper article:

> New York has become the first state to regulate the use of cell phones in cars, with a new law requiring drivers to use only hands-free technology such as headsets.
>
> Beginning in December, New York drivers caught holding a cell phone while driving will face a fine of up to $100. Another 41 states have proposed similar legislation, all of which is misguided and based on false perceptions, not facts. Already, roughly a dozen localities—from Westchester, N.Y., to Brooklyn, Ohio—have declared the front seat off-limits to hand-held cell phones.
>
> Backers of these proposals say that cell phones have been the cause of an extraordinarily large number of automobile accidents. But statistics reveal a very different picture.
>
> Far more distracting to drivers are things that happen outside the car, such as construction or roadside accidents, which contribute to nearly 30% of car wrecks, according to a May study by the University of North Carolina Highway Safety Research Center that employed government crash data.
>
> Adjusting a radio or CD player is also risky (11.4%), as is chatting with passengers (10.9%), which ranks third. Cell phones contribute to only 1.5% of accidents.
>
> Many people take the small risk of using a cell phone to notify their boss they'll be late for a meeting or to call their spouse to say they are on the way home. And every day cell phone users make an estimated 140,000 emergency calls, according to the Cellular Telecommunications Industry Association.[19]

---

[19] Helen Chaney, *Drive to Limit Cell Phones Based on Bad Information*, MILWAUKEE JOURNAL SENTINEL, July 1, 2001, at 02J.

A similar issue was presented by Justice Scalia, dissenting in *Lawrence v. Texas*.[20] Should the U.S. Supreme Court refuse to overturn a "bad" precedent, because its members choose to ignore other cases that could be considered "bad" precedent?

> Today's approach to *stare decisis* invites us to overrule an erroneously decided precedent (including an "intensely divisive" decision) *if*: (1) its foundations have been "eroded" by subsequent decisions; (2) it has been subject to "substantial and continuing" criticism; and (3) it has not induced "individual or societal reliance" that counsels against overturning. The problem is that *Roe* itself—which today's majority surely has no disposition to overrule—satisfies these conditions to at least the same degree as *Bowers*.
>
> . . . .
>
> I do not quarrel with the Court's claim that *Romer v. Evans* "eroded" the "foundations" of *Bowers*' rational-basis holding. But *Roe* and *Casey* have been equally "eroded" by *Washington v. Glucksberg*, which held that only fundamental rights which are "'deeply rooted in this Nation's history and tradition'" qualify for anything other than rational basis scrutiny under the doctrine of "substantive due process." *Roe* and *Casey*, of course, subjected the restriction of abortion to heightened scrutiny without even attempting to establish that the freedom to abort was rooted in this Nation's tradition.
>
> . . . .
>
> We have held repeatedly, in cases the Court today does not overrule, that *only* fundamental rights qualify for this so-called "heightened scrutiny" protection—that is, rights which are "'deeply rooted in this Nation's history and tradition.'"[21] (citations omitted; italics and parentheses in original; ellipses added).

Justice White, dissenting in *Harmelin v. Michigan*,[22] contended that Justice Kennedy relied upon evidence necessary to convict for distribution of drugs (straw man), rather than on evidence for prosecution under the possession statute:

> Both the State and Justice Kennedy, point to the fact that the amount and purity of the drugs and Harmelin's possession of a beeper, coded phone book, and gun all were noted in the presentence report and provided circumstantial evidence of an intent to distribute. None of

---

[20]539 U.S. 558 (2008).
[21]*Id.* at 587, 593.
[22]501 U.S. 957 (1991).

this information, however, was relevant to a prosecution under the possession statute. Indeed, because the sentence is statutorily mandated for mere possession, there was no reason for defense counsel to challenge the presence of this information in the presentence report. It would likewise be inappropriate to consider petitioner's characteristics in assessing the constitutionality of the penalty.[23] (citations omitted).

Does the pursuit of justice through the court system (as opposed to the legislature) qualify as "normal democratic means"? That issue is posed by Justice Scalia, in his dissent in *Lawrence v. Texas*,[24] involving the legality of private, consensual homosexual conduct: "Let me be clear that I have nothing against homosexuals, or any other group, promoting their agenda through normal democratic means."[25]

In the same case, Justice Thomas, who also dissented, raised the straw man argument that if he were a member of the Texas Legislature, he would vote to repeal the challenged statute. As a member of the U.S. Supreme Court, however, he could not find that the statute violated the Equal Protection Clause of the Fourteenth Amendment and a similar provision in the Texas Constitution:

> I join Justice Scalia's dissenting opinion. I write separately to note that the law before the Court today "is . . . uncommonly silly." If I were a member of the Texas Legislature, I would vote to repeal it. Punishing someone for expressing his sexual preference through noncommercial consensual conduct with another adult does not appear to be a worthy way to expend valuable law enforcement resources.
>
> Notwithstanding this, I recognize that as a member of this Court I am not empowered to help petitioners and others similarly situated. My duty, rather, is to "decide cases 'agreeably to the Constitution and laws of the United States.'"[26] (citations omitted).

Justice Kennedy, in *Allegheny County v. Greater Pittsburgh ACLU*,[27] likewise offered that he, as a member of the local legislature, would have voted to prohibit religious displays on county grounds:

> For these reasons, I might have voted against installation of these particular displays were I a local legislative official. But we have no

---

[23] *Id.* at 1025 n.6.
[24] *Supra* at 539 U.S. 558.
[25] *Id.* at 603.
[26] *Id.* at 605.
[27] *Supra* at 492 U.S. 573.

jurisdiction over matters of taste within the realm of constitutionally permissible discretion. Our role is enforcement of a written Constitution.[28]

There are any number of ways to respond to a straw man argument. Justice Stevens, in *Hill v. Colorado*,[29] denied that the majority based its decision on a straw man argument, and reiterated the disputed issue:

> The dissenters argue that we depart from precedent by recognizing a "right to avoid unpopular speech in a public forum." We, of course, are not addressing whether there is such a "right." Rather, we are merely noting that our cases have repeatedly recognized the interests of unwilling listeners in situations where "the degree of captivity makes it impractical for the unwilling viewer or auditor to avoid exposure." We explained in *Erznoznik* that "[t]his Court has considered analogous issues—pitting the First Amendment rights of speakers against the privacy rights of those who may be unwilling viewers or auditors—in a variety of contexts. Such cases demand delicate balancing." The dissenters, however, appear to consider recognizing any of the interests of unwilling listeners—let alone balancing those interests against the rights of speakers—to be unconstitutional. Our cases do not support this view.[30] (citations and footnote omitted; brackets in original).

Similarly, Justice Souter restated the issue, in *Alden v. Maine*,[31] and noted how the majority's straw man arguments did not resolve that issue, and, moreover, were not convincing:

> The Court does no better with its trio of arguments to undercut *Chisholm*'s legitimacy: that the *Chisholm* majority "failed to address either the practice or the understanding that prevailed in the States at the time the Constitution was adopted," that "the majority suspected the decision would be unpopular and surprising," *Ibid.*; and that "two Members of the majority acknowledged that the United States might well remain immune from suit despite" Article III. These three claims do not, of course, go to the question whether state sovereign immunity was understood to be "fundamental" or "inherent," but in any case, none of them is convincing.[32] (citations omitted).

Straw man arguments may be dismissed as "hair-splitting" and not relevant to the issue:

---

[28] *Id.* at 679.
[29] *Supra* at 530 U.S. 703.
[30] *Id.* at 718.
[31] 529 U.S. 706 (1999).
[32] *Id.* at 790.

The respondent makes much of the alleged fact that "Young's" statements to the county judge were not made under oath and thus not testimony. We find such legal hair-splitting immaterial on the question of whether the respondent violated the Code of Professional Responsibility.[33]

Justice Powell pointed out the undesirable consequences of the minority's straw man argument in *Booth v. Maryland*[34]:

> As evidenced by the full text of the VIS (victim impact statement) in this case, the family members were articulate and persuasive in expressing their grief and the extent of their loss. But in some cases the victim will not leave behind a family, or the family members may be less articulate in describing their feelings even though their sense of loss is equally severe. The fact that the imposition of the death sentence may turn on such distinctions illustrates the danger of allowing juries to consider this information. Certainly the degree to which a family is willing and able to express its grief is irrelevant to the decision whether a defendant, who may merit the death penalty, should live or die.[35] (parentheses added).
>
> . . . .
>
> We are troubled by the implication that defendants whose victims were assets to their community are more deserving of punishment than those whose victims are perceived to be less worthy. Of course, our system of justice does not tolerate such distinctions.[36] (citations omitted).

Justice White answered the majority's argument with a straw man argument of his own:

> The Court's reliance on the alleged arbitrariness that can result from the differing ability of victims' families to articulate their sense of loss is a makeweight consideration: No two prosecutors have exactly the same ability to present their arguments to the jury; no two witnesses have exactly the same ability to communicate the facts; but there is no requirement in capital cases that the evidence and argument be reduced to the lowest common denominator.[37]

---

[33] People v. Reichman, 819 P.2d 1035, 1036 n.4 (Colo. 1991).
[34] 482 U.S. 496 (1987).
[35] *Id.* at 505.
[36] *Id.* at 506 n.8.
[37] *Id.* at 517–18.

Responding to Justice O'Connor, in *Rogers v. Tennessee*,[38] Justice Scalia agreed with her definition of modern "common law decisionmaking," but noted that her definition (straw man) did not comport with the historical definition:

> The Court's opinion considers the judgment at issue here "a routine exercise of common law decisionmaking," whereby the Tennessee court "brought the law into conformity with reason and common sense," by "laying to rest an archaic and outdated rule." This is an accurate enough description of what modern "common law decisionmaking" consists of—but it is not an accurate description of the theoretical model of common-law decisionmaking accepted by those who adopted the Due Process Clause. At the time of the framing, common-law jurists believed (in the words of Sir Francis Bacon) that the judge's "office is *jus dicere*, and not *jus dare*; to interpret law, and not to make law, or give law."[39] (citations omitted; parentheses and italics in original).

In turn, Justice O'Connor declares that it is Justice Scalia who raises a straw man argument, by resurrecting a settled legal issue:

> Justice Scalia makes much of the fact that, at the time of the framing of the Constitution, it was widely accepted that courts could not change the law, and that (according to Justice Scalia) there is no doubt that the ExPost Facto Clause would have prohibited a legislative decision identical to the Tennessee courts decision here. This latter argument seeks at bottom merely to reopen what has long been settled by the constitutional text and our own decisions: that the ExPost Facto Clause does not apply to judicial decisionmaking. The former argument is beside the point. Common law courts at the time of the framing undoubtedly believed that they were finding rather than making law. But, however one characterizes their actions, the fact of the matter is that common law courts then, as now, were deciding cases, and in doing so were fashioning and refining the law as it then existed in light of reason and experience. Due process clearly did not prohibit this process of judicial evolution at the time of the framing, and it does not do so today.[40] (parentheses in original; citations omitted).

When facially challenging a statute's constitutionality, straw man applications that would make the statute unconstitutional may safely be ignored, so long as there are conceivable circumstances that render the statute constitutional:

---

[38] 532 U.S. 451 (2001).
[39] *Id.* at 472.
[40] *Id.* at 462.

Given Missouri's definition of "public facility" as "any public institution, public facility, public equipment, or any physical asset owned, leased, or controlled by this state or any agency or political subdivisions thereof," there may be conceivable applications of the ban on the use of public facilities that would be unconstitutional. Appellees and amici suggest that the State could try to enforce the ban against private hospitals using public water and sewage lines, or against private hospitals leasing state-owned equipment or state land. Whether some or all of these or other applications of 188.215 would be constitutional need not be decided here. *Maher, Poelker,* and *McRae* stand for the proposition that some quite straightforward applications of the Missouri ban on the use of public facilities for performing abortions would be constitutional and that is enough to defeat appellees' assertion that the ban is facially unconstitutional. "A facial challenge to a legislative Act is, of course, the most difficult challenge to mount successfully, since the challenger must establish that no set of circumstances exists under which the Act would be valid. The fact that the [relevant statute] might operate unconstitutionally under some conceivable set of circumstances is insufficient to render it wholly invalid, since we have not recognized an 'overbreadth' doctrine outside the limited context of the First Amendment."[41] (citations omitted; brackets in original).

A simple declaration that the majority's entire opinion was a straw man argument is the tactic used by Justice Stevens, in *Bennis v. Michigan*[42]:

Justice Ginsburg argues that Michigan should not be rebuked for its efforts to deter prostitution, but none of her arguments refutes the fact that the State has accomplished its ends by sacrificing the rights of an innocent person. First, the concession that the car itself may be confiscated provides no justification for the forfeiture of the co-owner's separate interest. Second, the assertion that the Michigan Supreme Court "stands ready to police exorbitant applications of the statute," has a hollow ring because it failed to do so in this case. That court did not even mention the relevance of innocence to the trial court's exercise of its "equitable discretion." Rather, it stated flatly that "Mrs. Bennis' claim is without constitutional consequence." Third, the blatant unfairness of using petitioner's property to compensate for her husband's offense is not diminished by its modest value. It is difficult, moreover, to credit the trial court's statement that it would have awarded the proceeds of the sale to petitioner if they had been larger,

---

[41]Webster v. Reproductive Health Services, 492 U.S. 490, 523-24 (1989) (O'Connor, J., concurring).
[42]516 U.S. 442 (1996).

for it expressly ordered that any remaining balance go to the State's coffers. Finally, the State's decision to deter "Johns from using cars *they* own (or co-own) to contribute to neighborhood blight," surely does not justify the forfeiture of that share of the car owned by an innocent spouse.[43] (citations omitted; italics and parentheses in original).

Justice Kennedy, in *Nevada Dept. of Human Resources v. Hibbs*,[44] claimed the majority's straw man argument was an unsupported hasty generalization:

> The Court's reliance on evidence suggesting States provided men and women with the parenting leave of different length, suffers from the same flaw. This evidence concerns the Act's grant of parenting leave, and is too attenuated to justify the family leave provision. The Court of Appeals' conclusion to the contrary was based on an assertion that "if states discriminate along gender lines regarding the one kind of leave, then they are likely to do so regarding the other." The charge that a State has engaged in a pattern of unconstitutional discrimination against its citizens is a most serious one. It must be supported by more than conjecture.[45] (citations omitted).

---

[43] *Id.* at 470–71 n.14.
[44] 538 U.S. 721 (2003).
[45] *Id.* at 748.

CHAPTER THIRTY

Division: Painting with the Same Brush

Membership in an organization does not lead reasonably to any inference as to the conduct of a member on a given occasion.

People v. Perez, 170 Cal. Rptr. 619, 622 (Cal. App. 2 Dist. 1981).

THIS CHAPTER AND THE NEXT ("One Bad Apple") involve comparisons among the whole or group and the individual or member. When the attributes or characteristics of the group are applied to an individual, the fallacy of division occurs. Conversely, when the attributes or characteristics of the individual are applied to the group, the fallacy of composition occurs. By way of example, do all the members of the Republican Party subscribe to all its tenets? Perhaps some conclusions can be drawn about general propositions, but as the quotation above suggests, being a Republican does not mean that each member agrees with the party on every issue. To make such an assumption is to commit the fallacy of division.

In mathematical terms, the fallacy of composition can be compared to the following fraction: X/5. The denominator (group) is "5," but the numerator (individual) "X" is undefined. When the numerator is "5," the group and the individual are identical, but a numerator of 1 to 4 means the group and the individual do not share the same characteristics, thus implicating the fallacy of division.

Formulating a response to the fallacy of division requires that the group and the individuals who belong to that group be identified. Next, the attribute or characteristic that is being applied must be identified. These are not necessarily easy tasks. In the case of division, however, a handy shortcut may sometimes be helpful: Does the argument rely on stereotypes? Stereotypes are attributes or characteristics assumed to be representative of a group and are applied to individuals. If all else fails, attack the conclusion as it applies to the group and the individual or member.

Chapter 1 discusses two examples of the fallacy of division arising out of Winona Ryder's trial. In the first example, the prosecutor wrote that the law does not say that "only poor people steal." The group is "all who steal," and the characteristic being applied to the individual is "stealing." Because Ryder, presumably a wealthy celebrity, would have no motive to steal, she is not one of the individuals who would steal, as that would only apply to "poor people." The second example involves the anticipated argument from the defense that "there's a higher standard of proof for celebrities." Because Ryder is a celebrity (group), and because the characteristic (higher standard of proof) is being applied to her, the anticipated defense argument commits the fallacy of division.

Criminal conspiracies, by their very nature, consist of multiple individuals setting out to commit a crime. The rights of the individual coconspirators are often impacted by their association with other members of the conspiracy. Mere association, however, is not a basis for finding an individual guilty:

> Appellants also contend that the prosecutor, in her closing argument, referred to previous crimes evidence in an improper manner by saying that "the company you keep says a lot about you." Defendants objected to the remark as improperly suggesting that conspiracy could be inferred from one's associations. The district court offered a cautionary instruction, advising the jury "that mere association of alleged conspirators without evidence of participation does not permit an inference of guilt." The court then instructed the jury to disregard the remark.[1]

Gang membership raises issues similar to those alleged in conspiracies. A prosecutor sought to introduce expert police testimony that the defendant was a member of a street gang:

> At the pretrial hearing on defendant's motion for a preliminary ruling on the admissibility of evidence, the prosecutor made an offer of proof as follows: "Your Honor, I have some deputies here, Deputy Grani and Valdemar, who are assigned to the Lynwood Station, experts in the street gang activities."
>
> "I intend to show through the testimony of these deputies two things: that the defendant in this case, Mr. Perez, is a member of a gang called the CV3 and that in addition to that the other codefendant in this

---

[1] United States v. Clarke, 24 F.3d 257, 270 (D.C. Cir. 1994).

case, who was identified by Mr. Bautista, is also a member of the CV3 gang, and the relevancy of this, first of all, shows an association between these two people which tends to corroborate the identification of Mr. Bautista, that is, Mr. Bautista picked out two people who have an association in the past and therefore he tends to be correct when he finds them as having been associated in this robbery against him. In other words, Mr. Perez and Ontiveros are not strangers to one another and that they associated in the past."[2] (citation omitted).

Guilt by Association

The Court concluded that a blanket proscription on the introduction of gang membership is unwarranted, because there are circumstances where the evidence may be relevant, but in this case, it could lead to "guilt by association":

> We agree with this basic proposition and state at the outset that evidence of gang membership is not per se inadmissible. In order to be admissible it must meet the test of relevancy.
>
> . . . .
>
> The asserted active membership in the "CV3" gang by defendant, as testified to by Deputy Valdemar, did not have any "tendency in reason" to prove a disputed fact, i.e., the identity of the person who committed the charged offense. Membership in an organization does not lead reasonably to any inference as to the conduct of a member on a given occasion. Hence, the evidence was not relevant. It allowed, on the contrary, unreasonable inferences to be made by the trier of fact that the defendant was guilty of the offense charged on the theory of "guilt by association."[3] (citation omitted; ellipses added).

"Guilt by association" has been defined as alien to the U.S. system of jurisprudence:

> The system used to condemn these organizations is bad enough. The evil is only compounded when a government employee is charged with being disloyal. Association with or membership in an organization found to be "subversive" weighs heavily against the accused. He is not allowed to prove that the charge against the organization is false. That case is closed; that line of defense is taken away. The technique is one of guilt by association—one of the most odious institutions of history. The fact that the technique of guilt by association was

---

[2]People v. Perez, 170 Cal. Rptr. 619, 620 (Cal. App. 2 Dist. 1981).
[3]*Id.* at 622.

used in the prosecutions at Nuremberg does not make it congenial to our constitutional scheme. Guilt under our system of government is personal. When we make guilt vicarious we borrow from systems alien to ours and ape our enemies. Those short-cuts may at times seem to serve noble aims; but we depreciate ourselves by indulging in them. When we deny even the most degraded person the rudiments of a fair trial, we endanger the liberties of everyone. We set a pattern of conduct that is dangerously expansive and is adaptable to the needs of any majority bent on suppressing opposition or dissension.[4] (footnote omitted).

The first line of defense to a claim of "guilt by association" is the First Amendment:

> The First Amendment . . . restricts the ability of the State to impose liability on an individual solely because of his association with another.
>
> . . . .
>
> Civil liability may not be imposed merely because an individual belonged to a group, some members of which committed acts of violence. For liability to be imposed by reason of association alone, it is necessary to establish that the group itself possessed unlawful goals and that the individual held a specific intent to further those illegal aims.[5] (citation omitted; ellipses added).

Then again, if a group has not engaged in any unlawful activity, there can be no "guilt by association":

> Respondents' supplemental brief also demonstrates that on the present record no judgment may be sustained against most of the petitioners. Regular attendance and participation at the Tuesday meetings of the Claiborne County Branch of the NAACP is an insufficient predicate on which to impose liability. The chancellor's findings do not suggest that any illegal conduct was authorized, ratified, or even discussed at any of the meetings. The Sheriff testified that he was kept informed of what transpired at the meetings; he made no reference to any discussion of unlawful activity. To impose liability for presence at weekly meetings of the NAACP would—ironically—not even constitute "guilt by association," since there is no evidence that the association possessed unlawful aims. Rather, liability could only be imposed on a "guilt *for* association" theory. Neither is permissible under the First Amendment.[6] (citations and footnotes omitted; italics in original).

---

[4]Anti-Fascist Comm. v. McGrath, 341 U.S. 123, 178–79 (1951).
[5]NAACP v. Claiborne Hardware Co., 458 U.S. 886, 918–20 (1982).
[6]*Id.* at 924–25.

In his final argument to the jury, a prosecutor drew a comparison between his work and that of defense counsel:

> Appellant asserts that the prosecutor engaged in prejudicial misconduct in final argument to the jury. The prosecutor commented that defense counsel "and I aren't any different in a couple of respects. I chose this side and he chose that side. My people are victims. His people are rapists, murderers, robbers, child molesters. He has to tell them what to say. He has to help them plan a defense. He does not want you to hear the truth." He later stated: "He [defense counsel] continues this copout too. He says, hey, look my is [sic] client testifying you ought to believe him. He says this was purely consent, but if you don't believe him, if you don't think it was consent then certainly you have a reason to believe he thinks it was consent. The attorney has a lot of faith in his own client if you don't believe consent then believe he thought he had consent."[7] (brackets in original).

Not only did the prosecutor denigrate the presumption of innocence and imply that defense counsel fabricated evidence, but he also inferred that all of defense counsel's clients were guilty:

> The prosecutor's comments, i.e., "[m]y people are victims. His people are rapists, murderers, robbers, child molesters. He has to tell them what to say. He has to help them plan a defense. He does not want you to hear the truth," were clearly improper and misconduct. His argument inferred (sic) that all those accused of crimes whom defense counsel represented are necessarily guilty of heinous crimes.[8] (brackets in original).

In *Hill v. Colorado*,[9] Justice Stevens, writing for the majority, argued that a "bright-line" rule prohibiting all demonstrators from entering the immediate space (an eight-foot boundary) around a health clinic is necessary, even if the prohibition precludes a demonstrator who would not engage in harassment:

> Justice Kennedy, however, argues that the statute leaves petitioners without adequate means of communication. This is a considerable overstatement. The statute seeks to protect those who wish to enter health care facilities, many of whom may be under special physical or emotional stress, from close physical approaches by demonstrators. In doing so, the statute takes a prophylactic approach; it forbids all unwelcome demonstrators to come closer than eight feet. We recognize that by doing so, it will sometimes inhibit a demonstrator whose

---

[7]People v. Herring, 25 Cal. Rptr. 213, 217 (Cal. App. 2 Dist. 1993).
[8]*Id.* at 218.
[9]530 U.S. 703 (2000).

approach in fact would have proved harmless. But the statute's prophylactic aspect is justified by the great difficulty of protecting, say, a pregnant woman from physical harassment with legal rules that focus exclusively on the individual impact of each instance of behavior, demanding in each case an accurate characterization (as harassing or not harassing) of each individual movement within the 8-foot boundary. Such individualized characterization of each individual movement is often difficult to make accurately. A bright-line prophylactic rule may be the best way to provide protection, and, at the same time, by offering clear guidance and avoiding subjectivity, to protect speech itself.[10] (citation omitted; parentheses in original).

Justice Stevens, in *Atkins v. Virginia*,[11] argued that not all mentally retarded offenders should be executed, because the severity of retardation varies by individual:

To the extent there is serious disagreement about the execution of mentally retarded offenders, it is in determining which offenders are in fact retarded. In this case, for instance, the Commonwealth of Virginia disputes that Atkins suffers from mental retardation. Not all people who claim to be mentally retarded will be so impaired as to fall within the range of mentally retarded offenders about whom there is a national consensus. As was our approach in *Ford v. Wainwright*, with regard to insanity, "we leave to the State[s] the task of developing appropriate ways to enforce the constitutional restriction upon its execution of sentences."[12] (brackets in original; citations and footnotes omitted).

The majority, in *Alden v. Maine*,[13] concluded that the Eleventh Amendment prohibited suits against a state brought by individuals in another state. Justice Souter, dissenting, argued that what is true of all the state's citizens is true of the individual citizen, a proposition rejected by the majority:

From the difference between the sovereignty of princes and that of the people, Chief Justice Jay argued, it followed that a State might be sued. When a State sued another State, as all agreed it could do in federal court, all the people of one State sued all the people of the other. "But why it should be more incompatible, that all the people of a State should be sued by *one* citizen, than by one hundred thousand, I

---

[10] *Id.* at 729.
[11] 536 U.S. 304 (2002).
[12] *Id.* at 317.
[13] 527 U.S. 706 (1999).

cannot perceive, the process in both cases being alike; and the consequences of a judgment alike."[14] (italics in original; citation omitted).

Can two different conclusions be drawn from membership in a single organization? This ostensible dichotomy was apparent in *United States v. Abel*,[15] where the U.S. Supreme Court both rejected the fallacy of division and permitted it. Quoting from the Ninth Circuit's opinion, the Court acknowledged that mere membership in an organization cannot result in a conviction:

> It is settled law that the government may not convict an individual merely for belonging to an organization that advocates illegal activity. Rather, the government must show that the individual knows of and personally accepts the tenets of the organization.[16] (citations omitted).

In contrast, membership alone can be a basis for concluding that any member of the organization is biased (ad hominem (circumstantial)):

> We hold that the evidence showing Mills' and respondent's membership in the prison gang was sufficiently probative of Mills' possible bias towards respondent to warrant its admission into evidence. Thus it was within the District Court's discretion to admit Ehle's testimony, and the Court of Appeals was wrong in concluding otherwise.[17]

The Boy Scouts' views on homosexuality were challenged in *Boy Scouts of America v. Dale*.[18] Chief Justice Rehnquist, writing for the majority, held that the First Amendment extended protection to the organization, even in the absence of unanimity among its members:

> [T]he First Amendment simply does not require that every member of a group agree on every issue in order for the group's policy to be "expressive association." The Boy Scouts takes an official position with respect to homosexual conduct, and that is sufficient for First Amendment purposes. In this same vein, Dale makes much of the claim that the Boy Scouts does not revoke the membership of heterosexual Scout leaders that openly disagree with the Boy Scouts' policy on sexual orientation. But if this is true, it is irrelevant.[19] (brackets added; footnote omitted).

---

[14] *Id.* at 785.
[15] 469 U.S. 45 (1984).
[16] *Id.* at 48–49.
[17] *Id.* at 49.
[18] 530 U.S. 640 (2000).
[19] *Id.* at 655.

Dissenting, Justice Stevens argued that a group could not cobble eclectic positions and rely on any one of them for First Amendment protection:

> We have never held, however, that a group can throw together any mixture of contradictory positions and then invoke the right to associate to defend any one of those views. At a minimum, a group seeking to prevail over an antidiscrimination law must adhere to a clear and unequivocal view.[20]

The dissent also noted that the Boy Scouts' policy amounted to "stereotyping":

> Consider, in this regard, that a heterosexual, as well as a homosexual, could advocate to the Scouts the view that homosexuality is not immoral. BSA acknowledges as much by stating that a heterosexual who advocates that view to Scouts would be expelled as well. ("[A]ny persons who advocate to Scouting youth that homosexual conduct is 'morally straight' under the Scout Oath, or 'clean' under the Scout Law will not be registered as adult leaders.") But BSA does not expel heterosexual members who take that view outside of their participation in Scouting, as long as they do not advocate that position to the Scouts. And if there is no reason to presume that such a heterosexual will openly violate BSA's desire to express no view on the subject, what reason—other than blatant stereotyping—could justify a contrary presumption for homosexuals?[21] (citations omitted; parentheses and brackets in original).

Gender Stereotyping

Gender "stereotyping" in the workplace, involving leave benefits, was challenged in *Nevada Dept. of Human Resources v. Hibbs*.[22] Chief Justice Rehnquist, on behalf of the majority, wrote:

> According to evidence that was before Congress when it enacted the FMLA, States continue to rely on invalid gender stereotypes in the employment context, specifically in the administration of leave benefits. Reliance on such stereotypes cannot justify the States' gender discrimination in this area. The long and extensive history of sex discrimination prompted us to hold that measures that differentiate on the basis of gender warrant heightened scrutiny; here, as in *Fitzpatrick*, the persistence of such unconstitutional discrimination by the States

---

[20] *Id.* at 676.
[21] *Id.* at 691 n.19.
[22] 538 U.S. 721 (2003).

justifies Congress' passage of prophylactic §5 legislation.²³ (citation omitted).

Men, as well as women, fall victim to gender "stereotyping":

> Stereotypes about women's domestic roles are reinforced by parallel stereotypes presuming a lack of domestic responsibilities for men. Because employers continued to regard the family as the woman's domain, they often denied men similar accommodations or discouraged them from taking leave. These mutually reinforcing stereotypes created a self-fulfilling cycle of discrimination that forced women to continue to assume the role of primary family caregiver, and fostered employers' stereotypical views about women's commitment to work and their value as employees. Those perceptions, in turn, Congress reasoned, lead to subtle discrimination that may be difficult to detect on a case-by-case basis.²⁴

Age and disability "stereotypes" have not fared as well as those that are gender-based:

> We reached the opposite conclusion in *Garrett* and *Kimel*. In those cases, the §5 legislation under review responded to a purported tendency of state officials to make age- or disability-based distinctions. Under our equal protection case law, discrimination on the basis of such characteristics is not judged under a heightened review standard, and passes muster if there is "a rational basis for doing so at a class-based level, even if it 'is probably not true' that those reasons are valid in the majority of cases." See also *Garrett* ("States are not required by the Fourteenth Amendment to make special accommodations for the disabled, so long as their actions toward such individuals are rational").²⁵ (citations omitted; parentheses in original).

Justice Scalia dissented, and personified the States by arguing that the sovereignty of one State could not be abridged on account of "guilt by association":

> I join Justice Kennedy's dissent, and add one further observation: The constitutional violation that is a prerequisite to "prophylactic" congressional action to "enforce" the Fourteenth Amendment is a violation *by the State against which the enforcement action is taken.* There is no guilt by association, enabling the sovereignty of one State to be abridged under §5 of the Fourteenth Amendment because of violations by another State, or by most other States, or even by 49 other States.

---

²³ *Id.* at 730.
²⁴ *Id.* at 736.
²⁵ *Id.* at 735.

. . . .

Congress has sometimes displayed awareness of this self-evident limitation. That is presumably why the most sweeping provisions of the Voting Rights Act of 1965—which we upheld in *City of Rome v. United States*, as a valid exercise of congressional power under §2 of the Fifteenth Amendment—were restricted to States "with a demonstrable history of intentional racial discrimination in voting."[26] (citations and footnote omitted; italics in original).

Peremptory Challenges

The Equal Protection Clause applies to peremptory challenges to exclude potential jurors based on characteristics of the group to which they belong. One of the earliest cases to consider removal of a potential juror based on group characteristics was *Batson v. Kentucky*,[27] which involved race-based peremptory challenges. In *Batson*, the Supreme Court "outlined a three-step process for evaluating claims that a prosecutor has used peremptory challenges in a manner violating the Equal Protection Clause"[28]:

> First, the defendant must make a prima facie showing that the prosecutor has exercised peremptory challenges on the basis of race. Second, if the requisite showing has been made, the burden shifts to the prosecutor to articulate a race-neutral explanation for striking the jurors in question. Finally, the trial court must determine whether the defendant has carried his burden of proving purposeful discrimination.[29] (citations omitted).

Six years later, the Supreme Court was presented with these facts:

> The trial court assembled a panel of 36 potential jurors, 12 males and 24 females. After the court excused three jurors for cause, only 10 of the remaining 33 jurors were male. The State then used 9 of its 10 peremptory strikes to remove male jurors; petitioner used all but one of his strikes to remove female jurors. As a result, all the selected jurors were female.[30]

The prosecution's argument for eliminating potential male jurors and selecting female jurors rested on stereotypes:

---

[26]*Id.* at 741–42.
[27]476 U.S. 79 (1986).
[28]Hernandez v. New York, 500 U.S. 352, 358 (1991).
[29]*Id.* at 358–59.
[30]J.E.B. v. Alabama, 511 U.S. 127, 129 (1994).

Far from proffering an exceptionally persuasive justification for its gender-based peremptory challenges, respondent maintains that its decision to strike virtually all the males from the jury in this case "may reasonably have been based upon the perception, supported by history, that men otherwise totally qualified to serve upon a jury might be more sympathetic and receptive to the arguments of a man alleged in a paternity action to be the father of an out-of-wedlock child, while women equally qualified to serve upon a jury might be more sympathetic and receptive to the arguments of the complaining witness who bore the child."[31]

Rejecting these stereotypes, the majority concluded that gender discrimination in jury selection violates the Equal Protection Clause:

> Striking individual jurors on the assumption that they hold particular views simply because of their gender is "practically a brand upon them, affixed by law, an assertion of their inferiority." It denigrates the dignity of the excluded juror, and, for a woman, reinvokes a history of exclusion from political participation. The message it sends to all those in the courtroom, and all those who may later learn of the discriminatory act, is that certain individuals, for no reason other than gender, are presumed unqualified by state actors to decide important questions upon which reasonable persons could disagree.[32] (citation and footnotes omitted).

Not all group characteristics, however, will invalidate jury selection:

> Parties may also exercise their peremptory challenges to remove from the venire any group or class of individuals normally subject to "rational basis" review. Even strikes based on characteristics that are disproportionately associated with one gender could be appropriate, absent a showing of pretext.[33] (citations omitted).

Justice Scalia, dissenting, offered this observation:

> The biases that go along with group characteristics tend to be biases that the juror himself does not perceive, so that it is no use asking about them. It is fruitless to inquire of a male juror whether he harbors any subliminal prejudice in favor of unwed fathers.[34]

Civil trials are subject to the same restrictions as criminal trials:

---

[31] *Id.* at 137–38.
[32] *Id.* at 142.
[33] *Id.* at 143.
[34] *Id.* at 162.

We have recognized that, whether the trial is criminal or civil, potential jurors, as well as litigants, have an equal protection right to jury selection procedures that are free from state-sponsored group stereotypes rooted in, and reflective of, historical prejudice.[35]

In *Shaw v. Reno*,[36] the Supreme Court noted stereotyping may be at play during political redistricting:

> Classifications of citizens solely on the basis of race "are by their nature odious to a free people whose institutions are founded upon the doctrine of equality." They threaten to stigmatize individuals by reason of their membership in a racial group and to incite racial hostility . . . These principles apply not only to legislation that contains explicit racial distinctions, but also to those "rare" statutes that, although race neutral, are, on their face, "unexplainable on grounds other than race."
>
> . . . .
>
> [R]edistricting legislation that is so bizarre on its face that it is "unexplainable on grounds other than race," demands the same close scrutiny that we give other state laws that classify citizens by race.[37] (ellipses added; citations omitted).

New York passed a rule disqualifying aliens, regardless of their individual qualifications, from serving as police officers. The U.S. Supreme Court, in *Foley v. Connelie*,[38] considered whether such a rule violated the Equal Protection Clause, and concluded it did not. As a matter of policy, Justice Stevens' dissent argued that New York could disqualify "Hercule Poirot or Sherlock Holmes," but could it disqualify all aliens?:

> [A] satisfactory answer to this question is essential to the validity of the rule: What is the group characteristic that justifies the unfavorable treatment of an otherwise qualified individual simply because he is an alien?[39]

Justice Stevens assumed that "foreign allegiance" was the disqualifying characteristic underlying New York's rule:

> No one suggests that aliens as a class lack the intelligence or the courage to serve the public as police officers. The disqualifying characteristic is apparently a foreign allegiance which raises a doubt concerning

---

[35] *Id.* at 128.
[36] 509 U.S. 630 (1993).
[37] *Id.* at 643–44.
[38] 435 U.S. 291 (1978).
[39] *Id.* at 308.

trustworthiness and loyalty so pervasive that a flat ban against the employment of any alien in any law enforcement position is thought to be justified. But if the integrity of all aliens is suspect, why may not a State deny aliens the right to practice law? Are untrustworthy or disloyal lawyers more tolerable than untrustworthy or disloyal policemen? Or is the legal profession better able to detect such characteristics on an individual basis than is the police department? Unless the Court repudiates its holding in *In re Griffiths*, it must reject any conclusive presumption that aliens, as a class, are disloyal or untrustworthy.[40] (citation and footnote omitted).

There may be a historical explanation why aliens have been excluded from some public employment positions:

A characteristic that all members of the class do possess may provide the historical explanation for their exclusion from some categories of public employment. Aliens do not vote. Aliens and their families were therefore unlikely to have been beneficiaries of the patronage system which controlled access to public employment during so much of our history. The widespread exclusion of aliens from such positions today may well be nothing more than a vestige of the historical relationship between nonvoting aliens and a system of distributing the spoils of victory to the party faithful. If that be true, it might explain, but cannot justify, the discrimination.[41] (footnote omitted).

Justice Stevens would find that it is permissible to preclude aliens from policy-making positions, but a State cannot foreclose them from other employment opportunities:

Although a State may deny the alien the right to participate in the making of policy, it may not deny him equal access to employment opportunities without a good and relevant reason. *Sugarman* plainly teaches us that the burgeoning public employment market cannot be totally foreclosed to aliens. Since the police officer is not a policy-maker in this country, the total exclusion of aliens from the police force must fall.[42]

---

[40] *Id.* at 308.
[41] *Id.* at 308–09.
[42] *Id.* at 311.

CHAPTER THIRTY-ONE

Composition: One Bad Apple

But to infer that examples of individual disloyalty prove group disloyalty and justify discriminatory action against the entire group is to deny that under our system of law individual guilt is the sole basis for deprivation of rights.

Korematsu v. United States, 323 U.S. 214, 240 (1944)
(Murphy, J., dissenting).

THE FALLACY OF COMPOSITION is often described in terms of a faggot, a bundle of sticks. Just because an individual stick can be broken, it does not mean that the entire bundle can be broken. Similarly, the characteristics of an individual or member cannot be imputed to the whole or group.

In defense of O.J. Simpson, at his first criminal trial, the assembled group of lawyers was known as the "dream team." Did that mean that because each was an outstanding lawyer in his own right, that the group was outstanding? Individual attorneys may have huge egos that prevent them from working well with others who have the same characteristic. Perhaps a group of highly skilled trial lawyers who were not as well known, but who could act as "team" players, would have accomplished the same objectives—with less cost. Given the trial's outcome, however, it is difficult to argue with success.

To continue the mathematical analogy begun in the preceding chapter, the fallacy of composition can be compared to the following fraction: $2/X$. When the denominator is "2," the characteristics of the individual and the group are identical; for any other denominator, the group (denominator) does not share the characteristics of the individual (numerator), resulting in the fallacy of composition.

As in the previous chapter, responding to this fallacy requires identification of the group or whole that is targeted and the members or individuals who comprise that group. Next, the characteristic that is applied to the group must be identified. The fallacy of composition occurs when it is assumed that the individual's characteristic can readily be attributed to the group. Defeating this fallacy entails proof that the group does not share the individual's characteristic.

In the Winona Ryder trial (Chapter 1), prosecutor Ann Rundle's chart of the top ten things the law does not say, included: "6. Only defense attorneys or celebrities can drive nice cars." The characteristic is "driving nice cars," the individuals are "defense attorneys or celebrities," and the group consists of all those who drive such cars. Here, Rundle expected the defense to argue that the only individuals who can drive nice cars are defense attorneys or celebrities. In other words, the characteristics of the individuals are being applied to the group, thus committing the fallacy of composition. Certainly, the group comprised of those who drive nice cars includes more than defense attorneys or celebrities—what about doctors, athletes, or top business leaders?

In the wake of the attack on Pearl Harbor, Congress passed a law authorizing, among other things, the President to issue an Executive Order restricting access to certain military areas or military zones. Pursuant to that Executive Order, the military commander for the West Coast, Lieutenant General DeWitt, imposed a curfew order, which "subjected all persons of Japanese ancestry in prescribed West Coast military areas to remain in their residences from 8 p.m. to 6 a.m."[1] The constitutionality of that curfew order, intended as a "protection against espionage and sabotage,"[2] was upheld in *Kiyoushi Hirabayashi v. United States*.[3] Along with the curfew order, Lieutenant General Dewitt promulgated another mandate, "which directed that after May 9, 1942, all persons of Japanese ancestry should be excluded from" certain West Coast military areas.[4]

Toyosaburo Korematsu, an American of Japanese descent, was convicted in a federal district court of violating the exclusion order for remaining in San Leandro, California, where he lived. The uncontradicted evidence established that he was a loyal citizen of the United States.

---

[1] Korematsu v. United States, 323 U.S. 214, 217 (1944).
[2] *Id.*
[3] 320 U.S. 81 (1943).
[4] *Korematsu, supra* at 216.

Upholding the constitutionality of the exclusion order, Justice Black, writing for the majority, proffered several arguments constituting fallacies of composition:

> (Quoting from the *Hirabayashi* case) "[W]e cannot reject as unfounded the judgment of the military authorities and of Congress that there were disloyal members of that population, whose number and strength could not be precisely and quickly ascertained. We cannot say that the war-making branches of the Government did not have ground for believing that in a critical hour such persons could not readily be isolated and separately dealt with, and constituted a menace to the national defense and safety, which demanded that prompt and adequate measures be taken to guard against it."[5] (parentheses added; ellipses in original).

In this instance, Justice Black assumed that because there were some "unknown," "disloyal" Japanese residing on the West Coast of the United States, Congress could justifiably subject all Japanese to the exclusion order. The disloyalty of "some" individuals was, therefore, applied to the entire Japanese population in the designated military area.

Justice Black continued his analysis with an argument similar to the one above:

> Like curfew, exclusion of those of Japanese origin was deemed necessary because of the presence of an unascertained number of disloyal members of the group, most of whom we have no doubt were loyal to this country. It was because we could not reject the finding of the military authorities that it was impossible to bring about an immediate segregation of the disloyal from the loyal that we sustained the validity of the curfew order as applying to the whole group.[6]

The justification for this treatment (concededly harsh), rested on the nature of war:

> We uphold the exclusion order as of the time it was made and when the petitioner violated it. In doing so, we are not unmindful of the hardships imposed by it upon a large group of American citizens. But hardships are part of war, and war is an aggregation of hardships. All citizens alike, both in and out of uniform, feel the impact of war in greater or lesser measure. Citizenship has its responsibilities as well as

---

[5] *Id.* at 218.
[6] *Id.* at 218–19.

its privileges, and in time of war the burden is always heavier. Compulsory exclusion of large groups of citizens from their homes, except under circumstances of direct emergency and peril, is inconsistent with our basic governmental institutions. But when under conditions of modern warfare our shores are threatened by hostile forces, the power to protect must be commensurate with the threatened danger.[7] (citations omitted).

Justice Roberts bluntly criticized the majority's opinion finding the exclusion order constitutional:

> This is not a case of keeping people off the streets at night as was *Hirabayashi v. United States,* nor a case of temporary exclusion of a citizen from an area for his own safety or that of the community, nor a case of offering him an opportunity to go temporarily out of an area where his presence might cause danger to himself or to his fellows. On the contrary, it is the case of convicting a citizen as a punishment for not submitting to imprisonment in a concentration camp, based on his ancestry, and solely because of his ancestry, without evidence or inquiry concerning his loyalty and good disposition towards the United States. If this be a correct statement of the facts disclosed by this record, and facts of which we take judicial notice, I need hardly labor the conclusion that Constitutional rights have been violated.[8] (citations omitted).

Justice Murphy, who wrote the quotation at the beginning of this chapter, captured the essence of the majority's fallacy of composition:

> The military necessity which is essential to the validity of the evacuation order thus resolves itself into a few intimations that certain individuals actively aided the enemy, from which it is inferred that the entire group of Japanese Americans could not be trusted to be or remain loyal to the United States. No one denies, of course, that there were some disloyal persons of Japanese descent on the Pacific Coast who did all in their power to aid their ancestral land. Similar disloyal activities have been engaged in by many persons of German, Italian and even more pioneer stock in our country.[9]

Conspiracy law may involve the application of individual characteristics to the group of coconspirators. Responding to defense counsel's arguments, a prosecutor referred to the defendant as a coconspirator, prompting an objection from defense counsel:

---

[7] *Id.* at 219–20.
[8] *Id.* at 225–26.
[9] *Id.* at 240.

Hall claims that the government, with the permission of the court, wrongfully referred to him as a co-conspirator during the trial. The reference occurred during the trial. The reference occurred during the examination of one of the other defendants in the case:

Objection: [By Hall's attorney] Your Honor, I would like the court to admonish the jurors that any statements made by another person out of this court that don't pertain to Mr. Birges or the person making that statement are hearsay as to Mr. Hall.

Prosecutor: The statements made by a co-conspirator in the course of a conspiracy are admissible against all conspirators.

Court: Yes, objection overruled, you may proceed.

A statement made by a coconspirator during the course of and in furtherance of the conspiracy is admissible against a party under Fed.R.Evid. 801(d)(2)(D). Hall's claim of error is not directed to the admission of such evidence. Instead he objected to the prosecutor's use of the word "conspirator," in the presence of the jury in responding to defense counsel's comments.[10]

The Ninth Circuit dismissed the appeal, citing harmless error:

The jury was properly instructed as to all of the essential elements of the offense of conspiracy. The jury was further instructed that it must find beyond a reasonable doubt (1) that a conspiracy existed and (2) that Hall was one of the members thereof before it could consider the statements of a co-conspirator.

The record does not demonstrate that the judge's ruling on the objection led the jury to believe that the court had conclusively determined that Hall was a conspirator. Any error which may have occurred in permitting the discussion concerning the admissibility of a co-conspirator's statement to occur in the presence of the jury was harmless in light of the court's conspiracy instruction.[11] (citation omitted).

A prosecutor's opening statement referring to the original number of defendants in a conspiracy, and then noting that a majority pled guilty, did not violate the rights of one of the defendants who chose to stand trial:

Wiggins also contends that she was prejudiced when, in his opening statement to the jury, the prosecutor noted that the indictment had originally named twenty-six defendants, and that a majority of these

---

[10] United States v. Birges, 723 F.2d 666, 673 (9th Cir. 1984).
[11] Id.

individuals had "decided they ought to plead guilty." A moment later he again noted that the defendants not presently before the jury had pled guilty.

. . . .

It may have been improper for the prosecutor to have highlighted the guilty pleas in the way that he did. Especially in view of the fact that a number of defendants who pleaded guilty would not testify, there was a danger that the jury might be led to draw improper inferences about the guilt of the defendants who had exercised their right to a trial. However, the district court instructed the jury on several occasions during the trial not to consider the guilty pleas of other defendants as evidence against the defendants on trial.[12] (citations omitted; ellipses added).

Another defendant in the case argued that the admission of the guilty pleas of five codefendants prejudicially altered the outcome of the trial:

[Defendant] also suggests that he was prejudiced when the government was permitted to introduce into evidence the guilty pleas of five codefendants who did not testify at trial. The government offered the pleas, and the district court allowed them into evidence, so as to place the charged conspiracy "into context," that is, to explain to the jury what became of the named codefendants who were not on trial and who had not testified. The court did not allow into evidence the stipulations of fact underlying each of the pleas.[13] (brackets added; citations omitted).

The Seventh Circuit agreed that admitting the plea agreements was improper:

We believe that the court erred in admitting the plea agreements into evidence. When a co-defendant pleads guilty and then testifies against another defendant, it is common for the co-defendant's plea agreement to be disclosed and possibly offered into evidence. From the defense perspective, the fact that the testifying co-defendant has pleaded guilty bears on the co-defendant's credibility, because it raises the possibility that he or she is testifying against the defendant in the hope of currying favor with the government and lessening his punishment. With that basis for impeachment in mind, the government often elects to place the plea into evidence at the outset of the co-defendant's testimony and thus to take the wind out of the defense's sails by establishing that the co-defendant has merely agreed to tell

---

[12]United States v. Carraway, 108 F.3d 745, 760–61 (7th Cir. 1997).
[13]*Id.* at 755.

the truth and has not been promised anything in return other than what is specified in the agreement.[14]

The court then noted that the plea agreements could lead the jury to conclude that the conspirator who elects to go to trial was also guilty:

> When the co-defendant does not testify, however, the fact of his plea, and the content of his plea agreement, typically will have little or no probative value—his or her credibility is not at issue. It is no doubt true, as the government points out, that the jury will wonder what happened to the co-defendants whose names have been mentioned in the indictment and in the course of the trial but who have not appeared before them. But the jury can be instructed simply not to concern itself with that question, and we have identified that as the preferred course. Disclosing the pleas, when the jury has never had an opportunity to hear from persons who pled guilty, presents the risk that the jury will impermissibly infer the guilt of the defendants on trial. Thus, where a missing co-defendant does not testify, "[i]t is generally accepted that absent agreement, 'courts and prosecutors generally are forbidden from mentioning that a co-defendant has either pled guilty or been convicted.'"[15] (citations omitted; brackets in original).

The plaintiff sued the administrator of the Small Business Administration (SBA) for alleged disability discrimination in a federal district court.[16] The Eleventh Circuit reversed the granting of backpay and attorney fees, and found that

> [the plaintiff] has failed to make a *prima facie* case of employment discrimination under the Rehabilitation Act because there was insufficient evidence that the SBA perceived him as a disabled person or that he was "otherwise qualified" for the position of construction analyst during the relevant time frame.[17] (brackets added).

One of the plaintiff's arguments about a theory of liability for disability claims committed the fallacy of composition:

> [The plaintiff] argues that the extent to which the SBA regarded him as impaired is irrelevant under a perception theory of disability discrimination. This reading of the Act is, of course, wrong as it would expand the Act to cover any impairment at all, so long as the employer knew of it. Under this theory, "a person in a group protected from adverse employment actions, i.e., anyone, could establish

---

[14]*Id.*
[15]*Id.*
[16]Sutton v. Lader, 185 F.3d 1203 (1999).
[17]*Id.* at 1211.

a *prima facie* discrimination case merely by demonstrating some adverse action against the individual and that the employer was aware that the employee's characteristic placed him or her in the group, *e.g.*, race, age, or sex [or disabled]."[18] (first brackets added; second brackets in original; citation omitted).

Taxpayer Standing

A vexatious concept taught in beginning classes of Constitutional Law is the requirement that individuals instituting a lawsuit must have "standing." In *Hein v. Freedom from Religion Foundation, Inc.*,[19] "an organization opposed to Government endorsement of religion and three of its members" sued the Director of the White House Office of Faith-Based and Community Initiatives for violating the Establishment Clause, "by organizing conferences that were designed to promote, and had the effect of promoting, religious community groups over secular ones."[20] The majority of the Supreme Court concluded that the individual taxpayers did not have standing to challenge the government expenditures in this case.[21]

Justice Scalia, who concurred in the judgment, argued that for individuals to have standing there must be injury in fact, and he noted that the Court had previously relied on two concepts of injury in fact: "Wallet Injury" and "Psychic Injury."[22] Describing Psychic Injury, Justice Scalia presented an example of the fallacy of composition:

> Psychic injury, on the other hand, has nothing to do with the plaintiff's tax liability. Instead, the injury consists of the taxpayer's *mental displeasure* that money extracted from him is being spent in an unlawful manner. This shift in focus eliminates traceability and redressability problems. Psychic Injury is directly traceable to the improper *use of* taxpayer funds, and it is redressed when the improper use is enjoined, regardless of whether that injunction affects the taxpayer's purse. *Flast* and the cases following its teaching have invoked a peculiarly restricted version of Psychic Injury, permitting taxpayer displeasure over unconstitutional spending to support standing *only if* the constitutional provision allegedly violated is a specific limitation on the taxing and spending power. Restricted or not, this conceptualiz-

---

[18]*Id.* at 1208 n.6.
[19]127 S. Ct. 2553 (2007).
[20]*Id.* at 2560–61.
[21]*Id.* at 2572.
[22]*Id.* at 2574.

ing of injury in fact in purely mental terms conflicts squarely with the familiar proposition that a plaintiff lacks a concrete and particularized injury when his only complaint is the generalized grievance that the law is being violated. As we reaffirmed unanimously just this Term: "'We have consistently held that a plaintiff raising only a generally available grievance about government—claiming only harm to his and every citizen's interest in proper application of the Constitution and laws, and seeking relief that no more directly and tangibly benefits him than it does the public at large—does not state an Article III case or controversy.'"[23] (italics in original; citations omitted).

Students at a school-sanctioned and school-supervised event who unfurled a banner stating, "BONG HITS 4 JESUS," as the Olympic Torch Relay passed, were directed to remove the banner by the high school principal. One of the students, Frederick, refused to take down the banner, and was later suspended. The U.S. Supreme Court held that Frederick's First Amendment rights were not violated.[24] Justice Stevens, dissenting, disagreed with the majority's assessment that the banner was an incitement to use drugs, and argued that while some students may be "dumb," not all are:

> To the extent the Court independently finds that "BONG HITS FOR JESUS" *objectively* amounts to the advocacy of illegal drug use—in other words, that it can *most* reasonably be interpreted as such—that conclusion practically refutes itself. This is a nonsense message, not advocacy. The Court's feeble effort to divine its hidden meaning is strong evidence of that . . . Frederick's credible and uncontradicted explanation for the message—he just wanted to get on television—is also relevant because a speaker who does not intend to persuade his audience can hardly be said to be advocating anything. But most importantly, it takes real imagination to read a "cryptic" message (the Court's characterization not mine), with a slanting drug reference as an incitement to drug use. Admittedly, some high school students (including those who use drugs) are dumb. Most students, however, do not shed their brains at the schoolhouse gate, and most students know dumb advocacy when they see it. The notion that the message on this banner would actually persuade either the average student or even the dumbest one to change his or her behavior is most implausible.[25] (citations and footnote omitted; italics and parentheses in original).

---

[23]*Id.* at 2574.
[24]Morse v. Frederick, 127 S. Ct. 2618 (2007).
[25]*Id.* at 2649.

Special Risk of Wrongful Execution

In *Atkins v. Virginia*,[26] the Supreme Court considered whether the States could execute mentally retarded offenders. Justice Stevens, writing for the majority, argued that because individual offenders have difficulty presenting, and assisting in, their defense, mentally retarded defendants, as a group, "face a special risk of wrongful execution"[27]:

> The reduced capacity of mentally retarded offenders provides a second justification for a categorical rule making such offenders ineligible for the death penalty. The risk "that the death penalty will be imposed in spite of factors which may call for a less severe penalty," is enhanced, not only by the possibility of false confessions, but also by the lesser ability of mentally retarded defendants to make a persuasive showing of mitigation in the face of prosecutorial evidence of one or more aggravating factors. Mentally retarded defendants may be less able to give meaningful assistance to their counsel and are typically poor witnesses, and their demeanor may create an unwarranted impression of lack of remorse for their crimes. As *Penry* demonstrated, moreover, reliance on mental retardation as a mitigating factor can be a two-edged sword that may enhance the likelihood that the aggravating factor of future dangerousness will be found by the jury. Mentally retarded defendants in the aggregate face a special risk of wrongful execution.[28] (footnotes and citations omitted).

Justice Scalia employed humor/ridicule to render a critique of the majority's fallacy of composition argument:

> The Court throws one last factor into its grab bag of reasons why execution of the retarded is "excessive" in all cases: Mentally retarded offenders "face a special risk of wrongful execution" because they are less able "to make a persuasive showing of mitigation," "to give meaningful assistance to their counsel," and to be effective witnesses. Special risk is pretty flabby language (even flabbier than "less likely")—and I suppose a similar "special risk" could be said to exist for just plain stupid people, inarticulate people, even ugly people. If this unsupported claim has any substance to it (which I doubt) it might support a due process claim in all criminal prosecutions of the mentally retarded; but it is hard to see how it has anything to do with an *Eighth Amendment* claim that execution of the mentally retarded

---

[26] 536 U.S. 304 (2002).
[27] *Id.* at 321.
[28] *Id.* at 320–21.

is cruel and unusual. We have never before held it to be cruel and unusual punishment to impose a sentence in violation of some *other* constitutional imperative.²⁹ (citation omitted; parentheses and italics in original).

It is not enough, argued Justice Souter, that some individuals of the framers' generation believed in a "natural law view" of sovereign immunity:

> There is almost no evidence that the generation of the Framers thought sovereign immunity was fundamental in the sense of being unalterable. Whether one looks at the period before the framing, to the ratification controversies, or to the early republican era, the evidence is the same. Some Framers thought sovereign immunity was an obsolete royal prerogative inapplicable in a republic; some thought sovereign immunity was a common-law power defeasible, like other common-law rights, by statute; and perhaps a few thought, in keeping with a natural law view distinct from the common-law conception, that immunity was inherent in a sovereign because the body that made a law could not logically be bound by it. Natural law thinking on the part of a doubtful few will not, however, support the Court's position.³⁰

Does a gay rights activist who happens to be a Boy Scout send a message that the organization supports homosexuality? The Supreme Court majority, in *Boy Scouts of America v. Dale*,³¹ answered this question affirmatively:

> We must then determine whether Dale's presence as an assistant scoutmaster would significantly burden the Boy Scouts' desire to not "promote homosexual conduct as a legitimate form of behavior." As we give deference to an association's assertions regarding the nature of its expression, we must also give deference to an association's view of what would impair its expression. That is not to say that an expressive association can erect a shield against antidiscrimination laws simply by asserting that mere acceptance of a member from a particular group would impair its message. But here Dale, by his own admission, is one of a group of gay Scouts who have "become leaders in their community and are open and honest about their sexual orientation." Dale was the copresident of a gay and lesbian organization at college and remains a gay rights activist. Dale's presence in the Boy Scouts would,

---

²⁹*Id.* at 352.
³⁰Alden v. Maine, 527 U.S. 706, 764 (1999).
³¹530 U.S. 640 (2000).

at the very least, force the organization to send a message, both to the youth members and the world, that the Boy Scouts accepts homosexual conduct as a legitimate form of behavior.[32] (citations omitted).

Writing for the dissent, Justice Stevens argued by analogy that not every activist would send a message contrary to the organization's goals:

> But surely many members of BSA engage in expressive activities outside their troop, and surely BSA does not want all of that expression to be carried on inside the troop. For example, a Scoutmaster may be a member of a religious group that encourages its followers to convert others to its faith. Or a Scoutmaster may belong to a political party that encourages its members to advance its views among family and friends. Yet BSA does not think it is appropriate for Scoutmasters to proselytize a particular faith to unwilling Scouts or to attempt to convert them from one religion to another. Nor does BSA think it appropriate for Scouts or Scoutmasters to bring politics into the troop. From all accounts, then, BSA does not discourage or forbid outside expressive activity, but relies on compliance with its policies and trusts Scouts and Scoutmasters alike not to bring unwanted views into the organization. Of course, a disobedient member who flouts BSA's policy may be expelled. But there is no basis for BSA to presume that a homosexual will be unable to comply with BSA's policy not to discuss sexual matters any more than it would presume that politically or religiously active members could not resist the urge to proselytize or politicize during troop meetings. As BSA itself puts it, its rights are "not implicated *unless* a prospective leader *presents himself* as a role model inconsistent with Boy Scouting's understanding of the Scout Oath and law."[33] (citations and footnotes omitted; italics in original).

Upholding the constitutionality of the Family Medical Leave Act, Chief Justice Rehnquist's majority opinion explained that the national law attacked "state-sanctioned stereotype(s)":

> By creating an across-the-board, routine employment benefit for all eligible employees, Congress sought to ensure that family-care leave would no longer be stigmatized as an inordinate drain on the workplace caused by female employees, and that employers could not evade leave obligations simply by hiring men. By setting a minimum standard of family leave for *all* eligible employees, irrespective of gender, the FMLA attacks the formerly state-sanctioned stereotype that only women are responsible for family caregiving, thereby reducing

---

[32] *Id.* at 653.
[33] *Id.* at 690–92.

employers' incentives to engage in discrimination by basing hiring and promotion decisions on stereotypes.[34] (italics in original)

In response to the majority's assault on the fallacy of division (stereotyping by the states), Justice Scalia maintained the majority engaged in the fallacy of composition:

> Today's opinion for the Court does not even attempt to demonstrate that each one of the 50 States covered by 29 U. S. C. §2612(a)(1)(C) was in violation of the Fourteenth Amendment. It treats "the States" as some sort of collective entity which is guilty or innocent as a body. "[T]he States' record of unconstitutional participation in, and fostering of, gender-based discrimination," it concludes, "is weighty enough to justify the enactment of prophylactic §5 legislation." This will not do. Prophylaxis in the sense of extending the remedy beyond the violation is one thing; prophylaxis in the sense of extending the remedy beyond the violator is something else.[35] (brackets in original; citation omitted).

The expression "the whole is greater than the sum of its parts" typically signals a rejection of the fallacy of composition. In other words, what is true of the parts cannot be true of the whole:

> Confronted with our decisions in *Fort Wayne Books* and *Arcara*—neither of which he challenges—petitioner's position boils down to this: Stiff criminal penalties for obscenity offenses are consistent with the First Amendment; so is the forfeiture of expressive materials as punishment for criminal conduct; but the combination of the two somehow results in a violation of the First Amendment. We reject this counterintuitive conclusion, which in effect would say that the whole is greater than the sum of the parts.[36]

---

[34] Nevada Dept. of Human Resources v. Hibbs, 538 U.S. 721, 737 (2003).
[35] *Id.* at 742.
[36] Alexander v. United States, 509 U.S. 544, 557–58 (1993).

CHAPTER THIRTY-TWO

Sweeping Generalizations

> *[A] thing may be within the letter of the statute and yet not within the statute, because not within its spirit, nor within the intention of its makers[.]*
>
> Holy Trinity Church v. United States, 143 U.S. 457, 459 (1892).

THE PRECEDING TWO CHAPTERS analyzed comparisons among the whole or group and the individual or member. This chapter examines the extent to which individual examples or cases inappropriately fall (or are swept up) within a general rule or principle. Although the individual examples or cases literally fall within a rule or principle, there may be reasons why they should not be included. An example or case may be excluded, as the quotation above illustrates, because it does not fall within the spirit or intent of the statute.

An advocate of a sweeping generalization will likely emphasize the literal inclusion of the example or case within the rule or principle's language, and argue that there is no basis for scrutinizing that language because it is not subject to ambiguity. Countering the sweeping generalization may require the concession that the example or case literally falls within the rule or principle, accompanied by a reasoned analysis why the rule or principle does not apply in this instance.

In *Zuni Public School District No. 89 v. Department of Education*,[1] a 5-4 majority of the U.S. Supreme Court held that Congress' intention must prevail over the literal reading of the statutory language in the case. Justice Breyer defined the issue as follows:

---

[1] 167 L. Ed. 2d 449 (2007).

A federal statute sets forth a method that the Secretary of Education is to use when determining whether a State's public school funding program "equalizes expenditures" throughout the State. The statute instructs the Secretary to calculate the disparity in per-pupil expenditures among local school districts in the State. But when doing so, the Secretary is to *"disregard" school districts "with per-pupil expenditures . . . above the 95th percentile or below the 5th percentile of such expenditures . . . in the State."* (citation omitted).

The question before us is whether the emphasized statutory language permits the Secretary to identify the school districts that should be "disregard[ed]" by looking to the *number of the district's pupils* as well as the size of the district's expenditures per pupil. We conclude that it does.[2] (italics and ellipses in original).

Justice Scalia dissented, concluding that the Secretary of Education's "preferred methodology for determining whether a State's school-funding system is equalized" did not fall within the statute's literal language. He accused the majority of overriding the plain language of the statute to include a meaning that did not fall within the statute, based solely on the perceived legislative intent. According to Justice Scalia, the majority swept within the statute an impermissible interpretation—"a judge-empowering proposition":

> In *Church of the Holy Trinity v. United States,* this Court conceded that a church's act of contracting with a prospective rector fell within the plain meaning of a federal labor statute, but nevertheless did not apply the statute to the church: "It is a familiar rule," the Court pronounced, "that a thing may be within the letter of the statute and yet not within the statute, because not within its spirit, nor within the intention of its makers." That is a judge-empowering proposition if ever there was one, and in a century since, the Court has wisely retreated from it, in words if not always in actions. But today *Church of the Holy Trinity* arises, Phoenix-like, from the ashes. This Court's contrary assertions aside, today's decision is nothing other than the elevation of judge-supposed legislative intent over clear statutory test. The plain language of the federal Impact Aid statute clearly and unambiguously forecloses the Secretary of Education's preferred methodology for determining whether a State's school-funding system is equalized. Her selection of that methodology is therefore entitled to zero deference under *Chevron U.S.A. Inc. v. Natural Resources Defense Council, Inc.*[3] (citations omitted).

---

[2] *Id.* at 455.
[3] *Id.* at 469–70.

SWEEPING GENERALIZATIONS 437

Justice Stevens's concurring arguments and Justice Scalia's dissent illustrate the various arguments, and responses, that may arise when considering a sweeping generalization.

Justice Stevens initiates his concurrence with an appeal to authority—former Chief Justice Rehnquist:

> In his oft-cited opinion for the Court in *Griffin v. Oceanic Contractors*, then-Justice Rehnquist wisely acknowledged that "in rare cases the literal application of a statute will produce a result demonstrably at odds with the intentions of the drafters, and those intentions must be controlling."[4] (citation omitted).

Beginning with a recitation of the facts and holding, Justice Scalia then argues that if *Griffin* was not a suitable case to rely on congressional intent, this one is not either:

> *Griffin* involved a maritime statute that required the master of a vessel to furnish unpaid wages to a seaman within a specified period after the seaman's discharge, and further provided that a master who failed to do so without sufficient cause "'shall pay to the seaman a sum equal to two days' pay for each and every day during which payment is delayed.'" We explained that "Congress intended the statute to mean exactly what its plain language says," and held that the seaman was entitled to double wages for every day during which payment was delayed, even for the period in which he had obtained alternative employment. The result was that the seaman would receive approximately $300,000 for his master's improper withholding of $412.50, even though "[i]t [was] probably true that Congress did not precisely envision the grossness of the difference . . . between the actual wages withheld and the amount of the award required by the statute." We suggested in dicta that there might be a "rare cas[e]" in which the Court could relax its steadfastness to statutory text, but if *Griffin* itself did not qualify, it is hard to imagine what would. The principle Justice Stevens would ascribe to *Griffin* is in fact the one he advocated in dissent. "[T]his is one of the cases in which the exercise of judgment dictates a departure from the literal text in order to be faithful to the legislative will."[5] (brackets and ellipses in original; citations omitted).

Noting that Justice Scalia provided the fifth vote in *United States v. Ron Pair Enterprises, Inc.*,[6] Justice Stevens offered a tu quoque argument: Justice Scalia previously found that intent trumped the statute's language:

---

[4]*Id.* at 467.
[5]*Id.* at 476.
[6]489 U.S. 235, 242 (1989).

And in *Ron Pair Enterprises, Inc.*, the Court began its analysis of the question of statutory construction by restating the proposition that "[i]n such cases, the intention of the drafters, rather than the strict language, controls." Justice Scalia provided the decisive fifth vote for the majority in that case.[7] (brackets in original; citation omitted).

Justice Scalia acknowledged that he provided the decisive fifth vote, but denied that he agreed with the principle attributed to him:

> The second case Justice Stevens relied upon, [*Ron Pair*], is equally inapt. The Court's opinion there (unlike the one here) explained that our analysis "must begin . . . with the language of the statute itself," and concluded that was "also where the inquiry should end, for where . . . the statute's language is plain, 'the sole function of the courts is to enforce it according to its terms.'" My "fifth vote" in *Ron Pair* was thus only "decisive," in reaffirming this Court's adherence to statutory text, decisively preventing it from falling off the precipice it plunges over today.[8] (brackets added; parentheses and ellipses in original; citations omitted).

Agreeing that overriding the language of the statute (based on a determination of Congress's intent) could lead to a "policy-driven interpretation," Justice Stevens, nonetheless, concludes that that is a proper role for the judiciary:

> Today he (Justice Scalia) correctly observes that a judicial decision that departs from statutory text may represent "Policy-driven interpretation." As long as that driving policy is faithful to the intent of Congress (or, as in this case, aims only to give effect to such intent)—which it must be if it is to override a strict interpretation of the text—the decision is also a correct performance of the judicial function.[9] (parentheses added; citations omitted; brackets in original).

Justice Scalia notes the apparent dangers in Justice Stevens's approach:

> But Justice Stevens' candor should not make his philosophy seem unassuming. He maintains that it is "a correct performance of the judicial function" to "override a strict interpretation of the text" so long as policy-driven interpretation "is faithful to the intent of Congress." But once one departs from "strict interpretation of the text" (by which Justice Stevens means the actual meaning of the text) fidelity to the intent of Congress is a chancy thing. The only thing we know for certain both Houses of Congress (and the President, if he signed the leg-

---

[7] 167 L. Ed. 2d at 467–68.
[8] *Id.* at 476.
[9] *Id.* at 468.

islation) agreed upon is the text. Legislative history can never produce a "pellucidly clear" picture of what the law was "intended" to mean, for the simple reason that it is never voted upon—or ordinarily even seen or heard—by the "intending" law-giving entity, which consists of both Houses of Congress and the President (if he did not veto the bill). Thus, what judges believe Congress "meant" (apart from the text) has a disturbing but entirely unsurprising tendency to be whatever judges think Congress *must* have meant, i.e. *should* have meant.[10] (parentheses in original; italics in original; citations omitted).

Unwilling to assume that every instance of "policy-driven interpretation" is improper, Justice Stevens accuses Justice Scalia of engaging in a hasty generalization, based solely on the holding of this case:

Justice Scalia's argument today rests on the incorrect premise that every policy-driven interpretation implements a judge's personal view of sound policy, rather than a faithful attempt to carry out the will of the legislature. Quite the contrary is true of the work of the judges with whom I have worked for many years. If we presume that our judges are intellectually honest—as I do—there is no reason to fear "policy-driven interpretation[s]" of Acts of Congress.[11] (brackets in original).

Justice Scalia cites the Court's decision in *Church of the Holy Trinity* to counter Justice Stevens's argument:

In *Church of the Holy Trinity*, every Justice on this Court disregarded the plain language of a statute that forbade the hiring of a clergyman from abroad because, after all (they thought), "this is a Christian nation," so Congress could not have meant what it said. Is there any reason to believe that those Justices were lacking that "intellectua[l] honest[y]" that *Justice Stevens* "presume[s]" all our judges possess? Intellectual honesty does not exclude a blinding intellectual bias. And even if it did, the system of judicial amendatory veto over texts duly adopted by Congress bears no resemblance to the system of lawmaking set forth in our Constitution.[12] (parentheses and brackets in original; citations omitted).

There exists, according to Justice Stevens, a congressional intent, apart from the statutory language:

In *Chevron U.S.A. Inc. v Natural Resources Defense Council, Inc.*[13] we acknowledged that when "the intent of Congress is clear [from the

---

[10]*Id.* at 475.
[11]*Id.* at 468.
[12]*Id.* at 475.
[13]467 U.S. 837, 842 (1984).

statutory text], that is the end of the matter." But we also made clear that "administrative constructions which are contrary to clear congressional intent" must be rejected. In that unanimous opinion, we explained:

> "If a court, employing traditional tools of statutory construction, ascertains that Congress had an intention on the precise question at issue, that intention is the law and must be given effect."[14] (brackets in original; citations omitted).

Justice Scalia expressed his dubiousness of an intent separate from the language of the statute:

> I do not purport to know what Congress thought it was doing when it amended the Impact Aid program in 1994. But even indulging Justice Stevens' erroneous premise that there exists a "legislative intent" separate and apart from the statutory text, I do not see how the Court can possibly say, with any measure of confidence, that Congress wished one thing rather than another.[15] (citation omitted).

According to Justice Stevens, when searching for congressional intent, the Court is not required to first consider the statutory language, but may begin with consideration of the legislative history:

> Analysis of legislative history is, of course, a traditional tool of statutory construction. There is no reason why we must confine ourselves to, or begin our analysis with, the statutory text if other tools of statutory construction provide better evidence of congressional intent with respect to the precise point at issue.
>
> As the Court's opinion demonstrates, this is a quintessential example of a case in which the statutory text was obviously enacted to adopt the rule that the Secretary administered both before and after the enactment of the rather confusing language found in [citation omitted]. That text is sufficiently ambiguous to justify the Court's exegesis, but my own vote is the product of a more direct route to the Court's patently correct conclusion. This happens to be a case in which the legislative history is pellucidly clear and the statutory text is difficult to fathom. Moreover, it is a case in which I cannot imagine anyone accusing any Member of the Court of voting one way or the other because of that Justice's own policy preferences.[16] (citations and footnotes omitted; brackets added).

---

[14]167 L. Ed. 2d at 468.
[15]*Id.* at 477.
[16]*Id.* at 468–69.

SWEEPING GENERALIZATIONS 441

The problem with that approach, argues Justice Scalia, is that legislative history is always ambiguous:

> Legislative history can never produce a "pellucidly clear" picture of what a law was "intended" to mean, for the simple reason that it is never voted upon—or ordinarily even seen or heard—by the "intending" lawgiving entity, which consists of both Houses of Congress and the President (if he did not veto the bill).[17] (citations omitted; parentheses in original).

Finally, Justice Stevens contends that he would not be bound by a sweeping generalization:

> Given the clarity of the evidence of Congress' "intention on the precise question at issue," I would affirm the judgment of the Court of Appeals even if I thought that petitioners' literal reading of the statutory text was correct. The only "policy' by which I have been driven is that which this court has endorsed on repeated occasions regarding the importance of remaining faithful to Congress' intent.[18] (footnote omitted).

Although he admires Justice Stevens' candor, Justice Scalia disagrees with his rationale:

> How then, if the text is so clear, are respondents managing to win this case? The answer can only be the return of that miraculous redeemer of lost causes, *Church of the Holy Trinity*. In order to contort the statute's language beyond recognition, the Court must believe Congress's intent so crystalline, the spirit of its legislation so glowingly bright, that the statutory text should simply not be read to say what it says. Justice Stevens is quite candid on the point: He is willing to contradict the text.[19] (citations omitted).

Overbreadth vs. Underbreadth

First Amendment challenges often involve claims that a particular statute is overbroad, i.e., it impermissibly sweeps within its ambit conduct that amounts to protected speech. "Underbreadth," however, is not a claim commonly heard. In *Hill v. Colorado*,[20] the Supreme Court upheld

---

[17] *Id.* at 475.
[18] *Id.* at 469.
[19] *Id.* at 474–75.
[20] 530 U.S. 703 (2000).

Colorado's law that prohibited anyone from entering an 8-foot buffer zone within 100 feet of the entrance of a medical facility. Justice Stevens's majority opinion argued that a statute that failed to include significant conduct the statute was intended to prohibit could be problematical:

> But a statute that restricts certain categories of speech only lends itself to invidious use if there is a significant number of communications, raising the same problem that the statute was enacted to solve, that fall outside the statute's scope, while others fall inside.[21] (citation omitted).

This case, however, did not present a statute that could be labeled "underbroad" because it did not exclude significant speech which the statute was intended to cover:

> Here, the statute's restriction seeks to protect those who enter a health care facility from the harassment, the nuisance, the persistent importuning, the following, the dogging, and the implied threat of physical touching that can accompany an unwelcome approach within eight feet of a patient by a person wishing to argue vociferously face-to-face and perhaps thrust an undesired handbill upon her. The statutory phrases, "oral protest, education, or counseling," distinguish speech activities likely to have those consequences from speech activities (such as Justice Scalia's "happy speech,") that are most unlikely to have those consequences. The statute does not distinguish among speech instances that are similarly likely to raise the legitimate concerns to which it responds. Hence, the statute cannot be struck down for failure to maintain "content neutrality," or for "underbreadth."[22] (citation omitted; parentheses in original).

There were claims that the Colorado statute in this case was overbroad:

> Petitioners argue that [the Colorado statute] is invalid because it is "overbroad." There are two parts to petitioners' "overbreadth" argument. On the one hand, they argue that the statute is too broad because it protects too many people in too many places, rather than just the patients at the facilities where confrontational speech had occurred. Similarly, it burdens all speakers, rather than just persons with a history of bad conduct. On the other hand, petitioners also contend that the statute is overbroad because it "bans virtually the universe of protected expression, including displays of signs, distribu-

---

[21]167 L. Ed. 2d at 723.
[22]*Id.* at 723–24.

SWEEPING GENERALIZATIONS 443

tion of literature, and mere verbal statements."[23] (citations and footnotes omitted; brackets added).

The fact that a statute included more conduct than originally was intended was of no moment, according to Justice Stevens:

> The first part of the argument does not identify a constitutional defect. The fact that the coverage of a statute is broader than the specific concern that led to its enactment is of no constitutional significance. What is important is that all persons entering or leaving health care facilities share the interests served by the statute. It is precisely because the Colorado Legislature made a general policy choice that the statute is assessed under [a less strict standard].[24]

It is the sweep of the statute that saves it from being an unreasonable restriction on protected speech activity:

> The cases cited by petitioners are distinguishable from this statute. In those cases, the government attempted to regulate nonprotected activity, yet because the statute was overbroad, protected speech was also implicated. In this case, it is not disputed that the regulation affects protected speech activity, the question is thus whether it is a "reasonable restrictio[n] on the time, place, or manner of protected speech." Here, the comprehensiveness of the statute is a virtue, not a vice, because it is evidence against there being a discriminatory governmental motive. As we have observed, "there is no more effective practical guaranty against arbitrary and unreasonable government than to require that the principles of law which officials would impose upon a minority must be imposed generally."[25] (citations omitted; brackets in original).

Justice Scalia dissented, and took issue with this argument, stating it may be true generally, but not when protected speech is involved:

> "The fact," the Court says, "that the coverage of a statute is broader than the specific concern that led to its enactment is of no constitutional significance." That is true enough ordinarily, but it is not true with respect to restraints upon speech, which is what the doctrine of overbreadth is all about. (Of course it is also not true, thanks to one of the other proabortion "firsts" announced by the current Court, with respect to restrictions upon abortion, which—as our decision in

---

[23]*Id.* at 730.
[24]*I.e.*, the constitutional standard set forth in *Ward* (Ward v. Rock Against Racism, 491 U.S. 781 (1989)), 491 U.S., at 791, rather than a more strict standard. *See* Madsen v. Women's Health Center, 512 U.S. 753 (1994).
[25]167 L. Ed. 2d at 731.

Stenberg v. Carhart exemplifies—has been raised to First Amendment status, even as speech opposing abortion has been demoted from First Amendment status.)[26] (citations omitted; parentheses in original).

Justice Scalia also argued that the majority's opinion swept protected activity within the statute's prohibition:

> And even with respect to those who *are* seeking to enter or exit the facilities, the statute does not protect them only from speech that is so intimidating or threatening as to impede access. Rather, it covers *all* unconsented-to approaches for the purpose of oral protest, education, or counseling (including those made for the purpose of the most peaceful appeals) and, perhaps even more significantly, every approach made for the purposes of leafletting or handbilling, which we have never considered, standing alone, obstructive or unduly intrusive. The sweep of this prohibition is breathtaking.[27] (parentheses and italics in original).

In the First Amendment context, asserted Justice Scalia, any law that involves broad prophylactic restrictions is suspect:

> In contrast to the laws approved in those cases, the law before us here enacts a broad prophylactic restriction which does not "respon[d] precisely to the substantive problem which legitimately concern[ed]" the State—namely (the only problem asserted by Colorado), the obstruction of access to health facilities. Such prophylactic restrictions in the First Amendment context—even when they are content-neutral—are not permissible. "Broad prophylactic rules in the area of free expression are suspect. . . . Precision of regulation must be the touchstone in an area so closely touching our most precious freedoms."[28] (citations omitted; ellipses, brackets, and parentheses in original).

He then cited a case involving legislation that limited protests on the sidewalks around the Supreme Court building, which the Court struck down because it improperly swept protected speech within its ambit:

> In *United States v. Grace*,[29] we declined to uphold a ban on certain expressive activity on the sidewalks surrounding the Supreme Court. The purpose of the restriction was the perfectly valid interest in security, just as the purpose of the restriction here is the perfectly valid interest in unobstructed access; and there, as here, the restriction furthered that interest—but it furthered it with insufficient precision

---

[26]*Id.* at 760.
[27]*Id.* at 755.
[28]*Id.* at 759.
[29]461 U. S. 171 (1983).

and hence at excessive cost to the freedom of speech. There was, we said, "an insufficient nexus" between security and all the expressive activity that was banned—just as here there is an insufficient nexus between the assurance of access and forbidding unconsented communications within eight feet.[30] (citations and footnote omitted).

The *Grace* decision was also cited for its affirmation of the overbreadth doctrine:

> Again, the Court says that the overbreadth doctrine is not applicable because this law simply "does not 'ban' any signs, literature, or oral statements," but "merely regulates the places where communications may occur." I know of no precedent for the proposition that time, place, and manner restrictions are not subject to the doctrine of overbreadth. Our decision in *Grace* demonstrates the contrary: Restriction of speech on the sidewalks around the Supreme Court was invalidated because it went further than the needs of security justified. Surely New York City cannot require a parade permit and a security bond for any individual who carries a sign on the sidewalks of Fifth Avenue.[31] (citations omitted).

Because there was no evidence that any individuals misbehaved, Justice Scalia asserted the statute necessarily included those who would not abuse their free speech rights:

> It is one thing to assume, as in *Schenck*, that a prophylactic injunction is necessary when the specific targets of that measure have demonstrated an inability or unwillingness to engage in protected speech activity without also engaging in conduct that the Constitution clearly does not protect. It is something else to assume that *all* those who wish to speak outside health care facilities across the State will similarly abuse their rights if permitted to exercise them. The First Amendment stands as a bar to exactly this type of prophylactic legislation. I cannot improve upon the Court's conclusion in *Madsen* that "it is difficult, indeed, to justify a prohibition on *all* uninvited approaches of persons seeking the services of the clinic, regardless of how peaceful the contact may be, without burdening more speech than necessary to prevent intimidation and to ensure access to the clinic. Absent evidence that the protestors' speech is independently proscribable (i.e., 'fighting words' or threats), or is so infused with violence as to be indistinguishable from a threat of physical harm, this provision cannot stand."[32] (citations omitted; parentheses and italics in original).

---

[30] 167 L. Ed. 2d at 759.
[31] *Id.* at 760–61.
[32] *Id.* at 761–62.

Finally, Justice Kennedy argued that overbreadth was a constitutional flaw, not a virtue:

> Rather than adhere to this rule, the Court turns it on its head, stating the statute's overbreadth is "a virtue, not a vice." The Court goes even further, praising the statute's "prophylactic approach; it forbids all unwelcome demonstrators to come closer than eight feet." Indeed, in the Court's view, "bright-line prophylactic rule[s] may be the best way to provide protection" to those individuals unwilling to hear a fellow citizen's message in a public forum. The Court is quite wrong. Overbreadth is a constitutional flaw, not a saving feature. Sweeping within its ambit even more protected speech does not save a criminal statute invalid in its essential reach and design.[33] (citations omitted; brackets in original).

In addition to a First Amendment defense to a sweeping generalization, due process may also constitute a defense, as Justice O'Connor wrote in *Rogers v. Tennessee*,[34] involving the year and a day rule:

> ([D]ue process bars courts from applying a novel construction of a criminal statute to conduct that neither the statute nor any prior judicial decision has fairly disclosed to be within its scope); (Due process protects against judicial infringement of "the right to fair warning" that certain conduct will give rise to criminal penalties); (upholding defendant's conviction under statute prohibiting "crimes against nature" because, unlike in *Bouie*, the defendant "[could] make no claim that [the statute] afforded no notice that his conduct might be within its scope"); (trial courts construction of the term "arrest" as including a traffic citation, and application of that construction to defendant to revoke his probation, was unforeseeable and thus violated due process); (reversing conviction under state obscenity law because it did "not giv[e] fair notice" that the location of the allegedly obscene exhibition was a vital element of the offense).[35] (citations omitted; parentheses and brackets in original).

Sweep of Criminal Statutes

The sweep of criminal statutes has been the subject of differing Supreme Court interpretations:

---

[33] *Id.* at 775.
[34] 532 U.S. 451 (2001).
[35] 167 L. Ed. 2d at 459–60.

SWEEPING GENERALIZATIONS 447

The mere fact that a false denial fits within the unqualified language of 18 U.S.C. §1001 is not, in my opinion, a sufficient reason for rejecting a well-settled interpretation of that statute. It is not at all unusual for this Court to conclude that the literal text of a criminal statute is broader than the coverage intended by Congress. (departing from "most natural grammatical reading" of statute because of "anomalies which result from this construction," and presumptions with respect to scienter in criminal statutes and avoiding constitutional questions); (stating that lower court interpretation of statute rejected by the Court was "quite obviously *the only grammatical reading*) . . . (holding that statute prohibiting the making of false statements to a bank was inapplicable to depositing of a "bad check" because "the Government's interpretation . . . would make a surprisingly broad range of unremarkable conduct a violation of federal law"); ("We are unable to conclude that it was the intention of the Congress in enacting [a Prohibition Act] statute that its processes of detection and enforcement should be abused by the instigation by government officials of an act on the part of persons otherwise innocent in order to lure them to its commission and to punish them") (holding that although "words 'any person or persons,' [in maritime robbery statute] are broad enough to comprehend every human being . . . general words must not only be limited to cases within the jurisdiction of the state, but also to those objects to which the legislature intended to apply them"). Although the text of §1001, read literally, makes it a crime for an undercover narcotics agent to make a false statement to a drug peddler, I am confident that Congress did not intend any such result. As Justice Ginsburg has explained, it seems equally clear that Congress did not intend to make every "exculpatory no" a felony. Even if that were not clear, I believe the Court should show greater respect of the virtually uniform understanding of the bench and the bar that persisted for decades with, as Justice Ginsburg notes, the approval of this Court as well as the Department of Justice.[36] (citations and footnotes omitted; ellipses, brackets, and italics in original).

Finally, in *Dickerson v. United States*,[37] Justice Scalia, with a bit of concluding humor, contended that the majority's decision was too sweeping, because it rejected confessions per se, rather than merely those that were coerced:

Thus, what is most remarkable about the *Miranda* decision—and what made it unacceptable as a matter of straight forward constitutional

---

[36] Brogan v. United States, 522 U.S. 398, 419–20 (1998).
[37] 530 U.S. 428 (2000).

interpretation in the *Marbury* tradition—is its palpable hostility toward the act of confession *per se*, rather than toward what the Constitution abhors, *compelled* confession. ("[F]ar from being prohibited by the Constitution, admissions of guilt by wrongdoers, if not coerced, are inherently desirable"). The Constitution is not, unlike the *Miranda* majority, offended by a criminal's commendable qualm of conscience or fortunate fit of stupidity.[38] (citations omitted; brackets and parentheses in original).

---

[38] *Id.* at 449–50.

CHAPTER THIRTY-THREE

Hasty Generalizations

The old saw that hard cases make bad law has its basis in experience. But petty cases are even more calculated to make bad law. The impact of a sordid little case is apt to obscure the implications of the generalization to which the case gives rise.

United States v. Rabinowitz, 339 U.S. 56, 68 (1950).
(Frankfurter, J., dissenting)

IN THE PREVIOUS CHAPTER, individual examples or cases are inappropriately swept up within a general rule or principle. This chapter, hasty generalizations, presents the opposite argument of the sweeping generalization—a general rule or principle is declared, based on inappropriate examples or cases. General rules or principles in the legal context may result from insufficient evidence or questionable precedent. Sometimes, as Justice Frankfurter noted above, a single case can produce a hasty generalization.

Making a hasty generalization is not difficult; almost any conclusion will do. The challenge is to successfully attack the underpinnings of the conclusion, in order to demonstrate the conclusion was inappropriately drawn. In turn, the proponent must then justify the conclusion, based on the supporting evidence.

Confronted with a hasty generalization, in or out of the courtroom, an attorney must thoroughly examine the bases for the conclusion. How large is the population from which the examples are drawn? Are there sufficient examples from which to draw the correct conclusion? Are the examples appropriately representative of the population? Are the examples relevant to the conclusion?

In *Dickerson v. United States*,¹ the Supreme Court majority found that *Miranda* warnings were constitutionally mandated. Justice Scalia's dissent criticizes the petitioner and the United States for reaching a conclusion based on (1) a relatively new practice, and (2) an infrequent Supreme Court custom of making prophylactic rules to give effect to constitutional guarantees:

> Petitioner and the United States contend that there is nothing at all exceptional, much less unconstitutional, about the Court's adopting prophylactic rules to buttress constitutional rights, and enforcing them against Congress and the States. Indeed, the United States argues that "[p]rophylactic rules are now and have been for many years a feature of this Court's constitutional adjudication." That statement is not wholly inaccurate, if by "many years" one means since the mid-1960's. However, in their zeal to validate what is in my view a lawless practice, the United States and petitioner greatly overstate the frequency with which we have engaged in it.² (citation omitted; brackets in original).

Justice Kennedy, writing for the majority in *Alden v. Maine*,³ argued that the Eleventh Amendment did not permit individuals to file suits against a State to enforce a federal statutory right under the Fair Labor Standards Act of 1938. In the excerpts below, he argues that the minimal evidence relied on by the minority to support its conclusion actually confirms the majority's conclusion:

> Although the dissent attempts to rewrite history to reflect a different original understanding, its evidence is unpersuasive. The handful of state statutory and constitutional provisions authorizing suits or petitions of right against States only confirms the prevalence of the traditional understanding that a State could not be sued in the absence of an express waiver, for if the understanding were otherwise, the provisions would have been unnecessary.⁴
>
> . . . .
>
> In short, the scanty and equivocal evidence offered by the dissent establishes no more than what is evident from the decision in *Chisholm*—that some members of the founding generation disagreed with Hamilton, Madison, Marshall, Iredell, and the only state conventions formally to address the matter. The events leading to the adoption of the Eleventh Amendment, however, make clear that the individuals

---

¹530 U.S. 428 (2000).
²*Id.* at 457.
³527 U.S. 706 (1999).
⁴*Id.* at 724.

who believed the Constitution stripped the States of their immunity from suit were at most a small minority.[5]

Justice Thurgood Marshall offered a dissenter's perspective of "feeble" evidence, in *Payne v. Tennessee*[6]:

> The majority does assert that *Booth* and *Gathers* "have defied consistent application by the lower courts," but the evidence that the majority proffers is so feeble that the majority cannot sincerely expect anyone to believe this claim. To support its contention, the majority points to Justice O'Connor's dissent in *Gathers*, which noted a division among lower courts over whether *Booth* prohibited prosecutorial arguments relating to the victim's personal characteristics. That, of course, was the issue expressly considered and resolved in *Gathers*. The majority also cites The Chief Justice's dissent in *Mills v. Maryland*[.] That opinion does not contain a *single* word about any supposed "[in]consistent application" of *Booth* in the lower courts. Finally, the majority refers to a divided Ohio Supreme Court decision disposing of an issue concerning victim-impact evidence. Obviously, if a division among the members of a single lower court in a single case were sufficient to demonstrate that a particular precedent was a "detriment to coherence and consistency in the law," *Patterson v. McLean Credit Union*, there would hardly be a decision in United States Reports that we would not be obliged to reconsider.[7] (citations omitted; italics and brackets in original).

Sovereign Immunity

Responding to the majority's conclusion, in *Alden v. Maine*, regarding sovereign immunity, Justice Souter challenged their reliance on "an assertion of historical fact" by a Justice of the Supreme Court:

> The Court claims that the doctrine of sovereign immunity was "universal in the States when the Constitution was drafted and ratified," but the examples of Connecticut and Rhode Island suggest that this claim is overstated. It is of course true that these States' preservation without comment of their colonial suability could be construed merely as a waiver of sovereign immunity, and not as a denial of the principle. But in light of these States' silence as to any change in their status as suable bodies, it would be tendentious so to understand it. The Court relies for its claim on Justice Iredell's statement in *Chisholm v. Georgia*,

---

[5]*Id.* at 726.
[6]501 U.S. 80 (1991).
[7]*Id.* at 849–50.

that there was "no doubt" that no State had "'any particular Legislative mode, authorizing a compulsory suit for the recovery of money against a State . . . either when the Constitution was adopted, or at the time the judicial act was passed.'" But as the cases of Rhode Island and Connecticut demonstrate, Justice Iredell was simply wrong. As I have had occasion to say elsewhere, that an assertion of historical fact has been made by a Justice of the Court does not make it so.[8] (citations omitted; ellipses in original).

A legal conclusion based on a single case is not justified, argued Justice Scalia in *Buckhannon v. West Virginia*,[9] in which the Court divided over the meaning of "prevailing party":

> The only case cited by the dissent in which the conclusion of acknowledgment of liability was rested on something other than a settlement is *Board of Ed. of Madison County v. Fowler*, which, in one of the states that considered settlement an acknowledgment of liability, analogized compliance with what had been sought by a mandamus suit to a settlement. This is a slim reed upon which to rest the broad conclusion of a catalyst theory.[10] (citations omitted).

Noting that the majority, in *Hill v. Colorado*,[11] contended there was abundant support for its conclusion, Justice Scalia pointed out that they cited only one case, and he thought that case was inapposite:

> The Court assures us that "we have emphasized" this proposition "on more than one occasion[.]" The only citation the Court provides, however, says no such thing. *Ward v. Rock Against Racism*, says only that narrow tailoring is not synonymous with "least restrictive alternative." It does not at all suggest—and to my knowledge no other case does either—that narrow tailoring can be relaxed when there are other speech alternatives.[12] (brackets added; citation omitted).

Similarly, in *Buckhannon*,[13] Justice Scalia wrote that the dissent's sole case citation was distinguishable:

> At the time 42 U. S. C. §1988 was enacted, I know of no case, state or federal, in which—either under a statutory invocation of "prevailing party," or under the common-law rule—the "catalyst theory" was enunciated as the basis for awarding costs. Indeed, the dissent cites only one case in which (although the "catalyst theory" was not

---

[8] *Id.* at 769 n.8.
[9] 532 U.S. 598 (2001).
[10] *Id.* at 613–614 n.2.
[11] 530 U.S. 703 (2000).
[12] *Id.* at 756.
[13] *Supra.*

expressed) costs were awarded for a reason that the catalyst theory would support, but today's holding of the Court would not: *Baldwin v. Chesapeake & Potomac*, where costs were awarded because "the granting of [appellee's] motion to dismiss the appeal has made it unnecessary to inquire into the merits of the suit, and the dismissal is based on an act of appellee performed after both the institution of the suit and the entry of the appeal." And that case is irrelevant to the meaning of "prevailing party," because it was a case in equity.[14] (citations omitted; brackets and parentheses in original).

Year and a Day Rule

A single case providing support for the "year and a day rule," in *Rogers v. Tennessee*,[15] was likewise inapposite, argued Justice O'Connor:

> While petitioner relies on this case for the proposition that the year and a day rule was firmly entrenched in the common law of Tennessee, we agree with the Supreme Court of Tennessee that the case cannot establish nearly so much. After reciting the rules just mentioned, the court in *Percer* went on to point out that the indictment was found on July 6, 1906; that it charged that the murder was committed sometime in May 1906; and that the only evidence of when the victim died was testimony from a witness stating that he thought the death occurred sometime in July, but specifying neither a date nor a year. From this, the court concluded that it did not affirmatively appear from the evidence whether the death occurred before or after the finding of the indictment. The court made no mention of the year and a day rule anywhere in its legal analysis or, for that matter, anywhere else in its opinion. Thus, whatever the import of the court's earlier quoting of the rule, it is clear that the rule did not serve as the basis for the *Percer* court's decision.[16] (citation omitted).

A single, exceptional case should not be the basis of a general rule, asserted Justice O'Connor, in *Associated General Contractors v. City of Jacksonville*[17]:

> The majority is therefore quite unconvincing in its assertion that the mootness question in this case "is controlled by" *City of Mesquite*. By treating that exceptional case as announcing a general rule favoring the exercise of jurisdiction, moreover, today's decision casts doubt on our other statutory-change cases and injects new uncertainty into

---

[14]*Id.* at 611–12.
[15]532 U.S. 451 (2001).
[16]*Id.* at 465.
[17]508 U.S. 656 (1993).

our mootness jurisprudence. In my view, the principles developed in the other decisions I have described should continue to apply in the ordinary case. Where, as here, a challenged statute is replaced with a more narrowly drawn version pending review, and there is no indication the legislature intends to reenact the prior version, I would follow *Diffenderfer*, vacate the lower court judgment, and direct that the plaintiff be permitted to challenge the new legislation.[18] (citation omitted).

Citing the oft-repeated saw about "hard" cases, Chief Justice Burger, in *Vlandis v. Kline*,[19] claimed the majority created new law from a "hard" case:

> I find myself unable to join the action taken today because the Court in this case strays from what seem to me sound and established constitutional principles in order to reach what it considers a just result in a particular case; this gives meaning to the ancient warning that "hard cases make bad law." The Court permits this "hard" case to make some very dubious law.[20]

"Easy" cases share the same fate as "hard" cases, argued Justice Stevens, in *Ankenbrandt v. Richards*[21]:

> The first Justice Harlan cautioned long ago that "'it is the duty of all courts of justice to take care, for the general good of the community, that hard cases do not make bad law.'" Courts should observe similar caution with regard to easy cases. Cf. *O'Bannon v. Town Court Nursing Center*. ("Easy cases make bad law"). An easy case is especially likely to make bad law when it is unnecessarily transformed into a hard case.[22] (citations omitted).

"Silly Cases"

Chief Justice Rehnquist suggested a third class of cases that make bad law: "silly" cases. In *Larkin v. Grendel's Den, Inc.*,[23] he reproached the majority for reaching a conclusion based on a single term—taken out of context:

---

[18] *Id.* at 677–78.
[19] 412 U.S. 441 (1973).
[20] *Id.* at 459.
[21] 504 U.S. 689 (1992).
[22] *Id.* at 717.
[23] 459 U.S. 116 (1982).

> Dissenting opinions in previous cases have commented that "great" cases, like "hard" cases, make bad law. Today's opinion suggests that a third class of cases—silly cases—also make bad law. The Court wrenches from the decision of the Massachusetts Supreme Judicial Court the word "veto," and rests its conclusion on this single term. The aim of this effort is to prove that a quite sensible Massachusetts liquor zoning law is apparently some sort of sinister religious attack on secular government reminiscent of St. Bartholemew's Night. Being unpersuaded, I dissent.[24] (citations omitted).

Justice Holmes, many years ago, added what would have been the fourth class of cases from which hasty generalizations are drawn— "great" cases:

> Great cases like hard cases make bad law. For great cases are called great, not by reason of their real importance in shaping the law of the future, but because of some accident of immediate overwhelming interest which appeals to the feelings and distorts the judgment. These immediate interests exercise a kind of hydraulic pressure which makes what previously was clear seem doubtful, and before which even well settled principles of law will bend.[25]

Three cases were cited by Chief Justice Rehnquist to justify the Supreme Court's rejection of the Florida Supreme Court's interpretation of State law, in *Bush v. Gore*.[26] Justice Ginsburg, dissenting, took issue with the Chief Justice's conclusion based on these cases:

> Rarely has this Court rejected outright an interpretation of state law by a state high court. *Fairfax's Devisee v. Hunter's Lessee*, *NAACP v. Alabama ex rel. Patterson*, and *Bouie v. City of Columbia*, cited by The Chief Justice, are three such rare instances.
>
> . . . .
>
> The Chief Justice's casual citation of these cases might lead one to believe they are part of a larger collection of cases in which we said that the Constitution impelled us to train a skeptical eye on a state court's portrayal of state law. But one would be hard pressed, I think, to find additional cases that fit the mold. As Justice Breyer convincingly

---

[24]*Id.* at 127-28.
[25]Northern Sec. Co. v. United States, 193 U.S. 197, 400–01 (1904) (Holmes, J., dissenting).
[26]531 U.S. 98 (2000).

explains, this case involves nothing close to the kind of recalcitrance by a state high court that warrants extraordinary action by this Court. The Florida Supreme Court concluded that counting every legal vote was the overriding concern of the Florida Legislature when it enacted the State's Election Code. The court surely should not be bracketed with state high courts of the Jim Crow South.[27] (citations omitted).

Although more than one case may support a proposition, if the cases do not establish a "widespread pattern," Chief Justice Rehnquist argued, in *Nevada Dept. of Human Resources v. Hibbs*,[28] the conclusion cannot be justified:

> Thus, in order to impugn the constitutionality of state discrimination against the disabled or the elderly, Congress must identify, not just the existence of age- or disability-based state decisions, but a "widespread pattern" of irrational reliance on such criteria.[29] (citation omitted).

Lacking a "widespread pattern" of states that prohibit the execution of mentally retarded persons, Justice Stevens, in *Atkins v. Virginia*,[30] asserted that "the direction" the states were taking on this issue was significant:

> It is not so much the number of these States that is significant, but the consistency of the direction of change. Given the well-known fact that anticrime legislation is far more popular than legislation providing protections for persons guilty of violent crime, the large number of States prohibiting the execution of mentally retarded persons (and the complete absence of States passing legislation reinstating the power to conduct such executions) provides powerful evidence that today our society views mentally retarded offenders as categorically less culpable than the average criminal. The evidence carries even greater force when it is noted that the legislatures that have addressed the issue have voted overwhelmingly in favor of the prohibition.[31] (footnotes omitted; parentheses in original).

Justice Scalia's dissent faulted Justice Stevens for committing the fallacy of accent on the way to his hasty generalization:

> The Court pays lip service to these precedents as it miraculously extracts a "national consensus" forbidding execution of *the* mentally retarded, from the fact that 18 States—less than *half* (47%) of the 38

---

[27]*Id.* at 139–40.
[28]538 U.S. 721 (2003).
[29]*Id.* at 735.
[30]536 U.S. 304 (2002).
[31]*Id.* at 315–16.

States that permit capital punishment (for whom the issue exists)—have very recently enacted legislation barring execution of the mentally retarded. Even that 47% figure is a distorted one. If one is to say, as the Court does today, that all executions of the mentally retarded are so morally repugnant as to violate our national standards of decency, surely the consensus it points to must be one that has set its righteous face against all such executions. Not 18 States, but only 7—18% of death penalty jurisdictions—have legislation of that scope. Eleven of those that the Court counts enacted statutes prohibiting execution of mentally retarded defendants *convicted after, or convicted of crimes committed after, the effective date of the legislation*; those already on death row, or consigned there before the statutes' effective date, or even (in those States using the date of the crime as the criterion of retroactivity) tried in the future for murders committed many years ago, could be put to death. That is not a statement of absolute moral repugnance, but one of current preference between two tolerable approaches. Two of these States permit execution of the mentally retarded in other situations as well: Kansas apparently permits execution of all except the severely mentally retarded; New York permits execution of the mentally retarded who commit murder in a correctional facility.[32] (citations and footnote omitted; parentheses and italics in original).

The U.S. Supreme Court majority's conclusion (that a rule which is appropriate for the Fifth Amendment is also appropriate for the Sixth Amendment) lacks evidentiary support, according to Chief Justice Rehnquist:

> The dispositive question in the instant cases, and the question the Court should address in its opinion, is whether the same kind of prophylactic rule is needed to protect a defendant's right to counsel under the Sixth Amendment. The answer, it seems to me, is clearly "no." The Court does not even suggest that the police commonly deny defendants their Sixth Amendment right to counsel. Nor, I suspect, would such a claim likely be borne out by empirical evidence. Thus, the justification for the prophylactic rules this Court created in *Miranda* and *Edwards*, namely, the perceived widespread problem that the police were violating, and would probably continue to violate, the Fifth Amendment rights of defendants during the course of custodial interrogations, is conspicuously absent in the Sixth Amendment context. To put it simply, the prophylactic rule set forth in *Edwards* makes no sense at all except when linked to the Fifth Amendment's prohibition against compelled self-incrimination.[33] (citations omitted).

---

[32] *Id.* at 342–43.
[33] Michigan v. Jackson, 475 U.S. 625, 639–40 (1986).

Justice Stewart also took issue with a transplanted conclusion, in *Bounds v. Smith*[34]:

> In view of the importance of the writ of habeas corpus in our constitutional scheme, "it is fundamental that access of prisoners to the courts for the purpose of presenting their complaints may not be denied or obstructed." From this basic principle the Court over five years ago made a quantum jump to the conclusion that a State has a constitutional obligation to provide law libraries for prisoners in its custody.[35] (citations omitted).

Similarly, Justice O'Connor, writing for the majority in *Rogers v. Tennessee*,[36] criticized the suggestion that "the strictures of the *Ex Post Facto* Clause" should be transferred to the common law:

> Petitioner observes that the Due Process and *Ex Post Facto* Clauses safeguard common interests—in particular, the interests in fundamental fairness (through notice and fair warning) and the prevention of the arbitrary and vindictive use of the laws. While this is undoubtedly correct, petitioner is mistaken to suggest that these considerations compel extending the strictures of the *Ex Post Facto* Clause to the context of common law judging. The *Ex Post Facto* Clause, by its own terms, does not apply to courts. Extending the Clause to courts through the rubric of due process thus would circumvent the clear constitutional text. It also would evince too little regard for the important institutional and contextual differences between legislating, on the one hand, and common law decisionmaking, on the other.[37] (citations omitted; parentheses in original).

Support for a conclusion may derive from more than one source. Justice Breyer, dissenting in *Bush v. Gore*,[38] disagreed with the concurring Justices' conclusion that both the Constitution and the lone case they cited justified the Supreme Court's intervention in the election dispute:

> While conceding that, in most cases, "comity and respect for federalism compel us to defer to the decisions of state courts on issues of state law," the concurrence relies on some combination of Art. II, §1, and 3 U. S. C. §5 to justify the majority's conclusion that this case is one of the few in which we may lay that fundamental principle

---

[34] 430 U.S. 817 (1977).
[35] *Id.* at 836.
[36] 532 U.S. 451 (2001).
[37] *Id.* at 640.
[38] *Supra.*

aside. The concurrence's primary foundation for this conclusion rests on an appeal to plain text: Art. II, §1's grant of the power to appoint Presidential electors to the State "Legislature." But neither the text of Article II itself nor the only case the concurrence cites that interprets Article II, *McPherson v. Blacker*, leads to the conclusion that Article II grants unlimited power to the legislature, devoid of any state constitutional limitations, to select the manner of appointing electors. (specifically referring to state constitutional provision in upholding state law regarding selection of electors). Nor, as Justice Stevens points out, have we interpreted the Federal constitutional provision most analogous to Art. II, §1—Art. I, §4—in the strained manner put forth in the concurrence.[39] (citations omitted; parentheses in original).

A combination of state legislation and case law was insufficient to overturn two previous decisions of the Supreme Court, argued Justice Stevens, in *Payne v. Tennessee*[40]:

> The dissents in *Booth* and *Gathers* and the majority today offer only the recent decision in *Tison v. Arizona*, and two legislative examples to support their contention that harm to the victim has traditionally influenced sentencing discretion. *Tison* held that the death penalty may be imposed on a felon who acts with reckless disregard for human life if a death occurs in the course of the felony, even though capital punishment cannot be imposed if no one dies as a result of the crime. The first legislative example is that attempted murder and murder are classified as two different offenses subject to different punishments. The second legislative example is that a person who drives while intoxicated is guilty of vehicular homicide if his actions result in a death but is not guilty of this offense if he has the good fortune to make it home without killing anyone.
>
> These three scenarios, however, are fully consistent with the Eighth Amendment jurisprudence reflected in *Booth* and *Gathers* and do not demonstrate that harm to the victim may be considered by a capital sentencer in the *ad hoc* and *post hoc* manner authorized by today's majority. The majority's examples demonstrate only that harm to the victim may justify enhanced punishment if the harm is both foreseeable to the defendant and clearly identified in advance of the crime by the legislature as a class of harm that should in every case result in more severe punishment.[41] (citations omitted).

---

[39] *Id.* at 148.
[40] 501 U.S. 808 (1991).
[41] *Id.* at 862–63.

Justice O'Connor attacked Justice Souter's statistical conclusion, in *Zelman v. Simmons-Harris*,[42] by describing the underlying data as too narrow to draw appropriate conclusions:

> Ultimately, Justice Souter relies on very narrow data to draw rather broad conclusions. One year of poor test scores at four community schools targeted at the most challenged students from the inner city says little about the value of those schools, let alone the quality of the 6 other community schools and 24 magnet schools in Cleveland. Justice Souter's use of statistics confirms the Court's wisdom in refusing to consider them when assessing the Cleveland program's constitutionality. What appears to motivate Justice Souter's analysis is a desire for a limiting principle to rule out certain nonreligious schools as alternatives to religious schools in the voucher program. But the goal of the Court's Establishment Clause jurisprudence is to determine whether, after the Cleveland voucher program was enacted, parents were free to direct state educational aid in either a nonreligious or religious direction. That inquiry requires an evaluation of all reasonable educational options Ohio provides the Cleveland school system, regardless of whether they are formally made available in the same section of the Ohio Code as the voucher program.[43] (citations omitted).

"Isolated" and "stale" are the terms Justice Kennedy used to describe the support for the majority's conclusion in *Nevada Dept. of Human Resources v. Hibbs*[44]:

> Even if this isolated testimony could support an inference that private sector's gender-based discrimination in the provision of parenting leave was parallel to the behavior by state actors in 1986, the evidence would not be probative of the States' conduct some seven years later with respect to a statutory provision conferring a different benefit. The Court of Appeals admitted as much: "We recognize that a weakness in this evidence as applied to Hibbs' case is that the BLS and Yale Bush Center studies deal only with parental leave, not with leave to care for a sick family member. They thus do not document a widespread pattern of precisely the kind of discrimination that §2612(a)(1)(C) is intended to prevent."[45] (citation omitted).

Just because the Federal Government discriminates, Justice Kennedy argued, that is insufficient reason to conclude that the states engaged in the same illegal conduct:

---

[42] 536 U.S. 639 (2002).
[43] *Id.* at 675–76.
[44] *Supra*.
[45] *Id.* at 748.

The study explicitly stated that its conclusions concerned federal employees: "'[I]n the absence of a national minimum standard for granting leave for parental purposes, the authority to grant leave and to arrange the length of that leave rests with individual supervisors, leaving Federal employees open to discretionary and possibly unequal treatment.'" A history of discrimination on the part of the Federal Government may, in some situations, support an inference of similar conduct by the States, but the Court does not explain why the inference is justified here.[46] (brackets in original; citation omitted).

The evidence of state discrimination, asserted Justice Kennedy, was not sufficient to violate the Constitution:

Considered in its entirety, the evidence fails to document a pattern of unconstitutional conduct sufficient to justify the abrogation of States' sovereign immunity. The few incidents identified by the Court "fall far short of even suggesting the pattern of unconstitutional discrimination on which §5 legislation must be based." Juxtaposed to this evidence is the States' record of addressing gender-based discrimination in the provision of leave benefits on their own volition.[47] (citations omitted).

In a fractured Supreme Court opinion, involving the regulation of campaign financing, Justice Thomas claimed the joint opinion reached a hasty generalization, based on "a relatively innocent fact," about why donors may contribute to both political parties:

The joint opinion also places a substantial amount of weight on the fact that "in 1996 and 2000, more than half of the top 50 soft-money donors gave substantial sums to *both* major national parties," and suggests that this fact "leav[es] room for no other conclusion but that these donors were seeking influence, or avoiding retaliation, rather than promoting any particular ideology." But that is not necessarily the case. The two major parties are not perfect ideological opposites, and supporters or opponents of certain policies or ideas might find substantial overlap between the two parties. If donors feel that both major parties are in general agreement over an issue of importance to them, it is unremarkable that such donors show support for both parties. This commonsense explanation surely belies the joint opinion's too-hasty conclusion drawn from a relatively innocent fact.[48] (italics and brackets in original; citation omitted).

---

[46]*Id.* at 749.
[47]*Id.* at 753–54.
[48]McConnell v. Federal Election Campaign Comm'n, 540 U.S. 93 (2003).

Unprovoked Flight

A false cause argument may also involve a hasty generalization. If an individual flees at the sight of an approaching police vehicle, what conclusion should be drawn about the runner's motives? Justice Stevens, in *Illinois v. Wardlow*,[49] contrasted contemporary law with previous law regarding flight from the authorities:

> Our ancestors, observing that guilty persons usually fled from justice, adopted the hasty conclusion that it was only the guilty who did so . . . so that under the old law, a man who fled to avoid being tried for felony forfeited all his goods even though he were acquitted. . . . In modern times more correct views have prevailed, and the evasion of or flight from justice seems now nearly reduced to its true place in the administration of the criminal law, namely, that of a circumstance—a fact which it is always of importance to take into consideration, and combined with others may afford strong evidence of guilt, but which, like any other piece of presumptive evidence, it is equally absurd and dangerous to invest with infallibility.[50]
>
> "Unprovoked flight," in short, describes a category of activity too broad and varied to permit a per se reasonable inference regarding the motivation for the activity. While the innocent explanations surely do not establish that the Fourth Amendment is always violated whenever someone is stopped solely on the basis of an unprovoked flight, neither do the suspicious motivations establish that the Fourth Amendment is never violated when a *Terry* stop is predicated on that fact alone. For these reasons, the Court is surely correct in refusing to embrace either *per se* rule advocated by the parties. The totality of the circumstances, as always, must dictate the result.[51] (citation and footnote omitted).

---

[49] 528 U.S. 119 (2000).
[50] *Id.* at 271–72.
[51] *Id.* at 135–36.

CHAPTER THIRTY-FOUR

Lies, Damn Lies, and Statistics

> *In the frame within which it was used, however, the statistic, though relevant, became an item of prejudicial overweight.*
>
> Marx & Co., Inc. v. Diners' Club, Inc., 550 F.2d 505, 511 (2d Cir. 1977).

STATISTICAL FALLACIES, like their nonstatistical counterparts, are noteworthy for their effectiveness. In fact, statistics, because they assume the aura of scientific evidence, must be carefully scrutinized to prevent their use in courtroom situations where they become prejudicial. In the case quoted above, the Second Circuit agreed that the statistic was relevant, but found that its introduction into evidence was prejudicial, under Federal Rule of Evidence 403:

> The issue for the jury was whether Diners' conduct was reasonable in the circumstances in which it found itself—not what a median statistic showed. The statistic could have served as a possible starting point for the discussion of the particular issue involved, but it should not have been given to the jury as if it were akin to a statute of limitations without regard to the particular facts.[1]

When the source of the statistic is not identified, the burden is effectively shifted to the opposing side to disprove the merit of the statistic. In a murder trial, the prosecution called an expert witness who testified that "there is an eight in one million probability that the teeth marks found on the deceased's breast were not made by appellant."[2] The court majority described the witness's credentials and his testimony:

---

[1] Marx & Co., Inc. v. Diners' Club, Inc., 550 F.2d 505, 511 (2d Cir. 1977).
[2] State v. Garrison, 585 P.2d 563, 566 (Ariz. 1978).

The witness, Campbell, is a board certified specialist in forensic dentistry and a member of the American Society of Orthodontology. His testimony is that the wounds in the deceased's breasts had ten points of similarity with appellant's teeth. He testified:

> "My conclusion was that the bite marks on the deceased, and the bite marks produced by the model that I received, were consistent, the marks were consistent with those being made by the teeth that I received."

He further testified:

> "... the probability factor of two sets of teeth being identical in a case similar to this is, approximately, eight in one million, or one in two hundred and fifty—one in a hundred and twenty-five thousand people."[3] (ellipses in original).

The source of the "eight in one million" statistic was derived from "unidentified" individuals:

> In the instant case, Dr. Campbell obtained the figure of eight in one million not from personal mathematical calculations, but from "articles written in the journals of the American Academy of Forensic Sciences" and two books, and "there are articles written throughout the literature that do mention the possibility of the numerical values of finding two [sets of teeth] the same."[4] (brackets in original).

Two of the Arizona Supreme Court Justices dissented from the majority's conclusion that the expert witness's testimony was admissible:

> A reading of Dr. Campbell's testimony reveals that, not only did he not perform any of his own mathematical calculations in reaching the eight in one million figure, but also that he was unaware of the formula utilized to arrive at that figure other than that it was "computerized", and that he was ignorant of the statistical weight assigned to each variable used in the equation ... In short, it is obvious that while Dr. Campbell may have a great deal of expertise in the actual comparison techniques of bite-mark identification, he is totally out of his field when the discussion turns to probability theory.
>
> . . . .
>
> Dr. Campbell's testimony provides a classic example of why a witness' memory of the contents of a writing is not a preferred method of proving those contents. As indicated in the majority opinion, Dr.

---

[3] *Id.*
[4] *Id.*

Campbell was unsure as to precisely where he obtained the figure "eight in one million."[5] (ellipses added).

An appeal to ignorance may occur not only when the source of the statistic is unidentified, but also may result from an attempt to shift the burden of proof to the opposing party. Chief Justice Rehnquist decried the majority's analogy to foreign law involving the execution of the mentally retarded, in *Atkins v. Virginia*,[6] and began his analysis with an appeal to ignorance:

> In reaching its conclusion today, the Court does not take notice of the fact that neither petitioner nor his *amici* have adduced any comprehensive statistics that would conclusively prove (or disprove) whether juries routinely consider death a disproportionate punishment for mentally retarded offenders like petitioner.[7] (parentheses in original).

When a source of statistics is cited, two issues can arise: (1) Is the source reputable? (appeal to authority), and (2) Is the source biased? (ad hominem (circumstantial)).

In *Ramdass v. Virginia*,[8] Justice Kennedy attacked a poll Justice Stevens cited, prompting Justice Stevens to cite other polls, not known for any bias. Justice Kennedy begins the exchange by noting the sponsors of the poll seek to have prisoners incarcerated, rather than executed: "The poll was supervised by the Southern Prisoners' Defense Committee, a group having an interest in obtaining life sentences for the inmates it represents."[9]

Similar polls were not trustworthy, argued Justice Kennedy, because they were conducted by defense attorneys (who, of course, are presumed to be biased in favor of their clients):

> The reporters of the poll contend other similar, limited studies support the results, yet those studies were conducted over the telephone "by defense attorneys in connection with motions for new trials."[10]

Justice Stevens responded by citing polls conducted by assertedly unimpeachable sources:

> Finally, the plurality questions the objectivity of one particular study. Even if the plurality were justified in that criticism, it surely has no

---

[5] *Id.* at 568–69.
[6] 536 U.S. 304 (2002).
[7] *Id.* at 324.
[8] 530 U.S. 156 (2000).
[9] *Id.* at 172.
[10] *Id.* at 173.

basis for questioning the many other sources cited. (Univ. of South Carolina's Institute for Public Affairs) (Gallup Poll and Virginia Tech's Center for Survey Research) (study by Associate Professor of Statistics, Dept. of Economic and Social Statistics, Cornell Univ.).[11] (citations omitted).

A party that seeks to introduce statistics without an expert runs the risk that the data may not be admitted:

> Appellant also contends that the trial court improperly excluded her general statistical evidence of Cerberonics' employment of minorities. The proffered evidence showed the percentage of qualified blacks in the greater Washington area relative to the percentage employed by Cerberonics. Appellant sought to introduce this evidence without expert testimony as to how the statistics were compiled or how they related to appellant's claim. Under these circumstances, we do not believe that the trial court erred in excluding this evidence under Fed. R. Evid. 403. Without expert testimony, the limited probative value of the evidence was plainly outweighed by the possibility it might mislead or confuse the jury.[12] (citation omitted).

Even an expert's testimony in support of statistical evidence may not suffice:

> "An expert who supplies nothing but a bottom line supplies nothing of value to the judicial process."[13] (citation omitted).

The preferred practice, when offering statistical evidence, is to present two experts: one with a statistical background and one with knowledge of the substantive area.[14]

Are Both Sides Presented?

When evaluating the worth of statistical data, two related concepts must be considered. Has certain data been emphasized, while relevant, contrary evidence has been minimized? (fallacy of accent). Or has certain data been suppressed? (fallacy of concealed evidence). An example of the latter would be a party's presentation of a survey completely supporting

---

[11]*Id.* at 199 n.28.
[12]Williams v. Cerberonics, Inc., 871 F.2d 452, 455 n.1 (4th Cir. 1989).
[13]Mid-State Fertilizer Co. v. Exchange Nat'l Bank, 877 F.2d 1333, 1339 (7th Cir. 1989).
[14]Toys "R" Us, Inc. v. Canarsie Kiddie Shop, Inc., 559 F. Supp. 1189, 1205 (E.D.N.Y. 1983).

his or her position, but omitting any mention of another survey, undertaken on behalf of the party, that produced a contrary result.

An example of the former is the weight afforded to anecdotal evidence, evidence of individual cases, usually gathered apart from the statistical data. The First Circuit considered an Equal Protection challenge to the City of Boston's policy of making race a determining factor in the admission of students in three renowned schools.[15] An expert on behalf of the defendants, Dr. William Trent, a sociologist, presented both statistical and anecdotal evidence. The majority rejected the anecdotal evidence:

> Dr. Trent's reliance on anecdotal evidence fares no better. As a general matter, anecdotal evidence is problematic because it does not tend to show that a problem is pervasive. ("While anecdotal evidence may suffice to prove individual claims of discrimination, rarely, if ever, can such evidence show a systematic pattern of discrimination necessary for the adoption of an affirmative action plan.") Thus, even though anecdotal evidence may prove powerful when proffered in conjunction with admissions or valid statistical evidence, anecdotal evidence alone can establish institutional discrimination only in the most exceptional circumstances.[16] (citations omitted; parentheses in original).

The dissenter noted the different views of anecdotal evidence, and how emphasis (fallacy of accent) can alter the outcome:

> The majority asserts that Dr. Trent's failure to conduct a survey of the type conducted in Kansas City disabled him from validly establishing that teachers had different expectations for minority students. Specifically, the majority criticizes Dr. Trent's reliance on "anecdotal" evidence about teacher attitudes supplied by school officials rather than the broad survey of teachers in Kansas City. Used pejoratively, the word "anecdotal" describes accounts of isolated instances few in number. Used descriptively, the word describes observational testimony that could embrace many instances of a phenomenon. We should be wary of dismissing as "anecdotal" the extensive observational accounts of experienced school administrators testifying about the prevalence of different teacher expectations in their school systems, particularly when, as is the case of Deputy Superintendent Jackson, the administrator is trained to make such observations.[17]

---

[15]Wessmann v. Gittens, 160 F.3d 790 (1st Cir. 1998).
[16]Id. at 805–06.
[17]Id. at 824.

Definition of "Average"

Equivocation is the change in meaning of a word or phrase in a given context. A common statistical term is "average," which, mathematically speaking, could be the "mean," the "mode," or the "median." Each term may give rise to a different number, its appropriateness determined by the context. A plaintiff suing an insurance company over the following language, contended the word "average" was ambiguous, and was subject to shifting meanings:

> HOSPITAL ROOM AND BOARD: Hospital room and board including all customary daily services and nursing charges. The room and board charge shall be limited to an **average** semi-private room rate.[18] (bold added).

The Tenth Circuit endorsed the trial court's analysis of the contractual language:

> Giving the policy language its common and ordinary meaning as a reasonable person in the position of a plan participant would have understood the words to mean, Gem's policy language is not ambiguous. The phrase "an average semi-private room rate" must be read in conjunction with the language of the "covered eligible expenses" provision, which imposes a limitation that Gem "will pay the lesser of the billed charges or the Usual and Customary charges as set forth in the Schedule of Benefits." "Usual and Customary" is defined as "(t)he currently prevailing charge made for a medical service or item by a majority of health care providers of the same discipline [or] type within the same geographical area as determined by the Company." Thus a reasonable person in the position of a plan participant would understand the words to mean that Gem would pay the lesser of the billed charge or, the prevailing, usual or average charge made for a semi-private room (as opposed to a private room rate) by a majority of health care providers of the same type within the same geographical area as determined by Gem.[19] (parentheses, brackets, and quotes in original; citation omitted).

Additionally, the Tenth Circuit rejected the argument that the language was ambiguous:

> The district court correctly found that the term "average" did not render the contract ambiguous:

---

[18]Hickman v. Gem Insurance Company, Inc., 299 F.3d 1208, 1210 (10th Cir. 2002).
[19]*Id.* at 1211.

While Plaintiffs have argued that the word "average" is ambiguous because it actually could mean the mode, the median, or the mean, and the parties have spent considerable time on and have provided extensive expert testimony regarding the various meanings of the word "average," and whether and how the word differs in meaning from the words "usual," "customary," "prevailing," etc. and what the average person would interpret "average" to mean, *the court finds that there is no material ambiguity created by the use of these various words,* particularly when Gem retains the discretion to determine the rate it will pay by use of the phrase "as determined by the company." Simply put, *a reasonable person in the position of a plan participant would not be [sic] interpret Gem's policy language to mean something materially different from what it states.* In other words, a reasonable plan participant would not be misled by Gem's policy language. There is nothing in the plan that requires Gem to pay a claim simply because most other carriers would pay the claim if it were presented to them.[20] (italics in original).

Statistical data may be presented in a form that leaves no room for alternative conclusions. (either/or fallacy). Mapes Casino, Inc. sued its insurer on two fidelity bonds, after having lost money on its operations.[21] The principal table games were craps, twenty-one, and roulette. Chips, for use at the tables, were issued for cash or credit, but were treated like cash, in that other casinos would readily accept them. Mapes received a report from another casino that an unusually large number of its chips were being cashed at the other casino. Other casinos were alerted, and they also reported similar chip-cashing activity. After a cashier from another casino identified an individual, Buster Collins, as someone who cashed a large number of Mapes chips, Collins was interrogated by the police and Mapes officials. Collins admitted that he cashed chips for unnamed Mapes employees at other casinos. A short time later, Collins named certain Mapes employees who were involved in the chip-cashing scheme. All were involved in the crap game, and subsequently discharged.

The district court described Mapes' calculation of loss in some detail:

> After disclosure of Collins' activities, Mapes Casino reexamined its records and determined that the percentage of win for the crap tables between (an almost two year period) was much lower than it should have been by mathematical calculation. In casino parlance, the

---

[20] *Id.* at 1212–13.
[21] Mapes Casino, Inc. v. Maryland Casualty Company, 290 F. Supp. 186 (D. Nev. 1968).

percentage of win to drop is the "per." A shift of a crap table, or other game, starts with a certain money value of chips in the bank. As the game progresses, money received from the players is dropped in that box, as are chips of other casinos. As the game progresses, the bank may become depleted and a fill of chips is brought from the cashier's cage; the amount is recorded on a fill slip which is also dropped in the box; and credit slips are dropped representing excess chips taken from the table. At the conclusion of the shift, the percentage which the game won or lost may be calculated by comparing the starting bank with the ending bank and the drop. The figure of $431,024 claimed by Mapes in its proof of loss was arrived at by calculation. The total drop for the crap games for (twenty-two months) was $3,162,797. Assuming a normal win percentage of twenty per cent, Mapes believes its crap games won $632,559 during this period. The books show a total win of $201,535, or 6.37% of the drop. The difference of $431,024 is the amount claimed due to filching of chips by employees. As defendant points out this represents 86,200 five dollar chips.[22]

Records introduced by Mapes demonstrated that the twenty-one and roulette games held their percentages during the 22-month period.

From this evidence, Mapes argued that the loss could only be due to employee dishonesty—akin to Hobson's either/or choice of take the horse at the door or no horse. The court disagreed with Mapes' argument:

> The preponderance of the evidence shows that while computation of the percentage of win from a game and calculation of an unusually low percentage of win are reliable proof of loss due to employee dishonesty. There are too many variables. A bad "per" on the books may be due to skimming (taking off the top before counting the drop), scamming (cheating by collusion between dealer and player), crossroading (professional cheaters among the players), bad fills, false fills, spotty play, the odds given by the house, and just plain bad luck. Reliable testimony indicates that each casino tends to establish its own normal percentages, and that they vary from house to house.[23] (parentheses in original).

Though it may not have been any consolation to Mapes, the court concluded the evidence supported other conclusions:

> While the statistical evidence of the gaming experience at the Mapes Casino is unpersuasive in proving the amount of employee defalcation, it is probative and pertinent evidence in other respects. Over a

---

[22] *Id.* at 192–93.
[23] *Id.* at 193.

period of several years, the house percentage of craps at the Mapes has averaged approximately 18%. During the twenty-two month period in question, the percentage of win was 6.37%. This is evidence that something was wrong, and employee dishonesty is one possibility. We consider that evidence to be probative in the following particulars:

1. It identifies the crap table as the locus of the problem.

2. It corroborates Collins's testimony of the period of time involved in the filching of chips by employees.

3. It is corroborative of other evidence that the losses due to employees were substantial and that Collins was probably not the only outside man, or woman, who was used to exchange the Mapes chips for money at other casinos.[24]

As mentioned earlier in this chapter, statistical data supporting a contrary conclusion may be concealed. For example, an expert may only present the results of the most favorable survey, omitting any mention of surveys yielding contrary conclusions. A practical guidebook to statistics litigation discusses this possibility, and presents an appropriate inquiry[25]:

It does not always occur to cross-examining counsel that the witness's recitation on direct examination may have been selective. However, there is a high likelihood of this in quantitative analysis. The expert may well have done substantially more arithmetic than the client knows of in any find (sic) detail. Counsel for the party-proponent, if thorough, will have covered just about every analyzed fact; however, anything not brought out on direct examination is gold for the party-opponent.

ATTORNEY: Did you do any analyses in connection with this case that have not been covered in your testimony?

Again, the odds are, in the case of the quantitative expert witness, that more was explored than reported and that anything left out is somehow detrimental to the party that has put forward the expert witness. The surprises, with only low-probability exception, can only be pleasant for the party-opponent....[26]

The possibility of stepping on a land mine, however, by asking the above question, exists:

---

[24]*Id.* at 193.
[25]Richard A. Wehmhoefer, Statistics in Litigation: Practical Applications for Lawyers 129 (1985).
[26]*Id.*

A remote possibility that needs to be considered by counsel for the party-opponent is that the witness would say: "What I did not report was that I did a whole variety of analyses, using different methods, all of which led to the same conclusion. I just reported one of them to save time."[27]

Arguing by Analogy

Statistical evidence, like its nonstatistical counterpart, may involve arguing by analogy. In the *Wessmann* case discussed above, involving the fallacy of accent, an expert sought to analogize data obtained from Kansas City and apply it to Boston. The First Circuit rejected this statistical analogy:

> The School Committee attempts to compensate for this shortcoming by pointing to certain alleged phenomena that it claims constitute substantial cause of the achievement gap. Chief among these is "low teacher expectations" vis-a-vis African-American and Hispanic students, a condition which the School Committee argues is an attitudinal remnant of the segregation era. To show the systemic nature of this alleged phenomenon, the School Committee leans heavily on the testimony of Dr. William Trent. Dr. Trent, a sociologist, identified teachers' low expectations of African-American and Hispanic students as a significant factor underlying the achievement gap in the Boston public schools. He based his conclusion on an analogy that he drew from studies he had performed in the Kansas City school system, including a "climate survey" of teacher attitudes and a multiple regression analysis designed to determine whether the low expectations reflected in teachers' answers to the questions posed in the climate survey might partially explain the achievement gap. Based on these materials, Dr. Trent had concluded that, in Kansas City, teacher "efficacy"—a term of art referring to a teacher's success in encouraging pupils to succeed—correlated with higher achievement test scores.
>
> One difficulty with Dr. Trent's testimony is that it relies on evidence from one locality to establish the lingering effects of discrimination in another. Dr. Trent noted, for example, that data he examined from the Boston public schools revealed patterns "consistent with" his findings concerning the Kansas City schools. *Croson*, however, reaffirmed the

---

[27] *Id.*

Court's longstanding teaching that we must staunchly resist attempts to substitute speculation about correlation for evidence of causation.[28] (citation omitted).

In the same case, the First Circuit discussed how statistics may fall short of proving a cause (false cause fallacy):

> With the admissions process eliminated as an illegitimate barrier to entry, the achievement gap statistics, by themselves, must specifically point to other allegedly discriminatory conduct in order to suggest a causal link between those discriminatory acts and the achievement gap. Unlike the focused inquiry characteristic of the employment discrimination cases, however, the raw achievement gap statistics presented in this case do not by themselves isolate any particular locus of discrimination for measurement. Without such a focus, the achievement gap statistics cannot possibly be said to measure the causal effect of any particular phenomenon, whether it be discrimination or anything else. As such, the achievement gap statistics, by themselves, do not even eliminate the possibility that they are caused by what the Court terms "societal discrimination." To be sure, gross statistical disparities at times may suffice to satisfy a state actor's burden of production. But the achievement gap statistics adduced here fail to do so because it is unclear exactly what causative factors they measure.[29] (citations omitted).

The court then explained what requisites statistics must meet in order to establish an appropriate cause:

> The *Croson* Court relied on precisely this reasoning when it concluded, in the contractor context, that low minority membership in a local trade association "standing alone cannot establish a prima facie case of discrimination." The Court reasoned there could be "numerous explanations for this dearth of minority participation, including past societal discrimination." Therefore, if such statistics are to be at all probative of discrimination, they must link cause and effect variables in a manner which would permit such an inference.
>
> . . . .
>
> We do not propose that the achievement gap bears no relation to some form of prior discrimination. We posit only that it is fallacious to maintain that an endless gaze at any set of raw numbers permits a

---

[28] 160 F.3d at 804.
[29] *Id.* at 803.

court to arrive at a valid etiology of complex social phenomena. Even strong statistical correlation between variables does not automatically establish causation. On their own, the achievement gap statistics here do not even identify a variable with which we can begin to hypothesize the existence of a correlation.[30] (citations omitted; ellipses added).

---

[30] *Id.* at 803–04.

Index

A

abstract concepts. *See* hypostatization
accent, 105–118
 ambiguity and, 7
 context and, 105–108, 115–117
 defined, 105
 depiction presented in case and, 108
 disagreement with conclusion and, 117–118
 hasty generalizations and, 456–457
 statistical argument and, 466, 467
 tone of voice and, 110–115
 verbatim quotes and, 106, 108–110
Adamo Wrecking Co. v. United States, 241–243
ad baculum, 279. *See also* threats, force, and fear
ad hominem (abusive), 39–53
 appealing to mob instinct and, 43–44
 blame and, 51–52, 53
 characterizing opponent as uncaring and, 48–49
 connotation and, 6–7
 consequences of, 41–43
 defined, 39
 disparagement and, 44–48
 genetic argument and, 365–366
 odious comparison and, 49–51
 techniques of, 40–41

ad hominem (circumstantial), 31, 33, 55–66
 connotation and, 6–7
 defined, 55–56
 division and epithets, 56–60
 expert bias and, 64–66
 genetic argument and, 365–366
 judicial bias and, 60–63
ad lapidem, 187–188. *See also* hurling epithets
admiralty law, 155–156
Aetna Insurance Co. v. Lavoie, 60–62
Alden v. Maine, 94–95
 accent argument and, 117
 appeal to ignorance and, 168
 division argument and, 412–413
 hasty generalizations and, 450–451, 451–452
 humor/ridicule argument and, 210
 hurling epithets and, 199
 straw man argument and, 402
Allegheny County v. Greater Pittsburgh ACLU, 51–52, 401–402
 accent argument and, 114–116
 begging the question argument and, 294, 299
 either/or argument and, 356–357
 false analogy and, 345
 genetic argument and, 370, 373, 378

Allegheny County v. Greater Pittsburgh ACLU (Continued)
  humor/ridicule argument and, 205–207
  hurling epithets and, 196–199
  hypostatization argument and, 148
  slippery slope argument and, 246
  straw man argument and, 396–397
  tu quoque argument and, 75–76
ambiguity, 7
American Association for Justice, 92
American Bar Association
  ABA Journal, 380–382
  Model Rules of Professional Conduct, 82, 89–90, 91–92
  Standards for Criminal Justice, 25–38
  "Standards Relating to the Prosecution Function and the Defense Function," 282
amphiboly, 133–146
  ambiguity and, 7
  contradiction and, 144–146
  criminal statutes and, 139–144
  defined, 133–134
  libelous headlines and, 134–139
analogy. *See* false analogy
Ankenbrandt v. Richards, 454
Anti-Drug Abuse Act, 136–139
Anti-Kickback Act, 164–165
appeal to authority, 93–104
  connotation and, 7
  defined, 93
  judicial use of, 96–100
  in lower court decisions, 95–96
  multiple lines of attack and, 94–95
  prosecutors and, 101–102
  vouching and, 102–104
  witness-vouching and, 30
appeal to ignorance, 159–172
  burden of proof and, 160–162
  compliance with law and, 171–172
  defined, 159–160
  emotional appeal and, 7
  iceberg metaphor and, 164–169
  judicial discretion and, 171–172
  nonappearing witnesses and, 161–164
  responding in kind and, 170–171

  statistical argument and, 465
  sui generis and, 171–172
appeal to mob, 215–235
  ad hominem (abusive) argument and, 43–44
  collective interests and, 215–216
  "conscience of the community" arguments and, 230–235
  defined, 215
  emotional appeal and, 7
  "message" by juries and, 218–220
  "overcrowded courtrooms" objection and, 223
  pecuniary interests of jurors and, 223–225
  "rally around the flag" arguments, 220–223
  regionalism and, 216–218
  religious beliefs and, 225–227
  "war on drugs" and, 227–229
appeal to sympathy, 34, 173–186
  defined, 173–174
  emotional appeal and, 7
  "golden rule" argument and, 174–178
  victim impact statements and, 182–186
  victim's perspective and, 178–182
"apples and oranges" comparison, false analogy and, 344–346
arguing by analogy, 472–474
argumentum ad ignorantiam, 159–160. *See also* appeal to ignorance
argumentum ad misericordiam, 173–174. *See also* appeal to sympathy
argumentum ad populum, 215. *See also* appeal to mob
argumentum ad verecundiam, 93. *See also* appeal to authority
Armitage, Richard, 40–41
Aryan Brotherhood, 56–59
Associated General Contractors v. City of Jacksonville, 453–454
Association of Trial Lawyers of America, 92
Atkins v. Virginia, 53
  composition argument and, 430–431
  division argument and, 412
  either/or argument and, 352

INDEX 477

false analogy and, 347
genetic argument and, 372
hasty generalizations and, 456–457
humor/ridicule and, 208–209
reductio ad absurdum and, 261–262
statistical argument and, 465
Atlantic Cleaners & Dyers v. United States, 123–126
"average," statistical argument and, 468–472

B

Batson v. Kentucky, 416
begging the question, 293–306
 defined, 293–296
 examples, 301–306
 "fair reading" and, 297–301
 questionable assumptions and, 8
 "reasonable" vs. "unreasonable," 297
Bennis v. Michigan, 116
 hypostatization and, 156–158
 reductio ad absurdum argument and, 259–260
 slippery slope argument and, 247
 straw man argument and, 405–406
"best defense is good offense" strategy, 21
bias. *See also* ad hominem (circumstantial)
 "actual bias," 60
 expert, 64–66
 judicial, 60–63
Blackmun, Harry, 51–52
Black's Law Dictionary
 either/or argument and, 360–362
 genetic argument and, 375
Blair, Tony, 83
bolstering, 104
Booth v. Maryland
 appeal to sympathy and, 182
 false analogy and, 344
 genetic argument and, 368–369
 red herring argument and, 390–391
 slippery slope and, 244
 straw man argument and, 403
Borden, 47–48
Bouie v. City of Columbia, 115–116

Bounds v. Smith, 458
Boy Scouts of America v. Dale, 170
 composition argument and, 431–432
 division argument and, 413
 genetic argument and, 375
 slippery slope argument and, 249
"bright-line" approach, to either/or argument, 360, 362–363
Brogan v. United States, 355
Buckhannon v. West Virginia, 95
 begging the question and, 298
 either/or argument and, 360
 equivocation argument and, 129–130
 genetic argument and, 369, 375
 hasty generalizations and, 452–453
 slippery slope argument and, 247–248
burden of proof
 appeal to ignorance and, 160–162
 false cause argument and, 323
Bush, George W., 71–72, 191, 259, 363, 382. *See also* Bush v. Gore
Bush v. Gore
 ad hominem (abusive) argument and, 51–52
 appeal to ignorance and, 170–171
 begging the question and, 297–299, 300, 302–304
 equivocation argument and, 122–123
 false analogy and, 349
 genetic argument and, 370–371
 hasty generalizations and, 455–456, 458–459
 slippery slope argument and, 243–244
 straw man argument and, 395–396
 tu quoque argument and, 74

C

Calderone v. Thompson, 88–89
"camel" analogy, 241–243
cause and effect. *See* false cause
CBOCS West, Inc. v. Humphries, 95–96
cell phones, 399
character attack, xv. *See also* ad hominem (abusive)
Cheney, Dick, 62–63, 71–72, 382
Church of the Holy Trinity, 439–441

circular reasoning, 293–296. *See also* begging the question
City of Boston, 467
civil cases. *See also individual names of cases*
   division argument and, 417–418
   red herring argument and, 386–387
"clean hands doctrine," 72–75
Clinton, Bill, 7, 72
   accent argument and, 107–108
   ad hominem (circumstantial) argument and, 65–66
   appeal to sympathy and, 185–186
   either/or argument and, 352–353, 362–363
   equivocation argument and, 119–121
   false cause argument and, 325–326
   Guinier nomination and, 202
   hurling epithets and, 189–191
   hypostatization argument and, 153–154
   reductio ad absurdum argument and, 252
   tu quoque argument and, 68–71
collective interests, appeal to mob and, 215–216
College Savings Bank v. Florida Prepaid Postsecondary Education Expense Board, 78–79
   appeal to ignorance and, 167
   begging the question argument and, 294–295
   humor/ridicule argument and, 210–211
Collins, Bruce, 181–182
Collins, Buster, 469–472
"common law decisionmaking," 404
comparisons. *See* composition; division
complex question, 307–321
   defined, 307
   fact not in evidence and, 318–321
   objections to, 308–318
   questionable assumptions and, 8
compliance with law, appeal to ignorance and, 171–172
composition, 421–433
   defined, 421–422
   erroneous conclusions, 8–9
   examples, 422–428

   risk of wrongful execution and, 430–433
   "standing" and, 428–429
Compton Petroleum Corporation, 270–273. *See also United States v. Young*
"conscience of the community" arguments, 230–235
conspiracy, composition argument and, 424–427
context, accent and, 105–108, 115–117
"convict to protect" argument, 280–282
credibility
   appeal to authority and, 102–104
   poisoning the well argument and, 83–90
crimen falsi, 84
criminal cases. *See also individual names of cases*
   amphiboly and, 139–144
   appeal to sympathy and, 178–186
   complex question argument in, 310–311
   sweeping generalizations and, 446–448
Cromwell, Oliver, 127
Currie, Betty, 325–326

D

Dahmer, Jeffrey, 338–339
Darrow, Clarence, 7, 239–241
"death for dangerousness" argument, 282–289
DeLay, Tom, xvi, 13–18
   humor/ridicule argument and, 201–202
   hurling epithets and, 189
   tu quoque argument and, 71
   depiction of case, accent and, 108
Detainee Treatment Act of 2005, 240–241
DeWitt, Lt. Gen., 422
Dickerson v. United States, 77
   accent argument and, 117
   begging the question argument and, 296
   genetic argument and, 367–368, 372
   hasty generalizations and, 450
   reductio ad absurdum and, 263

sweeping generalizations and, 447–448
two wrongs make a right argument and, 277
dilatory conduct, 70–71
dilemmas, either/or argument and, 354–356
disparagement, 44–48. *See also* ad hominem (abusive); humor and ridicule
District of Columbia v. Heller, 143–144, 146
division, 33, 407–419
   defined, 407–409
   Equal Protection Clause and peremptory challenges, 416–419
   erroneous conclusions, 8–9
   gender stereotyping and, 414–416
   "guilt by association" and, 409–414
"dream team" (Simpson trial), 421
Duckworth v. Eagan, 242–243

E

Earle, Ronnie, 13–18, 71
either/or argument, 9, 351–363
   alternatives to, 357–360
   Black's Law Dictionary on, 360–362
   "bright-line" approach to, 360, 362–363
   defined, 351–357
ejusdem generis, 133–134
Eleventh Amendment, 210–213
Embry, T. Eric, 60–62
emotional appeal, 7
Enron Corporation. *See also* Lay, Kenneth
   ad hominem (abusive) argument and, 44
   ad hominem (circumstantial) argument and, 64–65
   humor/ridicule argument and, 205
Equal Protection Clause, 416–419
equivocation, 119–131
   ambiguity and, 7
   defined, 119–121
   differing interpretations of one word/phrase, 127–131
   using one word in two ways, 121–126
   erroneous conclusions, 8–9

Establishment Clause test
   false analogy and, 345
   humor/ridicule argument and, 206–207
   tu quoque argument and, 75–76
ethics. *See also* prohibited arguments
   appeal to authority and, 93
   two wrongs make a right argument and, 266–270
evolution, slippery slope and, 239–241
Ewing v. California, 115–116
   begging the question and, 305–306
   either/or argument and, 361–362
   genetic argument and, 377
Ex Post Facto clause, 458
extrajudicial statements. *See* poisoning the well
"eye for an eye" argument, 383–384

F

fact not in evidence, 318–321
Fair Labor Standards Act, 94–95
"fair reading," 297–301
fair trial, complex question argument and, 310–313
fallacy, categories of, 5–9
false analogy, 337–349
   "apples and oranges" comparison and, 344–346
   defined, 337–340
   foreign law reliance and, 347–349
   infamous individuals and, 341–344
   questionable assumptions and, 8
false cause, 323–335
   cause of negligence and, 328–332
   defined, 323–328
   hasty generalizations and, 462
   questionable assumptions and, 8
   retirement vesting questions and, 332–335
false question. *See* complex question
"falsus in uno, falsus in omnibus," 84–86
Family Medical Leave Act, 432–433
Federal Election Commission v. Wisconsin Right to Life, 212
Federal Rules of Civil Procedure, 117–118

Federal Rules of Evidence
   bias and, 57
   on character evidence, 42
   on credibility, 83–84
   on demonstrating lack of evidence, 160–161
   false cause argument and, 334
Fifth Amendment, 290–292
Fiorina, Carly, 98
First Amendment, 78, 207–209, 410–411, 414, 429
Foley v. Connelie, 418
foreign law reliance, false analogy and, 347–349
Fourteenth Amendment, 279, 290
Fourth Amendment, 127–129
France, Anatole, 257
Frankfurter, Felix, 53
Furman v. Georgia, 199

G

gang membership, division argument and, 408, 409–410
Gavalik v. Continental Can Co., 333
gender stereotyping, 414–416
genetic argument, 265–278
   defined, 365–373
   long standing practices and, 377–378
   "novel" rationale and, 370–371, 373–377
Gentile v. State Bar of Nevada, 89–90, 91–92
Georges, Constantine, 205
Gervasio, Richard, 86–87
Gilmore, Gary, 338
Gingrich, Newt, 40–41
Ginsburg, Ruth Bader, 51
"golden rule" argument, 174–178
Goldman, Ronald, 134–136
Good News Club v. Milford Central School, 361
Grace, 445–446
Griffin v. Oceanic Contractors, 437
"guilt by association," division and, 409–414
Guinier, Lani, 202
Gustafson v. Alloyd Co., Inc., 146

H

Hagel, Chuck, 72
Hamdan v. Rumsfeld, 240
"happy speech" limitation, 207–209
Harmelin v. Michigan, 79
   appeal to ignorance and, 171
   begging the question and, 305
   either/or argument and, 363
   straw man argument and, 400–401
hasty generalizations, 8–9, 449–462
   defined, 449–451
   false cause and, 462
   "silly" cases and, 454–461
   sovereign immunity and, 451–453
   "year-and-a-day rule" and, 453–454
Hein v. Freedom from Religion Foundation, Inc.
   composition argument and, 428–429
   humor/ridicule argument and, 211–212
Hill v. Colorado, 52, 73
   division argument and, 411–412
   false analogy and, 345–346
   genetic argument and, 366–367, 373–374
   hasty generalizations and, 452
   humor/ridicule argument and, 207–209
   hurling epithets and, 198
   reductio ad absurdum argument and, 255, 257–260
   straw man argument and, 402
   sweeping generalizations and, 441–445
Hitler, Adolph, 341
Hobson, Tobias, 351–352
Hobson's choice, 351–352. *See also* either/or argument
"hooters and polluters" bill, 202–203
Howard, Michael, 83
Huber, Michael, 86–87
humor and ridicule, 201–213
   composition argument and, 430–431
   either/or argument and, 359
   Eleventh Amendment cases and, 210–213
   emotional appeal and, 7

INDEX

exceeding permissible boundaries
    and, 204–207
"happy speech" limitation and,
    207–209
use of, 201–204
hurling epithets, 187–199
    courts targeted by, 196–199
    defendants/judges targeted by,
        194–196
    defined, 187–188
    emotional appeal and, 7
    epithets as "unwarranted hyperbole,"
        199
    improper epithets and, 191–194
    lies and, 188–191
    reductio ad absurdum argument and,
        260
Hyde, Henry, 380–382
hypocrisy. *See* tu quoque
hypostatization, 147–158
    admiralty law and, 155–156
    ambiguity and, 7
    defined, 147–148
    privacy and, 150–155
    property and, 156–158
    res ipsa loquitur doctrine and,
        148–150

I

iceberg metaphor, 164–169
Illinois Department of Conservation, 134
Illinois v. Wardlow, 324–325
    either/or argument and, 357–358
    hasty generalizations and, 462
impeachment. *See* Clinton, Bill
improper conduct, threats/force/fear
    argument and, 289–290
infamous individuals, false analogy and,
    341–344
informal argument. *See also individual
    types of informal argument*
    defined, xv
    identifying, 5
    Rules of Legal Logic and, 19–22
    using combination of, 18
"invited response" doctrine, 32, 266,
    270–275

Iran-Contra hearings, 380–382
Iraq
    Iraqi parliament on voting
        requirements, 121–122
    Iraq War, 83
irrelevant arguments, 393–394. *See also*
    red herrings; straw man

J

J.C. Penney Co. v. NLRB, 110–114
J.E.B. v. Alabama
    equivocation and, 131
    reductio ad absurdum argument and,
        253–254, 259
J.E.B. v. United States, 198
Johnson v. United States, 23
Jones, Henry H., Jr., 340
Jones, Paula, 119
Jones v. United States, 139–143
    appeal to ignorance and, 172
    either/or argument and, 354–355
Jordan, James, 68–71
judges. *See also individual names of judges*
    appeal to authority and, 96–100
    appeal to ignorance and discretion of,
        171–172
    bias and, 60–63
    discretion of, and appeal to ignorance,
        171–172
    hurling epithets and, 194–196
    improper conduct and threats/force/
        fear argument, 289–290
juries
    appealing to the mob argument and,
        215–235
    red herrings as diverting attention of,
        391–392

K

Kaelin, Brian "Kato," 134–136
Kennedy, Anthony, 51–52
King, Rodney, 231
King Henry VI (Shakespeare), 105–106
Kiyoushi Hirabayashi v. United States,
    422–424
Kmart, 48–49, 161–162, 275–277

Korematsu, Toyosaburo, 422–424
Kunstler, William, 281–282

L

Larkin v. Grendel's Den, Inc., 454–455
Lawrence v. Texas, 115
    false cause argument and, 3335
    genetic argument and, 368, 371–372, 377–378
    humor/ridicule argument and, 211
    hypostatization argument and, 149–150
    reductio ad absurdum and, 262–263
    slippery slope argument and, 245–246
    straw man argument and, 400, 401
Lay, Kenneth, 44, 181–182. *See also* Enron Corporation
Ledbetter v. Goodyear Tire & Rubber Co., 300–301
"legal floodgates," slippery slope argument and, 243–246
Legal Logic Flow Chart, xv–xvii, 1, 5–18
    as argument generator, 18
    ethics and, 23–38
    fallacy/argument categories, 5–9
    illustration, 2–4
    Tom DeLay example and, 13–18
    Winona Ryder example and, 9–13
Lewinsky, Monica, 120, 326
lex talionis, 265–277
Libby, "Scooter," 382
libel, 134–139
lies. *See* statistical argument
loaded question. *See* complex question
logic, xv, 19–22. *See also* Legal Logic Flow Chart
long-standing practices, genetic argument and, 377–378

M

Maddalozzo, Rob, 205
Mapes Casino, Inc., 469–472
Marshall, Thurgood, 36
Masson v. New Yorker Magazine, Inc., 109–110
McCain, John, 202–203, 301–302

McCain-Feingold bill, 301–302
McConnell, Mitch, 301–302
McCormick on Evidence, 308
McElhaney, James W., 174
McKune v. Lile, 290–292
Microsoft, 20, 263
Miranda decision
    accent argument and, 117
    either/or argument and, 362
    genetic argument and, 367, 372
    hurling epithets and, 197
    reductio ad absurdum and, 263
    slippery slope and, 242–243
    tu quoque argument and, 76–79
    two wrongs make a right argument and, 277
misconduct claims, complex question argument and, 310–313
Mitchell, George, 380–382
Morse v. Frederick
    humor/ridicule argument and, 213
    tu quoque argument and, 78
Muscarello v. United States, 78
    appeal to authority and, 96–98
    equivocation argument and, 127
    false analogy and, 348
    humor/ridicule and, 209

N

National Examiner, 134–136
National Labor Relations Board, 99, 110–114
"natural presumption," 124
Neal, William, 267
negligence, false cause argument and, 328–332
Nevada Dept of Human Resources v. Hibbs, 296
    division argument and, 414–415
    hasty generalizations and, 456, 459–460
    straw man argument and, 406
New Yorker, 109–110
New York Times, 82–83
Nizer, Louis, 281–282
non causa pro causa, 323. *See also* false cause

INDEX

North, Oliver, 380–382
"Nose of the Camel: Extending the Public Policy Exception Beyond the Wrongful Discharge Context, The," 242
"novel" rationale, genetic argument and, 370–371, 373–377

O

objections, complex question argument and, 308–318
Occam's Razor, 21–22
Office of Independent Counsel (OIC). *See also* Starr, Kenneth
   ad hominem (circumstantial) argument and, 65–66
   complex question argument and, 308–310
   reductio ad absurdum argument and, 252, 254
   tu quoque argument and, 68–71
Olmstead v. United States, 265–266
Omnibus Crime Control and Safe Streets Act of 1968, 142–143
"one," accent argument and, 106
origin. *See* genetic argument
"overcrowded courtrooms," 223

P

patriotism, appeal to mob and, 220–223
Pautler, Mark, 267–269
Payne v. Tennessee
   appeal to sympathy and, 182–185
   false analogy and, 344
   genetic argument and, 367, 368–369, 376
   hasty generalizations and, 451, 459
   reductio ad absurdum argument and, 253
   slippery slope argument and, 244
pension benefits, false cause argument and, 332–335
"people," equivocation argument and, 128–129
peremptory challenges, 416–419
pity. *See* appeal to sympathy

plain error standard
   appeal to authority and, 103
   appeal to mob and, 228
   prohibited arguments and, 23, 30, 38
   two wrongs rarely make a right argument, 275–277
Plessy v. Ferguson, 239–240
Poindexter, John, 381–382
poisoning the well, 81–92
   connotation and, 6–7
   credibility and, 83–90
   defined, 81–82
   pre-trial publicity and, 82–83
Posner, Richard, 273–275
prejudice. *See* ad hominem (circumstantial)
pre-trial publicity, poisoning the well and, 82–83
principle of parsimony (Occam's Razor), 21–22
privacy, hypostatization and, 150–155
prohibited arguments, 23–38. *See also* ethics
   appeals to prejudice and, 33–35
   defined, 23–26
   injecting red herrings and, 35–38
   misconduct and, 28–30
   opinion of prosecutors and, 26–28, 30–33
property, hypostatization and, 156–158
prosecutors. *See also* prohibited arguments
   appeal to authority and, 99–100, 101–102
   personal opinion of, 26–28, 30–33
   "Standards Relating to the Prosecution Function and the Defense Function" (ABA), 282
public housing authorities (PHAs), 137

Q

questionable assumptions, 8

R

R. J. Reynolds Tobacco Company, 73, 243

"rally around the flag" arguments, 220–223
Ramdass v. Angelone
  begging the question and, 304–305
  either/or argument and, 358
  equivocation argument and, 130–131
  humor/ridicule argument and, 211
  slippery slope argument and, 248–249
Ramdass v. Virginia, 465–466
Reagan, Ronald, 380–382
red herrings, 379–392, 393
  defined, 379–380
  as diverting jurors' attention, 391–392
  ethics and, 35–38
  examples of, 380–391
reductio ad absurdum, 238, 251–263
  adverse consequences and, 8
  "considerable overstatement" and, 256–258
  decisions that signal "the end" and, 262–263
  defined, 251–252
  either/or argument and, 359
  exaggerated terms and, 252–254
  extreme examples of, 254–256
  genetic argument and, 370
  harsh penalties and, 261–262
  humor/ridicule and, 258–260
regionalism, appeal to mob and, 216–218
Rehnquist, William, 51
religious beliefs
  appeal to mob and, 225–227
  composition argument and, 428–429
  red herring argument and, 384–386
res ipsa loquitur doctrine, 148–150
responding in kind, appeal to ignorance and, 170–171
retirement vesting, false cause argument and, 332–335
Roe v. Wade, 238, 334–335
Rogers v. Tennessee, 20–21, 115
  begging the question argument and, 299–300
  genetic argument and, 373, 374–375, 376–377
  hasty generalizations and, 453, 458

  humor/ridicule and, 209
  slippery slope argument and, 245
  straw man argument and, 404
  sweeping generalizations and, 446
Ruemmler, Kathryn, 44, 205
rule of completeness, 107
Rules of Legal Logic, 19–22
Rummel v. Estelle, 262
Rundle, Ann, 9–13, 266
Ryder, Winona, xvi, 9–13
  appeal to authority and, 98
  appeal to ignorance and, 161
  composition argument and, 422
  division argument and, 408
  two wrongs make a right argument and, 266

S

Safire, William, 40–41
Sanders, Grady, 89–90
Scalia, Antonin, 52, 53
Schiavo v. Schiavo
  appeal to ignorance and, 171–172
  hurling epithets and, 188
Scopes trial, 239–241
selective quotation, 106, 108–110
self-incrimination privilege, 290–292
Seminole Tribe of Fla. v. Florida, 168
Sesame Street, 348
Shakespeare, William, 105–106
Shaw v. Reno, 418
Shell Oil Company, 154
Sherman Anti-Trust Act, 123–126
Sierra Club, 62–63, 134
"silly" cases, hasty generalizations and, 454–461
Simmons v. South Carolina, 130
Simpson, Nicole Brown, 134–136
Simpson, O. J., 134–136, 421
Sixth Amendment, 287–288
Skilling, Jeffrey, 44
slippery slope, 237–249, 251
  adverse consequences and, 8
  "camel" analogy and, 241–243
  defined, 237–238
  leading to "legal floodgates," 243–246

INDEX

point/counterpoint and, 246–249
refutations of slippery slope
  arguments, 238
Scopes trial and, 239–241
Small Business Administration (SBA),
  427–428
source. *See* genetic argument
South Carolina v. Gathers
  appeal to sympathy and, 182
  false analogy and, 344
  genetic argument and, 376
  slippery slope argument and, 244
sovereign immunity, hasty
  generalizations and, 451–453
"Standards Relating to the Prosecution
  Function and the Defense
  Function" (ABA), 282
"standing," composition argument and,
  428–429
stare decisis, 244, 369, 400
Starr, Kenneth. *See also* Office of
    Independent Counsel (OIC)
  accent argument and, 107–108
  hypostatization argument and,
    153–154
  tu quoque argument and, 68–71
State v. Raspberry, 280–282
statistical argument, 9, 463–474
  arguing by analogy and,
    472–474
  defined, 463–466
  lies and hurling epithets, 188–191
  presenting both sides and, 4
    66–467
  use of "average" and, 468–472
stereotypes, 414–416, 417, 418–419,
  432–433
Stewart, Potter, 241–243
straw man, 379, 393–406
  defined, 393–394
  examples, 394–406
subtlety, in legal logic, 21–22
sui generis, 171–172
sweeping generalizations, 435–448
  criminal statutes and, 446–448
  defined, 435
  erroneous conclusions, 8–9
  examples, 435–441

overbreadth *vs.* "underbreadth,"
  441–446

T

Texas v. Cobb, 347
Thomas, Cal, 82–83
threats, force, and fear, 279–292
  adverse consequences and, 8
  "convict to protect" argument,
    280–282
  "death for dangerousness" argument
    and, 282–289
  defined, 279–282
  improper conduct and, 289–290
  self-incrimination privilege and,
    290–292
"to carry," 9698
tone of voice, 106, 110–115
tort liability cases, false cause argument
  and, 323
Trent, William, 467
Tripp, Linda, 65–66, 308–310
tu quoque, 67–79, 266
  "clean hands doctrine" and, 72–75
  connotation and, 6–7
  defending against hypocrisy, 68–71
  defined, 67–68
  Establishment Clause test and,
    75–76
  Miranda rights and, 76–79
  sweeping generalizations and,
    437–438
  vulgarity and, 70–71
two wrongs rarely make a right
  argument, 67, 265–277
  adverse consequences and, 8
  defined, 265–266
  "invited response" rule and, 266,
    270–275
  justification for, 266–270
  lex talionis, 265–277
  "plain error" rule and, 275–277

U

"underbreadth," sweeping
  generalizations and, 441–446

486 INDEX

United States v. Abel
  ad hominem (circumstantial) argument and, 56–59
  division argument and, 413
United States v. Bass, 143
United States v. Emenogha, 59
United States v. Ron Pair Enterprises, Inc., 437–439
United States v. Russell, 346
United States v. Verdugo-Urquidez, 127
United States v. Young, 32, 270–273
U.S. Constitution
  ad baculum appeals and, 279
  composition argument and, 429
  constitutional arguments and appeal to authority, 94–95
  division argument and, 410–411, 414
  either/or argument and, 359
  equivocation argument and, 126, 127–129
  hasty generalizations and, 457–458, 461
  humor/ridicule argument and, 207–209, 210–213
  Miranda rights and, 77
  threats/force/fear argument and, 287–288, 290–292
  tu quoque and, 78
U.S. Department of Housing and Urban Development (HUD), 137
U.S. Supreme Court. *See individual names of cases; individual names of justices*
USA Patriot Act, 260

V

verbatim quotes, 108–110
victim impact statements
  appeal to sympathy and, 182–186
  red herring argument and, 390–392
Virginia Military Institute (VMI), 398
Vlandis v. Kline, 454
voir dire, poisoning the well argument and, 91–92
vulgarity, tu quoque argument and, 70–71

W

"war on drugs"
  appeal to mob and, 227–229
  red herring argument and, 389–390
Webb v. Texas, 288–289
Webster v. Reproductive Health Services, 52
  begging the question argument and, 295–296, 305
  genetic argument and, 374
  hurling epithets and, 198
  reductio ad absurdum argument and, 254, 261
  slippery slope argument and, 238, 246–247
Wessmann v. Gittens, 472
Whalen v. Roe, 151
"whole greater than the sum of its parts," composition argument and, 433
witnesses, 34
  appeal to ignorance and nonappearing witnesses, 161–164
  credibility and poisoning the well argument, 83–88
  threats to, 288–289
  vouching and, 30, 102–103

Y

Yagman, Stephen, 185
"year-and-a-day rule," 96, 453–454

Z

Zelman v. Simmons-Harris, 241–242
  begging the question and, 297
  false analogy and, 348
  hasty generalizations and, 459
Zuni Public School District No. 89 v. Department of Education
  amphiboly and, 145–146
  sweeping generalizations and, 435–437